Double Jeopardy

Recent Titles in
Reference Guides to the United States Constitution
Jack Stark, Series Editor

The Right to the Assistance of Counsel
James J. Tomkovicz

Prohibited Government Acts
Jack Stark

State Sovereign Immunity
Melvyn R. Durchslag

Constitutional Remedies
Michael Wells and Thomas A. Eaton

Privileges and Immunities
David Skillen Bogen

Searches, Seizures, and Warrants
Robert M. Bloom

The Supremacy Clause
Christopher R. Drahozal

Procedural Due Process
Rhonda Wasserman

Double Jeopardy

A Reference Guide to the United States Constitution

David S. Rudstein

Foreword by Albert W. Alschuler

REFERENCE GUIDES TO THE
UNITED STATES CONSTITUTION, NUMBER 9
Jack Stark, *Series Editor*

PRAEGER

Westport, Connecticut
London

Library of Congress Cataloging-in-Publication Data

Rudstein, David S. (David Stewart), 1946–
Double jeopardy: a reference guide to the United States Constitution/
David S. Rudstein; foreword by Albert W. Alschuler.
p. cm.—(Reference guides to the United States Constitution, ISSN 1539-8986; no. 9)
Includes bibliographical references and index.
ISBN 0-313-31180-3 (alk. paper)
1. Double jeopardy—United States. I. Title. II. Series.
KF9245.R83 2004
345.73'04—dc22 2004009840

British Library Cataloguing in Publication Data is available.

Library of Congress Catalog Card Number: 2004009840
ISBN: 0-313-31180-3
ISSN: 1539-8986

First published in 2004

Praeger Publishers, 88 Post Road West, Westport, CT 06881
An imprint of Greenwood Publishing Group, Inc.
www.praeger.com

Printed in the United States of America

The paper used in this book complies with the
Permanent Paper Standard issued by the National
Information Standards Organization (Z39.48-1984)

10 9 8 7 6 5 4 3 2 1

To Danielle and Jobie, the best daughters a father could ever hope for; and to the memory of my parents, Daniel and Delia, whose sacrifices made it all possible.

[T]he double jeopardy prohibition of the Fifth Amendment represents a fundamental ideal in our constitutional heritage.

—Justice Thurgood Marshall, *Benton v. Maryland,* 395 U.S. 784, 794 (1969)

Contents

Series Foreword

JACK STARK

One can conceive of the United States Constitution in many ways. For example, noting the reverence in which it has been held, one can think of it as equivalent to a sacred text. Unfortunately, most of its devotees have had less knowledge and even less understanding of the document than they have had reverence for it. Sometimes it is treated as primarily a political document and on that basis has been subjected to analysis, such as Charles Beard's *An Economic Interpretation of the Constitution of the United States.* One can plausibly argue that the Constitution seems most astounding when it is seen in the light of the intellectual effort that has been associated with it. Three brief but highly intense bursts of intellectual energy produced, and established as organic law, most of the Constitution as it now exists. Two of these efforts, sustained over a long period of time, have enabled us to better understand that document.

The first burst of energy occurred at the Constitutional Convention. Although some of the delegates' business, such as the struggle between populous and nonpopulous states about their representation in Congress, was political, much of it was about fundamental issues of political theory. A few of the delegates had or later achieved international eminence for their intellects. Among them were Benjamin Franklin, Alexander Hamilton, and James Madison. Others, although less well known, had first-rate minds. That group includes George Mason and George Wythe. Many of the delegates contributed intelligently. Although the Convention's records are less than satisfactory, they indicate clearly enough that the delegates worked mightily to constitute not merely a polity but a rational polity—one that would rise to the standards envisioned by the delegate's intellectual ancestors. Their product, though brief, is amazing. William Gladstone called it "the most wonderful work ever struck off."

Despite the delegates' eminence and the Constitution's excellence as seen from our place in history, its ratification was far from certain. That state of affairs necessitated the second burst of intellectual energy associated with that document: the debate over ratification. Soon after the Convention adjourned, articles and speeches—some supporting the Constitution and some attacking it—began to proliferate. A national debate commenced, not only about the document itself, but also about the nature of the polity that ought to exist in this country. Both sides included many writers and speakers who were verbally adroit and steeped in the relevant political and philosophical literature. The result was an accumulation of material that is remarkable for both its quantity and its quality. At its apex is *The Federalist Papers,* a production of Alexander Hamilton, James Madison, and John Jay that deserves a place among the great books of Western culture.

Another burst, not as impressive as the first two but highly respectable, occurred when the Bill of Rights was proposed. Some delegates to the Constitutional Convention had vigorously asserted that such guarantees should be included in the original document. George Mason, the principal drafter of the Virginia Declaration of Rights, so held, and he walked out of the Convention when he failed to achieve his purpose. Even those who had argued that the rights in question were implicit recognized the value of adding protection of them to the Constitution. The debate was thus focused on the rights that were to be explicitly granted, not on whether any rights *ought* to be explicitly granted. Again many writers and speakers entered the fray, and again the debate was solidly grounded in theory and was conducted on a high intellectual level.

Thus, within a few years a statement of organic law and a vital coda to it had been produced. However, the meaning and effect of many of that document's provisions were far from certain; the debates on ratification of the Constitution and the Bill of Rights had demonstrated that. In addition, the document existed in a vacuum, because statutes and actions had not been assessed by its standards. The attempt to resolve these problems began after Chief Justice John Marshall, in Marbury v. Madison, asserted the right of the U.S. Supreme Court to interpret and apply the Constitution. Judicial interpretation and application of the Constitution, beginning with the first constitutional case and persisting until the most recent, is one of the sustained exertions of intellectual energy associated with the Constitution. The framers would be surprised by some of the results of those activities. References in the document to "due process," which seems to refer only to procedures, have been held also to have a substantive dimension. A right to privacy has been found lurking among the penumbras of various parts of the text. A requirement that states grant the same "privileges and immunities" to citizens of other states that they granted to their own citizens, which seemed to guarantee important rights, was held not to be particularly important. The corpus of judicial interpretations of the Constitution is now as voluminous as that document is terse.

As the judicial interpretations multiplied, another layer—interpretations of interpretations—appeared, and also multiplied. This layer, the other sustained intellectual effort associated with the Constitution, consists of articles, most of them published in law reviews, and books on the Constitution. This material varies in quality and significance. Some of these works of scholarship result from meticulous examination and incisive thought. Others repeat earlier work, or apply a fine-tooth comb to matters that are too minute even for such a comb. Somewhere in that welter of tertiary material is the answer to almost every question that one could ask about constitutional law. The problem is finding the answer that one wants. The difficulty of locating useful guidance is exacerbated by the bifurcation of most constitutional scholarship into two kinds. In "Two Styles of Social Science Research," C. Wright Mills delineates macroscopic and molecular research. The former deals with huge issues, the latter with tiny issues. Virtually all of the scholarship on the Constitution is of one of those two types. Little of it is macroscopic, but that category does include some first-rate syntheses such as Jack Rakove's *Original Meanings*. Most constitutional scholarship is molecular and, again, some fine work is included in that category.

In his essay, Mills bemoans the inability of social scientists to combine the two kinds of research that he describes to create a third category that will be more generally useful. This series of books is an attempt to do for constitutional law the intellectual work that Mills proposed for social science. The author of each book has dealt carefully and at reasonable length with a topic that lies in the middle range of generality. Upon completion, this series will consist of thirty-seven books, each on a constitutional law topic. Some of the books, such as the book on freedom of the press, explicate one portion of the Constitution's text. Others, such as the volume on federalism, treat a topic that has several anchors in the Constitution. The books on constitutional history and constitutional interpretation range over the entire document, but each does so from one perspective. Except for a very few of the books, for which special circumstances dictate minor changes in format, each book includes the same components: A brief history of the topic, a lengthy and sophisticated analysis of the current state of the law on that topic, a bibliographical essay that organizes and evaluates scholarly material in order to facilitate further research, a table of cases, and an index. The books are intellectually rigorous—in fact, authorities have written them—but, due to their clarity and to brief definitions of terms that are unfamiliar to laypersons, each is comprehensible and useful to a wide audience, one that ranges from other experts on the book's subject to intelligent non-lawyers.

In short, this series provides an extremely valuable service to the legal community and to others who are interested in constitutional law, as every citizen should be. Each book is a map of part of the U.S. Constitution. Together they map all of that document's territory that is worth mapping. When this series is complete, each book will be a third kind of scholarly work that combines the macroscopic and the molecular. Together they will explicate all of the important constitutional topics. Anyone who wants assistance in understanding either a topic in constitutional law or the Constitution as a whole can easily find it in these books.

Foreword

Albert W. Alschuler
Julius Kreeger Professor of Law and Criminology
The University of Chicago

A well-dressed older woman once approached a zookeeper. "Mr. Zookeeper," she asked, "is that a male or a female hippopotamus?" "Madam," the zookeeper replied, "the answer to that question should be of interest only to another hippopotamus."

"Lawyer's law" is the law of interest only to lawyers. The twists and turns of double jeopardy law might seem to qualify.

On the surface, the idea looks simple. The Fifth Amendment of the United States Constitution provides, "[N]or shall any person be subject for the same offence to be twice put in jeopardy of life or limb." This language might have been read to do no more than incorporate three well established pleas of the English common law that could bar a defendant's trial—*autrefoits acquit* (formerly acquitted), *autrefoits convict* (formerly convicted), and *pardon* (formerly pardoned by the Crown). Each of these pleas told the court, "This matter has already been resolved." The core idea of the Double Jeopardy Clause—it has been decided, or *res judicata*—turns out, however, to be much trickier than the authors of the Fifth Amendment imagined. Moreover, in 1824—in its first construction of the clause—the Supreme Court held that it did more than incorporate the concept of *res judicata*.

Courts now discover answers to questions such as these in the nineteen words of the Double Jeopardy Clause:

- When a person has been acquitted of robbery, may he be tried for the same theft that was alleged to be part of the robbery? (Answer: No.)

- May a person be convicted at a single trial of both robbery and the theft that constituted a part of the robbery, and may a separate punishment be imposed for each crime? (Answer: Yes, if the legislature clearly wanted this result.)
- When a defendant alleged to have broken into a poker game and to have robbed six poker players is acquitted of robbing the first player, may he be tried for robbing the second? (Answer: No.)
- When a poker player has played ten hands of poker, may she be convicted of illegal gambling ten times? (Answer: Yes.)
- When a person has secured an acquittal of murder by bribing a judge, may he be tried for murder again? (Answer: Yes.)
- When a person has secured an acquittal of murder by bribing a witness to support her alibi, may she be tried for the murder again? (Answer: Probably no.)
- When the case of a 21-year-old defendant has been mistakenly assigned to a court with jurisdiction only over juveniles and the defendant has then been acquitted, may she be tried in an adult court? (Answer: Yes.)
- When someone has been acquitted of murder, may the family of the murder victim sue him to recover punitive damages? (Answer: Yes.)
- When a jury cannot agree on a verdict, may the judge declare a mistrial and order the defendant to stand trial again? (Answer: Sometimes yes and sometimes no.)
- When a man has hired a killer in Georgia, brought him to Alabama to abduct the man's wife, and paid the killer for murdering the wife in Georgia, may the husband be convicted of murder in both Georgia and Alabama? May he be sentenced to death in the second state's trial even if he managed to escape the death penalty in the first state? (Answer: Yes.)
- When an appellate court has reversed a defendant's conviction because the evidence presented at trial was insufficient to support her conviction, may she be tried again? (Answer: No.)
- When an appellate court has reversed a defendant's conviction because the jury heard evidence of an involuntary confession that should not have been admitted, may she be tried again? (Answer: Yes.)
- When an appellate court has reversed a defendant's conviction because the prosecutor, at the end of a trial, mentioned a confession the court had excluded from evidence, may the defendant be tried again? (Answer: Uncertain.)
- When a jury has acquitted a defendant of robbing a bank, may a court revoke the probated sentence the defendant received for an earlier crime and send him to prison on the ground that, despite the jury's verdict, he did rob the bank? (Answer: Yes.)

You need not be a lawyer to be intrigued by these questions and to be baffled by some of the answers. In this volume, America's foremost authority on the Double Jeopardy Clause, David S. Rudstein, describes the courts' answers to conundrums like these and explains why many of the answers make sense and many of them do not.

Rudstein begins with a chapter examining the origins of the double jeopardy principle, its development in England and America prior to the ratification of the Fifth Amendment, and its modern history, including its application to the States. He ends with a bibliographic essay summarizing all the significant scholarly writing on the topic. In between, he explores the law concerning such knotty subjects as when jeopardy attaches, when it ends, what constitutes the "same offense," when a trial may be cancelled prior to verdict and a new trial begun, when multiple punishments are permissible, when the government may appeal a ruling in favor of the defendant, when a defendant may be sentenced to a greater punishment on a retrial, when "collateral estoppel" applies, and when "the dual-sovereignty doctrine" permits a second trial.

Rudstein's meticulous scholarship ensures that this volume will be of value to lawyers. The intriguing and important law of the Double Jeopardy Clause, however, should not be simply "lawyer's law." The crisp prose and careful exposition of Rudstein's work now make this law accessible to zookeepers, curious visitors, and other non-lawyers who care about a provision of the Bill of Rights that, in the Supreme Court's words, is truly "fundamental to our scheme of justice."

Introduction

The Double Jeopardy Clause of the Fifth Amendment to the Constitution of the United States provides that "[n]o person shall ... be subject for the same offense to be twice put in jeopardy of life and limb. ..." As the United States Supreme Court recognized in *Benton v. Maryland* (1969), this guarantee against double jeopardy "represents a fundamental ideal in our constitutional heritage." When initially adopted, however, the Double Jeopardy Clause did not restrict the States in any way (Palko v. Connecticut, 1937; Brock v. North Carolina, 1953). Like the other provisions of the Bill of Rights (the first eight amendments to the Constitution), it placed limitations only upon the federal government (Barron v. Mayor and City Council of Baltimore, 1833; *accord* Adamson v. California, 1947). It was not until 1969 that the Supreme Court held that the United States Constitution barred the States from placing an individual in jeopardy twice for the same offense. In that year the Court determined that the Due Process Clause of the Fourteenth Amendment, which prohibits the States from "depriv[ing] any person of life, liberty, or property, without due process of law," "incorporated" the Double Jeopardy Clause of the Fifth Amendment and made its provisions fully applicable to the States (Benton v. Maryland, 1969). Technically, then, the protection against double jeopardy afforded by the Constitution to a defendant in a state criminal prosecution stems from the Fourteenth Amendment, not directly from the Fifth Amendment. However, for the sake of convenience, this text will refer to both the Fifth and Fourteenth Amendment protections against double jeopardy as the "Fifth Amendment protection against double jeopardy."

This text is divided into three major portions. Chapter 1 discusses the history of the protection against double jeopardy. It begins by showing that ancient Jewish law, early Greek and Roman law, and canon law all recognized some form of protection against double jeopardy. The chapter then studies the development of the protection against double jeopardy in English common law, beginning with the twelfth century dispute between King Henry II and Thomas à Becket (the Archbishop of Canterbury) and ending with the emergence of modern double jeopardy law in the late-seventeenth and eighteenth centuries. Next, chapter 1 explores the protection against double jeopardy in North America during the colonial period. It then traces the events during the First Congress leading up to the submission of the Double Jeopardy Clause to the States for ratification in 1789 and culminating with its inclusion two years later as part of the Fifth Amendment to the Constitution of the United States. Chapter 1 concludes with an examination of some of the major decisions of the United States Supreme Court interpreting and giving meaning to the guarantee against double jeopardy contained in the Fifth Amendment.

Chapter 2 contains an in-depth analysis of the current scope and content of the constitutional guarantee against double jeopardy. It commences with a detailed discussion of the policies underlying the protection against double jeopardy. After exploring the meaning of the term "jeopardy" and discussing the types of proceedings in which the protection against double jeopardy applies, it moves on to examine when two offenses are deemed to be the "same" for purposes of double jeopardy analysis. This latter section includes a discussion of the so-called "dual sovereignty" doctrine under which two separate sovereigns, such as a state and the federal government, can each prosecute an individual for the same conduct without violating the federal guarantee against double jeopardy. Chapter 2 then focuses upon the substantive limitations imposed by the Double Jeopardy Clause. The bulk of the analysis explores the circumstances in which the Double Jeopardy Clause bars successive prosecutions of an individual for the same offense and the circumstances in which it bars multiple punishments for the same offense. Next, chapter 2 briefly examines the limitations the double jeopardy provision places upon the resentencing of an individual convicted of a criminal offense; first in the context of the same proceeding and then in the situation in which an individual is convicted again for the same offense at a new trial following his successful appeal of his initial conviction. Chapter 2 concludes with an examination of the double jeopardy provision in the context of appeals, focusing primarily upon the limitations it places upon appeals by the government.

The final portion of this text contains a bibliographical essay discussing a variety of sources that examine the various aspects of the protection against double jeopardy addressed in the historical and analytical chapters of the text.

1

A History of the Guarantee Against Double Jeopardy

ORIGINS OF THE GUARANTEE

The Double Jeopardy Clause of the Fifth Amendment provides: "[N]or shall any person be subject for the same offence to be twice put in jeopardy of life or limb ...." In recent years, courts, jurists, and scholars have considered the protection against being placed in jeopardy twice for the same offense* to be a fundamental right. In *Benton v. Maryland* (1969), the Supreme Court of the United States stated that "[t]he fundamental nature of the guarantee against double jeopardy can hardly be doubted." A dozen years earlier, United States Supreme Court Justice Felix Frankfurter called the protection "an indispensable requirement of a civilized criminal procedure" (Green v. United States, 1957 (dissenting opinion)). Justice Ivan Rand of the Supreme Court of Canada made a similar claim, maintaining that this "cardinal principle" lies "[a]t the foundation of criminal law" (Cullen v. The King, 1949 (dissenting opinion)). One prominent scholar believes that "[n]o other procedural doctrine is more fundamental or all-pervasive."[1]

The precise origins of the guarantee against double jeopardy are unclear. Early in the twentieth century, one American court declared that the doctrine "seems to have been always embedded in the common law of England, as well as in the Roman law, and doubtless in every other system of jurisprudence, and, instead of having a specific origin, it simply always existed" (Stout v. State *ex rel.* Caldwell, 1913). This claim is certainly overstated. The Code of Hammurabi, for example, makes no reference to double jeopardy.[2] This, in part, led one scholar to conclude that "[t]he alleged universality of the double jeopardy principle is not apparent from a study of early law."[3] Indeed, the United States Supreme Court itself recognized in *Palko v. Connecticut* (1937) that "[d]ouble jeopardy ... is not everywhere forbidden."

Nevertheless, there can be no doubt that the protection against double jeopardy possesses a long history. Ancient Jewish law contains several references to principles encompassed by double jeopardy law. The Talmud, a compilation of the teachings of the ancient Hebrew sages, proclaims that in capital cases an acquittal may not be reversed.[4] In the Old Testament, Deuteronomy 25:2 states that when a dispute between men is brought before a court, a guilty man who deserves to be beaten shall be flogged in the presence of the judge "according to the measure of his misdeeds" or "according to his guilt."[5] The Talmud relates that Rabbi Akiba relied upon this verse to explain why Jewish law prohibited a person liable to a death penalty by a human tribunal from also being flogged. Rabbi Akiba interpreted the verse to mean that "you make [the guilty man] liable to punishment for *one* misdeed, but you cannot hold him liable [in two ways] for *two* misdeeds [*i.e.*, death and lashes]."[6] A modern writer construes Rabbi Akiba's statement to mean that "for one offense only one punishment might be inflicted."[7]

The Talmud also contains a discussion by Rabbi Johanan of the situation in which a man forcibly engages in sexual intercourse with his maiden sister. Sexual intercourse with a maiden was punishable by a fine, whereas forcible sexual intercourse by a man with his sister, after forewarning, was punishable by flogging. Rabbi Johanan explained that a man who engaged in forcible sexual intercourse with his maiden sister would be liable *only* for the lashes because Deuteronomy 25:2 means that "you punish him because of one guilt but not because of two guilts ...."[8]

United States Supreme Court Justice Hugo L. Black asserted in his dissenting opinion in *Bartkus v. Illinois* (1959) that "[f]ear and abhorrence of governmental power to try people twice for the same conduct is one of the oldest ideas found in western civilization. Its roots run deep into Greek and Roman times" (*see also* Benton v. Maryland, 1969). An examination of early Greek and Roman law bears out Justice Black's assertion. Both legal systems contained some form of protection against double jeopardy. In 355 B.C.E., the Greek orator Demosthenes stated that "the laws forbid the same man to be tried twice on the same issue, be it a civil action, a scrutiny, a contested claim, or anything else of the sort."[9] It is said that in ancient Athens, "[a] man could not be tried twice for the same offense."[10] Referring to the practice in the last half of the fifth century, one scholar wrote: "The main concern of a man brought into court was to win a verdict by one means or another, for once tried he could not be prosecuted again on the same charge, the rule *ne bis in eadem re* being accepted in Athens if not in Sparta ...."[11] This prohibition against double jeopardy may have been incomplete, for "the pleaders were not slow to find loopholes in the law and to employ various devices, including charges of false witness, for reopening questions which had apparently already been disposed of by the courts."[12]

In the Roman Republic, an acquittal by a magistrate in a criminal prosecution barred further proceedings of any kind against the accused.[13] The Roman Empire also provided some protection against double jeopardy. During the early years of the Empire, "there was no appeal and no chance of reviewing the verdict of a jury."[14] On one occasion during the reign of Tiberius in the first century, a jury acquitted a man Tiberius thought should have been convicted. Although Tiberius scolded the jury and charged the man with another crime, "he could not affect the verdict already given."[15] Shortly thereafter, the rulers of Rome began providing substitutes for jury trials[16] and allowed an accuser to seek review of an acquittal in the imperial appeal courts.[17] Despite these new judicial procedures, some protection against double jeopardy still existed. Iulius Paulus, a leading Roman jurist at the turn of the second and third centuries, stated that "[a]fter a public acquittal a defendant can again be prosecuted by his informer within thirty days, *but after that time [has passed] this cannot be done*."[18] The *Digest of Justinian* (a collection and abridgment of juristic writings on then-existing Roman law compiled under the Byzantine emperor Justinian I and published in 533) provided that "[t]he governor must not allow a man to be charged with the same offense of which he has already been acquitted ...."[19]

The Roman law most likely contained the maxim *nemo debet bis puniri pro uno delicto*,[20] that is, "[n]o one ought to be punished twice for one offense."[21] Nonetheless, the protection against double jeopardy afforded by Roman law differed significantly from that accorded an individual under modern double jeopardy principles, primarily because criminal prosecutions generally were not brought by the state. Rather, under Roman law, a criminal prosecution could be brought by the victim of the crime or by any Roman citizen.[22] In most cases, a person injured by the conduct of another could elect[23] to bring either a criminal action against the wrongdoer, or alternatively, a delictual action[24] against him (*i.e.*, a private action seeking a penalty—not compensation—from the wrongdoer). Thus, after its statement that "[t]he governor must not allow a man to be charged with the same offense of which he has already been acquitted ...," the *Digest of Justinian* explains that this principle merely means that the individual cannot be charged *by the same accuser*; at least "if the person who has now come forward as accuser be pursuing his own injury and shows that he had not known that an accusation had [previously] been brought by another, if there is good reason he is to be allowed to be an accuser."[25]

The canon law, which began its development near the end of the Roman Empire, also contained a prohibition against double jeopardy.[26] The *Gregorian Decretals*, a compilation of papal decretals (mainly written answers to specific questions put to the pope) promulgated by Pope Gregory IX in 1234,[27] contains a chapter, taken from a canon of an earlier church council, proclaiming: "An accusation cannot be repeated with respect to those crimes of which the accused has been absolved."[28] The commentary on this chapter states this principle as: "[I]f anyone is absolved of a crime of which he was accused, he should not again be accused of the same thing."[29] Even earlier, around 1140, Gratian, a Camaldolese monk who taught in Bologna, published his *Concordantia discordantium canonum* (*Concordance of discordant canons*), known as the *Decretum*, which contained a mass of authorities from the past, including canons of church councils, scriptural passages, and decisions of popes.[30] The *Decretum* contains at least two references to double jeopardy. At one point it states: "The Scripture holds, 'God does not punish twice in the same matter,'"[31] while at another it proclaims: "Whether one is condemned or absolved, there can be no further action involving the same crime."[32]

The canon law's prohibition against double jeopardy emanated from an interpretation given by Saint Jerome in 391 to Nahum 1:9, a verse in the Old Testament (Bartkus v. Illinois, 1959 (Black, J., dissenting)).[33] The Douay version of the Bible translates this verse as: "there shall not rise a double affliction;" the King James version reads: "affliction shall not rise up the second time." Saint Jerome interpreted the verse to mean that God does not punish twice for the same act (*see* Bartkus v. Illinois, 1959 (Black, J., dissenting)).[34] It was reasoned that if this were so before God, it should be the same on earth.[35] Saint Jerome's interpretation of the verse entered church canons as early as 847,[36] subsequently to be stated as, "Not even God judges twice for the same act" (Bartkus v. Illinois, 1959 (Black, J., dissenting)).[37]

ENGLISH COMMON LAW

By the middle of the thirteenth century, the English common law recognized some form of protection against double jeopardy. Over the next four hundred years, the guarantee against double jeopardy became firmly entrenched in the common law in the form of the pleas of *autrefoits acquit* (a former acquittal), *autrefoits convict* (a former conviction), and pardon.[38] By the second half of the eighteenth century, Sir William Blackstone, perhaps the most important writer on the common law, could say that the principle that "no man is to be brought into jeopardy of his life, more than once for the same offense," upon which the pleas were based, constitutes a "universal maxim of the common law."[39]

Scholars have advanced three different theories explaining the introduction of the double jeopardy principle into English common law. One theory postulates that the principle came from the Continent, either through canon law, which was introduced into England after the Norman conquest in 1066;[40] or through Roman law, which influenced treatise writers and judges.[41] These writers, as the theory goes, supplemented the relatively undeveloped common law with the more refined and sophisticated jurisprudence of the Roman law. In addition, the earliest judges of the common law courts, as well as the chancellors in England, were members of the clergy who had studied Roman law. When called upon to formulate principles, it is contended, they naturally turned to the ideas with which they were familiar from their studies.

The second theory advocates that the posthumous victory of Thomas à Becket, the Archbishop of Canterbury, in the twelfth century power struggle between the Church and King Henry II, led to the introduction of the principle.[42] Following his conquest of England, William the Conqueror (William I), perhaps to repay the Pope for supporting his conquest[43] or perhaps to help him gain control over the

English Church,[44] encouraged the establishment of a system of ecclesiastical courts to exist side-by-side with the royal courts.[45] These ecclesiastical courts claimed jurisdiction not only over spiritual matters,[46] but also over all criminal and civil cases in which a clerk (cleric) stood accused of committing a crime or a wrong.[47]

The relationship between the Church and the King deteriorated after William's death in 1087. In the middle of the twelfth century, Henry II sought to regain jurisdiction over clerics who committed secular offenses.[48] What motivated Henry remains a matter of conjecture. Some contend he sought to curb the power of the Church generally,[49] while others maintain he wanted to strengthen law enforcement in the realm and believed that ecclesiastical courts, which could impose neither the death penalty nor a penalty involving the shedding of blood, did not punish criminal clerics severely enough.[50] Still others claim that Henry sought to regain jurisdiction over clerics because he needed money to finance overseas campaigns and coveted the revenue generated for the Church through fines and forfeitures imposed by ecclesiastical courts.[51]

Whatever his motivation, Henry held a council of the magnates of the realm in 1164. This council resulted in the issuance of the Constitutions of Clarendon, a formal statement embodying the previous customs concerning the jurisdiction of the Church in certain matters. The third clause of that document provided:

> Clergyman charged and accused of anything shall, on being summoned by a justice of the [K]ing, come into his court, to be responsible there for whatever it may seem to the [K]ing's court they should there be responsible for; and [to be responsible] in the ecclesiastical court [for what] it may seem they should there be responsible for—so that the [K]ing's justice shall send into the court of holy church to see on what ground matters are there to be treated. And if the clergyman is convicted, or [if he] confesses, the church should no longer protect him.[52]

This clause in the Constitutions meant that a clergyman suspected of committing a crime had to be brought to the royal court and accused there; unless he admitted his guilt, he would be sent to the ecclesiastical court for trial in the presence of royal officers; if convicted in the ecclesiastical court, he would be stripped of his clerical status and returned to the royal court and then be sentenced—it is unclear whether there would be a further trial—to the layman's punishment, either death or mutilation.[53] In addition, his property would be forfeited to the King.[54]

Archbishop Becket objected to this scheme. He claimed, among other things, that clerics could be tried and punished only in an ecclesiastical court and that a cleric convicted in such a court and deposed from his orders could not subsequently be brought to the royal court for punishment. To do so, argued Becket, would be to punish him twice for the same offense in violation of the maxim *nec enim Deus iudicat bis in idipsum* (or a variation thereof) and of canon law.[55] The conflict between Henry and Becket continued for several years with Becket, at one point, fleeing to France and excommunicating several of the King's ministers after Henry seized the revenues of the see of Canterbury. Becket and Henry eventually reached a compromise and Becket returned to England. Shortly thereafter, in 1170, four of Henry's knights murdered Becket inside Canterbury Cathedral.[56] Six years later, and after the canonization of Becket by Pope Alexander III, Henry renounced the provision in the Constitutions that allowed a degraded cleric to be further punished in the royal court.[57] Archbishop Becket's martyrdom and Henry's capitulation, as this theory argues, must have made an impression on the King's judges—many of whom were bishops and archdeacons—and convinced them that the maxim Becket espoused was worthy of consideration.[58]

The third theory explaining the introduction of the protection against double jeopardy into the English common law suggests that "the protection evolved from Anglo-Saxon criminal procedure as a practical and obvious procedural assumption by the courts."[59] The proponent of this theory argues that the relative unimportance of the protection during the first five hundred years of its existence, as illustrated by its numerous exceptions and its vulnerability to legislative interference on two occasions[60] without public or judicial uproar over the loss of liberties, in conjunction with its slow development, points towards procedural evolution rather than introduction from Roman law. Had the protection been a product of Roman law, the proponent contends, it probably would have established a rule of fundamental doctrine from its inception.[61] Similarly, she claims that the appearance of the plea of a former acquittal in 1203,[62] so soon after the clash between Becket and Henry II, shows that the conflict could not have played a major role in the introduction of the protection into English common law.[63] She reasons that such "a novel principle would take much longer to percolate through to [the] courts [and] establish itself as a commonplace rule ...."[64]

Regardless of the theory to which one subscribes, scholars generally agree that the origin of the protection against double jeopardy "is, and undoubtedly will remain, a matter of speculation,"[65] because "much of Western law derives from a common fund of shared judicial concepts."[66]

The extent to which the common law protected a person against double jeopardy before Henry II's capitulation is difficult to ascertain. Some evidence suggests that the earliest rulers after the Norman Conquest paid little heed to questions of double jeopardy. William II ("Rufus"), who reigned from 1087–1100, once tried fifty Englishmen by the ordeal of the hot iron. When they escaped unhurt, and hence were acquitted, William purportedly "declared he would try them again by the judgment of his court, and would not abide by this pretended judgment of God ...."[67] The Charter of Liberties, issued by Henry I in 1101, did not mention a protection against double jeopardy.[68] In 1163, Henry II's claim that he could retry a cleric, Philip de Brois, following his acquittal in an ecclesiastical court of murdering a knight,[69] brought his dispute with Becket to a head and constituted a complete rejection of a protection against double jeopardy.[70] Three years later, Henry II included in the Assize of Clarendon a provision that a person acquitted by the ordeal must abjure the realm (*i.e.*, depart the country under an oath never to return) if he was of bad character,[71] once again violating the principle against double jeopardy.

Even after Becket's murder and Henry's capitulation, a general prohibition against double jeopardy did not exist in England. An examination of the earliest treatise on the common law, purportedly written by Glanville in the last part of the twelfth century,[72] reveals no mention of a protection against double jeopardy.[73] Magna Carta, originally issued by King John in 1215[74] and reaffirmed by King Edward I in 1297,[75] also lacks a protection against double jeopardy.[76]

Thomas à Becket's successor, Archbishop Richard, did not oppose the form of dual punishment contained in the Constitutions of Clarendon. Upset that Becket's murderers had not been punished for their misdeed, he wanted laymen who murdered clerics to be excommunicated in the ecclesiastical court and then turned over to the royal courts to be hanged. He assured several of the King's justices that such a procedure would not punish a person twice for the same offense.[77] He argued that "there is no duplication where what is begun by one is completed by another"[78]—the exact position Henry had taken with respect to offenses committed by clerics. Indeed, after Henry II's death, Pope Innocent III issued a decree providing that the forgers of papal letters should be handed over to the secular courts and declared that such a procedure was sanctioned by the *Decretum*.[79] That position, too, was consistent with Henry's claim in his controversy with Becket.

The principle against double jeopardy was also violated by a statute enacted in 1315–16 in an attempt to ensure that the royal courts remained paramount to the ecclesiastical courts in those situations in which both possessed jurisdiction over the act of an individual.[80] That statute allowed the royal courts to ignore the determination of, and punishment imposed by, an ecclesiastical court. It provided that "[w]hen any one [c]ase is debated before [j]udges, [s]piritual [or] [t]emporal, as ... upon the [c]ase of laying violent hands on a [c]lerk, [it is thought,] that notwithstanding the [s]piritual [j]udgement, the King's Court shall discuss the same [m]atter ...."[81]

Situations not involving clergy, however, show some recognition of the principle against double jeopardy following the Henry II–Becket dispute, but its development and emergence into modern double jeopardy law was slow. One explanation for its slow growth is that the power to prosecute for offenses had not yet coalesced in the state. At least since the Norman Conquest, criminal prosecutions could be brought not only by the King by means of an indictment (*i.e.*, a formal written accusation of a crime), but also by a private subject in a suit against another demanding punishment for the particular wrong he suffered, *i.e.*, a "suit of vengeance,"[82] rather than for the offense against the public.[83] This latter method of prosecution, known as an "appeal," initially could be used for a variety of offenses, although by the end of the thirteenth century its use was limited to serious ones.[84] By its very nature, the protection against double jeopardy constitutes a limitation upon the power of the state to prosecute and punish an individual. As one scholar put it, "[t]he state's gathering of the power to institute suit is a prerequisite to a true double jeopardy situation."[85]

In the thirteenth century, a judgment of acquittal in a suit brought on an indictment by the King barred a further suit on an indictment by the King.[86] By the middle of the thirteenth century, a judgment of acquittal in an appeal brought by a private individual barred a further suit by that individual,[87] as well as by any other individual.[88] It is unclear whether, in the thirteenth century, an acquittal on an appeal by a private individual barred an indictment by the King, and *vice-versa*. Bracton, in a treatise written sometime between 1220 and 1256, stated that an acquittal on an appeal of homicide barred a suit by the King for the same death.[89] On the other hand, Britton, writing around 1290, said that "although [an appellee of homicide] acquit himself as to our [*i.e.*, the King's] suit, yet the suit of any other, who will prosecute within the year and day, is not thereby taken away."[90] One modern scholar asserts that "at least up to the mid-fourteenth century, if a verdict of acquittal at the suit of the King preceded an appeal the courts would hold the earlier acquittal null and void ...."[91]

Conviction of a felony at this time carried a mandatory death penalty; therefore, a prohibition against a second conviction was irrelevant.[92] If the King pardoned an individual convicted on an appeal, the pardon operated to prevent a subsequent prosecution by the King for the same offense.[93] On the other hand, a conviction on an indictment, followed by a pardon, would not bar an appeal by a private party, "for the pardon invariably was on the condition that the defendant 'stand to right' (*stet recto*) to answer the suit of the party."[94]

During the fifteenth century, an acquittal on an appeal barred a prosecution for the same offense by indictment,[95] and an acquittal on an indictment barred an appeal for the same offense.[96] In such situations, the accused could plead the former acquittal as a bar to the subsequent prosecution.[97]

In 1487, however, a statute created a limited exception to the plea of a former acquittal.[98] By that time a general practice had developed in homicide cases in favor of appeals. An individual could not be tried on an indictment for homicide until more than a year and a day after the death of the victim[99]—a year and a day being the period within which an appeal could be brought by those entitled to prosecute an appeal of death.[100] Frequently, though, witnesses died during that time period or the matter was forgotten. To remedy this situation, the statute provided for the immediate prosecution of an indictment for homicide, without waiting for the bringing of an appeal. In addition, it removed the plea of a former acquittal as a bar to the prosecuting of an appeal for the same death, so long as the appeal was brought within a year and a day.[101]

This "loophole" created by the statute, however, proved to be of little practical significance (Bartkus v. Illinois, 1959 (Black, J., dissenting)). Courts construed it extremely narrowly, and it was never broadened beyond homicide cases.[102] Moreover, the statute soon fell into disuse (*see* Bartkus v. Illinois, 1959 (Black, J., dissenting)).[103] Although Parliament did not formally abolish prosecution by appeal until 1819,[104] by the early part of the eighteenth century that method of prosecution was "all but practically obsolete."[105] Nevertheless, as late as 1709, an appeal was brought after an acquittal (Young v. Slaughterford, 1709). In that case, Chief Justice Holt *ordered* an appeal for murder to be brought against a man who previously had been acquitted on an indictment for the same offense. A jury convicted the man on the appeal, and he apparently was sentenced to death. Indeed, it was an appeal after an acquittal for murder (see Ashford v. Thornton, 1818) that prompted Parliament to abolish prosecutions by appeal.[106]

Perhaps because of the statute of Henry VII in 1487,[107] the sixteenth century proved to be a "dark period" in the development of a rule prohibiting double jeopardy.[108] In an apparent attempt to prevent Welsh criminals from receiving favorable treatment from Welsh juries,[109] a statute was enacted in 1534 allowing individuals acquitted of felonies committed in Wales to be tried in the adjoining English county within two years of the alleged offense.[110] In 1591, the Court of King's Bench, the highest court in England, held in *Vaux's Case* that the accused acquitted of an offense under an insufficient indictment could be tried again under a new indictment, because he was never in jeopardy under the defective indictment. This was one of several judicial decisions "stultify[ing] the widening of the protection [against double jeopardy]."[111]

Nevertheless, despite these "significant lapses"[112] in the rational development of the rules against double jeopardy, the sixteenth century saw a legal text for the first time describe the pleas of *autrefoits acquit* (a former acquittal) and *autrefoits convict* (a former conviction) in detail and present them as principles of law. This text, written by Sir William Staunford in 1557,[113] was the first to use the Norman-French labels to describe the pleas and the first to mention the plea of a former conviction, although in a form bearing little resemblance to its manifestation in modern double jeopardy law.[114] At that time, though, the pleas "still represented little more than a set of rules of procedure of no great pre-eminence."[115]

Modern double jeopardy law began to emerge in England in the last half of the seventeenth century.[116] By that time, prosecutions by the King had begun replacing private prosecutions by appeal as the preferred method of prosecution,[117] thereby fulfilling the "prerequisite to a true double jeopardy situation ...."[118] In addition, Sir Edward Coke's *Institutes* had been published posthumously in 1641 and 1644. In his *Third Institutes*,[119] Lord Coke, whom one scholar has called "a fountainhead of double jeopardy law,"[120] described the basis for double jeopardy, clarifying the concept and emphasizing its importance.[121] Largely restating earlier writers, Coke incorporated "the slowly growing body of case law" concerning double jeopardy that "by and large led the law deeper and deeper into a mire of tangled technical and artificial rules."[122] Coke's work did not indicate any important advances in the application of the pleas of *autrefoits acquit*, *autrefoits convict*, and pardon, which "remained the only manifestations of the rule against double jeopardy."[123] Indeed, the Bill of Rights enacted in 1689 made no mention of a protection against double jeopardy.[124]

Shortly after the publication of Coke's Institutes, Sir Matthew Hale wrote *The History of the Pleas of the Crown* (*Historia Placitorium Coronae*). Like Coke, Hale detailed the pleas of *autrefoits acquit*, *autrefoits convict*, and pardon,[125] but also like Coke, "many of his observations are studded with legal anachronism."[126] Whether Hale's work influenced the development of double jeopardy law during the seventeenth century is unclear because it was not published until 1736–39, more than sixty years after his death.

During the last half of the seventeenth century, English courts began dealing with a variety of double jeopardy issues,[127] such as whether an individual acquitted of an offense could be re-indicted for a different offense based upon the same conduct for which he had been acquitted (*see* Turner, 1664; Jones and Bever, 1665). In the 1660s, the Court of King's Bench expanded the protection against double jeopardy considerably. Among other things, the Court held that a prosecutor could not seek a new trial following an acquittal (The King v. Read, 1660). It also held that a bill of exceptions (*i.e.*, a written statement—signed by the trial judge and presented to a reviewing court—containing the objections taken by a party during trial and the grounds upon which they were based) could not be employed in criminal cases (Sir Henry Vane's Case, 1662). In so holding, the Court refused to expand the scope of review by writ of error, which was limited to errors on the face of the trial record. Because a second proceeding was permitted when a conviction was reversed on a writ of error,[128] had the Court not limited the use of a bill of exceptions, further trials would have been permitted in criminal cases.[129]

It also became clear during the last half of the seventeenth century that the Court of King's Bench would recognize judgments of other criminal courts in England so that an acquittal in any such court that had jurisdiction over the matter barred a subsequent prosecution for the same crime in the Court of King's Bench.[130] The Court of King's Bench also held that an acquittal in another country barred a subsequent prosecution for the same offense in England. In *Rex v. Hutchinson* (1677) (discussed in Beak v. Thyrwhit, 1688; *see also* The King v. Roche, 1775), the Court held that Hutchinson's previous acquittal of murder in Portugal barred his prosecution in England for the same killing.

During that same period, the Court of King's Bench also dealt with the practice frequently engaged in by trial judges of discharging the jury when it appeared an acquittal was imminent, thereby affording the prosecuting attorney the opportunity to bring a stronger case in a new trial. In *The King v. Perkins* (1698), the Court prohibited the practice, with Chief Justice Lord Holt stating, "it was the opinion of all the Judges of England, upon debate between them, that in all capital cases, a juror cannot be withdrawn, though the parties consent to it; that in criminal cases, not capital, a juror may be withdrawn, if both parties consent, but not otherwise ...."

By the second half of the eighteenth century, the pleas of *autrefoits acquit*, *autrefoits convict*, and pardon were fixtures in English common law. In his monumental treatise, Sir William Blackstone set forth the following rules that applied to all but homicide cases, which were governed by the statute of 1487:[131]

> First, [under] the plea of *autrefoits acquit*, or a former acquittal, ... when a man is once fairly found not guilty upon any indictment, or other prosecution, before any court having competent jurisdiction of the offence, he may plead such acquittal in bar of any subsequent accusation for the same crime. Therefore an acquittal on an appeal is a good bar to an indictment on the same offense. And so also was an acquittal on an indictment a good bar to an appeal, by the common law ....
>
> Secondly, the plea of *autrefoits convict*, or a former conviction for the same identical crime, though no judgment was ever given, or perhaps will be, ... is a good plea in bar to an indictment ....
>
> Lastly, a *pardon* may be pleaded in bar; as at once destroying the end and purpose of the indictment, by remitting that punishment which the prosecution is calculated to inflict.[132]

DOUBLE JEOPARDY PROTECTION IN AMERICA BEFORE THE ADOPTION OF THE FIFTH AMENDMENT

While double jeopardy law continued to develop in England during the seventeenth century, it began to take root in England's colonies in North America. In 1639, the Maryland General Assembly enacted the Act for the Liberties of the People, which has been called "the first American Bill of Rights."[133] Although the Act did not contain an express protection against double jeopardy, it reaffirmed the principle that the inhabitants of the Colony (with the exception of slaves) "[s]hall have and enjoy all such rights[,] liberties[,] immunities[,] priviledges [sic][,] and free customs ... as any naturall [sic] born subject of England hath or ought to have or enjoy in the Realm of England by force or vertue [sic] of the common law or [s]tatute [l]aw of England ...."[134]

The first colonial enactment containing an express guarantee against double jeopardy appeared in 1641 when the General Court, or legislature, of the Massachusetts Bay Colony enacted the Body of Liberties. This detailed charter of liberties served as the model for other colonies and was "the most important ... forerunner of the federal Bill of Rights."[135] Paragraph 42 of the Body of Liberties stated that "[n]o man shall be twise [sic] sentenced by [c]ivill [sic] [j]ustice for one and the same [c]rime, offence, or [t]respasse [sic]."[136] Seven years later came the Laws and Liberties of 1648. This code included the double jeopardy provision contained in the Body of Liberties.[137] It also contained a provision stating that "everie [sic] [a]ction between partie [sic] and partie [sic] and in proceedings against delinquents in *criminal* [c]auses shall be ... entered in the *rolls* of everie [sic] [c]ourt by the *Recorder* thereof, that such [a]ctions be not afterwards brought again to the vexation of any man."[138]

Connecticut also adopted a provision against double jeopardy. The Connecticut Code of 1652 included a clause, which its authors took from the Massachusetts Bay

Colony's Body of Liberties, providing that "no [p]erson shall be twice sentenced by [c]ivil [j]ustice for one and the same [c]rime ...."[139] In addition, the Fundamental Constitutions of Carolina, a document drafted by the political philosopher John Locke but never adopted, contained a provision stating that "[n]o cause shall be twice tried in any one court, upon any reason or pretence whatsoever."[140]

After the Revolutionary War, the former colonies formed the United States of America under the Articles of Confederation. While guaranteeing the free inhabitants of each state "all privileges and immunities of free citizens in the several [s]tates,"[141] the Articles of Confederation did not contain a bill of rights or an express protection against double jeopardy. Similarly, most state constitutions at that time did not contain an express guarantee against double jeopardy, although some provided that the common law of England should remain in force unless altered by statute.[142] The common law of England, of course, recognized the pleas of *autrefoits acquit* and *autrefoits convict*.[143]

The first state constitution to incorporate an express protection against double jeopardy was the New Hampshire Constitution of 1784. Section XVI of the Constitution's Bill of Rights provided: "No subject shall be liable to be tried, after an acquittal, for the same crime or offence."[144] Shortly after New Hampshire's adoption of a constitutional protection against double jeopardy, Pennsylvania followed suit. In 1790, it ratified a new constitution containing the following double jeopardy clause: "No person shall, for the same offence, be twice put in jeopardy of life or limb."[145]

In addition to statutes and constitutional provisions recognizing a protection against double jeopardy, several colonies and, after independence, a number of states also recognized a prohibition against double jeopardy through case law. For example, Virginia courts acknowledged the English common law pleas of a former conviction, a former acquittal, and a pardon for the identical crime charged.[146] Thus, "[o]n a verdict of not guilty, the prisoner was forever discharged so far as that particular accusation was concerned."[147] Not surprisingly, the decisions in the Virginia courts involving these pleas tended to follow English precedent. In one case decided in 1735, a jury convicted an individual for stealing a horse. On a motion in arrest of judgment, the trial court declared a mistrial (*i.e.*, terminated the proceeding before entering a judgment on the fact finder's verdict) after finding that the order directing the sheriff to assemble a jury to try the case had been issued to the wrong county. The trial court nevertheless remanded the case for a new trial before a jury assembled in the proper county. It concluded that the maxim that a man should not be twice put in danger of his life did not bar a second trial of the individual for the horse theft because the jury that initially tried the case had no power to convict the accused.[148] The result reached by the Virginia court in this case was consistent with that reached in England in *Vaux's Case* (1591), in which the Court of King's Bench held that an individual acquitted of an offense charged in an insufficient indictment could be tried for the same offense under a new indictment because he was never in jeopardy under the original one.

New York courts also recognized the defenses of a previous conviction and a previous acquittal. In 1699, a grand jury in New York City charged three men with vending bread of unlawful assize. Two years earlier, the men had been convicted and fined for making bread contrary to the laws of New York City. The same act apparently constituted the basis for both charges, for the court dismissed the second charge because the men "ha[d] been fined before for the same fact."[149] Nearly seventy years later, George Klock, Jr., was charged in the Supreme Court of New York with contempt for rescuing his father from the sheriff. Klock pleaded *autrefoits convict* and the court discharged him, "[i]t appearing to the Court by the examination of the defendant taken in [c]ourt on [o]ath that the [d]efendant had been indicted in the Court of ... [General Sessions] ... for Albany for the [r]escue aforesaid and had been fined the sum of ten pounds for the same and had paid said [f]ine ...."[150] Although judicial records in colonial New York do not show any sign of a plea of *autrefoits acquit*, it has been suggested that this "can be attributed to the solicitude of royal officials that there be no double prosecutions."[151] Such solicitude also may explain the infrequency of a plea of *autrefoits convict*.[152]

In Connecticut, too, the courts recognized a protection against double jeopardy. In *Hannaball v. Spalding* (1783), a private individual, Spalding, brought a combined criminal prosecution and civil action for damages against Hannaball for the theft of a handkerchief. The county court acquitted Hannaball, but subsequently granted Spalding a new trial on the civil portion of the case on the ground of newly discovered evidence. At his second trial, Hannaball was found liable, and the court entered a judgment against him. The appellate court reversed that judgment, holding that a prosecutor could not obtain a new trial in a criminal case following the acquittal of the accused and that a new trial could not be granted only on the civil portion of a combined criminal prosecution and civil action for damages. Four years later, another appellate court in Connecticut reached a similar result. In *Coit v. Geer* (1787), the court held that an individual who brought a combined criminal prosecution and civil action for damages for theft could not appeal a verdict of not guilty. The court reasoned that "[n]o one is to be twice drawn in jeopardy for the same crime, which might be the case if this appeal is sustained."

Pennsylvania courts also recognized a protection against double jeopardy. In *Respublica v. Shaffer* (1788), Chief Justice Thomas McKean of the Supreme Court of Pennsylvania addressed a grand jury that was considering whether to charge a particular individual with a criminal offense. Chief Justice McKean told the grand jurors that the individual could not summon witnesses to testify before the grand jury in his behalf. He explained that allowing the putative defendant to call witnesses would turn the grand jury proceeding into a trial, with the grand jury's decision being tantamount to a verdict of acquittal or guilt. The Chief Justice continued: "[T]his would involve us in another difficulty; for by the law, it is declared, that no man shall be twice put in jeopardy for the same offence: and, yet, it is certain, that the inquiry now proposed by the grand jury, would necessarily introduce the oppression of a double trial."

THE ADOPTION OF THE FIFTH AMENDMENT GUARANTEE AGAINST DOUBLE JEOPARDY

As originally submitted by the Constitutional Convention to the States for ratification, the Constitution did not contain a bill of rights. Its failure to do so created an outcry from the populace.[153] In his Inaugural Address to Congress, President George Washington mentioned the widespread call for amendments to the Constitution.[154] Thomas Jefferson, in a series of letters he wrote to his political mentor and intimate friend James Madison—the father of the Constitution—demanded that a bill of rights be added.[155] In a number of states, ratification of the Constitution occurred only after its supporters at the ratifying convention assured hesitant state delegates that a bill of rights would be added to the Constitution in the form of subsequent amendments.[156] George Mason and Elbridge Gerry, two of the framers of the Constitution, relied partially upon the lack of a bill of rights as a ground to oppose ratification of the Constitution. To be sure, many of those clamoring for a bill of rights viewed the proposed Constitution as too great an infringement upon the sovereignty of the individual states and actually opposed ratification of the Constitution on that ground; yet, their expressions of alarm would not have received a favorable response from the masses unless the citizenry felt genuine concern about the absence of a bill of rights.[157]

When the First Congress convened in 1789, James Madison introduced in the House of Representatives a series of proposed amendments, including all those that ultimately became the Bill of Rights (the first eight amendments to the Constitution).[158] One of those proposals was the forerunner of the Double Jeopardy Clause. Madison proposed that "[n]o person shall be subject, except in cases of impeachment, to more than one punishment or one trial for the same offence ...."[159]

The House of Representatives first referred Madison's proposed amendments to a Committee of the Whole[160] and then to a Select Committee,[161] which redrafted the clause on double jeopardy to read: "No person shall be subject, [except] in case of impeachment, to more than one trial or one punishment for the same offence ...."[162] When the House of Representatives, sitting as a Committee of the Whole, eventually considered the proposed amendments to the Constitution, Representative Egbert Benson of New York opposed the provision on double jeopardy. He claimed that its meaning "appeared rather doubtful" and asserted that its language prohibiting more than one trial for the same offense contradicted established law. He presumed that the clause intended to express the guarantee that no man's life should be put in jeopardy more than once for the same offense, but pointed out that an individual was frequently entitled to more than one trial for the same offense. Benson noted that the "humane" objective of a guarantee against double jeopardy was to prevent more than one punishment for a single offense. For that reason, he moved to amend the clause by striking the words "one trial or."[163]

Representative Roger Sherman of Connecticut agreed with Benson. Sherman thought that the courts would never think of trying and punishing an individual twice for the same offense, and that a person acquitted in his first trial should not be tried a second time. He argued, however, that a convicted individual should be entitled to a second trial if prejudicial error infected his initial trial. As the clause stood, Sherman contended, it deprived such a person of that opportunity.[164]

Representative Samuel Livermore of New Hampshire spoke in favor of the proposed amendment. He thought the clause was "essential" and that it declared the state of the law as it then stood. Striking the words "one trial or," as proposed by Representative Benson, would imply that the House intended to change the current law and expose an individual to the danger of more than one trial for the same offense. He noted that in many cases a guilty person obtains an acquittal because the prosecution failed to introduce sufficient evidence to prove his guilt and that in such cases, both in Great Britain and the United States, the individual cannot be tried again for the same offense. Accordingly, Livermore argued, the clause was proper.[165]

Representative Theodore Sedgwick of Massachusetts sided with Benson. He proclaimed that instead of securing the liberty of an individual, the clause would abridge the privileges of those accused of a crime.[166] Nevertheless, Benson's motion "lost by a considerable majority."[167]

Representative George Partridge of Massachusetts then moved to amend the proposal by inserting the words "by any law of the United States" after the words "same offence."[168] That amendment "lost also."[169]

Several days later, the House of Representatives adopted the proposed amendment concerning double jeopardy.[170] After a committee arranged the proposed articles of amendments, the House adopted a resolution to send the proposed amendments to the States for ratification.[171] The House then sent the proposed articles of amendments to the Senate for its concurrence.[172]

The Senate struck the words "except in case of impeachment, to more than one trial, or one punishment," and in its place substituted the phrase "be twice put in jeopardy of life or limb by any public prosecution."[173] Shortly thereafter, the Senate eliminated the words "by any public prosecution" and, after joining the clause on double jeopardy with several other clauses, approved the following proposed amendment dealing with double jeopardy: "[N]or shall any person be subject for the same offence to be twice put in jeopardy of life or limb ...."[174] The House of Representatives agreed to the Senate's version of the proposed amendment,[175] and after the Senate agreed to several changes in other proposed amendments,[176] Congress submitted it to the States for ratification.[177] This clause became part of the Fifth Amendment to the Constitution following its ratification by the States in 1791.

THE PROTECTION AGAINST DOUBLE JEOPARDY AFTER RATIFICATION OF THE FIFTH AMENDMENT

The Double Jeopardy Clause and State Criminal Prosecutions

The provisions of the Bill of Rights originally placed restrictions only upon the federal government (Barron v. Mayor and City Council of Baltimore, 1833; Adamson v. California, 1947); they were "not directed to the [S]tates" (Palko v.

Connecticut, 1937). As a result, the Double Jeopardy Clause of the Fifth Amendment did not prohibit the States from placing an individual in jeopardy twice for the same offense (Palko v. Connecticut, 1937; Brock v. North Carolina, 1953).

In 1868, following the Civil War, the States ratified the Fourteenth Amendment to the Constitution. The Due Process Clause of that Amendment provides that "[n]o [s]tate shall ... deprive any person of life, liberty, or property, without due process of law ...." After the ratification of the Fourteenth Amendment, the question arose whether the Due Process Clause incorporated the entire Bill of Rights and made its provisions fully applicable to the States. Over the years, a number of individual Justices of the United States Supreme Court, most notably Justice Hugo L. Black in his dissenting opinion in Adamson v. California (1947), argued that it did (*see also* Duncan v. Louisiana, 1968 (Black, J., concurring); Wolf v. Colorado, 1949 (Black, J., concurring); Betts v. Brady, 1942 (Black, J., dissenting)), but a majority of the Supreme Court never subscribed to this view; rather, the Court consistently held that the Due Process Clause does not totally incorporate the provisions of the Bill of Rights (*e.g.*, Adamson v. California, 1947; Palko v. Connecticut, 1937; Wolf v. Colorado, 1949; Twining v. New Jersey, 1908). The Supreme Court did, however, recognize that due process of law encompassed those rights—whether or not included in the specific provisions of the Bill of Rights—that are "fundamental" (Twining v. New Jersey, 1908), or as the Court put it in Palko v. Connecticut (1937), that are "implicit in the concept of ordered liberty" (*see also* Wolf v. Colorado, 1949; Adamson v. California, 1947).

Under this test, the Supreme Court held that several guarantees contained in the Bill of Rights applied to the States through the Due Process Clause of the Fourteenth Amendment, including the right to a public trial (*In re* Oliver, 1948) and the protection against unreasonable searches and seizures (albeit not the rule excluding illegally seized evidence from the government's case at trial) (Wolf v. Colorado, 1949). For the most part, though, the Supreme Court refused to hold that various other rights guaranteed to those accused of criminal conduct applied to the States through the Fourteenth Amendment. For example, in Hurtado v. California (1884), the Court held that due process of law did not require a grand jury indictment to institute serious criminal charges against an individual; while in *Twining v. New Jersey* (1908), it held that the privilege against self-incrimination is not so fundamental as to be required by due process of law. The Court reached the same result in *Betts v. Brady* (1942) with respect to the right to counsel, holding that due process did not require the States to appoint counsel to represent indigent individuals accused of committing felony offenses.

The issue whether due process of law protects an individual against double jeopardy was first presented to the United States Supreme Court in *Dreyer v. Illinois* (1902). In that case, Edward Dreyer, the former treasurer of the West Chicago Park Commissioners, contended that the State of Illinois placed him in jeopardy twice for the same offense when it retried him for failing to turn over funds and other personal property to his successor in office after his first trial for that offense ended in a mistrial (*i.e.*, the trial judge terminated the trial before the fact finder determined the factual guilt or innocence of the accused) because the jury could not agree upon a verdict. The Supreme Court did not, however, consider the merits of Dreyer's claim. Rather, the Court held that even if the due process of law required by the Fourteenth Amendment embraced the guarantee against double jeopardy, Dreyer's retrial following a hung jury did not place him in jeopardy twice for the same offense (*see* United States v. Perez, 1824).

The Supreme Court next faced the issue in *Palko*, in which the State of Connecticut charged Frank Palko with murder in the first degree. A jury convicted him of murder in the second degree, and the trial judge sentenced him to life imprisonment. The State, acting pursuant to a state statute and with the permission of the trial judge, appealed. It claimed that the judge committed a number of errors of law prejudicial to the government, including erroneously instructing the jury concerning the difference between first-degree murder and second-degree murder. The Connecticut Supreme Court of Errors reversed Palko's conviction and ordered that he be tried again for murder in the first degree (State v. Palko, 1936). Prior to his retrial, Palko claimed that the new trial would place him in jeopardy twice for the same offense, in violation of the Fourteenth Amendment. The judge rejected Palko's claim, and the trial proceeded. This time the jury convicted Palko of first-degree murder, and the trial judge sentenced him to the punishment of death.

The Supreme Court of the United States, with only a single justice dissenting, concluded that Palko's second trial did not deprive him of due process of law under the Fourteenth Amendment. The Supreme Court acknowledged that a "closely divided" Court in *Kepner v. United States* (1904) held that the prohibition against double jeopardy contained in the Fifth Amendment forbids putting an individual in jeopardy a second time, not only in a different case, but also in the same case if the new jeopardy is at the insistence of the government and not the accused. Nevertheless, after reviewing its previous decisions concerning the relationship between the Bill of Rights and the Due Process Clause of the Fourteenth Amendment, the Supreme Court concluded that the rights encompassed by due process of law, and hence applicable against the States, were only those "implicit in the concept of ordered liberty." The Court stated that the right must be such that abolishing it would "violate a 'principle of justice so rooted in the traditions and conscience of our people as to be ranked as fundamental.' ... [N]either liberty nor justice would exist if [it] were sacrificed." Allowing the government to appeal errors of law, the Court decided, would neither subject an accused to "a hardship so acute and shocking that our policy will not endure it," nor "violate those 'fundamental principles of liberty and justice which lie at the base of all our civil and political institutions.'" The Supreme Court reasoned:

> The state is not attempting to wear the accused out by a multitude of cases with accumulated trials. It asks no more than this, that the case against him shall go on until there shall be a trial free from the corrosion of substantial legal error. This is not cruelty at all, nor

even vexation in any immoderate degree. If the trial had been infected with error adverse to the accused, there might have been review at his instance, and as often as necessary to purge the vicious taint. A reciprocal privilege, subject at all times to the discretion of the presiding judge, has now been granted to the state. There is here no seismic innovation. The edifice of justice stands, its symmetry, to many, greater than before.

Indeed, earlier in its opinion, the Supreme Court stated that the dissenting opinions in *Kepner* show how much could be said in favor of a ruling in that case that the Fifth Amendment does *not* forbid putting an individual in jeopardy in the same case if the new jeopardy is following a successful appeal by the government. The Court continued:

Right-minded men, as we learn from those [dissenting] opinions, could reasonably, even if mistakenly, believe that a second trial was lawful in prosecutions subject to the Fifth Amendment, if it was all in the same case. Even more plainly, right-minded men could reasonably believe that in espousing that conclusion they were not favoring a practice repugnant to the conscience of mankind.

Sixteen years later, in *Brock v. North Carolina* (1953), the Supreme Court again faced the issue whether due process protects an individual against double jeopardy. In that case, the State of North Carolina charged Brock and two others involved in a labor dispute with firing shots into a house from a passing automobile. The government tried the two others first and obtained convictions for assault with a deadly weapon. At Brock's separate trial, the government called his two alleged accomplices to corroborate the testimony of its other witnesses. Each of the alleged accomplices represented to the trial judge that he intended to appeal his conviction and invoked his privilege against self-incrimination. Upon their refusal to testify, the trial judge declared a mistrial. After the Supreme Court of North Carolina affirmed the convictions of Brock's alleged accomplices, the government brought Brock to trial a second time. Brock objected, claiming that a second trial would place him in jeopardy twice for the same offense and thereby deny him due process of law under the Fourteenth Amendment. The trial court overruled the objection, and Brock was tried, convicted, and sentenced to two years' imprisonment. The Supreme Court of North Carolina affirmed Brock's conviction (State v. Brock, 1951).

When Brock appealed to the United States Supreme Court, the State of North Carolina argued that Brock's second trial did not place him in jeopardy twice for the same offense "because [a] trial court has the discretion to declare a mistrial and require the defendant to be presented before another jury if it be in the interest of justice to do so" (Brock v. North Carolina, 1953). The Supreme Court agreed, holding that the second trial did not deny Brock due process of law. As in *Palko*, the Supreme Court concluded that the second trial did not subject the accused to "a hardship so acute and shocking that our policy will not endure it," and that it did not "violate those fundamental principles of liberty and justice which lie at the base of all our civil and political institutions" (internal quotation marks omitted). The Court stated that under the Double Jeopardy Clause of the Fifth Amendment it had "long favored the rule of discretion in the trial judge to declare a mistrial and to require another panel to try the defendant if the ends of justice will be best served." The Court explained:

"[A] trial can be discontinued when particular circumstances manifest a necessity for so doing, and when failure to discontinue would defeat the ends of justice." Justice to either or both parties may indicate to the wide discretion of the trial judge that he declare a mistrial and require the defendant to stand trial before another jury. As in all cases involving what is or is not due process, so in this case, no hard and fast rule can be laid down. The pattern of due process is picked out in the facts and circumstances of each case. The pattern here, long in use in North Carolina, does not deny the fundamental essentials of a trial, "the very essence of a scheme of ordered justice," which is due process.

During the 1960s, the United States Supreme Court altered its approach concerning the relationship between the Bill of Rights and the requirement of due process of law. Beginning with *Mapp v. Ohio* (1961), the Supreme Court held that the Due Process Cause of the Fourteenth Amendment "selectively" incorporated (*see* Duncan v. Louisiana, 1968 (Black, J., concurring)) various provisions of the first eight amendments and made them fully applicable to the States. Under this approach, the Court held that the Fourth Amendment rule excluding evidence obtained by means of an illegal search and seizure (Mapp v. Ohio, 1961) and various other rights, including the Sixth Amendment right to counsel (Gideon v. Wainwright, 1963); the Fifth Amendment privilege against self-incrimination (Malloy v. Hogan, 1964); and the Sixth Amendment right to a trial by jury (Duncan v. Louisiana, 1968), apply in state criminal prosecutions. The Court in *Duncan v. Louisiana* (1968) explained the test for determining whether a particular provision of the Bill of Rights is "incorporated" into the Due Process Clause of the Fourteenth Amendment:

The recent cases ... have proceeded upon the valid assumption that state criminal processes are not imaginary and theoretical schemes but actual systems bearing virtually every characteristic of the common-law system that has been developing contemporaneously in England and in this country. The question thus is whether given this kind of system a particular procedure is fundamental—whether, that is, a procedure is necessary to an Anglo-American regime of ordered liberty.

In *Benton v. Maryland* (1969), the Supreme Court faced the question whether the Due Process Clause of the Fourteenth Amendment "incorporated" the double jeopardy provision of the Fifth Amendment. There, the State of Maryland charged John Benton with the crimes of burglary and larceny. A jury found him not guilty of the larceny charge, but convicted him of the burglary charge, for which the trial judge sentenced him to ten years' imprisonment. After the trial, it was determined that both the grand jury that indicted Benton and the jury that tried him had been unlawfully selected. The trial court gave Benton the option of demanding re-indictment and retrial. Benton chose to have his conviction set aside, and the State again charged him with both larceny and burglary. Benton moved to dismiss the larceny charge, arguing that because the first jury acquitted him of that crime, retrial would unconstitutionally place him in jeopardy twice for the same offense. The trial judge denied the motion, and the trial proceeded on both charges. This time the jury convicted Benton of both larceny and burglary, and the trial judge sentenced him to a total of fifteen years in prison.

Overruling its decision in *Palko*, the United States Supreme Court held that the Double Jeopardy Clause applies to the States through the Due Process Clause of the Fourteenth Amendment. The Supreme Court began its analysis by noting that in recent years it had "'increasingly looked to the specific guarantees of the [Bill of Rights] to determine whether a state criminal trial was conducted with due process of law'" and that "[i]n an increasing number of cases, [it] ha[d] rejected the notion that the Fourteenth Amendment applies to the States only a watered-down, subjective version of the individual guarantees of the Bill of Rights ...." (internal quotation marks omitted). The Court continued:

> Our recent cases have thoroughly rejected the *Palko* notion that basic constitutional rights can be denied by the States as long as the totality of the circumstances does not disclose a denial of "fundamental fairness." Once it is decided that a particular Bill of Rights guarantee is "fundamental to the American scheme of justice," the same constitutional standards apply against both the state and federal governments.

The Supreme Court then concluded that the protection against double jeopardy contained in the Fifth Amendment "represents a fundamental ideal in our constitutional heritage." The Court stated:

> The fundamental nature of the guarantee against double jeopardy can hardly be doubted. Its origins can be traced to Greek and Roman times, and it became established in the common law of England long before this [n]ation's independence. As with many other elements of the common law, it was carried into the jurisprudence of this [c]ountry through the medium of Blackstone, who codified the doctrine in his Commentaries. "[T]he plea of *autrefoits acquit*, or a former acquittal," he wrote "is grounded on this universal maxim of the common law of England, that no man is to be brought into jeopardy of his life more than once for the same offence." Today, every [s]tate incorporates some form of the prohibition in its constitution or common law.... [The] underlying notion [that the [s]tate, with all its resources and power, should not be allowed to make repeated attempts to convict an individual for an alleged offense] has from the very beginning been part of our constitutional tradition.... [I]t is clearly "fundamental to the American scheme of justice."

Judging the validity of Benton's larceny conviction by federal double jeopardy standards, the Supreme Court held that that conviction could not stand. Benton's initial acquittal of larceny barred his second trial. The Supreme Court explained that under its holding in *Green v. United States* (1957), the State of Maryland could not condition the appeal of Benton's burglary conviction upon his coerced surrender of a valid plea of former jeopardy on the larceny charge. Moreover, Benton was placed in "jeopardy" for larceny at his first trial, despite the defect in the original indictment. At most, reasoned the Court, the defect rendered that indictment "voidable," not "void."

Developing the Contours of the Guarantee Against Double Jeopardy

Since the adoption of the Fifth Amendment in 1791, the United States Supreme Court has given meaning to the Double Jeopardy Clause by applying its provisions in specific cases. The Supreme Court rendered its first significant opinion concerning the Double Jeopardy Clause in 1824. In *United States v. Perez* (1824), the government tried Josef Perez for a capital offense. When the jury could not agree upon a verdict, the trial judge, without Perez's consent, discharged the jury and declared a mistrial. The Supreme Court held that the double jeopardy provision did not bar the government from trying Perez anew for the same offense. In an opinion written by Justice Joseph Story, the Court stated:

> The prisoner has not been convicted or acquitted, and may again be put upon his defence. We think, that in all cases of this nature, the law has invested [c]ourts of justice with the authority to discharge a jury from giving any verdict, whenever, in their opinion, taking all the circumstances into consideration, there is a manifest necessity for the act, or the ends of public justice would otherwise be defeated. They are to exercise a sound discretion on the subject; and it is impossible to define all the circumstances, which would render it proper to interfere.... We are aware that there is some diversity of opinion and practice on this subject in the American [c]ourts; but, after weighing the question with due deliberation, we are of opinion that such a discharge constitutes no bar to further proceedings, and gives no right of exemption to the prisoner from being again put upon trial.

Perez thus settled the specific question whether a mistrial declared because of a "hung jury," and without the consent of the accused, bars reprosecution for the same offense; however, the significance of its holding goes beyond that narrow issue. The Supreme Court in *Perez* decided that a mistrial declared without the consent of the accused—*for whatever reason*—does not bar retrial, so long as a "manifest necessity" existed for the trial judge's action, or the ends of public justice would otherwise have been defeated, but that absent such circumstances, the Double Jeopardy Clause bars a subsequent prosecution for the same offense. This decision made it clear that the protection against double jeopardy under the Fifth Amendment extends further than the English pleas of *autrefoits acquit* and *autrefoits convict*, because both of those pleas require that a trial culminate in a final judgment to afford the accused protection against reprosecution.

The next significant decision on double jeopardy rendered by the United States Supreme Court was *Ex parte Lange* (1874). There, Edward Lange raised a double jeopardy claim in a case involving the crime of appropriating to his own use mail-bags belonging to the Post Office Department, an offense punishable by imprisonment for up to one year *or* a fine not exceeding $200. The Supreme Court upheld Lange's claim that he had been punished twice for the same offense in violation of the constitutional guarantee against double jeopardy when the trial judge imposed a sentence of one year's imprisonment *and* a fine of $200. In doing so, the Court made it clear that the words "life or limb" contained in the Double Jeopardy Clause do not limit the protection afforded by that provision to capital offenses or other serious crimes. Rather, it extends to *all* criminal offenses, including less serious offenses such as misdemeanors. The Court reasoned:

> If we reflect that at the time [the] maxim [that a person should not be placed in peril of legal penalties more than once upon the same accusation] came into existence almost every offense was punished with death or other punishment touching the person, and that [the] pleas [of *autrefoits acquit*, and *autrefoits convict*] are now held valid in felonies, minor crimes, and misdemeanors alike, and on the difficulty of deciding when a statute under modern systems does or does not describe a felony when it defines and punishes an offense, we shall see ample reason for holding that the principle intended to be asserted by the constitutional provision [against double jeopardy] must be applied to all cases ....

In 1896, the United States Supreme Court decided *United States v. Ball*, its last significant double jeopardy decision of the nineteenth century. In that case, a grand jury indicted John C. Ball and Robert E. Boutwell for murder. Following a jury trial, they were convicted and sentenced to death. On appeal, the Supreme Court reversed the convictions and ordered the indictment dismissed. The Supreme Court found that the indictment under which the two men were tried was fatally defective because it did not allege when and where the victim died (Ball v. United States, 1891). A grand jury subsequently returned a new indictment charging Ball and Boutwell with the same murder charged in the first indictment. Each man entered a plea of former conviction. The trial court overruled the pleas, and both men were again convicted and sentenced to death. The United States Supreme Court affirmed the convictions. It rejected the claim that the Double Jeopardy Clause barred the retrial and set forth the principle that an individual who succeeds in getting a conviction set aside upon appeal or otherwise may be tried anew for the same offense.

Perhaps the next major double jeopardy case the United States Supreme Court decided was *United States v. Lanza* (1922). There, a grand jury charged Lanza and several others with various offenses under the National Prohibition Act. The defendants filed a plea of former conviction, asserting that they previously had been convicted and fined in a Washington state court for the same acts. The trial court sustained the plea and dismissed the charges (United States v. Peterson,

1920). On appeal, the Supreme Court, in an opinion written by Chief Justice William Howard Taft, rejected the defendants' double jeopardy claim. The Court reasoned:

> We have here two sovereignties, deriving power from different sources, capable of dealing with the same-subject matter within the same territory. Each may, without interference by the other, enact laws to secure prohibition .... Each government in determining what shall be an offense against its peace and dignity is exercising its own sovereignty, not that of the other.
>
> It follows that an act denounced as a crime by both national and state sovereignties is an offense against the peace and dignity of both and may be punished by each .... Here the same act was an offense against the State of Washington, because a violation of its law, and also an offense against the United States under the National Prohibition Act. The defendants thus committed two different offenses by the same act, and a conviction by a court of Washington of the offense against that [s]tate is not a conviction of the different offense against the United States, and so is not double jeopardy.

In reaching this result, the Supreme Court established the so-called "dual sovereignty" doctrine, under which the United States and an individual state, or two separate states, or a foreign country and either the United States or an individual state, can prosecute an individual for the same act without violating the prohibition against double jeopardy. The doctrine not only conflicts with the rule in England (*see* The King v. Thomas, 1664; Beak v. Thyrwhit, 1688 (discussing Rex v. Hutchinson, 1677); *see also* The King v. Roche, 1775), but also appears to conflict with the intent of Congress in drafting the Double Jeopardy Clause and submitting it to the States for ratification. As previously discussed, in 1789, James Madison introduced a proposal in the House of Representatives to amend the Constitution by adding the clause "[n]o person shall be subject, except in cases of impeachment, to more than one punishment or one trial for the same offence ...." During the debate on this proposal, Representative George Partridge of Massachusetts moved to insert the words "by any law of the United States" after the words "same offence."[178] If added, those words may have implied that an individual convicted in a federal court could be tried and convicted of the same offense in a state court.[179] According to one scholar, "Partridge's motion certainly would have been adopted if Congress had shared his desire to open [a] loophole [to allow successive federal and state convictions for the same offense]."[180] Its failure to pass the motion may indicate that Congress intended the double jeopardy provision to protect individuals against successive federal and state prosecutions, a result contrary to the Supreme Court's holding in *Lanza*. Nevertheless, on numerous occasions, the Supreme Court has reaffirmed its holding in *Lanza* (*e.g.*, Abbate v. United States, 1959; Heath v. Alabama, 1985; *see also* Bartkus v. Illinois, 1959).

Ten years after its decision in *Lanza*, the United States Supreme Court determined when two statutory offenses constitute the "same offence" for purposes of the Double Jeopardy Clause. In *Blockburger v. United States* (1932), a jury convicted Blockburger of two separate offenses under the Harrison Narcotic Act—unlawfully selling a narcotic drug not in or from its original stamped package and unlawfully selling a narcotic drug not in pursuance of a written order of the purchaser of the drug on a form issued for that purpose by the Commissioner of Internal Revenue. Both convictions were based upon the same sale of eight grains of morphine hydrochloride. The trial court sentenced Blockburger to a term of imprisonment and a fine for *each* of the offenses.

The United States Supreme Court rejected Blockburger's claim that his single sale of the narcotic drug constituted only one offense and that the trial judge therefore could impose only a single penalty. The Supreme Court held that "where the same act or transaction constitutes a violation of two distinct statutory provisions, the test to be applied to determine whether there are two offenses or only one, is whether each provision requires proof of a fact which the other does not." The two offenses in question were separate offenses for double jeopardy purposes, concluded the Court, because each required proof of a fact that the other did not: the offense of selling a forbidden drug not in or from its original package did not require proof that the sale was not in pursuance of a written order of the purchaser, while the offense of selling a forbidden drug not in pursuance of a written order of the purchaser did not require proof that the drug sold was not in or from its original package.

Although the Supreme Court subsequently expanded the test for determining when two offenses constitute the "same offense" (Grady v. Corbin, 1990), it shortly thereafter returned to the *Blockburger* test as the sole test for determining whether two offenses are the "same" for purposes of double jeopardy analysis (United States v. Dixon, 1993).

Several years after it decided *Blockburger*, the United States Supreme Court made it clear in *Helvering v. Mitchell* (1938) that the Double Jeopardy Clause does not apply in civil actions or to civil sanctions, and that the legislature therefore "may impose both a criminal and a civil sanction in respect to the same act or omission" without running afoul of the double jeopardy provision. In *Helvering*, the Commissioner of Internal Revenue instituted an action against Charles. E. Mitchell under the Revenue Act of 1928 to collect a tax deficiency and a 50% penalty for his alleged fraudulent underpayment of his income taxes. The Supreme Court held that the action was not "essentially criminal" in character and that the Double Jeopardy Clause did not apply in such a proceeding. In an opinion written by Justice Louis D. Brandeis, the Court concluded that the sanction of an addition to the unpaid tax is remedial in character, primarily intended to serve as a safeguard for the protection of the revenue and to reimburse the Government for its expenses in investigating the fraud and its losses from the fraud. Although the Supreme Court later held in *United States v. Halper* (1989) that a sanction imposed in a civil proceeding could, in rare cases, constitute "punishment" for double jeopardy purposes, it reversed its position several years later and essentially overruled *Halper*, returning to the position it set forth in *Helvering* (Hudson v. United States, 1997).

During the middle part of the twentieth century, the United States Supreme Court decided only a few cases involving the Double Jeopardy Clause and none of particular importance. The 1970s, however, saw a dramatic increase in the number of double jeopardy issues decided by the Supreme Court, most likely because of the Court's 1969 decision holding the Double Jeopardy Clause applicable to the States through the Due Process Clause of the Fourteenth Amendment (*see* Benton v. Maryland, 1969).

Perhaps the first significant case the Supreme Court decided during this decade was *Ashe v. Swenson* (1970). In that case, the Court held that the Double Jeopardy Clause embodies the principle of collateral estoppel, meaning: "[W]hen an issue of ultimate fact has once been determined by a valid and final judgment, that issue cannot again be litigated between the same parties in any future lawsuit." An acquittal therefore bars not only a subsequent prosecution for the "same" offense, but also a subsequent prosecution for a *different* offense if in the second prosecution the government must relitigate factual issues already resolved in the defendant's favor by the first trial.

In *Ashe*, three or four masked men broke into a home, robbed each of six men who were engaged in a late-night poker game, and fled in an automobile belonging to one of the robbery victims. The State of Missouri charged Bob Fred Ashe and three others with seven separate offenses in connection with the incident—the armed robbery of each of the six poker players and the theft of the car. The State first brought Ashe to trial on the charge of robbing one of the participants in the poker game. At that trial, the State presented unassailable evidence that an armed robbery had occurred, but its evidence that Ashe had been one of the robbers was weak. Defense counsel's cross-examination of the State's witnesses was brief and was aimed primarily at exposing the weakness of their identification testimony. Defense counsel made no attempt to question their testimony regarding the robbery itself or their claims as to their losses.

The jury found Ashe "not guilty due to insufficient evidence." Several weeks later, following Ashe's unsuccessful motion to dismiss the charge on the basis of his previous acquittal, the State of Missouri tried Ashe for the armed robbery of one of the other participants in the poker game. This time the State presented a stronger case on the issue of Ashe's identity, and the jury convicted him of armed robbery.

The United States Supreme Court held that Ashe's conviction could not stand, because the collateral estoppel component of the Double Jeopardy Clause barred his prosecution for the armed robbery of the second poker player. The Court reasoned:

Straightforward application of the [constitutional principle of collateral estoppel] to the present case can lead to but one conclusion. For the record is utterly devoid of any indication that the first jury could rationally have found that an armed robbery had not occurred, or that [the first poker player] had not been a victim of that robbery. The single rationally conceivable issue in dispute before the jury was whether [Ashe] had been one of the robbers. And the jury by its verdict found that he had not. The [constitutional principle of collateral estoppel], therefore, ... make[s] a second prosecution for the robbery of [another of the poker players] wholly impermissible.

The Supreme Court in *Ashe* explained why the principle of collateral estoppel constitutes an integral part of the guarantee against double jeopardy. It stated:

After the first jury had acquitted [Ashe] of robbing [the first victim], Missouri could certainly not have brought him to trial again upon that charge. Once a jury had determined upon conflicting testimony that there was at least a reasonable doubt that [Ashe] was one of the robbers, the State could not present the same or different identification evidence in a second prosecution for the robbery of [the first victim] in the hope that a different jury might find that evidence more convincing. The situation is constitutionally no different here, even though the second trial related to another victim of the same robbery. For the name of the victim, in the circumstances of this case, had no bearing whatever upon the issue of whether [Ashe] was one of the robbers.

In this case the State ... has frankly conceded that following [Ashe's] acquittal, it treated the first trial as no more than a dry run for the second prosecution: "No doubt the prosecutor felt the [S]tate had a provable case on the first charge and, when he lost, he did what every good attorney would do—he refined his presentation in light of the turn of events at the first trial." But this is precisely what the constitutional guarantee [against double jeopardy] forbids.

During the 1970s, the Supreme Court also dealt with the double jeopardy ramifications of a mistrial declared at the request of the accused, or with his consent, and the midtrial dismissal of a charge upon motion of the accused. In *Dinitz v. United States* (1976), the trial judge excluded Dinitz's lead attorney from the trial for engaging in improper conduct during his opening statement to the jury. Dinitz subsequently moved for a mistrial, which the trial court granted. The United States Supreme Court held that even if the trial judge had overreacted in excluding Dinitz's lead attorney, the Double Jeopardy Clause did not bar the government from retrying Dinitz, because, even though he could have continued the trial before the jury that had already been selected, Dinitz *requested* the trial judge to declare the mistrial. The Supreme Court explained:

Even when judicial or prosecutorial error prejudices a defendant's prospects of securing an acquittal, he may nonetheless desire "to go to the first jury and, perhaps, end the dispute then and there with an acquittal." Our prior decisions recognize the defendant's right to pursue this course in the absence of circumstances of manifest necessity requiring a *sua sponte* judicial declaration of a mistrial. But it is evident that when judicial or prosecutorial error seriously prejudices a defendant, he may have little interest in completing the trial and obtaining a verdict from the first jury. The defendant may reasonably conclude that a continuation of the tainted proceeding would result in a conviction followed by a lengthy appeal and, if a reversal is secured, by a second prosecution. In such circumstances, a defendant's mistrial request has objectives not unlike the interests served by the Double Jeopardy Clause—the avoidance of the anxiety, expense, and delay occasioned by multiple prosecutions.

Consequently, under *Dinitz*, when prosecutorial or judicial error of a magnitude sufficient to warrant a mistrial has occurred, "[t]he important consideration, for purposes of the Double Jeopardy Clause, is that the defendant retain primary control over the course to be followed ...."

The Supreme Court reached a similar result in *United States v. Scott* (1978). In that case, it held that if a defendant successfully moves to dismiss the charge against him and terminate his trial on a ground unrelated to his factual guilt or innocence, and one that contemplates that the proceedings will end then and there in his favor, the Double Jeopardy Clause does not bar the government from appealing the trial court's order dismissing the charge, and if it succeeds in obtaining a reversal of that order, prosecuting the defendant anew for the charge that had been erroneously dismissed.

In *Scott*, after the jury had heard all the evidence in the case, the trial judge granted the defendant's motion to dismiss two counts of a three-count indictment on the ground that the government's delay in charging him with the narcotics transactions alleged in those counts prejudiced his defense and thereby deprived him of his constitutional right to due process of law. The trial judge's action in *Scott* constituted a "dismissal," rather than an "acquittal," because he based his resolution of the case in the defendant's favor on a ground not related to the defendant's factual guilt or innocence of the offense charged. The Supreme Court first held that the government could appeal the order of dismissal. The Court then concluded that the trial judge erred in dismissing the charges against Scott and held that the double jeopardy provision did not bar the government from prosecuting Scott anew. It reasoned that an order dismissing a charge on a ground not related to the factual guilt or innocence of the accused does not constitute an "acquittal," even when the trial judge based his ruling upon facts outside the face of the charging instrument or upon the ground that the accused simply could not be convicted of the offense charged. Moreover, said the Court, the government's appeal of the midtrial dismissal of a charge, granted by the court at the request of the accused,

scarcely [presents] a picture of an all-powerful state relentlessly pursuing a defendant who had either been found not guilty or who had at least insisted on having the issue of guilt submitted to the first trier of fact. It is instead a picture of a defendant who chooses to avoid conviction and imprisonment, not because of his assertion that the [g]overnment has failed to make out a case against him, but because of a legal claim that the [g]overnment's case against him must fail even though it might satisfy the trier of fact that he was guilty beyond a reasonable doubt.

Furthermore, according to the Supreme Court in *Scott*, a defendant who "deliberately choos[es]" to seek to terminate the proceedings against him on a ground unrelated to guilt or innocence is not deprived of his "valued right" to have his trial completed before the first fact finder; rather, "the public has been deprived of its valued right to 'one complete opportunity to convict those who have violated its laws.'"

It was during the 1970s that the Supreme Court also decided the point in a criminal proceeding when jeopardy "attaches" under the Double Jeopardy Clause, that is, the point after which a second trial could conceivably constitute "double" jeopardy. In *Crist v. Bretz* (1978), the Supreme Court held that jeopardy "attaches" in a jury trial when the jury is empaneled and sworn.

In *Crist*, a prosecuting attorney filed an information (*i.e.*, a formal criminal charge made by a prosecutor without a grand jury indictment) charging L.R. Bretz and another person with the offenses of grand larceny, obtaining money and property by false pretenses, and preparing or offering false evidence. After the jury had been empaneled and sworn, but before the first witness was sworn, the prosecuting attorney moved to dismiss the information so he could correct a typographical error concerning the date of the defendants' alleged illegal conduct. The judge granted the motion and dismissed the jury. The prosecuting attorney subsequently filed a new information alleging the correct date of the offense. Prior to their trial, the defendants moved to dismiss the new information on double jeopardy grounds. The trial court denied the motion on the ground that the defendants had not been placed in jeopardy under the first information because, under state law, jeopardy attached only when the first witness was sworn. Following a trial, the defendants were convicted and sentenced to terms of imprisonment.

The United States Supreme Court reversed the conviction. The Supreme Court recognized that although the Double Jeopardy Clause initially was understood to encompass the English common law rule that an individual has been placed in jeopardy only when there has been a conviction or acquittal after a complete trial,[181] its decision in *United States v. Perez* (1824) established that an individual can be placed in jeopardy even if the prosecution did not result in a conviction or acquittal. The Court held that under the Double Jeopardy Clause, jeopardy attaches in a jury trial when the jury is empaneled and sworn, even though no witnesses have testified, or even been sworn, and no evidence has been presented. The Court reasoned that it is at that point that the need arises to protect the individual's interest in "retaining [the] chosen jury," that is, his "valued right to have his trial completed by [that] particular tribunal," one that the individual may perceive to be favorably inclined towards him and his case.

During the last part of the twentieth century and into the twenty-first century, the United States Supreme Court decided numerous cases involving the Double Jeopardy Clause. Perhaps the most important of these were *Grady v. Corbin* (1990), in which the Supreme Court expanded the definition of the "same offense" for purposes of successive prosecutions, and *United States v. Halper* (1989), in which the Court held that the penalty imposed in a civil proceeding could, in some circumstances, constitute "punishment" for purposes of double jeopardy analysis. As previously mentioned, however, the Supreme Court subsequently overruled both of these cases (*see* United States v. Dixon, 1993; Hudson v. United States, 1997).

NOTES

*The Fifth Amendment uses the English spelling of the word "offense" ("offence"). Henceforth, the American spelling is used in the text, except when quoting material that uses the English spelling.

1. Martin L. Friedland, *Double Jeopardy* 3 (Clarendon Press 1969).
2. Jay A. Sigler, *Double Jeopardy: The Development of a Legal and Social Policy* 3 n. 6 (Cornell University Press, 1969); Note, *Double Jeopardy and Dual Sovereigns*, 35 Indiana Law Journal 444–445 (1960). *But see* George C. Thomas III, *Double Jeopardy: The History, The Law* 1 (New York University Press 1998) ("[L]aws against changing a final judgment can be traced to the Code of Hammurabi.").
3. Sigler, *supra* note 2, at 3 n.6.
4. *The Babylon Talmud* (Isidore Epstein ed., Jacob Shachter trans., Soncino Press 1935). *See also* Hyman E. Goldin, *Hebrew Criminal Law and Procedure* 108–09 & n.6 Twayne Publishers, Inc. 1952); Samuel Mendelsohn, *The Criminal Jurisprudence of the Ancient Hebrews: Compiled from the Talmud and other Rabbinical Writings, and Compared with Roman and English Penal Jurisprudence* 150 & n.358 (Hermon Press, 2nd ed. 1968).
5. The *King James Bible* translates this verse as "according to his fault," while the *Revised Standard Version* of the Bible translates it as "in proportion to his offense."
6. *The Babylon Talmud* (Isidore Epstein ed., H.M. Lazarus trans., Soncino Press 1935), *Makkoth* 13b (first brackets added).
7. George Horowitz, *The Spirit of Jewish Law: A Brief Account of Biblical and Rabbinical Jurisprudence with a Special Note on Jewish Law and the State of Israel* 170 (Bloch Publishing Co. 1973). *See also* Mendelsohn, *supra* note 4, at 35 & n.62.
8. *The Babylon Talmud* (Isidore Epstein ed., Samuel Daiches trans., Soncino Press 1936), *Kethuboth* 32b.
9. Demosthenes, *Speech Against Leptines* (XX:147), in *Demosthenes: Orations I-XVII, XX: Olynthiacs • Philippics • Minor Public Orations* 589 (J.H. Vince trans., Harvard University Press 1998).
10. Robert J. Bonner, *Lawyers and Litigants in Ancient Athens: The Genesis of the Legal Profession* 195 (University of Chicago Press 1927).
11. J. Walter Jones, *Law and Legal Theory of the Greeks: An Introduction* 148 (Clarendon Press 1956).
12. *Id.* at 149.
13. H.F. Jolowicz, *Historical Introduction to the Study of Roman Law* 325 (Cambridge University Press, 2nd ed. 1952); 1 James Leigh Strachan-Davidson, *Problems of the Roman Criminal Law* 155 (Clarendon Press 1912).
14. 2 Strachan-Davidson, *supra* note 13, at 157.
15. *Id.*
16. *Id.*

17. *Id.* at 177; Pandias M. Schisas, *Offences Against the State in Roman Law* 221–22, 232 (University of London Press Ltd. 1926).

18. *The Opinions of Paulus*, Book V, Title XVII, translated in 1 S.P. Scott, *The Civil Law* 323 (AMS Press, Inc. 1973) (italics added).

19. *Digest of Justinian*, Book 48, Title 2, Note 7, as contained in 4 Theodor Mommsen, Paul Kreuger & Alan Watson, *Digest of Justinian* 797 (University of Pennsylvania Press 1985).

20. Sigler, *supra* note 2, at 2.

21. *Black's Law Dictionary* 1660 (West Group, 7th ed. 1999).

22. Max Radin, *Handbook of Roman Law* § 176 (West Publishing Co. 1927); Jolowicz, *supra* note 13, at 331.

23. Radin, *supra* note 22, § 176.

24. See *id* § 44; Wolfgang Kunkel, *An Introduction to Roman Legal and Constitutional History* 29 (J.M. Kelley trans., Oxford University Press, 2nd ed. 1973).

25. *Digest of Justinian, supra* note 19, at 797.

26. R.H. Helmholz, *The Spirit of Classical Canon Law* 284, 286–87 (University of Georgia Press 1996); Friedland, *supra* note 1, at 5, 326–27; Sigler, *supra* note 1, at 3.

27. Helmholz, *supra* note 26, at 11–13.

28. *Id.* at 286, citing *Decretals Gregorii IX*, Book 5, Title 1, Ch. 6.

29. *Id.*, discussing the *glossa ordinaria*, or gloss, to *Decretals Gregorii IX*, Book 5, Title 1, Ch. 6 at 286.

30. *Id.* at 7.

31. *Id.* at 286, citing *Decretum Gratiani*, Distinctio 81 canon 12.

32. *Id.*, citing *Decretum Gratiani*, Causa 2, quaestio 1, canon 14.

33. *See also* Friedland, *supra* note 1, at 5, 327; Helmholz, *supra* note 27, at 287; 1 Frederick Pollock & Frederic William Maitland, *The History of English Law* 448–49 n.2 (Cambridge University Press, 2nd ed. 1898); Sigler, *supra* note 2, at 3; Thomas, *supra* note 2, at 72.

34. *See also* Z.N. Brooke, *The English Church and the Papacy* 205 & n. 1. (Cambridge University Press 1989).

35. Helmholz, *supra* note 26, at 287.

36. Brooke, *supra* note 34, at 205 n.1.

37. *See also id.*; Helmholz, *supra* note 26, at 286; Thomas, *supra* note 2, at 72.

38. 4 William Blackstone, *Commentaries* *335, *336, *337–38.

39. *Id.* at *335.

40. Helmholz, *supra* note 26, at 286; Max Radin, *Handbook of Anglo-American Legal History* 228 (West Publishing Co. 1936); Sigler, *supra* note 2, at 3; Note, *supra* note 2, at 446–47.

41. Note, *supra* note 2, at 446–47.

42. Friedland, *supra* note 1, at 5-6, 328; Sigler, *supra* note 2, at 3.

43. Jill Hunter, *The Development of the Rule Against Double Jeopardy*, 5 Journal of Legal History 3, 5 (1984).

44. Brooke, *supra* note 34, at 135–37.

45. Hunter, *supra* note 43, at 5.

46. Pollock & Maitland, *supra* note 33, at 125–30.

47. *Id.* at 130.

48. Hunter, *supra* note 43, at 5.

49. Austin Lane Poole, *From Domesday Book to Magna Carta 1087–1216* 200–02 (Clarendon Press, 2nd ed. 1955).

50. *Id.* at 202; W.L. Warren, *Henry II* 461, 464–65 (University of California Press 1973).

51. Hunter, *supra* note 43, at 5, 17 n.16.

52. The Constitutions of Clarendon c. 3 (1164), *reprinted in* Michael Evans & R. Ian Jack, *Sources of English Legal and Constitutional History* 12 (Butterworths 1984).

53. Pollock & Maitland, *supra* note 33, at 447–48 & n.1.

54. Hunter, *supra* note 43, at 6.

55. Friedland, *supra* note 1, at 5 & n.3, 326 & n.5; Helmholz, *supra* note 26, at 284; Pollock & Maitland, *supra* note 33, at 448; Poole, *supra* note 49, at 206; Hunter, *supra* note 43, at 6.

56. Poole, *supra* note 49, at 208–14; Goldwin Smith, *A Constitutional and Legal History of England* 90 (Charles Scribner's Sons 1955).

57. Brooke, *supra* note 34, at 212; Pollock & Maitland, *supra* note 33, at 124; Poole, *supra* note 49, at 218; Smith, *supra* note 56, at 90.

58. Friedland, *supra* note 1, at 5-6, 328.

59. Hunter, *supra* note 43, at 4.

60. 3 *Henry VII*, c. 1 (1487); 26 *Henry VIII*, c. 6 (1534). See *infra* text accompanying notes 98–101 & notes 109–10.

61. Hunter, *supra* note 43, at 4-5.

62. See *id.* at 16 n.3 (asserting that the first recorded mention of the plea of a previous acquittal was in 1203).

63. *Id.* at 6–7.

64. *Id.* at 7.

65. *Id.* at 4.

66. Sigler, *supra* note 2, at 3.

67. 1 *Reeves' History of the English Law, from the Time of the Romans to the End of the Reign of Elizabeth* 456 (W.F. Finlason ed., William S. Hein & Co. 1981; originally published: M. Murphy 1880).

68. The Charter of Liberties (1101), *reprinted in* Evans & Jack, *supra* note 52, at 49–50.

69. Poole, *supra* note 49, at 202–03; Warren, *supra* note 50, at 466.

70. Poole, *supra* note 49, at 203; Friedland, *supra* note 1, at 330.

71. Pollock & Maitland, *supra* note 33, at 152; Friedland, *supra* note 1, at 328.

72. John Beames, *A Translation of Glanville* Fred Rothman & Co. 1980; originally published: W. Reed 1812); *The Treatise on the Laws and Customs of the Realm of England Commonly Called Glanvill* (G.D.G. Hall ed., Clarendon Press 1993).

73. Friedland, *supra* note 1, at 7 n.1; Sigler, *supra* note 2, at 11-12; Hunter, *supra* note 43, at 18 n.36.

74. Magna Carta (1215), *reprinted in* Ray Stingham, *Magna Carta: Fountainhead of Freedom* 227 (Aqueduct Books 1966).

75. Magna Carta (1297), *reprinted in* Evans & Jack, *supra* note 52, at 51–55.

76. Sigler, *supra* note 2, at 4.

77. Pollock & Maitland, *supra* note 33, at 457; Friedland, *supra* note 1, at 7.

78. Brooke, *supra* note 34, at 220.

79. Pollock & Maitland, *supra* note 33, at 455 & n.1.

80. *See* Friedland, *supra* note 1, at 333–34.

81. 9 *Edward II*, stat. 1, c. 6 (1315-16).

82. Marion S. Kirk, *"Jeopardy" During the Period of the Year Books*, 82 University of Pennsylvania Law Review 602, 605 (1934).

83. *See* Blackstone, *supra* note 38, at *312–17; 1 James Fitzjames Stephen, *A History of the Criminal Law of England* 244–50 (MacMillan & Co. 1883); Hunter, *supra* note 43, at 8–9; Kirk, *supra* note 82, at 605–06.

84. Blackstone, *supra* note 38, at *314; 2 William S. Holdsworth, *A History of English Law* 257 (Metheun & Co. and Sweet & Maxwell, Ltd., 4th ed. 1936); Kirk, *supra* note 82, at 605.

85. Sigler, *supra* note 2, at 9.

86. Friedland, *supra* note 1, at 8. *See also* Kirk, *supra* note 82, at 607 & nn.27 & 29.

87. Friedland, *supra* note 1, at 8; Kirk, *supra* note 82, at 607 & n.29.

88. Hunter, *supra* note 43, at 9.

89. *Bracton on the Laws and Customs of England* 391 (Belknap Press 1968).

90. *Britton: An English Translation and Notes* 94 (Francis Morgan Nichols trans., John Byrne & Co. 1901). *See also* Friedland, *supra* note 1, at 8-9; Kirk, *supra* note 82, at 607 & n.26.

91. Hunter, *supra* note 43, at 11–12.

92. *Id.* at 18 n.37; Kirk, *supra* note 82, at 607 n.25.

93. Kirk, *supra* note 82, at 607 n.25.

94. *Id.* at 608.

95. Friedland, *supra* note 1, at 9; Sigler, *supra* note 2, at 10; Kirk, *supra* note 82, at 607 n.25.

96. Friedland, *supra* note 1, at 9; Sigler, *supra* note 2, at 8, 10; Hunter, *supra* note 43, at 12; Kirk, *supra* note 82, at 607 n.26, 608.

97. *See* Blackstone, *supra* note 38, at *335-36; 1 Joseph Chitty, *A Practical Treatise on the Criminal Law* *452, *461 (G & C. Merriam 1836).

98. 3 *Henry VII*, c. 1 (1487).

99. Blackstone, *supra* note 38, at *335; Friedland, *supra* note 1, at 9.

100. Blackstone, *supra* note 38, at *314–15; Kirk, *supra* note 82, at 605–06 & n.20.

101. Blackstone, *supra* note 38, at *335–36; Friedland, *supra* note 1, at 9-10; Sigler, *supra* note 2, at 8; Stephen, *supra* note 83, at 248–49; Hunter, *supra* note 43, at 12; Kirk, *supra* note 82, at 607 n.26, 608.

102. Friedland, *supra* note 1, at 10.

103. *See also id.* ("Because the use of the procedure of appeal was on the decline by this time, the dual procedure was probably not widely employed."); Stephen, *supra* note 83, at 249 (stating that the result of the trial on an indictment was "practically conclusive," unless it resulted in an acquittal "under circumstances which greatly dissatisfied the parties concerned").

104. 59 *George III*, c. 46 (1819).

105. Stephen, *supra* note 83, at 247.

106. *See id.* at 249; Friedland, *supra* note 1, at 8; Hunter, *supra* note 43, at 19 n.57; Kirk, *supra* note 83, at 608–09.

107. Friedland, *supra* note 1, at 10.

108. Hunter, *supra* note 43, at 13.

109. *Id.* at 12.

110. 26 *Henry VIII*, c. 6 (1534).
111. Hunter, *supra* note 43, at 13.
112. Friedland, *supra* note 1, at 10.
113. 2 William Staunford, *Les Plees Del Coron* 105–08 (P.R. Glazebrook ed., London Professional Books, Ltd. 1971).
114. Hunter, *supra* note 43, at 13.
115. *Id.* at 14.
116. *See generally* Friedland, *supra* note 1, at 11–13.
117. *See* Stephen, *supra* note 83, at 247. *See generally* Holdsworth, *supra* note 84, at 360–61.
118. Sigler, *supra* note 2, at 9.
119. Edward Coke, *The Third Part of the Institutes of the Laws of England* 213–14, 233–40 (W. Lee & D. Parkman 1644).
120. Sigler, *supra* note 2, at 17.
121. *Id.* at 16.
122. Hunter, *supra* note 43, at 14.
123. *Id.*
124. 1 *William & Mary*, sess. 2, c. 2 (1689).
125. 2 Matthew Hale, *The History of the Pleas of the Crown (Historia Placitorium Coronae)* *240–55.
126. Sigler, *supra* note 1, at 16.
127. *See* Friedland, *supra* note 1, at 11–13.
128. *Id.* at 238.
129. *Id.* at 11–12.
130. *Id.* at 12.
131. See *supra* text accompanying notes 98–101.
132. Blackstone, *supra* note 38, at *335-36, *337.
133. 1 Bernard Schwartz, *The Bill of Rights: A Documentary History* 67 (Chelsea House Publishers in association with McGraw Hill Book Co. 1971).
134. Maryland Act for the Liberties of the People (1639), *reprinted in* Schwartz, *supra* note 133, at 68.
135. Schwartz, *supra* note 133, at 69.
136. Massachusetts Body of Liberties, para. 42 (1641), as reprinted in Richard L. Perry & John C. Cooper, *Sources of Our Liberties: Documentary Origins of Individual Liberties in the United States Constitution and Bill of Rights* 153 (Associated College Presses, 1959).
137. *The Laws and Liberties of Massachusetts: Reprinted from the Copy of the 1648 Edition in the Henry E. Huntington Library* 46 (Max Farrand ed., Harvard University Press 1929).
138. *Id.* at 47.
139. *See* Christopher Collier, *The Common Law and Individual Rights in Connecticut Before the Federal Bill of Rights*, 76 Connecticut Bar Journal 1, 12 (2002).
140. Fundamental Constitutions of Carolina, ¶ 64 (1669), *reprinted in* 5 Francis Newton Thorpe, *The Federal and State Constitutions, Colonial Charters, and Other Organic Laws of the States, Territories, and Colonies 1492–1908* 2780 (Government Printing Office 1909).
141. Articles of Confederation, art. IV (1778).

142. *E.g.*, Del. Const. of 1776, art. 25; N.J. Const. of 1776, ¶ XXII; N.Y. Const. of 1777, ¶ XXXV. *See also* Md. Const. of 1776, A Declaration of Rights, &c., ¶ III.

143. Blackstone, *supra* note 38, at *335–36, *337.

144. N.H. Const. of 1784, Part. I, art. XVI.

145. Pa. Const. of 1790, art. IX, § 10.

146. Arthur P. Scott, *Criminal Law in Colonial Virginia* 81–82 (University of Chicago Press 1930).

147. *Id.* at 102.

148. *Virginia Colonial Decisions: The Reports by Sir John Randolph and Edward Barradall of Decisions of the General Court of Virginia 1728–1741* B50 (R.T. Barton ed., Boston Book Co. 1909).

149. Minutes of the General Quarter Sessions of the Peace for the City and County of New York 1694-1731/32 30, 51, 53, discussed in Julius Goebel, Jr., & T. Raymond Naughton, *Law Enforcement in Colonial New York* 588 (Commonwealth Fund 1944).

150. Minutes of the Supreme Court of Judicature of the Province of New York 1766-69 (Engrossed Minutes) 504, 505, discussed in Goebel & Naughton, *supra* note 149, at 588–89.

151. Goebel & Naughton, *supra* note 149, at 589.

152. *Id.*.

153. Irving Brant, *The Bill of Rights: Its Origin and Meaning* 39 (Bobbs-Merrill Co., Inc. 1965); Edward Dumbauld, *The Bill of Rights: And What It Means Today* 9 (Greenwood Press 1979; originally published: University of Oklahoma Press 1957); Leonard W. Levy, *Origins of the Bill of Rights* 32 (Yale University Press 1999).

154. George Washington, First Inaugural Address, April 30, 1789, *reprinted in* 1 *Annals of Congress* 27–30 (Joseph Gales ed., 1789).

155. Dumbauld, *supra* note 153, at 8–9. *See also* Levy, *supra* note 153, at 32–34; 2 Francis Newton Thorpe, *The Constitutional History of the United States* 212–13 (Callahan & Co. 1901).

156. Levy, *supra* note 153, at 31–32.

157. Brant, *supra* note 153, at 39.

158. 1 *Annals of Congress* 450–53 (Joseph Gales ed., 1789).

159. *Id.* at 451–52.

160. *Id.* at 468.

161. *Id.* at 690.

162. *Id.* at 781.

163. *Id.* at 781–82.

164. *Id.* at 782.

165. *Id.*

166. *Id.*

167. *Id.*

168. *Id.*

169. *Id.*

170. *House of Representatives Journal*, 1st Cong., 1st Sess. 85 (1789).

171. 1 *Annals of Congress* 809 (Joseph Gales ed., 1789).

172. *Id.*

173. *Senate Journal*, 1st Cong., 1st Sess. 71 (1789).

174. Senate Pamphlet, *reprinted in* Neil H. Cogan, *The Complete Bill of Rights: The Drafts, Debates, Sources, and Origins* 303 (Oxford University Press 1997).

175. *House of Representatives Journal*, *supra* note 170, at 121.

176. *Senate Journal*, *supra* note 173, at 88.

177. 1 Statutes at Large 98 (1789).

178. 1 *Annals of Congress* 782 (Joseph Gales ed., 1789). *See also* Brant, *supra* note 153, at 64; Cogan, *supra* note 174, at 310–11.

179. Bryant, *supra* note 153, at 64.

180. *Id.*

181. 2 Joseph Story, *Commentaries on the Constitution of the United States: With a Preliminary Review of the Constitutional History of the Colonies and States Before the Adoption of the Constitution* § 1787 (Little, Brown, and Co., 4th ed. 1873).

2

Analysis

UNDERLYING POLICIES

The Double Jeopardy Clause of the Fifth Amendment provides that "[n]o person shall ... be subject for the same offense to be twice put in jeopardy of life or limb ...." This provision had its origin in the common law pleas of *autrefoits acquit* (a former acquittal), *autrefoits convict* (a former conviction), and pardon, which barred the retrial of an individual who previously had been acquitted, convicted, or pardoned for the same offense (United States v. DiFrancesco, 1980; United States v. Scott, 1978). Like the other provisions contained in the first eight amendments to the Constitution (Barron v. Mayor and City Council of Baltimore, 1833; Adamson v. California, 1947), collectively known as the Bill of Rights, the Double Jeopardy Clause originally placed restrictions only upon the federal government (Palko v. Connecticut, 1937; Brock v. North Carolina, 1953). In 1969, however, the United States Supreme Court recognized that the prohibition against double jeopardy contained in the Fifth Amendment "represents a fundamental ideal in our constitutional heritage" and is "'fundamental to the American scheme of justice.'" The Supreme Court stated:

> The fundamental nature of the guarantee against double jeopardy can hardly be doubted. Its origins can be traced to Greek and Roman times, and it became established in the common law of England long before this nation's independence. As with many other elements of the common law, it was carried into the jurisprudence of this country through the medium of Blackstone, who codified the doctrine in his Commentaries. "[T]he plea of *autrefoits acquit*, or a former acquittal," he wrote "is grounded on this universal maxim of the common law of England, that no man is to be brought into jeopardy of his life more than once for the same offence." Today, every [s]tate incorporates some form of the prohibition in its constitution or common law.... [The] underlying notion [that the state should not be allowed to make repeated attempts to convict an individual for an alleged offense] has from the very beginning been part of our constitutional tradition.

Accordingly, the Fifth Amendment's protection against double jeopardy has been "incorporated" (Duncan v. Louisiana, 1966), or "absorbed" (Palko v. Connecticut, 1937), into that portion of the Fourteenth Amendment that prohibits a state from "depriv[ing] any person of life, liberty, or property, without due process of law" and applies to the same extent against the individual states as it does against the federal government (Benton v. Maryland, 1969).

The constitutional guarantee against double jeopardy today encompasses several protections. First, it bars the government from prosecuting a person[1] a second time for the same offense after he already has been tried and *acquitted* (Smalis v. Pennsylvania, 1986; Sanabria v. United States, 1978; United States v. Martin Linen Supply Co., 1977; United States v. Sisson, 1970; Benton v. Maryland, 1969; Fong Foo v. United States, 1962; Kepner v. United States, 1904; United States v. Ball, 1896). Second, it bars the government from prosecuting a person a second time for the same offense after he already has been *convicted* (United States v. Dixon, 1993; Harris v. Oklahoma, 1977; Brown v. Ohio, 1977; *In re* Nielsen, 1889). Third, it bars the government from imposing multiple punishments upon a person for the same offense (Hudson v. United States, 1997; Missouri v. Hunter, 1983; North Carolina v. Pearce, 1969; *Ex parte* Lange, 1874). Finally, in some circumstances, it bars the government from prosecuting a person a second time for the same offense after a judge prematurely terminated that individual's first trial, either by declaring a mistrial (United States v. Jorn, 1971; Downum v. United States, 1963) or by dismissing the charge against him before the fact finder reached a verdict in the case (United States v. Govro, 1987; *see also* United States v. Scott, 1978).

The text of the Double Jeopardy Clause mentions only harms to "life or limb." Nevertheless, the policies underlying the provision apply equally when less severe penalties are involved. It is well settled that the Double Jeopardy Clause covers imprisonment and monetary penalties (Department of Revenue of Montana v. Kurth Ranch, 1994; Jeffers v. United States, 1976), and applies in proceedings involving misdemeanors (relatively minor offenses, generally punishable by less than one year's imprisonment) (*Ex parte* Lange, 1874), municipal ordinance violations (Waller v. Florida, 1970), and allegations of delinquency (Breed v. Jones, 1975), as well as felonies (serious offenses, generally punishable by more than one year's imprisonment).

The overall design of the Double Jeopardy Clause was perhaps best expressed by Justice Hugo L. Black, writing for the United States Supreme Court in *Green v. United States* (1957). Justice Black stated:

> The constitutional prohibition against "double jeopardy" was designed to protect an individual from being subjected to the hazards of trial and possible conviction more than once for an alleged offense....
>
> The underlying idea, one that is deeply ingrained in at least the Anglo-American system of jurisprudence, is that the state with all its resources and power should not be allowed to

make repeated attempts to convict an individual for an alleged offense, thereby subjecting him to embarrassment, expense and ordeal and compelling him to live in a continuing state of anxiety and insecurity, as well as enhancing the possibility that even though innocent he may be found guilty.

As indicated in Justice Black's opinion in *Green*, a number of related policy considerations underlie the constitutional ban on double jeopardy. By prohibiting the government from reprosecuting a person following his acquittal or conviction, the ban "preserve[s] the finality of judgments" (Crist v. Bretz, 1978) and protects the "integrity" of those judgments (United States v. Scott, 1978). That is, once the government tries an individual for a particular offense and the fact finder either convicts or acquits that individual, the government must respect that judgment in the future. It cannot relitigate the charge, even if it is dissatisfied with the result reached by the fact finder or the punishment imposed by the sentencing authority. This constitutional recognition of the finality of a judgment allows the defendant, whether acquitted or convicted of the offense charged, to consider the matter closed and to plan his future accordingly, without the threat of a subsequent prosecution and possible punishment for the same offense hanging over his head.

This policy of protecting the integrity of a final judgment is not unique to the double jeopardy provision. A similar purpose is served in civil (*i.e.*, noncriminal) cases by the doctrine of *res judicata*. Under that doctrine, a valid final judgment based upon the merits of the claim prevents the party who brought the action from suing the defendant a second time on the same claim, and, conversely, precludes the defendant from subsequently raising any new defense to defeat the enforcement of a judgment rendered against him in the action.[2] As the United States Supreme Court explained in *Angel v. Bullington* (1947), "Litigation is the means for vindicating rights, but it may also involve unwarranted friction and waste. The doctrine of *res judicata* reflects the refusal of law to tolerate needless litigation. Litigation is needless if, by fair process, a controversy has once gone through the courts to conclusion."

In the context of the prohibition against double jeopardy, the bar on relitigating adjudicated charges serves the public interest by conserving scarce prosecutorial and judicial resources and by promoting efficiency. It allows the prosecutor the opportunity to convict an individual of a particular offense in a single trial, but prevents the prosecutor from spending additional time and money, and from tying up courtrooms, judges, and law enforcement personnel, prosecuting the same individual for the same offense again and again until the prosecutor achieves the desired result.

The constitutional bar on relitigating adjudicated criminal charges, however, primarily serves the interests of the defendant. Barring a second trial following the *acquittal* of an individual precludes the government from successively retrying that person before a different fact finder in the hope that the second fact finder will reach a conclusion different from that reached by the first. Absent such a prohibition the government could use the first trial as a "dry run" (Ashe v. Swenson, 1970) or "dress rehearsal" (United States v. Dixon, 1993 (Souter, J., concurring in the judgment and dissenting)) for the presentation of its proof. It could find out which of its evidence proved persuasive to the fact finder and which areas of its case needed strengthening. It also could learn the strengths and weaknesses of the defendant's case. With such knowledge, the government could hone its trial strategies, attempt to supply evidence it failed to muster in the first proceeding, and otherwise perfect its case (Grady v. Corbin, 1990; Tibbs v. Florida, 1982; United States v. DiFrancesco, 1980).

Ashe v. Swenson (1970), which involved a conviction ultimately overturned by the United States Supreme Court on double jeopardy grounds, aptly illustrates this point. In that case, three or four armed masked men broke into the basement of a home in Lee's Summit, Missouri, robbed each of six men who were engaged in a poker game, and fled in an automobile belonging to one of the robbery victims. The State of Missouri charged Bob Fred Ashe and three others with seven separate offenses in connection with the incident—the armed robbery of each of the six poker players and the theft of the car. At Ashe's trial on the charge of robbing Donald Knight, one of the participants in the poker game, the prosecuting attorney called Knight and three of his fellow poker players as witnesses. Although the State presented unassailable evidence that an armed robbery had occurred, its evidence that Ashe had been one of the robbers was weak. Two of the State's witnesses thought there had been only three robbers altogether, and neither of those witnesses could identify Ashe as one of the robbers. Another of the State's witnesses could say only that Ashe's voice "sounded very much like" that of one of the robbers. The fourth witness for the State identified Ashe, but only by his "size and height, and his actions." After hearing all the evidence, the jury found Ashe not guilty of robbing Knight.

Six weeks later the State of Missouri brought Ashe to trial for the armed robbery of Ray Roberts, another participant in the poker game. Although the witnesses for the government were for the most part the same as in Ashe's trial for robbing Knight, this time their testimony was substantially stronger on the issue of Ashe's identity. Two witnesses who at the first trial had been wholly unable to identify Ashe as one of the robbers testified at the second trial that Ashe's features, size, and mannerisms matched those of one of the robbers. The witness who at the first trial had identified Ashe only by his size and actions testified at the second trial that he also remembered Ashe by the unusual sound of his voice. The government further refined its case at the second trial by declining to call as a witness the participant in the poker game whose identification testimony at the first trial had been conspicuously negative. This time the jury found Ashe guilty of armed robbery. When Ashe appealed his conviction, the State readily conceded that "when [the prosecuting attorney] lost [the first trial], he did what every good attorney would do—he refined his presentation in light of the turn of events at the first trial."

In addition to permitting the government to perfect its case, allowing a subsequent trial following an acquittal would permit the government, with its vastly superior resources, to wear down the accused—both emotionally and financially—and "create a risk of conviction through sheer governmental perseverance" (Tibbs v. Florida, 1982). It would also put the defendant in a position where he could never effectively be acquitted, no matter how many fact finders found him not guilty. For a prosecutor could disregard any number of acquittals and keep trying him until he found one fact finder that would convict.

Allowing the government several attempts to convict an individual would, of course, increase the risk that an innocent person would be wrongfully convicted. A person accused of a crime he did not commit might successfully fend off the government in one trial, but if he could be tried numerous times for the same offense, his chances of ultimately being convicted would increase. One commentator explained:

> [I]f the evidence [in a particular case] were such that one in four juries would convict, and three in four might acquit, the probability of conviction if the defendant is tried once is, of course, one in four (4/16). If two trials were permitted the defendant would have to convince two juries of his innocence and the probability of one of the two convicting would be 1—(3/4 × 3/4) = (7/16); assuming the independence of each jury and the absence of other variables. If he had to convince five juries his probability of conviction by one would rise to over three in four.[3]

Regardless of whether this mathematical formulation is correct, it makes the point that the more trials an innocent person must undergo, the greater the chance that he ultimately will be convicted. To put it another way, "[i]f you play with something long enough, you are likely to break it; and if the government is allowed to prosecute an innocent defendant enough times and disregard all acquittals, eventually it is likely to convict an innocent (by hypothesis) person."[4]

The Double Jeopardy Clause also prohibits reprosecution of an individual following an acquittal in order to protect the "'jury's prerogative to acquit against the evidence'" (United States v. DiFrancesco, 1980), that is, to find a person not guilty despite sufficient evidence of his guilt. In such situations the fact finder exercises its authority to nullify the law in individual cases by applying a standard different from, and more lenient than, that prescribed by the legislature in enacting the offense. Some scholars contend that this is the primary value underlying the Double Jeopardy Clause.[5]

Barring a second trial following the *conviction* of an individual prevents that person from being subjected to multiple punishments for the same offense (Justices of Boston Municipal Court v. Lydon, 1984; United States v. Wilson, 1975). It also precludes the government from successively retrying that person in the hope of securing a greater penalty than that originally imposed. Absent such a prohibition a prosecuting attorney who, for example, obtains a murder conviction against a defendant, but who is dissatisfied with the trial judge's imposition of a sentence of a term of years in prison, could prosecute the defendant a second time for the same murder in the hope that following a second conviction the new trial judge would impose either the death penalty or a sentence of life imprisonment.

Ciucci v. Illinois (1958) demonstrates that, absent the Double Jeopardy Clause, a prosecuting attorney might engage in such conduct. In that case, the State of Illinois charged Vincent Ciucci in four separate indictments with murdering his wife and three children. The State first tried Ciucci for killing his wife. At that trial the government introduced into evidence details of all four deaths. The jury convicted Ciucci of murder and sentenced him to twenty years' imprisonment. The prosecuting attorney expressed extreme dissatisfaction with the prison sentence and announced a determined purpose to prosecute Ciucci until the jury imposed the death penalty. The State then tried Ciucci for killing one of his daughters, once again introducing into evidence at trial details of all four killings. The jury in this second trial convicted Ciucci of murder and sentenced him to forty-five years' imprisonment. Once again the prosecuting attorney vowed to prosecute Ciucci until the jury sentenced him to death. Finally, following Ciucci's trial for killing his son, at which the government again introduced evidence of all four deaths, the jury convicted Ciucci of murder and imposed the death penalty. Although the case did not directly involve the prohibition against double jeopardy because the Double Jeopardy Clause had not yet been held applicable to the States, Justice William O. Douglas of the United States Supreme Court reached the heart of the matter when he observed in his dissenting opinion that the State of Illinois "in effect tried the accused for four murders three consecutive times," relentlessly prosecuting him "until it got the result it wanted," a capital verdict.

In protecting the integrity of a final judgment, the ban on double jeopardy safeguards an individual from the expense, embarrassment, anxiety, and excessive harassment of repeated criminal prosecutions. Defending oneself against a criminal charge is costly. A criminal defendant who has the funds to do so nearly always retains an attorney to represent him.[6] In many cases the defendant also hires an investigator to help locate witnesses and discover evidence helpful to his case, as well as experts to assist in preparing his defense and to testify in his behalf at trial. Moreover, a criminal charge generally causes an individual embarrassment and anxiety. His friends, neighbors, colleagues, and even relatives might disapprove of him, be suspicious of him, or be distrustful of him. He almost certainly will be concerned about the effect the pending charges could have on his family life and his employment. But even more than that, he will be concerned about his upcoming trial and the possibility that he will be convicted and punished. Such expense, embarrassment, and anxiety inevitably accompany any criminal charge, and there is no way to eliminate them. Allowing the government to bring successive prosecutions, however, would exacerbate the problem and permit the government to use the criminal process as a means to harass an individual. Consequently, except in limited situations, the double jeopardy provision precludes a second prosecution for the same offense following a final judgment of acquittal or conviction.

Barring reprosecution in some circumstances following the termination of a defendant's trial before the jury has reached a verdict, such as by the declaration of a mistrial at the behest of the prosecuting attorney, also helps to protect an individual against excessive harassment by the government. More importantly, though, it helps to protect the defendant's "valued right ... to have his trial completed by the particular tribunal summoned to sit in judgment on him" (Downum v. United States, 1963), that is, his interest in "'being able, once and for all, to conclude his confrontation with society through the verdict of a tribunal he might believe to be favorably disposed to his fate'" (Arizona v. Washington, 1978). Thus, it precludes the trial judge from affording the government a more favorable opportunity to convict the accused by declaring a mistrial when the government's case is going badly and it appears that the jury might not convict the defendant—perhaps because the jury appears unsympathetic to the government or because the prosecuting attorney poorly prepared and presented his case (Gori v. United States, 1961).

Finally, the guarantee against double jeopardy recognizes the injustice inherent in punishing an individual more than once for the same offense (United States v. Halper, 1989; United States v. Ewell, 1966; *Ex parte* Lange, 1874). As the Supreme Court stated in Louisiana *ex rel.* Francis v. Resweber (1947), "[o]ur minds rebel against permitting the same sovereignty to punish an accused twice for the same offense."

"JEOPARDY"

The Nature of "Jeopardy"

The Double Jeopardy Clause guarantees that the government will not place an individual in "jeopardy of life or limb" twice for the same offense. It is axiomatic that a proceeding brought by the government against an individual cannot run afoul of the Double Jeopardy Clause unless that individual previously faced "jeopardy" for the same offense. For it is a "fundamental principle that an accused must suffer jeopardy before he can suffer double jeopardy" (Serfass v. United States, 1975).

As used in the double jeopardy provision of the Fifth Amendment, "jeopardy" connotes "the risk that is traditionally associated with a criminal prosecution" (Breed v. Jones, 1975), that is, the risk that a person will be convicted of a criminal offense (Price v. Georgia, 1970). With the possible exception of summary criminal contempt of court proceedings, such risk is present in all criminal prosecutions. As a general matter, though, it is not present in civil proceedings. Accordingly, the Double Jeopardy Clause does not apply in civil actions between private parties and ordinarily does not apply in civil actions brought by the government. Only if a civil proceeding brought by the government is "essentially criminal in character" (United States v. One Assortment of 89 Firearms, 1984; *see also* Breed v. Jones, 1975), such as a hearing to determine whether a juvenile is "delinquent"

(Breed v. Jones, 1975), will the protection apply. Even in a proceeding in which the double jeopardy provision applies, "jeopardy" does not "attach" at the outset of the proceeding; only at a specific point in the proceeding can it be said that the individual faced "jeopardy" within the meaning of the Double Jeopardy Clause.

Proceedings in Which the Protection Applies

Criminal Prosecutions

Although the language of the Double Jeopardy Clause—"jeopardy of life or limb"—suggests that its protections apply only in proceedings in which the most serious penalties can be imposed, the Clause means something far broader than its literal language. Today, it is well settled that the provision extends not just to prosecutions for felonies (*i.e.*, those offenses of the most serious nature, which under the English common law were punishable by forfeiture of land or goods and the possible loss of life or a bodily part), but, with one possible exception, also to prosecutions for any offense punishable by imprisonment or by a fine or other monetary penalty (*see* Department of Revenue of Montana v. Kurth Ranch, 1994), including misdemeanors (Grady v. Corbin, 1990; Brown v. Ohio, 1977) and municipal ordinance violations (Robinson v. Neil, 1973; Waller v. Florida, 1970).

Referring to the maxim that "no man shall more than once be placed in peril of legal penalties upon the same accusation," upon which the common law pleas of *autrefoits acquit* and *autrefoits convict*—as well as the Double Jeopardy Clause itself—are based, the United States Supreme Court in *Ex parte Lange* (1874) explained:

> If we reflect that at the time this maxim came into existence almost every offence was punished with death or other punishment touching the person, and that [the] pleas [of *autrefoits acquit* and *autrefoits convict*] are now held valid in felonies, minor crimes, and misdemeanors alike, and on the difficulty of deciding when a statute under modern systems does or does not describe a felony when it defines and punishes an offence, we shall see ample reason for holding that the principle intended to be asserted by the constitutional provision [against double jeopardy] must be applied to all cases where a second punishment is attempted to be inflicted for the same offence by judicial sentence.

The only criminal prosecutions that the Double Jeopardy Clause might not encompass are summary proceedings for direct contempt of court. Direct contempt, sometimes called "in-court" contempt, involves conduct committed inside the courtroom that interferes with the orderly administration of the ongoing judicial proceeding, such as a witness' refusal to testify after being directed to do so by the judge; an attorney's failure to heed the judge's rulings on evidentiary or procedural matters; or a defendant's disrespectful conduct toward the judge. Unlike the situation involving contemptuous conduct committed outside the courtroom (*i.e.*, indirect or "out-of-court" contempt), such as an individual's violation of a court order, a judge can punish a person summarily for direct contempt of court, either immediately upon observing the contemptuous conduct, or at the end of the ongoing judicial proceeding; that is, without giving the person notice of the charges or affording him a hearing, the judge can find the person guilty of criminal contempt and sentence him to up to six months' imprisonment (Taylor v. Hayes, 1974; Codispoti v. Pennsylvania, 1974 (plurality opinion and Blackmun, J., dissenting); *Ex parte* Terry, 1888).

A judge can punish direct criminal contempt summarily because, in contrast to indirect contempt, the judge observed the individual's conduct and personally possesses all the facts necessary to conclude that the individual committed the offense (Sacher v. United States, 1952; Cooke v. United States, 1925). The summary power to punish for direct criminal contempt is thought by some to be "absolutely essential to the protection of the courts in the discharge of their functions" (Yates v. United States, 1957; *see also* Harris v. United States, 1965; Offutt v. United States, 1954).

In *United States v. Dixon* (1993), the United States Supreme Court held that criminal contempt of the sort enforced through *nonsummary* proceedings, *i.e.*, following notice and a hearing, is "'a crime in the ordinary sense'" and that the protection afforded by the Double Jeopardy Clause encompasses *nonsummary* criminal contempt of court prosecutions. The Supreme Court, however, expressly left open the question whether the double jeopardy provision applies to *summary* criminal contempt prosecutions.

Nearly every lower court that has considered the issue has concluded that the protection against double jeopardy does not extend to summary criminal contempt of court prosecutions for contumacious conduct committed inside the courtroom (*e.g.*, United States v. Rollerson, 1971; United States v. Mirra, 1963; People v. Totten, 1987; State v. Warren, 1982; Commonwealth v. Warrick, 1992; Maples v. State, 1978; *contra* Yarbro v. State, 1981; *see also* Ellis v. State, 1994; State v. Goodnow, 1995; State v. Bowling, 1987). For example, in *United States v. Rollerson* (1971), the United States Court of Appeals for the District of Columbia Circuit held that the summary criminal contempt of court conviction of Roosevelt Rollerson for hitting a federal prosecutor with an ice-filled plastic water pitcher during trial did not bar the government from subsequently prosecuting Rollerson for assault with a dangerous weapon and assault on a federal officer engaged in the performance of his duties, even though all three charges were based upon the same act.

Courts offer several justifications for holding the Double Jeopardy Clause inapplicable to summary criminal contempt prosecutions. First, some reason that application of the provision to such proceedings would place judges on the horns of "an unenviable dilemma" when faced with contumacious conduct (State v. Warren, 1982). On one hand, the judge could summarily find the contemnor guilty of criminal contempt of court, thereby effectively granting him immunity from prosecution for a substantive criminal offense based upon the same conduct—an offense that is likely to be a more serious one than criminal contempt. On the other hand, the judge, fearful of immunizing the individual from prosecution for a substantive criminal offense, could refrain from summarily holding him in criminal contempt, but at the cost of relinquishing his ability to maintain the dignity and decorum of the court and prevent defendants, attorneys, and others from impeding the orderly administration of justice through unruly and disrespectful conduct (*e.g.*, United States v. Mirra, 1963; State v. Warren, 1982; Maples v. State, 1978).

Second, some courts reason that the guarantee against double jeopardy does not apply to summary criminal contempt of court prosecutions because the crime of contempt of court and the underlying substantive offense protect distinct interests: the offense of direct contempt attempts to protect the dignity and decorum of the court, and hence the orderly administration of justice, while the underlying substantive offense seeks to protect the public from harmful conduct (*e.g.*, United States v. Rollerson, 1970; Maples v. State, 1978).

Finally, some courts reason that a criminal prosecution based upon the same conduct that served as the basis for a summary criminal contempt of court conviction does not offend the policy underlying the guarantee against double jeopardy because a person held in contempt without an adversary-type proceeding and then subsequently prosecuted for the same conduct does not suffer the harassment of successive trials (*e.g.*, United States v. Rollerson, 1971; United States v. Mirra, 1963; People v. Totten, 1987; State v. Warren, 1982; Commonwealth v. Warrick, 1985).

None of these asserted justifications can withstand analysis. The fear that judges will be forced either to, in effect, grant immunity from prosecution to contumacious defendants, attorneys, or others, or else lose control of their courtroom, seems "exaggerated" (United States v. Rollerson, 1971; *see also* State v. Goodnow, 1995). The power summarily to convict an individual of criminal contempt is not the only weapon a judge can wield to maintain the dignity, order, and decorum of court proceedings; a judge can also control an obstreperous *defendant* by binding and gagging him, or by ordering him removed from the courtroom until he promises to conduct himself properly (Illinois v. Allen, 1970). Alternatively, a judge can imprison the defendant for *civil* contempt, which does not implicate the protection against double jeopardy, and adjourn the trial until the defendant agrees to behave himself (Illinois v. Allen, 1970). In fact, in many circumstances these options will be more effective in maintaining order than would citing the defendant for criminal contempt of court. For example, a disruptive defendant being tried for a serious crime punishable by a severe sentence, such as life imprisonment, might not be affected by a mere criminal contempt of court conviction and sentence.

A judge also possesses a strong weapon, other than the summary contempt power, to deal with *attorneys* who disrupt proceedings by engaging in contumacious conduct that also constitutes a violation of the substantive criminal law. When confronted with such conduct a judge can refer the matter to the appropriate body charged with disciplining members of the bar. An attorney can be suspended or even disbarred for engaging in conduct that violates the applicable rules of professional responsibility or that tends to defeat the administration of justice. Moreover, because the double jeopardy provision does not apply in attorney disciplinary proceedings, any sanction imposed in such a proceeding would not bar a subsequent criminal prosecution based upon the same act, and *vice versa* (*e.g.*, *In re* Cardwell, 2002; *In re* Sharp, 1996; *In re* Chastain, 2000).

Similarly, a trial judge can deal with a disruptive *spectator* by immediately ordering the unruly individual removed from the courtroom (United States *ex rel.* Orlando v. Fay, 1965; Commonwealth v. Bohmer, 1978; *see also* Gannett Co. v. DePasquale, 1979 (Blackmun, J., concurring in part and dissenting in part)). The trial can then proceed unhindered and, if deemed necessary, the spectator can later be prosecuted for his disruptive conduct.

The fact that the crime of contempt protects the dignity, order, and decorum of the court, while the underlying substantive offense protects the public from harmful conduct, also should not preclude application of the double jeopardy provision in summary criminal contempt of court prosecutions. The United States Supreme Court has never held that the government can *prosecute* an individual twice for the same act merely because each trial involves an offense protecting a different interest than the other; nor has it ever held that the government can *punish* an individual twice for the same act merely because the two offenses for which he was convicted protect separate interests. Indeed, in *Dixon*, a majority of the Supreme Court rejected the "separate interests" argument in the context of multiple prosecutions (*see also* State v. Goodnow, 1995).

Finally, although an individual prosecuted for a substantive criminal offense following a summary contempt of court conviction for the same conduct does not suffer the harassment of successive trials and does not twice have to marshal the resources and energies necessary to defend himself for the same acts, the Double Jeopardy Clause guards against more than successive prosecutions for the same offense. Over 130 years ago, the United States Supreme Court concluded in *Ex parte Lange* (1874) that "the Constitution was designed as much to prevent the criminal from being twice punished for the same offense as from being twice tried for it." When a court summarily convicts an individual for contempt of court and sentences him for that contempt, he has been punished once for his contumacious act. If the government then convicts him of a substantive criminal offense based upon that same act, any punishment for that offense would be a second punishment for the same act and, at that point, the Double Jeopardy Clause's policy against multiple punishments becomes relevant. The Supreme Court has never held that a defendant who pleads guilty to an offense can later be tried for that same offense because the first conviction did not stem from a trial. The Double Jeopardy Clause therefore must apply to summary criminal contempt of court prosecutions so it can protect individuals against multiple punishments for the same offense (*see* State v. Goodnow, 1995).

Nevertheless, even if the guarantee against double jeopardy *applies* to summary criminal contempt prosecutions, that provision does not necessarily bar the government from prosecuting and punishing a person for a substantive criminal offense based upon the same act for which a court previously summarily convicted and punished him for contempt of court. As with any other crime, the Double Jeopardy Clause would preclude the subsequent prosecution and punishment only if the contempt of court and the substantive crime are the "same offense" for constitutional purposes (an issue discussed later in this Analysis). Under the current test for determining whether two offenses are the "same" for double jeopardy purposes (the so-called *Blockburger*, or "same-elements," test), it is unlikely that they would be deemed the same. For example, in *State v. Cox* (2002), the Court of Appeals of Washington assumed that the Double Jeopardy Clause encompasses summary criminal contempt prosecutions, but held that the clause did not bar the State from prosecuting a probationer for the crime of attempted escape following his summary conviction of criminal contempt, even though both crimes were based upon the individual's single act of running out of the courtroom during a probation revocation hearing after being warned by the judge not to leave. The court reasoned that summary contempt and attempted escape do not constitute the "same offense" for purposes of double jeopardy analysis because each requires proof of a fact that the other does not—summary contempt requires proof of disobedient, disorderly, or contemptuous conduct committed in the presence of the judge, which attempted escape does not; while conversely, attempted escape requires proof of an attempt to escape from detention, which summary contempt does not (*see also* Ellis v. State, 1994).

Of course, under a broader test for determining when two offenses are the "same" for purposes of double jeopardy analysis—such as the "same-conduct" test that the United States Supreme Court adopted in *Grady v. Corbin* (1990), but abandoned three years later in *Dixon* (1993); or the "same-transaction" test consistently urged by Justice William J. Brennan, Jr., but never adopted by a majority of the United States Supreme Court—summary contempt of court and a substantive criminal offense could constitute the "same offense" when based upon the same underlying conduct, so that a conviction of the former would preclude a subsequent prosecution for the latter. The Supreme Court of New Hampshire reached this result under its state constitution. It held that an individual's summary contempt conviction for attacking several police officers during a court hearing barred his subsequent prosecution for the offense of "assault by a prisoner," because the assault charge would be proved by the same evidence as the summary contempt conviction (State v. Goodnow, 1995).

After a defendant is convicted, the trial court holds a hearing at which it determines the appropriate sentence to impose. That sentencing proceeding may involve the testimony of witnesses and the introduction of other evidence. Nevertheless, the double jeopardy protection does not generally apply to such sentencing proceedings, "because the determinations at issue do not place a defendant in jeopardy for an 'offense'" (Monge v. California, 1998). The United States Supreme Court thus held in *Monge v. California* (1998) that a convicted defendant who received an enhanced sentence because of his prior conviction of a "serious felony" can be subjected to a second sentencing proceeding to determine the truth of the prior conviction allegation after an appellate court concludes that the government failed to introduce sufficient evidence to support that allegation at the defendant's initial repeat-offender sentencing proceeding.

An exception to the rule that the double jeopardy guarantee does not apply to sentencing proceedings exists for capital sentencing hearings in which the sentencing authority—be it a jury or a judge—makes the sentencing decision in a separate proceeding that resembles a trial on the issue of guilt or innocence and the government has the burden of proving certain elements beyond a reasonable doubt before the death penalty can be imposed (Bullington v. Missouri, 1981; *accord* Arizona v. Rumsey, 1984). The ramifications of this exception are discussed later in this Analysis in connection with the imposition of the death penalty at a defendant's retrial following his successful appeal of a conviction for which he received a sentence of life imprisonment.

Juvenile Court Proceedings

Every state and the District of Columbia has established a special court system to deal with the problems of youth, including those manifested by antisocial behavior. With limited exceptions, the Juvenile Court (or Family Court as it is known in some states) initially possesses exclusive jurisdiction of minors under a specified age who are alleged to be "delinquent" for having engaged in conduct that would be criminal if committed by an adult. In certain cases, the Juvenile Court can waive its jurisdiction and transfer the proceedings to an adult criminal court if, after an adversary hearing, it concludes that the welfare of the community requires the criminal prosecution of the minor. Absent a valid waiver of jurisdiction, however, an adult criminal court lacks the authority to try such a person. If the Juvenile Court retains jurisdiction of a child, it conducts an "adjudicatory" hearing at which it hears evidence and determines whether the youth violated the criminal law and is delinquent. If the court finds the child to be delinquent, it conducts a "dispositional" hearing to determine how best to deal with the child. Among the available alternatives are to make the child a ward of the court and commit the child to a state institution, such as an "industrial school," a "training school," or a "receiving home," for the remainder of his minority.

The Juvenile Court movement in the United States began at the end of the nineteenth century. At that time, children accused of violating the criminal law were treated the same as adults. They were tried in criminal courts and could be convicted of crimes, sentenced to lengthy prison terms, and intermingled in penal institutions with hardened criminals. In contrast, the Juvenile Court was intended not to determine whether a child was "guilty" or "innocent" of a criminal offense, but rather to ascertain what steps the State should take in the interest of the child and of society to "save" the child from a life of crime. The focus was to be upon "treating" and "rehabilitating" the child, not punishing the child. Toward this end, reformers envisioned a juvenile court proceeding as an informal and nonadversarial one, with the State acting as *parens patriae*, that is, in place of the parent for the purpose of protecting the child. The proceeding was to be "one in which a fatherly judge touched the heart and conscience of the erring youth by talking over his problems, by paternal advice and admonition, and in which, in extreme situations, benevolent and wise institutions of the State provided guidance and help 'to save him from a downward career'" (*In re* Gault, 1967). Delinquency proceedings were viewed as "civil" in nature, not "criminal," and subject to neither the rules of criminal procedure nor the constitutional requirements restricting the State when it seeks to deprive a person of his liberty.

In a series of cases beginning in 1966, however, the United States Supreme Court recognized that a gap existed in delinquency proceedings "between the originally benign conception of the [Juvenile Court] system and it realities" (Breed v. Jones, 1975). In *Kent v. United States* (1966), the Supreme Court stated:

> There is much evidence that some juvenile courts ... lack the personnel, facilities and techniques to perform adequately as representatives of the State in a *parens patriae* capacity, at least with respect to children charged with law violation. There is evidence, in fact, that there may be grounds for concern that the child receives the worst of both worlds: that he gets neither the protections accorded to adults nor the solicitous care and regenerative treatment postulated for children.

In *In re Gault* (1967), the Court observed that, despite the "'civil' label-of convenience" attached to delinquency proceedings, "[a] proceeding where the issue is whether the child will be found to be 'delinquent' and subjected to the loss of his liberty for years is comparable in seriousness to a felony prosecution" (*accord In re* Winship, 1970). It found it "of no constitutional consequence—and of limited practical meaning—that the institution to which [a delinquent child] is committed is called an Industrial School," because "[t]he fact of the matter is that, however euphemistic the title, a 'receiving home' or an 'industrial school' for juveniles is an institution of confinement in which the child is incarcerated for a greater or lesser time." The Court therefore held many of the constitutional guarantees associated with traditional criminal prosecutions applicable in juvenile delinquency proceedings, including the right to notice of the charges, the right to retained or appointed counsel, the rights of confrontation and cross-examination, and the privilege against self-incrimination (*In re* Gault, 1967), as well as the standard of proof beyond a reasonable doubt (*In re* Winship, 1970), although not the right to a trial by jury (McKeiver v. Pennsylvania, 1971).

The United States Supreme Court dealt with the guarantee against double jeopardy in *Breed v. Jones* (1975). There, after eschewing "the 'civil' label-of-convenience" and "'candidly apprais[ing]'" the juvenile process, the Supreme

Court held that the double jeopardy provision applies to delinquency proceedings in a Juvenile Court (*accord* Illinois v. Vitale, 1980; Swisher v. Brady, 1978). The Court reasoned that the potential consequences of a finding of delinquency, which include both the loss of liberty and the stigma inherent in a determination that the youth violated a criminal statute, are much the same as those of a traditional criminal prosecution and that therefore the risk faced by a juvenile in a delinquency proceeding is comparable to that faced by an individual in a criminal prosecution. Accordingly, the government may not criminally prosecute a youth following a delinquency proceeding for the same act, as in *Breed*, and *vice-versa (e.g., In re* Michael W., 2001); nor may it bring successive delinquency proceedings against a youth for the same act (*e.g., In re* Mitchell G., 1990; *In re* James C.F., 1984; *In re* J.O., 1990; *In re* Drakeford, 1977).

In addition to having jurisdiction of children alleged to be delinquent for having violated a criminal law, the Juvenile Court also typically has jurisdiction of children alleged to be "in need of supervision" because they are either habitually truant from school or beyond the control of their parents. To find a child "in need of supervision," the Juvenile Court need not—as it must with a finding of delinquency—determine that the youth committed an act that violated a criminal statute (although in some cases such an act may be the basis for the court's conclusion that the child is beyond the control of his parents). Moreover, the potential loss of liberty in a proceeding to determine whether a child is in need of supervision may not be as great as in a delinquency proceeding. Some states, for example, do not permit a child in need of supervision to be placed in a training school or similar facility, limiting the most serious disposition to court supervision in the child's own home, subject to conditions upon his liberty imposed by a probation officer or other designated official.

Despite these differences, lower courts have concluded that the potential consequences of a determination that a child is in need of supervision are "substantially similar" to those of a determination of delinquency, in that both can deprive the child of some personal freedom and both impose a stigma upon the child. They therefore hold that the guarantee against double jeopardy applies to juvenile court proceedings to determine whether a child is in need of supervision (*In re* R.L.K., 1978; A.R. v. State, 1984). Under this view, the government may neither bring successive proceedings to determine whether a child is in need of supervision when both are based upon the same conduct (*e.g.*, A.R. v. State, 1984), nor bring either a delinquency proceeding (*e.g., In re* R.L.K., 1978) or a criminal prosecution (*see* Breed v. Jones, 1975) following an "in need of supervision" proceeding based upon the same conduct, and *vice-versa*.

The Juvenile Court normally also has jurisdiction of children alleged to be abused or without proper parental care and for that reason abandoned, neglected, dependent, or otherwise in need of assistance. If the court finds the allegation true, it can—among other things—place the child in the legal custody of a social service agency or in foster care, or it can commit the child to a state-run residential institution. Quite clearly, a determination that a child is abused, abandoned, neglected, or dependent differs in significant respects from a decision that a child is delinquent, or even in need of supervision. A determination of dependency or the like requires no finding of wrongdoing on the part of the child, and in most circumstances, no stigma attaches to the child as a result of such a determination. Unlike a proceeding to determine whether a child is delinquent, a proceeding to determine whether a child is dependent or the like cannot be said to be comparable to a criminal prosecution of the child. For that reason it has been held that such a proceeding does not place a child in jeopardy, even in cases in which the allegation of dependency is based upon the child's having engaged in conduct that would be criminal if done by an adult and in which the youth can be committed to a state-run residential facility for juveniles (*In re* Spause, 1989). Accordingly, the Double Jeopardy Clause does not bar the government from either bringing a delinquency proceeding against a child, or prosecuting him criminally, following a determination that the child is "dependent," and *vice-versa*, even when both proceedings are based upon the same act by the child (*In re* Spause, 1989).

Moreover, because the purpose of an abuse, neglect, or dependency proceeding is to examine the child's environment and determine whether he or she is receiving proper care, the person who allegedly abused or neglected the child or caused his dependency does not face conviction and the possible loss of liberty in the Juvenile Court proceeding and therefore is not placed in "jeopardy" in that proceeding (*e.g.*, Joiner v. State, 1986; Fariss v. State, 1990; Hunter v. State, 1977; *In re* Neil C., 1987; Adoption of Iris, 1998; *In re* John P., 1988; Custody of a Minor, 1978; *In re* R.G., 1994; *In re* Commissioner of Social Services of New York *ex rel.* Denise R., 1995; *but see* Bowling v. State, 1984). As a result, the government can bring successive proceedings to determine whether a child is abandoned, abused, neglected, or dependent (*e.g.*, Adoption of Iris, 1998; *In re* John P., 1988; Custody of a Minor, 1978; *In re* R.G., 1994). It also can prosecute the person responsible for a child's condition following a proceeding to determine the child's dependency or the like (*e.g.*, Joiner v. State, 1986; Fariss v. State, 1990; Hunter v. State, 1977; *but see* Bowling v. State, 1984), and *vice-versa* (*In re* Neil C., 1987; *In re* Commissioner of Social Services of New York *ex rel.* Denise R., 1995), even though the successive proceedings are based upon the same conduct. With respect to the latter situation, one court commented that if the Double Jeopardy Clause applied to bar the criminal prosecution, the government would have to choose between either removing a child from an undesirable home situation or prosecuting an abusive or neglectful person for a criminal offense (Joiner v. State, 1986).

In cases involving the abuse, neglect, or abandonment of a child, the State may at some point ask the Juvenile Court to terminate the parental rights of the child's biological or adoptive parents. Although a parental termination proceeding focuses upon the conduct of the parents, the purpose of such a proceeding is to protect the child. The parents face no risk of punishment, only the termination of their parental rights. That risk is not sufficient to constitute "jeopardy," and the guarantee against double jeopardy does not apply in such proceedings (*e.g.*, *In re* B.G., 1997; Adoption of Iris, 1998; *In re* Theodore W., 1996; *In re* H.J., 1993; Malone v. State, 1993; *see also* Santosky v. Kramer, 1982; *In re* Roderick U., 1993). This means that "[i]f the State initially fails to win termination ..., it always can try once again to cut off the parents' rights after gathering more or better evidence" (Santosky v. Kramer, 1982; *e.g.*, Adoption of Iris, 1998; *In re* H.J., 1993). It also means that a proceeding to terminate parental rights does not bar a subsequent criminal prosecution of the parent based upon the same conduct that was the subject of the parental termination proceeding (*e.g.*, *In re* B.G., 1997; Malone v. State, 1993), and *vice versa* (*e.g.*, *In re* Theodore W., 1996).

Civil Actions Between Private Parties

Whereas "jeopardy," or the risk that is "traditionally associated with 'actions intended to authorize criminal punishment to vindicate public justice'" (Breed v. Jones, 1975), is present in all criminal prosecutions (with the possible exception of summary criminal contempt of court) and in juvenile delinquency proceedings, it is not present in civil actions brought by one person against another. Consequently, "[t]he protections of the Double Jeopardy Clause are not triggered by litigation between private parties" (United States v. Halper, 1989; *see also* Browning-Ferris Industries of Vermont, Inc. v. Kelco Disposal, Inc., 1989). A criminal prosecution of an individual for certain conduct therefore does not bar a private litigant from subsequently bringing a civil suit against that same person to recover damages, including punitive damages (*i.e.*, damages awarded in addition to actual damages to punish and thereby deter blameworthy acts), for the same conduct (*e.g.*, Stewart v. Roe, 1991; Tillis Trucking Co. v. Moses, 1999; Olson v. Walker, 1989; Jines v. Seiber, 1990; Whittaker v. Dail, 1991; Tuttle v. Raymond, 1985; Wittman v. Gilson, 1988; Coakley v. Daniels, 1992), and *vice-versa* (*see* United States v. Heffner, 1996; *see also* United States v. Randy, 1996; United States v. Beszborn, 1994).

The highly-publicized cases involving former professional football player and actor O.J. Simpson aptly illustrate this point. In 1994, the State of California charged Simpson, the 1968 Heisman Memorial Trophy winner and a member of the National Football League's Hall-of-Fame, with murdering his former wife, Nicole Brown Simpson, and her friend Ronald Goldman. Following the so-called "trial of the century," which lasted more than nine months, the jury deliberated less than four hours before finding Simpson not guilty. Meanwhile, during the pendency of the criminal prosecution, both Ronald's parents and Nicole's parents filed civil suits against O.J. Simpson seeking to recover damages for Simpson's wrongfully causing the death of their children. Although the Double Jeopardy Clause certainly precluded a second murder trial of Simpson following his acquittal in the criminal proceeding, neither the criminal prosecution itself nor Simpson's acquittal in that proceeding barred the civil actions or the subsequent judgments awarding Goldman's parents $8.5 million in compensatory damages and the estates of each of the victims $12.5 million in punitive damages, based upon the jury's finding that Simpson intentionally and wrongfully committed the homicides (*see* Rufo v. Simpson, 2001).

For the same reason the double jeopardy provision also does not prohibit either multiple lawsuits by private parties seeking punitive damages for the same wrongful act or multiple awards of punitive damages to private litigants for the same wrongful act (Racich v. Celotex Corp., 1989; Hansen v. Johns-Manville Products Corp., 1984; Delta School of Commerce, Inc. v. Harris, 1992; Spaur v. Owens-Corning Fiberglas Corp., 1994). For example, during the 1970s and 80s, thousands of individuals filed civil lawsuits against Johns-Manville Products Corporation, a manufacturer of asbestos, seeking to recover compensatory and punitive damages for deaths and physical harm caused by asbestos-related diseases. Many of these individuals succeeded in obtaining punitive damages awards. Because the actions were brought by private parties, and not by the government, the guarantee against double jeopardy did not preclude any litigant from bringing his or her own action or limit the amount of punitive damages any of the litigants could recover (*see* Hansen v. Johns-Manville Products Corp., 1984).[7]

In recent years, state legislatures have attacked the growing problem of domestic violence by enacting statutes granting the spouse, former spouse, live-in companion, and family members of an individual the right to petition a court for an "order of protection from abuse" by that individual. Typically, such an order can include provisions restraining the individual from committing further acts of physical and sexual abuse and from contacting or attempting to contact the petitioner; granting the petitioner exclusive possession of the shared residence and temporary possession of specified personal property, such as a motor vehicle; and awarding the petitioner temporary custody of the children of the parties. An individual who violates a protective order can be prosecuted criminally for contempt of court or for the separate offense of violation of a protective order.

Courts hold that the Double Jeopardy Clause does not apply to proceedings to obtain a protective order (State v. Manista, 1994; Nixon v. United States, 1999; City of Cleveland v. Hogan, 1998; Commonwealth v. Smith, 1988; Donley v. Donley, 1996; *see also* State v. Ohm, 2000); they reason that the purpose of a protective order is to help protect the victim against acts of violence or abuse and therefore is remedial—not punitive—in nature. Although the conclusion reached by these courts undoubtedly is correct, a better rationale for holding that an individual's action seeking a protective order does not implicate the double jeopardy provision is that the person bringing the action is a private party—not the government—and thus the proceeding is merely a civil action between two private litigants. The court in *State v. Morton* (1996) relied upon this latter rationale in holding that a proceeding brought by a beating victim against her boyfriend pursuant to New Jersey's Domestic Violence Act, and resulting in a judgment against him of $21,561 for reimbursement of medical expenses and $250,000 as compensation for pain and suffering, did not bar the State from subsequently prosecuting the boyfriend criminally for aggravated assault—even though both proceedings arose out of the same incident.

The Double Jeopardy Clause also does not apply in civil contempt of court proceedings brought by a private party in a lawsuit against an opposing party in that lawsuit, based upon the opposing party's failure to comply with a court's order, such as one requiring a parent to make support payments for a minor child or commanding a litigant to produce certain documents (*e.g.*, People v. Batey, 1986; Sanders v. Shephard, 1989; Eliker v. Eliker, 1980; *see also* Yates v. United States, 1957). Civil contempt is a sanction employed to coerce a party into compliance with an order of the court, and where necessary, to compensate the complaining party for any losses or damages sustained because of the noncompliance (McComb v. Jacksonville Paper Co., 1949). In contrast to criminal contempt of court, it is not intended to punish the noncomplying party or vindicate the authority of the court; rather, it is remedial and for the benefit of the complaining party (Hicks *ex rel.* Feiock v. Feiock, 1988; Gompers v. Buck's Stove & Range Co., 1911). Moreover, a fine imposed as a sanction for civil contempt is paid to the complaining party, rather than to the court, or if payable to the court, can be avoided simply by the party's performing the act required by the court's order; and unlike a sentence of imprisonment imposed for criminal contempt, a sentence of imprisonment for civil contempt of court is conditional in that the party can avoid the sanction by performing the act required by the court's order (Hicks *ex rel.* Feiock v. Feiock, 1988; Maggio v. Zeitz, 1948; Gompers v. Buck's Stove & Range Co., 1911). Consequently, the noncomplying party in a civil contempt of court proceeding does not face "the risk that is traditionally associated with a criminal prosecution" (Breed v. Jones, 1975) and is not in "jeopardy" for purposes of the double jeopardy provision.

Civil Actions Brought by the Government

The legislature "may impose both a criminal and a civil sanction in respect to the same act or omission," because "the double jeopardy clause prohibits merely punishing twice, or attempting a second time to punish *criminally*, for the same offense" (Helvering v. Mitchell, 1938) italics added. Nevertheless, the fact that the legislature designated a particular type of action brought by the government to be "civil" in nature does not necessarily mean that the Double Jeopardy Clause does not apply in such a proceeding. For "a 'civil label is not always dispositive'" (Kansas v. Hendricks, 1997). *Breed v. Jones* (1975), involving a juvenile delinquency proceeding, established that the "jeopardy" described in the double jeopardy provision is present in actions brought by the government that are "essentially criminal" in nature, even though they are labeled "civil" proceedings.

In *United States v. One Assortment of 89 Firearms* (1984), the United States Supreme Court articulated the test for determining whether a particular type of proceeding is "essentially criminal in character" and therefore subject to the double jeopardy provision. "The question," stated the Supreme Court, "is whether [the] proceeding is intended [by the legislature] to be, or by its nature necessarily is, criminal and punitive, or civil and remedial." This test requires a two-step analysis. First, it must be determined through an examination of the statute in question "'whether [the legislature], in establishing the penalizing mechanism, indicated either expressly or impliedly a preference for one label or the other.'" Second, when the legislature has indicated an intention to establish a civil penalty, it must be determined "'whether the statutory scheme [is] so punitive either in purpose or effect as to negate that intention.'" With respect to the latter inquiry, "[o]nly the clearest proof that the purpose and effect of the [sanction] are punitive will suffice to override [the legislature's] manifest preference for a civil sanction." Among the factors to be considered in determining whether a particular sanction is punitive in character are:

> Whether the sanction involves an affirmative disability or restraint, whether it has historically been regarded as a punishment, whether it comes into play only on a finding of *scienter* [a culpable mental state], whether its operation will promote the traditional aims of punishment—retribution and deterrence, whether the behavior to which it applies is already a crime, whether an alternative purpose to which it may rationally be connected is assignable for it, and whether it appears excessive in relation to the alternative purpose assigned ...."

This list of factors is "'neither exhaustive nor dispositive.'"

Applying this test in *89 Firearms*, the Supreme Court held that a gun owner's acquittal on criminal charges alleging that he engaged in the business of dealing in firearms without a license did not bar a subsequent proceeding pursuant to the Gun Control Act of 1968 for the forfeiture of the firearms involved in the criminal prosecution. The Court concluded that the forfeiture mechanism set forth in the statute "is not an additional penalty for the commission of a criminal act, but rather is a separate civil sanction, remedial in nature," aimed at "[k]eeping potentially dangerous weapons out of the hands of unlicensed [gun] dealers." An *in rem* forfeiture proceeding (*i.e.*, an action brought against the goods themselves) under the Act therefore is a civil proceeding that does not put the gun owner in "jeopardy."

In reaching this result, the Supreme Court first found that "Congress ... 'indicate[d] clearly that it intended a civil, not a criminal, sanction.'" The Court noted that Congress provided that an action to enforce a forfeiture under the Act is an *in rem* proceeding and that, "[i]n contrast to the *in personam* nature of criminal actions [*i.e.*, actions against the person], actions *in rem* have traditionally been viewed as civil proceedings, with jurisdiction dependent upon seizure of a physical object." The Court also pointed out that Congress authorized a summary administrative procedure for forfeiture of items valued at less than $2500 and provided that notice of a seizure of such an item could be by publication in a newspaper, rather than by personally informing the owner, which are "distinctly civil procedures." In addition, the Court found it apparent from the differences in the language between the substantive criminal provisions of the Act and the forfeiture provisions that Congress meant the latter to be broader in scope than the criminal sanctions. Finally, the Court concluded that the forfeiture provision "plays an important role in furthering the prophylactic purposes of the 1968 gun control legislation by discouraging unregulated commerce in firearms and by removing from circulation firearms that have been used or intended for use outside regulated channels of commerce," a goal the Court characterized as "plainly more remedial than punitive."

With respect to the second part of the inquiry—whether the statutory scheme is so punitive either in purpose or effect as to negate the legislature's intention to establish a civil remedial mechanism—the Supreme Court found that only one of the relevant factors—namely, that conduct giving rise to forfeiture proceedings also could entail the criminal penalties of another section of the Act—suggested that the forfeiture provision imposed a criminal penalty. The Court noted, however, that Congress may impose both a criminal penalty and a civil sanction in respect to the same conduct. It then found that "[b]ecause the sanction embodied in [the forfeiture provision] is not limited to criminal misconduct, the forfeiture remedy cannot be said to be coextensive with the criminal penalty" and that what overlap there is between the two sanctions is insufficient to show that the forfeiture proceeding cannot legitimately be viewed as civil in nature.

Prior to its decision in *89 Firearms*, the Supreme Court applied a comparable test and reached a similar result in *One Lot Emerald Cut Stones v. United States* (1972). There, the Court held that an *in rem* proceeding brought by the United States under the Tariff Act of 1930 seeking the forfeiture of jewels smuggled into the country and a monetary penalty equal to the value of those jewels was not essentially a criminal proceeding. The Double Jeopardy Clause therefore did not apply in such a proceeding, so that the owner's prior acquittal of smuggling the jewels into the country without submitting to the required customs procedures did not bar the forfeiture action.

In determining the character of the forfeiture proceeding, the Court first concluded that Congress intended the forfeiture to be a civil sanction. It reasoned that the sanctions contained in the Tariff Act were aimed at aiding the enforcement of tariff regulations by preventing forbidden merchandise from circulating in the country and, through its monetary penalty, by providing a reasonable form of liquidated damages (*i.e.*, a specified amount fixed as the measure of damages) for violation of the inspection provisions and by serving to reimburse the government for investigation and enforcement expenses—purposes that typically characterize remedial rather than punitive sanctions. The Court then concluded that the measure of recovery fixed by Congress in the Act was not so unreasonable or excessive that it transformed what was clearly intended as a civil remedy into a criminal penalty. It stated:

> Forfeiture of goods or their value and the payment of fixed or variable sums of money are ... sanctions which have been recognized as enforceable by civil proceedings .... In spite of their

comparative severity, such sanctions have been upheld against the contention that they are essentially criminal and subject to the procedural rules governing criminal prosecutions.

The Supreme Court applied the two-part test from *89 Firearms* to hold in *United States v. Ursery* (1996) that *in rem* proceedings to forfeit property used in connection with a federal drug offense or involved in money-laundering transactions are civil—not criminal—in nature, and that the guarantee against double jeopardy does not apply in such proceedings. Indeed, the Court in *Ursery* held that "civil forfeitures generally ... do not constitute 'punishment' for purposes of the Double Jeopardy Clause." Such proceedings therefore do not place an individual in "jeopardy."

On a number of occasions the United States Supreme Court has examined whether particular proceedings brought by the federal government to recover monetary penalties from those who allegedly defrauded the government or who violated statutes or regulations governing federally-regulated businesses are civil or criminal in nature. In each of these cases the Court concluded that the proceeding was civil in nature, even though the monetary penalty may have exceeded the amount of "actual" damages suffered by the government.

In *Helvering v. Mitchell* (1938), for example, the Supreme Court held that a proceeding instituted by the United States under the Revenue Act of 1928 to collect a tax deficiency and a 50% penalty from a taxpayer who fraudulently underpaid his income taxes was not "essentially criminal" and that the Double Jeopardy Clause did not apply in such a proceeding. The Court, in an opinion written by Justice Louis D. Brandeis, concluded that the sanction of an addition to the unpaid tax is remedial in character, primarily intended to serve as a safeguard for the protection of the revenue and to reimburse the government for its expenses in investigating the fraud and for the loss resulting from the fraud.

So too, in *United States ex rel. Marcus v. Hess* (1943), a *qui tam* action brought by a private individual on his own behalf and in the name of the United States (which by statute would share equally in any damages recovered by the individual) against a group of electrical contractors who allegedly defrauded the government. The United States Supreme Court concluded that a proceeding under a statute authorizing recovery of $2000 for each false claim against the government, plus double the amount of actual damages, was remedial in character and imposed a civil sanction. The Supreme Court found that the primary purpose of the statute was "to provide for restitution to the government of money taken from it by fraud, and that the device of double damages plus a specific sum was chosen to make sure that the government would be made completely whole." The Court stated that the remedy did "not lose the quality of a civil action because more than the precise amount of so-called actual damage is recovered." The Court reasoned:

As to the double damage provision, it cannot be said that there is any recovery in excess of actual loss for the government, since in the nature of the qui tam action the government's half of the double damages is the amount of actual damages proved. But in any case, Congress

might have provided here as it did in the anti-trust laws for recovery of "threefold damages ... sustained and the cost of suit, including a reasonable attorney's fee." Congress could remain fully in the common law tradition and still provide punitive damages. "By the common as well as by statute law, men are often punished for aggravated misconduct or lawless acts by means of a civil action and the damages inflicted by way of penalty or punishment, given to the party injured." This Court has noted the general practice in state statutes of allowing double or treble or even quadruple damages. Punitive or exemplary damages have been held recoverable under a statute like this which combines provision for criminal punishment with others which afford a civil remedy to the individual injured. The law can provide the same measure of damage for the government as it can for an individual.
(*See also* Hudson v. United States, 1997; Rex Trailer Co. v. United States, 1956.)

The United States Supreme Court also has indicated that proceedings brought by the government seeking to commit sexually violent predators are likely to be deemed civil in nature, even though those proceedings can result in the loss of liberty. In *Kansas v. Hendricks* (1997), the Supreme Court held that proceedings under a Kansas statute providing for the civil commitment of individuals who have been convicted of or charged with a sexually violent offense and who, due to a mental abnormality or personality disorder, are likely to engage in predatory acts of sexual violence are civil in character and that therefore the double jeopardy provision does not apply in such proceedings. The Court reasoned, in part, that the Kansas legislature intended the statute to protect the public from harm and that restricting the freedom of those mentally ill individuals who present a danger to the public by involuntarily committing them is "a legitimate nonpunitive governmental objective" (*see also* Martin v. Reinstein, 1999; Westerheide v. State, 2002; *In re* Detention of Samuelson, 2000; *In re* Detention of Garren, 2000).

The Supreme Court's conclusion in *Hendricks* is consistent with earlier lower court decisions holding that the Double Jeopardy Clause is not implicated in proceedings in which the government seeks to commit a person to a mental health facility involuntarily because he suffers from a mental illness and constitutes a danger to himself or others (*e.g.*, Edwards v. State, 1997; *In re* Katz, 1994; *In re* Lomax, 1976; Wiggins v. State, 1984; People v. Sansone, 1974; State v. Hudson, 1981; *see also* People v. Francis, 2002; People v. Superior Court (Williams), 1991; *In re* Vandenberg, 1980). Although an involuntary commitment proceeding can result in a significant deprivation of liberty, the purpose of the proceeding is not to ascertain the individual's guilt or innocence of a criminal offense and to punish him for such an offense, but rather to determine the person's mental condition and dangerousness, and if necessary, to commit him for treatment of his mental illness (Edwards v. State, 1997; *In re* Lomax, 1976; State v. Hudson, 1981; *see also* People v. Superior Court (Williams), 1991).

Finally, the United States Supreme Court indicated in *Hudson v. United States* (1997) that administrative proceedings brought by the government to debar an individual from engaging in a particular occupation will be deemed civil in nature and therefore not subject to the guarantee against double jeopardy. In *Hudson*, the Office of the Comptroller of the Currency (OCC) concluded that several officers and directors of two banks in Oklahoma violated various federal banking statutes and regulations. The OCC imposed monetary penalties upon the individuals and barred them from further participation in the conduct of any banking institution. The Supreme Court concluded that the administrative proceedings that led to the imposition of the sanctions were civil, not criminal, in nature, and that the guarantee against double jeopardy did not apply in such proceedings. The Court explained that while the occupational debarment (and the monetary penalties) were intended to deter future wrongdoing (a traditional goal of criminal punishment), they also served to promote the stability of the banking industry, a non-punitive purpose. More importantly, though, the Court believed that prohibiting the individuals from further participating in the banking industry was "certainly nothing approaching the 'infamous punishment' of imprisonment."

Beginning in the early 1900s, the practice of releasing prisoners on parole before the end of their sentences became the norm in the United States. The primary purpose of parole is to help those imprisoned for committing a crime reintegrate into society as constructive citizens as soon as they are able, without being confined for the full term of the sentence imposed upon them. Parole also eliminates the costs to society of keeping a person in prison. Release from prison on parole is conditional, however, for the danger exists that the offender will not have been rehabilitated and will again engage in criminal conduct. To help protect society from this possibility, the conditions of parole require a parolee to abide by certain rules that restrict his activities substantially beyond the ordinary restrictions imposed by law upon an individual citizen. For example, in addition to not violating any criminal laws, a parolee typically must refrain from using alcohol and associating with certain categories of undesirable people and must obtain permission before engaging in certain activities, such as changing jobs or living quarters, marrying, and traveling outside the community. To help assure that the parolee abides by the conditions of his parole, a parole officer is assigned to supervise him. If a parolee violates any of the conditions, the parole board can revoke his parole and incarcerate him for the remainder of his sentence (*see generally* Morrissey v. Brewer, 1972).

Revocation of parole is not a stage of a criminal prosecution (Morrissey v. Brewer, 1972). Parole arises after the end of a criminal prosecution, including the imposition of sentence. The decision whether to revoke parole is made by an administrative agency (the parole board), not by a court. Although the revocation of parole deprives the parolee of liberty, it is not of the absolute liberty to which every person is entitled, but only of the conditional liberty that is dependent upon the parolee's observance of special restrictions. More importantly, proceedings to revoke parole are not designed to punish the parolee for violating the criminal law. They are conducted to determine whether the individual violated the terms of his conditional release, and if he did, whether the interests of society and of the parolee require that he be incarcerated for the duration of his original sentence. Any imprisonment that results from the revocation of parole is punishment for his original crime, not for any new offense. A parole revocation proceeding cannot result in a conviction of a criminal offense and therefore does not put a parolee in "jeopardy" within the meaning of the Double Jeopardy Clause. Accordingly, a parole revocation proceeding based upon the parolee's alleged commission of a criminal act does not bar the government from subsequently prosecuting him criminally for the same act (*e.g.*, Stringer v. Williams, 1998; United States v. Hanahan, 1986 People v. Gallegos, 1995; People v. Marrow, 1995; State v. Black, 1998; *Ex parte* Peralta, 2002), and *vice-versa* (*e.g.*, Dantzler v. Travis, 1998). For the same reason, the double jeopardy provision does not bar successive parole revocation proceedings based upon the same conduct (*e.g.*, Turner v. United States Parole Comm'n, 1991; New Jersey State Parole Bd. v. Mannson, 1987).

Probation is a sentence of conditional release imposed by a court upon a convicted individual as an alternative to incarceration. In many cases, a sentencing judge will impose a prison sentence upon a convicted offender, but suspend all or part of the sentence and place the individual on probation for a specified period of time. In other cases, the judge will place the convicted offender on probation for a specified period of time and defer sentencing him for his crime.

The goal of probation is to integrate the convicted offender back into the community. Like parole, probation benefits both the offender and society. The offender benefits by avoiding imprisonment, while society gains by being relieved of the burden of caring for another prison inmate. At the same time, however, probation presents a threat to society because of the possibility that the probationer will revert to his pattern of criminal conduct. To reduce the chances of this occurring, a court granting probation typically imposes a number of conditions that the probationer must observe during the probationary period, such as not violating any criminal law, obtaining employment, remaining within the jurisdiction, and refraining from possessing or using any alcohol or controlled substance. Such conditions are intended to aid in the rehabilitation of the offender and to protect the community while he is at large. To help assure that the probationer observes these conditions, a probation officer is assigned to supervise him. If a probationer violates any of the conditions, the sentencing court can revoke his probation and incarcerate him for the term of his original suspended sentence, or, if the court originally deferred sentencing, it can sentence the probationer for his original crime (*see generally* United States v. Knights, 2001; Griffin v. Wisconsin, 1987).

A probation revocation proceeding constitutes only a reconsideration of the original sentence imposed by the trial court (People v. Preuss, 1995), and as such, is merely a continuation of the original criminal prosecution for the previous offense (Gagnon v. Scarpelli, 1973). The probationer does not face the risk of conviction for a new criminal offense, but merely incarceration for the previous offense. He therefore is not in "jeopardy" for purposes of double jeopardy analysis. For that reason, a probation revocation proceeding based upon the individual's alleged commission of a criminal act does not bar a subsequent criminal prosecution for that act (*e.g.*, United States v. Woods, 1997; United States v. Miller, 1986; State v. McDowell. 1997; State v. Daniels, 2000; Commonwealth v. Holmgren, 1995; State v. Monk, 1999; State v. Brunet, 2002), and *vice-versa* (*e.g.*, Johnson v. United States, 2000); nor does it bar successive probation revocation proceedings based upon the same conduct (*e.g.*, Perry v. State, 1994; Shumate v. State,1999; Davenport v. State, 1978), or for a parolee concurrently serving a sentence of probation, successive probation revocation and parole revocation hearings based upon the same conduct (United States v. Whitney, 1981; Ashba v. State, 1991).

The federal system abolished parole in 1987. Federal law now provides that a court, in imposing a sentence of imprisonment upon an individual convicted of a criminal offense, may include as part of the sentence a requirement that the individual be placed on a term of supervised release after imprisonment. Unlike parole, supervised release does not replace part of a term of imprisonment; rather it is imposed by a court in addition to a term of imprisonment. Like an individual on parole, however, an offender on supervised release must abide by certain conditions. If he violates any of the conditions, his supervised release can be revoked and he can be imprisoned for all or part of his term of supervised release (*see generally* Johnson v. United States, 2000; United States v. Reyes, 2002).

A proceeding to revoke an offender's supervised release is essentially a continuation of the original criminal prosecution for the previous offense (Jones v. United States, 1995; *see also* United States v. Johnson, 2000). It does not constitute a new criminal prosecution of the offender, and the court cannot convict him of a criminal offense. Any incarceration that results from the revocation of the supervised release is attributable to the original offense and conviction. An offender facing the revocation of his supervised release therefore is not in "jeopardy" as the double jeopardy provision uses that term. Consequently, an offender can be prosecuted for a criminal offense based upon the same act that served as the basis for a hearing to revoke his supervised release (United States v. Wyatt, 1996; United States v. Soto-Olivas, 1995; Jones v. United States, 1995), and *vice-versa*. The Double Jeopardy Clause also does not bar the government from bringing successive proceedings to revoke an individual's supervised release based upon the same act, or for an offender also serving a sentence of probation, a proceeding to revoke supervised release following a proceeding to revoke probation based on the same act (United States v. Clark, 1993).

Individuals charged with a crime frequently can remain free from custody pending their trial by posting money or property as bail, or, in many jurisdictions, on their own recognizance (*i.e.*, by promising to appear for trial). A person on pretrial release must abide by certain conditions imposed by the court, such as not violating any law; avoiding contact with the victim of the crime in question or any potential witnesses in the case; and not leaving the jurisdiction without permission. If he violates any of the conditions, the court can revoke his pretrial release and incarcerate him until his trial.

Although a hearing to revoke an individual's pretrial release is related to a pending criminal prosecution and can result in the loss of liberty for the individual, such a proceeding is not "essentially criminal" in nature and is not "intended to authorize criminal punishment to vindicate public justice" (United States *ex rel.* Marcus v. Hess, 1943). In a proceeding to revoke an individual's pretrial release, the court does not determine the guilt or innocence of the individual; rather, it determines whether the individual violated any of the conditions of his release, and if he did, whether his presence at trial and the safety of the community can still be assured if he is allowed to remain at liberty. Any incarceration the individual may suffer as a result of his violation of a pretrial release condition does not constitute punishment for the act constituting the violation. Its purposes are merely to assure the individual's presence at his trial for the initial criminal offense and to protect the community. An individual therefore is not in "jeopardy" at such a proceeding, and the Double Jeopardy Clause does not apply. Accordingly, when a court revokes the pretrial release of an individual on the basis of an act that also constitutes a criminal offense, the revocation hearing does not preclude the government from subsequently prosecuting the individual criminally for the same act (United States v. Grisanti, 1993; Wilcox v. State, 2001; *see also* Showery v. Samaniego, 1987).

A hearing to deport an alien is "a purely civil action" (INS v. Lopez-Mendoza, 1984; *accord* Harisiades v. Shaughnessy, 1952). The purpose of such a hearing is to determine the eligibility of an alien to remain in this country, not to punish an unlawful entry (INS v. Lopez-Mendoza, 1984). Moreover, deportation itself is not a punishment; it is merely a refusal by the government to harbor individuals whom it does not want (Harisiades v. Shaughnessy, 1952; Bugajewitz v. Adams, 1913). Indeed, a deportation hearing is held before an immigration judge, whose "sole power is to order deportation; the judge cannot adjudicate guilt or punish the respondent for any crime related to unlawful entry or presence in this country" (INS v. Lopez-Mendoza, 1984). Not surprisingly, the Double Jeopardy Clause does not apply in proceedings to deport an individual (*In re* Yacoubian, 1994; Zuniga v. Greene,1999; United States v. Garay-Burgos, 1997; Chukwurah v. United States, 1993; *see also* Helvering v. Mitchell, 1938).

As explained earlier in this section, the Double Jeopardy Clause does not apply when a private party to a lawsuit seeks a civil contempt of court citation against an opposing party in the lawsuit for disobeying an order of a court. The same is true in civil contempt proceedings brought by the government, such as when a witness called at a trial refuses, without a valid reason, to comply with the court's order to answer questions posed to him (Yates v. United States, 1957) or when an individual refuses to comply with a court's order to testify before a grand jury despite being granted immunity from prosecution (*e.g.*, United States v. Ryan, 1988; *In re* Grand Jury Proceedings (Horak), 1980; *see also* Shillitani v. United

States, 1966). A civil contempt of court action, even when brought by the government, involves a remedial sanctions employed to coerce an individual into compliance with a court's order and to compensate the complaining party for any losses sustained. The sanction case is not intended to punish the party failing to comply with the order; rather, they are remedial and for the benefit of the complaining party (Local 28 of the Sheet Metal Workers' Int'l Ass'n v. Equal Employment Opportunity Comm'n, 1986.) Unlike a sanction imposed for criminal contempt (*see* Yates v. United States, 1957), a sanction imposed by a court for civil contempt is conditional, in that the contemnor can avoid it merely by performing the act required by the court's order (Shillitani v. United States, 1966). Even when contemnors are imprisoned for their contempt, they "carry 'the keys of their prison in their own pockets'" (Shillitani v. United States, 1966.) Consequently, even in a civil contempt of court proceeding brought by the government, the person disobeying a court order does not face "the risk that is traditionally associated with a criminal prosecution" (Breed v. Jones, 1975) and therefore the double jeopardy provision does not apply.

Lower courts have held the Double Jeopardy Clause inapplicable in various other types of proceedings brought by a governmental department or agency, including disciplinary proceedings against attorneys (*e.g.*, Fitzsimmons v. State Bar of California, 1983; *In re* Cardwell, 2002; *In re* Asher, 2001; *In re* Sheaffer, 1995; *In re* Chastain, 2000; *In re* Discipline of Babilis, 1997), physicians (*e.g.*, Arthurs v. Board of Registration in Medicine, 1981; Thangavelu v. Department of Licensing & Regulation, 1986), judges (*e.g.*, *In re* Quirk, 1997; *In re* Larsen, 2002), and others required to have a government-issued license to engage in their business or profession (*e.g.*, Rondberg v. Arizona Bd. of Chiropractic Examiners, 1995; Nicoletti v. State Bd. of Vehicle Mfrs., Dealers and Salespersons, 1998; Reed v. Alcoholic Beverage Control Div., 1988); disciplinary proceedings against public employees, such as police officers (*e.g.*, Price v. Board of Fire and Police Comm'rs of Beardstown, 1985; Cross v. State *ex rel.* Linton, 1981; Louisville Civil Service Bd. v. Blair, 1986), teachers (*e.g.*, Heath v. Alabama State Tenure Comm'n, 1981), and school bus drivers (*e.g.*, Colburn v. Tuscaloosa County Bd. of Ed., 1997); and disciplinary proceedings brought by prison authorities against inmates (*e.g.*, People v. Jones, 1998; State v. McKinney, 1998; Russo v. New Jersey Dept. of Corrections, 1999; State v. Thompson, 1999).

Though disciplinary proceedings against professionals and other licensees can result in the suspension or revocation of their license to engage in their profession or business, such proceedings are "free of the punitive criminal element" (Helvering v. Mitchell, 1938) and therefore not "essentially criminal" in nature. The primary purpose of such a proceeding is not to punish the individual; rather, such proceedings are intended to protect the public from those who are deemed unfit to practice the particular profession or engage in the particular occupation, and to maintain the public's confidence in the particular profession or business, and in the case of attorneys, in the administration of justice.

When a governmental department or agency institutes proceedings to reprimand, suspend, or discharge a public employee, the government is not acting in its sovereign capacity seeking to punish a wrongdoer for violating a criminal statute. In undertaking such a proceeding, it is acting in its capacity as an employer and, like any private employer, is attempting to enhance its efficiency or productivity by taking steps to improve the performance of a lazy or careless employee or by ridding itself completely of an incompetent—perhaps even corrupt—employee by terminating the employment relationship. In a broad sense, such disciplinary proceedings are aimed at "protecting" the public from the harm that can result from government employees not adequately performing their jobs. In addition, disciplinary action taken against careless, incompetent, or corrupt government workers can help to prevent an erosion in the public's confidence in the government's ability to provide essential services.

Disciplinary proceedings against prison inmates present a closer question. As a result of such a proceeding, an inmate can, among other things, be placed in solitary confinement; lose "good time" credits and have his mandatory release date extended. Such sanctions appear to serve the purposes of punishment—gaining retribution for the prisoner's misdeeds and deterring that prisoner, as well as other inmates, from engaging in disruptive behavior and violating prison rules in the future. Nevertheless, courts conclude that prison disciplinary proceedings are not primarily undertaken to punish inmates for their misconduct and therefore are not "essentially criminal in character." According to these courts, such proceedings are aimed at maintaining order and safety in the institution and rehabilitating the inmates.

By like reasoning, courts also hold that the guarantee against double jeopardy does not apply in proceedings to suspend or revoke an individual's driver's license (*e.g.*, Reynolds v. State, 1999). Statutory schemes providing for the revocation or suspension of an individual's driver's license for conduct involving the use of a motor vehicle, such as driving while intoxicated or refusing to take a breathalyzer test, clearly serve a remedial, not punitive, purpose. They are intended to protect the public safety by removing dangerous drivers from the roads. As one court explained:

> The revocation of a driver's license is part of a civil/regulatory scheme that serves a vastly different governmental purpose from criminal punishment. Our state's interest is to foster safety by temporarily removing from public thoroughfares those licensees who have exhibited dangerous behavior, which interest is grossly different from the criminal penalties that are available in a driving while under the influence prosecution (State v. Maze, 1992).

The suspension or revocation of an individual's driver's license may, of course, deter that person and others from engaging in the conduct that led to the suspension or revocation. It also may prove extremely inconvenient to most individuals and can have severe monetary ramifications on those who use a motor vehicle in their occupation or profession. Nevertheless, these are merely incidental effects and should not transform an otherwise civil proceeding into an "essentially criminal" one for purposes of the Double Jeopardy Clause.

The Attachment of Jeopardy

The criminal prosecution of an individual for a particular offense cannot run afoul of the Double Jeopardy Clause unless that individual previously suffered "jeopardy" for the same offense. It is not surprising, then, that the United States Supreme Court has stated that the time at which an individual is placed in jeopardy in a criminal proceeding—that is, the point in the proceeding when jeopardy "'attaches'—serves as the lynchpin for all double jeopardy jurisprudence" (Crist v. Bretz, 1978).

Unlike in Great Britain, where an accused is put in jeopardy only after a complete trial that results in either his conviction or acquittal,[8] an individual may be placed in jeopardy under the double jeopardy provision of the Fifth Amendment even in a criminal trial that ends inconclusively (Crist v. Bretz, 1978). Jeopardy "attaches" under the Double Jeopardy Clause at that point in a proceeding when the accused is "'put to trial before the trier of facts, whether the trier be a jury or a judge'" (Serfass v. United States, 1975). It is at that point in the proceeding that the accused faces the risk of conviction (Serfass v. United States, 1975) and that the policies underpinning the constitutional guarantee against double jeopardy are implicated (Serfass v. United States, 1975; United States v. Jorn, 1971 (plurality opinion)).

To illustrate, in *Serfass v. United States* (1975), the Supreme Court held that jeopardy had not yet attached when the trial court granted the defendant's pretrial motion to dismiss the indictment against him, even though the trial court based its dismissal upon a legal ruling made after it examined records and an affidavit setting forth evidence to be adduced at trial. The Court reasoned that because the defendant had not waived his right to a jury trial and no jury had been selected, the trial court lacked power to make any determination regarding the defendant's guilt or innocence, so that he never had been "put to trial before the trier of facts." The Court explained:

> When a criminal prosecution is terminated prior to trial, an accused is often spared much of the expense, delay, strain, and embarrassment which attend a trial. Although an accused may raise defenses or objections before trial which are "capable of determination without the trial of the general issue [of guilt or innocence]," and although he must raise certain other defenses or objections before trial, in neither case is he "subjected to the hazards of trial and possible conviction." Moreover, in neither case would an appeal by the [government] "allow the prosecutor to seek to persuade a second trier of fact of the defendant's guilt after having failed with the first."

For the same reason, jeopardy does not attach at various stages of a criminal prosecution that take place before the actual trial, such as at a hearing to determine whether an individual should be extradited from the United States to another country (Collins v. Loisel, 1923), or from one state to another state (Laverty v. State, 1998; Shields v. State, 1970; McCrary v. Scully, 1989; *Ex parte* Shoels, 1982), to face criminal charges; a preliminary hearing to determine whether probable cause exists to believe that a suspect committed a criminal offense and should be held to stand trial (Commonwealth v. Friend, 1984; People v. Robbins, 1997; State v. Foley, 2000; State v. Brickey, 1986; *see also* United States *ex rel.* Rutz v. Levy, 1925; Collins v. Loisel, 1923); an arraignment at which the accused enters a plea to the charge against him (Bassing v. Cady, 1908; Commonwealth v. Aldrich, 1985; State v. Ferreira, 1985; State v. Todd, 1983); a hearing to determine whether the accused possesses sufficient mental competency to stand trial (*e.g.*, Parker v. Estelle, 1974; State v. Breuhl, 2000); a hearing on the defendant's motion to suppress evidence against him on the ground that the government obtained the evidence through illegal means (*e.g.*, State v. Barksdale, 1988; State v. Pfortmiller, 1981; Commonwealth v. Smith, 1990; *Ex parte* Ueno, 1998); or a hearing to determine whether a potential witness is competent to testify at trial (State v. Marr, 1996). Similarly, in a delinquency proceeding in Juvenile Court, jeopardy does not attach at a hearing conducted solely to determine whether to transfer the youth to the criminal court for prosecution as an adult (*e.g.*, W.T.K. v. State, 1992; State v. Belcher, 1998; Livingston v. State, 1996; People v. P.H., 1991; Proctor v. State, 1992; State *ex rel.* Vance v. Maynard, 1986).

The precise point at which jeopardy attaches in a criminal proceeding differs depending upon whether the case will be tried by a jury or to a judge alone. In a jury trial, jeopardy attaches when the entire jury, including alternates (*e.g.*, People v. McDermott, 2002; Livingston v. State, 1989; *contra* People v. Innis, 1992), has been selected and sworn, even though no witnesses have testified, or even been sworn, and no evidence has been presented (Crist v. Bretz, 1978; Downum v. United States, 1963). It is at that point that the accused faces the risk of being convicted and punished. More importantly, perhaps, once the jury has been empaneled and sworn, the need arises to protect the individual's interest in "retaining [the] chosen jury" (Crist v. Bretz, 1978), that is, his "'valued right to have his trial completed by [that] particular tribunal'" (Crist v. Bretz, 1978), one that the individual may perceive to be favorably inclined towards him and his case. Under this rule governing the attachment of jeopardy in a jury trial, an accused is not placed in jeopardy when only some jurors have been selected (*e.g.*, People v. Pontillo, 1994; People v. Moyer, 2002; Commonwealth v. Pursell, 1999; Jones v. State, 1992) or when the entire jury has been selected, but its members have not yet been sworn *as a collective body* (*e.g.*, United States v. Osteen, 2001; United States v. Albanese, 1999; Barela v. State, 1992; Fassi v. State, 1991), even though they may have been sworn individually or in groups (People v. Turner, 1989; State v. Tuckson, 2001; Koonce v. State, 1983; *contra* People v. Innis, 1992).

In a trial in which the judge rather than a jury serves as the fact finder, commonly known as a bench trial, jeopardy attaches when the judge begins to hear evidence in the case (Lee v. United States, 1977; United States v. Martin Linen Supply Co., 1977; Breed v. Jones, 1975; Serfass v. United States, 1975). This typically occurs when the first witness is sworn (Crist v. Bretz, 1978), regardless of whether the witness actually testifies (Goolsby v. Hutto, 1982; People v. Brower, 1987; *contra* R.A.C. v. State, 1999; State v. Clark, 1986); for once a witness is called and sworn, the accused is subject to conviction. Sometimes, in a bench trial, however, the prosecuting attorney and the defendant agree to allow the judge to decide the question of guilt or innocence solely on the basis of written evidence, such as an agreed statement of facts or the transcript of a preliminary hearing, and/or evidentiary exhibits. In such circumstances, a judge "begins to hear evidence," and jeopardy attaches, when the parties submit the written evidence or the evidentiary exhibits to the judge for his consideration (Finch v. United States, 1977).

At the commencement of a criminal trial, before the government calls any witnesses or introduces any evidence, the prosecuting attorney and defense counsel usually make opening statements to the fact finder in which they summarize what they expect the evidence to be presented at trial will show. These statements by the attorneys do not constitute evidence; thus, in a bench trial, jeopardy does not attach when the prosecutor commences his opening statement to the judge, or even upon the completion of his, or defense counsel's, opening statement (District of Columbia v. Whitley, 1994; Cummings v. Commonwealth, 1997; *see also* State v. Despertt, 1988). Of course, in a jury trial, the attorneys make their opening statements to the jury, which necessarily occurs at a point after the members of the jury have been selected and sworn, and thus after the attachment of jeopardy.

The overwhelming majority of criminal prosecutions in the United States, however, are resolved without a trial at all; rather, they culminate in the defendant's pleading guilty, or in some cases, *nolo contendere* (no contest), which has the same legal effect as a guilty plea. The United States Supreme Court has yet to decide when jeopardy attaches in a case involving either of these pleas. In *Ricketts v. Adamson* (1987), the trial court accepted a plea agreement and proposed sentence entered into between an accused murderer and the prosecuting attorney, but withheld imposition of the sentence for nearly two years until the accused fulfilled his obligations to testify against other parties involved in the murder. The Supreme Court "assume[d]" for purposes of that case that "jeopardy attached *at least* when [the accused] was sentenced ... on his plea of guilty" (italics added). This statement by the Court should not be interpreted to mean that jeopardy attaches *only* when the trial court imposes a sentence upon a defendant who pleads guilty or *nolo contendere*, because the precise point at which jeopardy attached in *Adamson* made no difference to the Court's analysis in that case. Nevertheless, some lower courts conclude that jeopardy does not attach in a case involving a plea of guilty or *nolo contendere* until the trial court sentences the defendant (*e.g.*, State v. Stevens, 1984; People v. Johnson, 1976; State v. Morton,

1998), while others hold it does not attach until the trial court imposes a sentence *and* enters a final judgment of conviction (United States v. Santiago Soto, 1987; United States v. Combs, 1980; State v. Angel, 2002). According to these latter courts, "[t]he mere acceptance of a guilty plea does not carry the same expectation of finality and tranquility that comes with a jury's verdict or with an entry of judgment and sentence [upon a plea of guilty or *nolo contendere*]" (United States v. Santiago Soto, 1987), and therefore the Double Jeopardy Clause's policy of preserving the finality of judgments does not come into play until that point.

The vast majority of courts that have considered the issue, however, hold that jeopardy attaches when the trial court unconditionally accepts a defendant's tendered plea of guilty or *nolo contendere* (*e.g.*, United States v. Faber, 1995; People v. Scott, 1997; Pettis v. State, 2002; People v. Jackson, 1987; Peiffer v. State, 2002; Sampson v. State, 1991; State v. Knaff, 1998; State v. Harrocks, 2001; State v. Comstock, 1992). These courts reason that once the trial court unconditionally accepts the plea, the defendant is bound by it and cannot withdraw it in the absence of exceptional circumstances, such as mistake, fraud, or coercion (Pettis v. State, 2002; Peiffer v. State, 2002; Sampson v. State, 1991); and that even though no sentence has yet been imposed and no judgment entered, the defendant is considered to be convicted at that time—the same as if a jury had returned a verdict of guilty against him (United States v. Hecht, 1981; State v. Keith, 1985; *see also* United States v. Smith, 1990). As one judge explained:

> Jeopardy means exposure to the risk of a determination of guilt or innocence. A defendant who pleads guilty and has his guilty plea accepted by the court obviously faces the risk of a determination of guilt. This risk is worthy of double jeopardy protection. By pleading guilty, the defendant admits all material facts alleged in the charge and waives nonjurisdictional defects in the proceeding. He also waives several constitutional rights, including the privilege against self-incrimination, the right to trial by jury, and the right to confront accusers, as well as his right to object to some, though not all, antecedent constitutional violations. A plea of guilty leaves the court nothing to do but impose sentence and enter judgment. (United States v. Combs, 1980 (McKay, J., concurring in part and dissenting in part)).

For that reason, the defendant's interest in "finality" may arise at the time the trial court accepts his plea of guilty or *nolo contendere*. Moreover, many of the other policies underlying the Double Jeopardy Clause are implicated at that point. If the trial court proceeds to trial on the same offense after accepting such a plea, the defendant will be subject to the same "embarrassment, expense and ordeal" and will suffer the same level of "anxiety and insecurity" (Green v. United States, 1957), regardless of whether the trial court has sentenced him or entered a formal judgment on his plea (United States v. Combs, 1980 (McKay, J., concurring in part and dissenting in part)).

Under any of these views, it is clear that jeopardy does not attach when the trial court *rejects* a defendant's tendered plea of guilty or *nolo contendere* (*e.g.*, Renye

v. State, 1999; State v. Wallace, 1997; State v. Wilkins, 1992; Commonwealth v. Lark, 1997), or when it "conditionally" accepts the plea pending its study of the presentence report (*e.g.*, United States v. Patterson, 2002; United States v. Cordova-Perez, 1995; Commonwealth v. Branch, 1992; State v. Akins, 1993). *A fortiori*, jeopardy does not attach merely upon a defendant's being sworn prior to testifying at a hearing to determine whether the court will accept his tendered plea of guilty or *nolo contendere* (United States v. Carreon, 1980).

In a juvenile delinquency proceeding, jeopardy attaches at least when the Juvenile Court judge begins receiving evidence at the adjudicatory hearing (Breed v. Jones, 1975). Some jurisdictions, however, allow the Juvenile Court to appoint a master or referee to conduct delinquency hearings and to make proposed findings of fact and recommendations to the Juvenile Court judge, who ultimately makes the final determination of whether the minor is delinquent. Although the Supreme Court in *Swisher v. Brady* (1978) found it unnecessary to decide whether jeopardy attaches at a hearing before a master or referee, it strongly indicated that it does.

To render a valid judgment in a criminal case, a trial court must have the power to exercise authority over the defendant (jurisdiction of the person) and the power to hear and decide a case involving the offense with which the defendant is charged (jurisdiction over the offense). For example, some trial courts may be vested by statute with jurisdiction to try only minor offenses, such as misdemeanors and ordinance violations. Such a court lacks subject matter jurisdiction over more serious offenses and therefore cannot try an individual charged with a felony. Proceedings in a case before a court that lacks jurisdiction over either the defendant or the offense are "absolutely void" (United States v. Ball, 1896), and therefore an individual is not placed in jeopardy in such a trial (Woodring v. United States, 1964; Bradley v. State, 2000; B.D.T. v. State, 2000; State v. Mesman, 1986; State v. Hamilton, 1998; Commonwealth v. Keenan, 1987). Consequently, neither an acquittal (United States v. Ball, 1896; United States v. Kahn, 1987; B.D.T. v. State, 2000; Commonwealth v. Simeone, 1972) nor a conviction (Woodring v. United States, 1964; Bradley v. State, 2000; People v. Brancoccio, 1994; State v. Hazzard, 1987; Hoang v. State, 1993) in a court that lacks jurisdiction bars the government from subsequently prosecuting the defendant in a court that possesses jurisdiction.

Some lower courts also hold that jeopardy does not attach in a "sham" trial in which the prosecutor does not actively participate and in which the trial judge seeks to prevent the government from subsequently prosecuting the accused for the "same offense" (*e.g.*, People v. Rudi, 1984; People v. Deems, 1980). In *People v. Deems* (1980), for example, the prosecuting attorney, on the date set for the defendant's trial for knowingly receiving stolen property, conceded to the trial judge that the defendant was not guilty of that offense and moved to dismiss that charge so he could obtain a new indictment charging the defendant with theft. The trial judge concluded that the prosecuting attorney was in effect seeking a continuance and that the defendant was entitled to an immediate trial. Although the judge preferred to dismiss the original indictment with prejudice (*i.e.*, a dismissal prohibiting the government from again bringing that charge against the accused), state law precluded him from doing so. Instead, he obtained a jury waiver from the defendant, called the case for trial, and swore the defendant as a witness. When the prosecuting attorney stated he had no witnesses to call, the judge found the defendant not guilty and acquitted him.

The State of Illinois subsequently obtained an indictment charging Deems with theft, but the trial court in that case, relying upon the defendant's previous acquittal on the receiving stolen property charge, dismissed the indictment on double jeopardy grounds. The Supreme Court of Illinois vacated the judgment of acquittal for receiving stolen property and reversed the dismissal of the theft charge. The court concluded that despite the technical attachment of jeopardy when a witness was sworn, the defendant's "trial" for receiving stolen property was merely an artifice used by the trial judge to dismiss the indictment with prejudice, a result he could not accomplish directly. It therefore was a "sham" trial that did not in fact subject the defendant to jeopardy, and the "acquittal" in that proceeding did not bar the State from subsequently prosecuting the defendant for theft, even though that charge constituted the "same offense" as receiving stolen property for purposes of double jeopardy analysis (*but see* Goolsby v. Huto, 1982; Daff v. Maryland, 1989; People v. Brower, 1987).

Jeopardy also *may* not attach in a trial in which the defendant obtains an acquittal through fraud or collusion, such as by bribing or blackmailing the judge in a bench trial. A number of text writers and legal encyclopedias allude to such a rule,[9] and several courts either hold (Price v. State, 1913; State v. Johnson, 1966) or state in *dicta* (*i.e.*, statements not essential to the decision in the case) (*e.g.*, State v. Lee, 1894; State v. Jones, 1849; Edwards v. Commonwealth, 1930; State v. Swepson, 1878; State v. Howell, 1951; McFarland v. State, 1887) that a fraudulently-obtained acquittal does not bar a subsequent prosecution of the acquitted individual for the same offense. The Illinois Appellate Court reached this result in *People v. Aleman* (1996). It held that the State of Illinois could prosecute Harry Aleman for murder sixteen years after his acquittal in a bench trial for the same crime because he had procured that acquittal by bribing the judge. The United States Court of Appeals for the Seventh Circuit, in reviewing this decision, concluded that Aleman endured none of the risks associated with criminal prosecution in his first trial, "because he 'fixed' his case," and therefore was not in jeopardy at that trial (Aleman v. Honorable Judges of the Circuit Court of Cook County, 1998).

The Termination of Jeopardy

For the Double Jeopardy Clause to bar the trial of an individual for a particular offense, that individual must not only have previously been placed in jeopardy for that offense, but some event must have terminated that original jeopardy

(Sattazahn v. Pennsylvania, 2003; Richardson v. United States, 1984). An acquittal, whether by a jury or by a judge in a bench trial, is one such event (Smalis v. Pennsylvania, 1984; Justices of Boston Municipal Court v. Lydon, 1984; Price v. Georgia, 1970). Similarly, an unreversed determination by a reviewing court that the evidence introduced at a convicted defendant's trial was legally insufficient to prove his guilt beyond a reasonable doubt terminates that individual's initial jeopardy (Burks v. United States, 1978).

On the other hand, in a juvenile delinquency proceeding, a recommendation by a master or referee that the Juvenile Court judge find a child not to be delinquent does not terminate any jeopardy that may have attached at the hearing before the master or referee. In a jurisdiction that allows a Juvenile Court judge to appoint a master or referee to conduct an adjudicatory hearing and make proposed findings of fact and recommendations, there is but a single proceeding that commences with the hearing before the master or referee and culminates with an adjudication of the child's status by the Juvenile Court judge (Swisher v. Brady, 1978).

A conviction of a criminal offense terminates jeopardy only if the defendant does not successfully challenge it (*see* United States v. Dixon, 1993; Harris v. Oklahoma, 1977; Brown v. Ohio, 1977). As discussed later in this Analysis, the Double Jeopardy Clause does not bar retrial of a convicted defendant who succeeds in having his conviction overturned on appeal. In reaching this result in *United States v. Ball* (1896), the United States Supreme Court effectively formulated a concept of "continuing jeopardy" that applies when criminal proceedings against an individual have not run their full course (Price v. Georgia, 1970).

The Supreme Court relied upon this "continuing jeopardy" rationale in *Justices of Boston Municipal Court v. Lydon* (1984). *Lydon* involved a two-tier system of courts for trying minor crimes under which a defendant convicted after electing a bench trial in a first-tier court had an absolute right to a trial *de novo* (a new trial on both questions of fact and issues of law) in a second-tier court. The Court in *Lydon* held that the double jeopardy provision does not bar a trial *de novo* of a convicted defendant even if the evidence presented in the first-tier court was, as a matter of law, insufficient to prove the defendant's guilt beyond a reasonable doubt. The Court reasoned that the conviction in the first-tier court—even if erroneous—did not terminate the defendant's jeopardy. The Court viewed the trial in the first-tier court and the trial *de novo* in the second-tier court as a "'single, continuous course of judicial proceedings,'" not as two separate trials.

The termination of a trial before the fact finder renders a decision on the defendant's guilt or innocence ordinarily does not end the defendant's original jeopardy, and the double jeopardy provision therefore does not bar the government from retrying the accused for the same offense. A defendant's initial jeopardy continues when the trial judge aborts the proceeding by declaring a mistrial in response to a request by the defendant (unless the prosecution "goaded" him into making the request) or with the defendant's consent (State v. Bostwick, 1986; Sullivan v. State, 1994; *see also* United States v. Dinitz, 1976). It also continues when, regardless of the defendant's consent, the trial judge declares a mistrial because of a "manifest necessity" (Richardson v. United States, 1984; State v. Large, 2000). For example, the inability of the jury to reach a verdict after hearing all the evidence long has been accepted as an instance of "manifest necessity" allowing the trial judge to declare a mistrial and retry the defendant (United States v. Perez, 1824). In *Richardson v. United States* (1984), the Supreme Court made it clear that a mistrial declared because of a "hung jury" does not terminate the defendant's original jeopardy. There, Richardson, whose first trial ended in a deadlocked jury, contended that the Double Jeopardy Clause barred his retrial because the evidence introduced by the government at his first trial failed to prove his guilt beyond a reasonable doubt. He argued that, under the circumstances, the mistrial should be treated as the equivalent of an acquittal. The Court rejected this argument, concluding that "the [g]overnment ... is entitled to resolution of the case by verdict from the jury ...."

The declaration of a mistrial does, however, terminate a defendant's original jeopardy when the trial judge declares a mistrial without the consent of the defendant and in the absence of a "manifest necessity" (*Ex parte* McAfee, 1988; *see also* United States v. Jorn, 1971 (plurality opinion); Downum v. United States, 1963), or at the request of the defendant when the prosecuting attorney "goaded" the defendant into moving for a mistrial (*see* Oregon v. Kennedy, 1982).

A trial judge's dismissal of a charge against the defendant on a ground consistent with reprosecution of the accused for the offense charged, such as a procedural defect in the charging instrument, is "functionally indistinguishable from a declaration of a mistrial" (Lee v. United States, 1977) and terminates the defendant's initial jeopardy only in those situations that the declaration of a mistrial would terminate it (*see* Lee in United States, 1977).

When the trial judge aborts the trial by dismissing the charge on a basis that contemplates that the proceedings will end then and there in favor of the defendant, the dismissal does not terminate the defendant's original jeopardy if the judge acted in response to a request by the defendant. In such circumstances, the government can try the defendant anew if it succeeds in overturning the dismissal on appeal (United States v. Scott, 1978). On the other hand, if the trial judge acted upon his own motion and over the objection of the defendant, the dismissal terminates the defendant's initial jeopardy and the double jeopardy provision bars the government from trying the defendant a second time for the offense charged, even if the trial judge erred in dismissing that charge (*see* United States v. Gaytan, 1997; United States v. Govro, 1987; State v. Bell, 2000; State v. Vestal, 1998; *but see* State v. Calhoun, 1985).

THE "SAME OFFENSE"

By its terms, the Double Jeopardy Clause prohibits the government from putting an individual twice in jeopardy "for the same offense"; therefore, the scope of protection afforded by this Clause therefore depends upon when two offenses are the "same" for purposes of double jeopardy analysis.

Factual Identity: The Same Act or Transaction

For two offenses to be the "same" for double jeopardy purposes, they must be based upon the same act or transaction. For example, in *Blockburger v. United States* (1932), the government obtained a five-count indictment charging Blockburger with violating provisions of the Harrison Narcotic Act. Count two of the indictment alleged that on a specified day, Blockburger sold to a particular individual ten grains of morphine hydrochloride (a narcotic drug) not in or from the original stamped package. The third count of the indictment alleged that on the following day, Blockburger sold to the same purchaser eight grains of the same drug not in or from the original stamped package. The evidence presented at trial showed that shortly after Blockburger delivered the morphine hydrochloride that was the subject of the first sale, the buyer paid for an additional quantity of the drug, which Blockburger delivered the next day. The jury convicted Blockburger on both counts.

On appeal, Blockburger contended that the two sales constituted a single offense because they were made to the same person and followed each other with no substantial interval of time between the delivery of the drug in the first transaction and the payment for the second quantity sold. The United States Supreme Court rejected Blockburger's contention. The Supreme Court concluded that the sales charged in the two counts constituted "distinct and separate sales made at different times." The Court reasoned that the first sale of the drug had already been completed when the purchaser paid for the second quantity, and that the payment for the additional drug, however closely following the first sale, was "the initiation of a separate and distinct sale completed by its delivery."

The Supreme Court in *Blockburger* nevertheless acknowledged that some offenses are continuous in character, that is, the crime consists of a course of conduct committed over a period of time and does not consist of merely an isolated act. Individual acts of the accused that are part of the continuing offense do not constitute separate offenses for double jeopardy purposes. The Court in *Blockburger* pointed to the offense of cohabiting with more than one woman, the crime involved in *In re Snow* (1887), as an example of a continuing offense. That offense is continuous, explained the Court in *Snow*, because it is committed when a man lives or dwells for a period of time in the same house with two or more women whom he holds out to the world as his wives. Each day, week, month, or even year that a man lives or dwells with more than one woman does not constitute a separate offense.

The more recent case of *Brown v. Ohio* (1977) also provides an example of a continuing offense. In that case, police in Wickliffe, Ohio, arrested Nathaniel Brown on December 8, 1973, for driving a car that had been stolen on November 29, 1973, from a parking lot in East Cleveland, Ohio. The Wickliffe police filed a complaint charging Brown with the misdemeanor offense of "joyriding." The complaint charged that "on or about December 8, 1973, ... Nathaniel H. Brown did unlawfully and purposely take, drive or operate a certain motor vehicle ... without the consent of the owner ...." After Brown pleaded guilty to the charge and served a sentence of thirty days in jail, a grand jury in Cuyahoga County, Ohio, returned an indictment charging that "on or about the 29th day of November 1973," Brown committed the felony of "auto theft" by stealing the same car in which the Wickliffe police discovered him joyriding.

Under Ohio law, joyriding constituted a lesser-included offense of auto theft (*i.e.*, every element of the crime of joyriding was also an element of the crime of auto theft) because auto theft required the taking or operating of a motor vehicle without the consent of the owner—the act constituting the offense of joyriding—as well as the additional element of an intent on the part of the thief permanently to deprive the owner of possession of the vehicle. As will be shown later in this Analysis, the two offenses constituted the "same statutory offense" for purposes of double jeopardy analysis. The trial court, however, rejected Brown's double jeopardy claim that his conviction of joyriding barred his subsequent prosecution for auto theft, and Brown pleaded guilty to the latter offense while preserving his right to appeal on double jeopardy grounds. The Ohio Court of Appeals affirmed the conviction. It held that Brown could be convicted of both crimes, despite their being the same statutory offense, because they focused on different parts of his nine-day joyride.

The United States Supreme Court disagreed. It concluded that the joyriding and auto theft statutes, as written by the Ohio Legislature and construed by the courts of that state, made the theft and operation of a single car a single offense. The joyriding statute did not provide that each day on which the automobile was operated without the owner's consent constituted a separate offense. The Supreme Court therefore held that the specification of different dates in the joyriding and auto theft charges could not alter the fact that the State of Ohio twice placed Brown in jeopardy for the same offense in violation of the protection against double jeopardy. "The Double Jeopardy Clause is not such a fragile guarantee," stated the Court, "that prosecutors can avoid its limitations by the simple expedient of dividing a single crime into a series of temporal or spatial units."

In contrast, the Supreme Court in *Blockburger* rejected Blockburger's claim that the two sales of the narcotic drug could not be separately punished because they constituted a single continuing offense. The Court stated that the Harrison Narcotic Act, under which the government prosecuted Blockburger, did not create the offense of "engaging in the business of selling narcotic drugs"; rather, it penalized any sale of a forbidden drug not in or from the original stamped package. As a result, "[e]ach of several successive sales constitutes a distinct offense, however closely they may follow each other."

The Supreme Court reached the same result in *Ebeling v. Morgan* (1915). There, it held that under the applicable statute an individual who, in the same transaction, successively tears or cuts mail bags of the United States, with the intent to rob or steal the contents of those bags, commits a separate offense for each act of tearing or cutting with the requisite intent. The Supreme Court reasoned that the words of the statute

> plainly indicate that it was the intention of the lawmakers to protect each and every mail bag from felonious injury and mutilation. Whenever any one mail bag is thus torn, cut, or injured, the offense is complete. Although the transaction of cutting the mail bags was in a sense continuous, the complete statutory offense was committed every time a mail bag was cut in the manner described, with the intent charged. The offense as to each separate bag was complete when that bag was cut, irrespective of any attack upon, or mutilation of, any other bag.... Congress evidently intended to protect the mail in each sack, and to make an attack thereon in the manner described a distinct and separate offense.

As *Blockburger*, *Brown*, and *Ebeling* reveal, whether a particular offense is a continuing one whose constituent acts constitute only a single offense for double jeopardy purposes depends upon the language of the statute defining the offense and the intent of the legislature in enacting that statute.

Successive prosecutions may be deemed to involve the same offense when the second prosecution requires relitigation of factual issues already resolved by the first prosecution. In *Ashe v. Swenson* (1970), for example, the United States Supreme Court held that Bob Fred Ashe's acquittal on a charge of robbing one of six men engaged in a poker game established that Ashe was not present at the robbery and that the principles of collateral estoppel embodied in the Double Jeopardy Clause barred prosecutions of Ashe for robbing the other poker players. The doctrine of collateral estoppel, "or, in modern usage, issue preclusion" (Schiro v. Farley, 1994), is discussed more fully later in this Analysis.

Legal Identity: The Same Statutory Offense

The Blockburger (Same-Elements) Test

For two offenses to be the "same" for double jeopardy purposes, they must not only be based upon the same act or transaction, they also must constitute the same statutory offense. Sometimes an individual will perform a single act or engage in a single transaction that violates two separate statutes. In such situations, it must be determined whether there are two offenses or merely one. Separate statutory offenses need not be identical—either in constituent elements or actual proof—to constitute the same offense for purposes of the Double Jeopardy Clause (Brown v. Ohio, 1977). In *Blockburger*, the United States Supreme Court held that "where the same act or transaction constitutes a violation of two distinct statutory provisions, the test to be applied to determine whether there are two offenses or only one, is whether each provision requires proof of a fact which the other does not" (*accord* United States v. Dixon, 1993; Illinois v. Vitale, 1980; Brown v. Ohio, 1977; Iannelli v. United States, 1975).

The *Blockburger* test "focuses on the proof necessary to prove the statutory elements of each offense, rather than on the actual evidence to be presented at trial" (Illinois v. Vitale, 1980; *accord* Brown v. Ohio, 1977). If each statute requires proof of a fact that the other does not, they constitute two separate offenses, "notwithstanding a substantial overlap in the proof offered to establish the crimes" (Iannelli v. United States, 1975).

To illustrate, in *Blockburger*, a jury found that Blockburger sold eight grains of morphine hydrochloride on a particular occasion and for that one sale convicted him of two separate offenses under the Harrison Narcotic Act—unlawfully selling a narcotic drug not in or from its original stamped package and unlawfully selling a narcotic drug not in pursuance of a written order of the purchaser of the drug on a form issued for that purpose by the Commissioner of Internal Revenue. The trial court sentenced Blockburger to five years' imprisonment and a fine of $2000 for each of the offenses, with the prison terms to run consecutively (*i.e.*, the sentence for the second offense would not commence until Blockburger finished serving his sentence for the first offense). The United States Supreme Court rejected Blockburger's claim that his single sale of the narcotic drug constituted only one offense and that therefore only a single penalty could be imposed. The Supreme Court concluded that the two offenses in question were separate offenses because each required proof of a fact that the other did not: the offense of selling a forbidden drug not in or from its original package did not require proof that the sale was not in pursuance of a written order of the purchaser, while the offense of selling a forbidden drug not in pursuance of a written order of the purchaser did not require proof that the drug sold was not in or from its original package.

The Supreme Court originally used the *Blockburger*, or same-elements, test to determine when a trial court can impose consecutive sentences in a single trial for the violation of two different statutory provisions without running afoul of the double jeopardy provision's prohibition against multiple punishments for the same offense.[10] Subsequently, however, the Court held that if two offenses are the same under the *Blockburger* test for purposes of barring consecutive sentences in a single trial, they necessarily are the same for purposes of barring successive prosecutions (Brown v. Ohio, 1977; *accord* United States v. Dixon, 1993; Illinois v. Vitale, 1980). The Court in *Brown* explained: "Where the judge is forbidden to impose cumulative punishment for two crimes at the end of a single proceeding, the prosecutor is forbidden to strive for the same result in successive proceedings."

Some offenses constitute lesser-included offenses of other, more serious, offenses. That is, the greater offense comprises all the elements of the lesser offense plus one or more additional elements, so that a person who commits the greater offense necessarily commits the lesser-included offense. The offense of "possession of cocaine," for example, is a lesser-included offense of "possession of cocaine with intent to distribute," and "robbery" is a lesser-included offense of "armed robbery," because each of the greater offenses (possession with intent to distribute and armed robbery) encompasses all the elements of the lesser-included offense (possession of cocaine and robbery) as well as an additional element (intent to distribute the drug and being armed with a weapon).

Under the *Blockburger* test, greater and lesser-included offenses constitute the "same offense" for double jeopardy purposes, because the lesser-included offense inevitably "requires no proof beyond that which is required for conviction of the greater" (Brown v. Ohio, 1977; *accord In re* Nielsen, 1889). For instance, in *Brown*, the United States Supreme Court concluded that the lesser offense of "joyriding"—taking or operating a motor vehicle without the consent of the owner—constituted the "same statutory offense" for double jeopardy purposes as the greater offense of auto theft—taking a vehicle without the owner's consent with the intent permanently to deprive the owner of possession—because joyriding required no proof beyond that which was required for conviction of auto theft.

For purposes of determining whether the double jeopardy provision allows successive prosecutions of an individual, a lesser-included offense constitutes the same offense as the greater offense even when the *Blockburger* test technically is not met because the greater offense incorporates the lesser offense without specifying the latter's elements. For example, in *Harris v. Oklahoma* (1977), the United States Supreme Court held that a conviction of felony-murder (an unintentional killing during the commission of a felony), based upon a killing committed during an armed robbery, precluded a subsequent prosecution for the same armed robbery. The Supreme Court reached this result even though the felony-murder statute, on its face, did not require proof of robbery, but only of *some* felony, and armed robbery did not require proof of a death. The Court subsequently explained that "for double jeopardy purposes, 'the crime generally described as felony murder' is not 'a separate offense distinct from its various elements'" (United States v. Dixon, 1993), so that in *Harris*, it "treated a killing in the course of a robbery as itself a separate statutory offense, and the robbery as a species of lesser-included offense" (Illinois v. Vitale, 1980).

Similarly, the Supreme Court in *In re Nielsen* (1887) held that for the purpose of prohibiting successive prosecutions, the offenses of adultery and cohabiting with more than one woman constituted the same offense when the adultery charge alleged that during the period of cohabitation the defendant committed the offense with one of the two women with whom he cohabited. The Court reached this result even though the offenses of unlawfully cohabiting with more than one woman and adultery each required proof of a fact that the other did not—adultery required proof that the defendant engaged in sexual intercourse with one woman while married to another and cohabiting with more than one woman required proof that the defendant lived with more than one woman at the same time. The Court reasoned that in the circumstances presented in *Nielsen*, the material part of the adultery charge—sexual intercourse—was contained within the unlawful cohabitation charge, and thus constituted a lesser-included offense of that crime.

The "Same-Conduct" Test

For many years, the United States Supreme Court applied the *Blockburger*, or "same-elements," test as the sole test for determining whether two offenses are the "same," both for the purpose of imposing cumulative punishment and for the purpose of barring successive prosecutions. In 1990, however, a bare majority of the Supreme Court in *Grady v. Corbin* recognized that the *Blockburger* test does not adequately protect individuals from the burdens of multiple trials. The Court stated: "Even when [the government] can bring multiple charges against an individual under *Blockburger*, a tremendous additional burden is placed on that defendant if he must face each of the charges in a separate proceeding." In a 5 to 4 decision, the Court in *Grady* rejected *Blockburger* as the exclusive test for determining whether successive prosecutions impermissibly involve the same offense.

In *Grady*, Thomas Corbin drove his automobile across the double yellow line of a New York highway and struck an oncoming vehicle, killing its driver and seriously injuring a passenger. Police issued Corbin two traffic tickets charging him with two offenses under New York law: driving while intoxicated (a misdemeanor) and failing to keep right of the median. Corbin pleaded guilty to both offenses. He was sentenced to pay a $350 fine and had his driver's license revoked for six months. The State of New York subsequently obtained an indictment charging Corbin with several additional offenses arising from the automobile accident, including reckless manslaughter, criminally negligent homicide, and reckless assault. In a bill of particulars (a document supplied by the government to the defendant giving him more information about the crime than provided in the indictment charging him with the crime), the State announced that it intended to prove the charges by relying upon the following reckless or negligent acts of Corbin: (1) operating an automobile in an intoxicated condition; (2) failing to keep right of the median; and (3) driving too fast for existing conditions.

Under the *Blockburger* test, the offenses of reckless manslaughter, criminally negligent homicide, and reckless assault constituted separate offenses from both driving while intoxicated and driving left of the median. The two homicide offenses (reckless manslaughter and criminally negligent homicide) each required proof of a death, which neither of the traffic offenses required; while neither homicide offense required proof of either driving while intoxicated or driving left of the median. Similarly, reckless assault required proof of physical injury to another, which neither of the traffic offenses required, and did not require proof of either driving while intoxicated or driving left of the median. The Double Jeopardy Clause, as interpreted by the Supreme Court until then, therefore would not have barred prosecution of Corbin for the homicide and assault offenses following his guilty plea to the traffic offenses. Indeed, the Supreme Court in *Grady* recognized that

> [i]f *Blockburger* constituted the entire double jeopardy inquiry in the context of successive prosecutions, the State [of New York] could try Corbin in four consecutive trials: for failure to keep right of the median, for driving while intoxicated, for assault, and for homicide. The State could improve its presentation of proof with each trial, assessing which witnesses gave the most persuasive testimony, which documents had the greatest impact, and which opening and closing arguments most persuaded the jurors. Corbin would be forced either to contest each of these trials or to plead guilty to avoid the harassment and expense.

To avoid that possibility, the Supreme Court in *Grady*—over the strong dissent of Justice Antonin Scalia—adopted a suggestion it originally made ten years earlier in *Illinois v. Vitale* (1980). The Court held that even if the *Blockburger* ("same-elements") test did not prohibit two successive prosecutions, the Double Jeopardy Clause nonetheless "bar[red] any subsequent prosecution in which the government, to establish an essential element of an offense charged in that prosecution, [would] prove conduct that constitute[d] an offense for which the defendant ha[d] already been prosecuted." Similarly, the Court concluded that "if in the course of securing a conviction for one offense the [government] necessarily ... proved the conduct comprising all of the elements of another offense not yet prosecuted (a 'component offense'), the Double Jeopardy Clause ... bar[red] subsequent prosecution of the component offense." The Court emphasized that the critical inquiry under this test was the *conduct* the government would prove, not the *evidence* it would use to prove that conduct, so that the government could not avoid the dictates of the Double Jeopardy Clause merely by using in the subsequent prosecution different evidence to prove the same conduct.

Applying this new interpretation of the double jeopardy provision in *Grady*, the Supreme Court held that the State of New York could not prosecute Thomas Corbin for the homicide and assault offenses because it admitted in its bill of particulars that it would prove the entirety of the conduct for which Corbin already had been convicted—driving while intoxicated and failing to keep right of the median—to establish the essential elements (recklessness or negligence) of the newly-charged offenses. The Court acknowledged, however, that its holding would not bar a subsequent prosecution of Corbin on the homicide and assault charges if the bill of particulars had revealed that the State would rely solely on conduct for which Corbin had not already been convicted, such as driving too fast for conditions, to establish recklessness or negligence.

Even under the "same-conduct" test adopted by the United States Supreme Court in *Grady*, if in one prosecution the government presented *evidence* of misconduct by the defendant that might ultimately be charged as a criminal offense in a second prosecution of that same individual, the Double Jeopardy Clause would not bar the latter prosecution. For "the introduction of relevant evidence of particular misconduct in a case is not the same thing as prosecution for that conduct" (United States v. Felix, 1992). Thus, in *United States v. Felix* (1992), the Supreme Court held that Frank Felix's trial in federal court for various drug offenses allegedly committed by him in Oklahoma during June and July of 1987 was not barred by the government's introduction into evidence of those drug transactions (to establish Felix's criminal intent) at his previous trial in which the government charged him with attempting to manufacture illegal drugs in Missouri during August of 1987.

The Supreme Court in *Felix* also held that the "same-conduct" test it adopted in *Grady* did not alter the long-established rule (*e.g.*, United States v. Bayer, 1947; Pinkerton v. United States, 1946; *see also* Garrett v. United States, 1985; Iannelli v. United States, 1975) that "a substantive crime and a conspiracy to commit that crime are not the 'same offence' for double jeopardy purposes." Under this rule, the prosecution of an individual for conspiracy (*i.e.*, the agreement to commit a crime), when certain of the overt acts relied upon by the government to support the conspiracy charge are based upon substantive offenses for which the individual previously has been convicted, does not violate the Double Jeopardy Clause. In *Felix*, this meant that the government's prosecution of Frank Felix in Missouri for attempting to manufacture methamphetamine between August 26 and August 31, 1987 (based upon his receiving in Joplin, Missouri, precursor chemicals and equipment for the manufacture of methamphetamine), did not bar the government from subsequently prosecuting him in Oklahoma for conspiring with five others between May 1 and August 31, 1987, to manufacture, possess, and distribute methamphetamine; even though two of the overt acts supporting the conspiracy were based upon conduct that had been the subject of the earlier Missouri prosecution—namely, that (1) on August 26, 1987, while in Tulsa, Oklahoma, he provided money for the purchase of chemicals and equipment necessary in the manufacture of methamphetamine, and (2) on August 31, 1987, while at a location in Missouri, he possessed chemicals and equipment necessary in the manufacture of methamphetamine.

The "same-conduct" test adopted by the United States Supreme Court in *Grady* as an additional test for determining whether two offenses are the "same" for purposes of prohibiting successive prosecutions proved to be short-lived. Only three years after its decision in *Grady*, and after the retirement of Justice William J. Brennan, Jr., the author of the Court's opinion in *Grady*, the Supreme Court, in another 5 to 4 decision, concluded in *United States v. Dixon* (1993) that its holding in *Grady* was a "mistake," and it overruled that decision. In an opinion written by Justice Antonin Scalia, the Court in *Dixon* returned to its pre-*Grady* position that the *Blockburger* ("same-elements") test is the sole test under the Double Jeopardy Clause for determining whether successive prosecutions impermissibly involve the "same offense."

The Court in *Dixon* first reasoned that *Grady* was "wrong in principle." It explained that "[u]nlike *Blockburger* analysis, whose definition of what prevents two crimes from being the 'same offense' has deep historical roots and has been accepted in numerous precedents of this Court, *Grady* lacks constitutional roots. The 'same-conduct' rule it announced is wholly inconsistent with earlier Supreme

Court precedent and with the clear common-law understanding of double jeopardy." The Court concluded that there was no authority, other than *Grady*, for the proposition that the term "same offense" has a different meaning in the context of successive prosecutions than in the context of cumulative punishments. It surmised that "[t]hat is perhaps because it is embarrassing to assert that the single term 'same offense' (the words of the Fifth Amendment at issue here) has two different meanings—that what *is* the same offense is yet *not* the same offense."

The Court in *Dixon* also reasoned that in the three years since it had decided *Grady*, its holding in that case had "already proved unstable in application" and "a continuing source of confusion." The Court pointed out that just two years after *Grady*, in *Felix*, it was forced to recognize a "large exception" to its holding in *Grady* by acknowledging that a crime and a conspiracy to commit that crime are different offenses for purposes of double jeopardy analysis. In addition, the Court noted that state courts and lower federal courts had found *Grady* difficult to apply.

The "Same-Transaction" Test

On numerous occasions in dissenting or concurring opinions, United States Supreme Court Justice William J. Brennan, Jr., frequently joined by one or more other Justices, urged the adoption of a "same-transaction" test to determine whether the government had already prosecuted the defendant for the "same offense" (*e.g.*, Jones v. Thomas, 1989 (Brennan, J., dissenting); Morris v. Mathews, 1986 (Brennan, J., dissenting); Harris v. Oklahoma, 1977 (Brennan, J., concurring); Brown v. Ohio, 1977 (Brennan, J., concurring); Simpson v. Florida, 1971 (Brennan, J., concurring); Ashe v. Swenson, 1970 (Brennan, J., concurring); Waller v. Florida, 1970 (Brennan, J., concurring); Abbate v. United States, 1959 (Brennan, J., separate opinion)). Under such a test, the government (except in very limited circumstances) would be constitutionally required "to join at one trial all the charges against a defendant that grow out of a single criminal act, occurrence, episode, or transaction" (Ashe v. Swenson, 1970 (Brennan, J., concurring)).

The "same-transaction" test affords greater protection against multiple prosecutions than either the *Blockburger* ("same-elements") test or the "same-conduct" test adopted in *Grady* and rejected shortly thereafter in *Dixon*. For example, when a single act or transaction violates two distinct statutory provisions that are separate offenses under the *Blockburger* test because each requires proof of a fact that the other does not, the "same-transaction" test normally bars successive prosecutions, even in cases in which the "same-conduct" test would not. To illustrate, in *Grady*, under the "same conduct" test, Thomas Corbin could have been prosecuted for reckless homicide, criminally negligent homicide, and reckless assault if the State of New York had sought to establish recklessness or negligence by relying upon conduct other than that for which Corbin previously had been convicted—driving while intoxicated and failing to keep right of the median. But under the "same-transaction" test, the subsequent prosecution would be barred, regardless of how the government sought to establish the essential elements of those offenses, because all the offenses arose from the same episode or transaction.

Unlike the other tests, the "same-transaction" test also bars multiple prosecutions when a single transaction is divisible into chronologically discrete crimes. It would therefore prohibit the result reached in *Johnson v. Commonwealth* (1923), in which the Court of Appeals of Kentucky held that the government could prosecute an individual separately for each of seventy-five or more hands of poker that he played because each hand constituted a separate offense of illegal gambling on a game of chance.

Similarly, when a single criminal episode involves several victims, the "same-transaction" test precludes the government from bringing a separate prosecution as to each victim, even though the other tests would not. For example, in *Ciucci v. Illinois* (1958), the State of Illinois, in successive trials, obtained convictions of Vincent Ciucci, first, for the murder of his wife, then for the murder of his daughter, and finally for the murder of his son. Although the killings all occurred during the same transaction, each trial involved a different victim and neither the *Blockburger* ("same-elements") test nor the "same-conduct" test would have barred the successive prosecutions. Under the "same-transaction" test, however, the State could have prosecuted Ciucci for the three murders only if it did so in a single trial.

In his separate opinion in *Abbate v. United States* (1959), Justice Brennan explained why the "same transaction" test is necessary. He stated:

> [S]eparate prosecutions of the same criminal conduct can be far more effectively used by a prosecutor to harass an accused than can the imposition of consecutive sentences for various aspects of that conduct. It is always within the discretion of the trial judge whether to impose consecutive or concurrent sentences, whereas, unless the Fifth Amendment applies, it would be solely within the prosecutor's discretion to bring successive prosecutions based on the same acts, thereby requiring the accused to defend himself more than once. Furthermore, separate prosecutions, unlike multiple punishments based on one trial, raise the possibility of an accused acquitted by one jury being subsequently convicted by another for essentially the same conduct. Thus to permit the [g]overnment statutorily to multiply the number of offenses resulting from the same acts, and to allow successive prosecutions of the several offenses, rather than merely the imposition of consecutive sentences after one trial of those offenses, would enable the [g]overnment to "wear the accused out by a multitude of cases with accumulated trial."

Justice Brennan recognized, however, that the "same-transaction" test must contain an exception to allow a separate prosecution "where a crime is not completed or not discovered, despite due diligence on the part of the police, until after the commencement of a prosecution for other crimes arising from the same transaction" (Ashe v. Swenson, 1970 (Brennan, J., concurring)). The Supreme Court of Michigan, which previously had adopted the "same-transaction" test under its state constitution, embraced such an exception in *People v. Harding* (1993). In that case, it held that the defendants' previous convictions for armed robbery, assault with intent to commit murder, and possession of a firearm during the commission of a felony did not bar the State of Michigan from subsequently prosecuting them for felony-murder for a death resulting from the same transaction, because the victim died four years after the incident and after the defendants' trial for armed robbery and the related offenses.

The persuasiveness of Justice Brennan's arguments in favor of the "same transaction" test are confirmed by its adoption by a number of state courts as a matter of state law (*e.g.*, People v. White, 1973; State v. Gregory, 1975; State v. Brown, 1972; Commonwealth v. Campana, 1974) and by the enactment of statutes in many states requiring the prosecution in a single proceeding of all offenses arising out of the same criminal episode.[11] Nevertheless, despite Justice Brennan's constant urging, "the same-transaction test ... has been consistently rejected by the [United States Supreme] Court" (United States v. Dixon, 1993; *see also* Grady v. Corbin, 1990).

The Dual Sovereignty Doctrine

Since 1847, the United States Supreme Court consistently has interpreted the Double Jeopardy Clause to bar successive prosecutions *only* when they are brought by the same sovereign entity (*e.g.*, Fox v. Ohio, 1847; United States v. Marigold, 1850; United States v. Lanza, 1922; Abbate v. United States, 1959; United States v. Wheeler, 1978; Heath v. Alabama, 1985). If a person performs a single act that violates the laws of two different sovereigns, such as the United States and an individual state, or two states, the Double Jeopardy Clause does not bar his separate prosecution, conviction, and punishment by each of those sovereigns (Heath v. Alabama, 1985; Abbate v. United States, 1959; United States v. Lanza, 1922).

To illustrate, in August of 1981, Larry Heath hired two men to kill his pregnant wife, Rebecca. He met with the two men in Georgia, just across the border from his home in Alabama, and then led them back to his residence and gave them the keys to his house and car. The two men kidnapped Rebecca Heath, took her into Georgia, and shot her in the head, killing her. Several days later, Georgia authorities arrested Heath, and he confessed to arranging his wife's kidnapping and murder. A Georgia grand jury indicted Heath for murder. Heath, who faced the possibility of a death sentence if convicted, pleaded guilty to the murder charge in exchange for a sentence of life imprisonment. Three months later an Alabama grand jury charged Heath with the capital offense of "murder during a kidnapping" in connection with the death of his wife. Although the killing occurred in Georgia, the State of Alabama could try Heath for the homicide because the crime commenced within its borders. The trial court in Alabama rejected Heath's claim that under the Double Jeopardy Clause, his conviction in Georgia for the murder of his wife barred his prosecution in Alabama for the same killing. Heath was then tried and convicted of "murder during a kidnapping" and sentenced to death.

The United States Supreme Court agreed with the trial court that the Double Jeopardy Clause did not prohibit the second prosecution and conviction because the State of Georgia and the State of Alabama are separate sovereign entities (Heath v. Alabama, 1985).

In justifying this so-called "dual sovereignty" doctrine, the United States Supreme Court focuses solely upon the interests of the sovereign entities. The Supreme Court reasons that one of the most important prerogatives a sovereign nation or state possesses is the power to enact and enforce a criminal code; and each sovereign entity, in the exercise of its sovereign power, can determine what conduct shall constitute an offense against it. When two different sovereigns denounce the same act as a crime, that act constitutes "an offense against the peace and dignity of both and may be punished by each" (United States v. Lanza, 1922). As the Court explained in *Moore v. Illinois* (1852):

> An offence, in its legal signification, means the transgression of a law.... Every citizen of the United States is also a citizen of a [s]tate or territory. He may be said to owe allegiance to two sovereigns, and may be liable to punishment for an infraction of the laws of either. The same act may be an offence or transgression of the laws of both.... That either or both may (if they see fit) punish such an offender, cannot be doubted. Yet it cannot be truly averred that the offender has been twice punished for the same offence; but only that by one act he has committed two offences, for each of which he is justly punishable.

Interpreting the Double Jeopardy Clause to prohibit successive prosecutions by different sovereign entities would, according to the Supreme Court, lead to "undesirable consequences" (Abbate v. United States, 1959). A prosecution of an individual by one sovereign for a relatively minor offense might bar a subsequent prosecution of that individual by another sovereign for a much more serious offense, thereby depriving the latter sovereign of the right to enforce its own criminal laws (United States v. Wheeler, 1978; Bartkus v. Illinois, 1959; United States v. Lanza, 1922; *see also* Abbate v. United States, 1959). To illustrate the problem, the Supreme Court in *Bartkus v. Illinois* (1959) pointed to *Screws v. United States* (1945), which involved a prosecution by the United States of three Georgia law enforcement officers for beating to death an African-American man they had arrested for stealing a tire. The civil rights statute the officers were convicted of violating authorized a maximum penalty of one year in prison and a fine of $1000; whereas, under Georgia law, their acts constituted the crime of murder, an offense punishable by death. Absent the dual sovereignty doctrine, the conviction of the officers in federal court for the relatively minor federal civil rights offense might have barred any subsequent prosecution of them by the State of Georgia for the much more serious crime of murder.

Even if two offenses are of equal magnitude, explained the Supreme Court in *Heath v. Alabama* (1985), depriving a sovereign entity of its power to enforce its criminal laws because another sovereign has "won the race to the courthouse" cannot be justified on the ground that its legitimate penal interests will be satisfied through a prosecution conducted by the other sovereign. For a sovereign entity's "interest in vindicating its sovereign authority through enforcement of its laws by definition can never be satisfied by another [sovereign entity's] enforcement of *its* own laws." Each sovereign entity must be entitled to decide that a prosecution by another sovereign entity has not vindicated *its* legitimate penal interests.

The "dual sovereignty" doctrine applies only when the two entities seeking successively to prosecute a person for the same act or course of conduct can be deemed *separate* sovereigns. Two entities are considered separate sovereigns under this doctrine if they draw their authority to punish the individual from distinct sources of power (Heath v. Alabama, 1985; United States v. Wheeler, 1978).

A foreign nation draws its authority to punish individuals from a separate source of power than either the United States or any of the individual states and therefore constitutes a separate sovereign from both the United States and the individual states. Thus, the prosecution of an individual by a foreign country, does not bar a subsequent prosecution in the United States, either by the federal government or by a state (United States v. Rashed, 2000; United States v. Rezaq, 1998; United States v. Guzman, 1996).[12] Nor does the prosecution of an individual in the United States, either by the federal government or by a state, prevent the individual's extradition to a foreign nation for prosecution in that country for an offense based upon the same conduct forming the basis for his prosecution in this country (Elcock v. United States, 2000).

The individual states of the United States are separate sovereigns with respect to each other. As the Supreme Court explained in *Heath*:

> [The] powers [of the states] to undertake criminal prosecutions derive from separate and independent sources of power and authority originally belonging to them before admission to the Union and preserved to them by the Tenth Amendment [to the Constitution]. The states are equal to each other "in power, dignity and authority, each competent to exert that residuum of sovereignty not delegated to the United States by the Constitution itself." Thus, "[e]ach has the power, inherent in any sovereignty, independently to determine what shall be an offense against its authority and to punish such offenses, and in doing so each 'is exercising its own sovereignty, not that of the other.'"

(*See also* United States v. Lanza, 1922.) The Double Jeopardy Clause therefore does not bar successive prosecutions of an individual by two states for the same conduct, as occurred in *Heath*, which was discussed previously in this section.[13]

Similarly, because each state derives its power to prosecute individuals from its own "inherent sovereignty," and not from the federal government, the states are separate sovereigns with respect to the United States (Abbate v. United States, 1959; United States v. Lanza, 1922; *see also* Heath v. Alabama, 1985). As a result, a state can prosecute an individual despite his previous prosecution by the federal government for the same conduct (Bartkus v. Illinois, 1959; Lynn v. West, 1998; Pope v. Thone, 1982; Booth v. State, 1983; People v. Porter, 1993).[14] For example, in *Bartkus*, the Supreme Court held that the State of Illinois did not violate the Constitution when it prosecuted Alfonse Bartkus under state law for the crime of robbery following his previous acquittal in a prosecution brought by the United States for the crime of "robbery of a federally insured savings and loan institution," even though both prosecutions were based upon the same robbery of the General Savings and Loan Association of Cicero, Illinois.[15]

Conversely, the Double Jeopardy Clause does not prohibit the federal government from prosecuting an individual who previously has been prosecuted by a state for the same conduct (Abbate v. United States, 1959; United States v. Lanza, 1922). For instance, in *Abbate v. United States* (1959), the United States Supreme Court held that the prohibition against double jeopardy did not preclude the federal government from prosecuting two individuals for the offense of conspiracy, based upon their conspiring to dynamite communications facilities operated and controlled by the United States—even though the two previously had pleaded guilty in an Illinois court to an indictment, based upon the same acts as those supporting the federal indictment, charging them with violating a state statute making it an offense to conspire to injure the property of another.

Although the double jeopardy provision does not bar a federal prosecution following a state prosecution for the same conduct, either a statute[16] or the Department of Justice's *Petite* policy may do so. The *Petite* policy, which takes its name from the case of *Petite v. United States* (1960), provides, among other things, that a federal prosecution can follow a state prosecution for the same act or acts only when compelling reasons exist and the prosecutor obtains prior authorization from an appropriate Assistant Attorney General (*see* Thompson v. United States, 1980; Rinaldi v. United States, 1977); however, because it is merely a government *policy*, an individual may not seek dismissal of a federal prosecution on the ground that the government brought the prosecution in violation of the policy (United States v. Basile, 1997; United States v. Gary, 1996).

Before the Europeans arrived in what is now the United States, the Indian tribes that are now physically within the territory of the United States were self-governing, sovereign, political communities possessing the inherent power to prescribe laws for their members and to punish violations of those laws. Over the years, through their acceptance of the protection of the United States, by specific treaty provision, and through Acts of Congress, these Indian tribes have given up or been divested of some—but not all—of their sovereign powers. The sovereignty that Indian tribes retain today is of limited character and exists only at the sufferance of Congress. Nevertheless, unless yielded in a treaty with the United States, the power to enact criminal laws and enforce those laws against members of their tribe is one of the sovereign powers an Indian tribe retains, and for purposes of the double jeopardy provision, such an Indian tribe is deemed a separate sovereign from both the United States and each of the individual states (United States v. Wheeler, 1978; *see also* United States v. Lara, 2004). Consequently, the double jeopardy provision does not bar either successive tribal and federal prosecutions (United States v. Lara, 2004; United States v. Wheeler, 1978), or successive tribal and state prosecutions (State v. Mitchell, 1998; Booth v. State, 1995).

The dual sovereignty doctrine does not apply, however, in every situation in which successive prosecutions are brought by nominally different prosecuting entities. For example, the United States Armed Forces derives its authority to try members of the military from the government of the United States. The dual sovereignty doctrine therefore does not allow a soldier to be tried in a United States District Court following his trial for the same offense by a court-martial, and *vice-versa*. For both the court-martial and the civil court derive their authority from the same sovereign entity, the United States (Grafton v. United States, 1907).[17]

Similarly, neither a city nor a county is a separate sovereign entity from the state of which it is a political subdivision; rather, cities and counties are merely agencies of the state, created by the state to assist it in carrying out its governmental functions. Any power a city or county possesses to create and punish offenses stems from the power granted to it by the state. Because municipalities and counties derive their power to prosecute individuals from the same organic law that empowers the state to prosecute, the Double Jeopardy Clause bars successive prosecutions by the state and one of its municipalities (Waller v. Florida, 1970), or by the state and one of its counties (Henderson v. State, 1992).

In *Waller v. Florida* (1970), for example, Joseph Waller, along with a number of other people, removed a canvas mural from a wall inside the City Hall of St. Petersburg, Florida, and carried it through the streets of the city until police officers confronted them. After a scuffle, the officers recovered the mural in a damaged condition. The City of St. Petersburg charged Waller with violating two ordinances: destruction of city property and disorderly breach of the peace. Following Waller's conviction in the municipal court of both offenses, the State of Florida tried him for grand larceny for taking the mural from City Hall. Acting under the assumption that the ordinance violations constituted included offenses of the grand larceny offense, the United States Supreme Court held this second trial impermissible under the Double Jeopardy Clause.

The government of a territory of the United States is entirely the creation of Congress. When such a government enacts and enforces criminal statutes to regulate its inhabitants, it is acting as an agency of the federal government, not as an independent political community. As the United States Supreme Court explained in *United States v. Wheeler* (1978):

> [I]n a federal [t]erritory and the [n]ation, as in a city and a [s]tate, '[t]here is but one system of government, or of laws operating within [its] limits.' City and [s]tate, or [t]erritory and [n]ation, are not two separate sovereigns to whom the citizen owes separate allegiance in any meaningful sense, but one alone. And the 'dual sovereignty' concept ... does not permit a single sovereign to impose multiple punishment for a single offense merely by the expedient of establishing multiple political subdivisions with the power to punish crimes."

For example, the Virgin Islands is not a separate sovereign from the United States for purposes of the Double Jeopardy Clause (United States v. Hodges, 2000; Virgin Islands v. Dowling, 1980). As a result, a prosecution in a territorial court of the Virgin Islands for violating a local law precludes a subsequent criminal prosecution in a federal court for the same offense, and *vice-versa* (Virgin Islands *ex rel.* Robinson v. Schneider, 1995; *see also* Puerto Rico v. Shell Co. (P.R.) Ltd., 1937; Grafton v. United States, 1907 (Philippine Islands)).

Consistent with this rule, when Puerto Rico was considered a territory of the United States, it was not deemed a separate sovereign for purposes of the double jeopardy provision (Puerto Rico v. Shell Co. (P.R.) Ltd., 1937). Today, however, Puerto Rico is a Commonwealth rather than a territory. It is unclear whether this change in status renders it a separate sovereign for purposes of double jeopardy analysis. The United States Circuit Court of Appeals for the Eleventh Circuit concluded in *United States v. Sanchez* (1993) that despite Congress' decision to allow self-governance in Puerto Rico through passage of the Federal Relations Act in 1950, Puerto Rico is not a separate sovereign for purposes of the Double Jeopardy Clause. Rather, "[t]he authority with which Puerto Rico brings charges as a prosecuting entity derives from the United States as sovereign," and therefore it is "still constitutionally a territory, and not a separate sovereign." Under this view, successive prosecutions of an individual for the same offense in a federal court and a local Puerto Rican court are constitutionally prohibited.

On the other hand, the United States Circuit Court of Appeals for the First Circuit reached the opposite result in *United States v. Lopez Andino* (1987). It concluded that Congress, in enacting the Federal Relations Act, intended "'to accord Puerto Rico the degree of autonomy and independence normally associated with States of the Union,'" and that therefore the criminal laws of Puerto Rico, "like those of a state, emanate from a different source than the federal laws." Under this latter view, Puerto Rico must be "treated as a state for purposes of the Double Jeopardy Clause," which means that the double jeopardy provision does not bar successive prosecutions in a federal court and a local Puerto Rican court (United States v. Lopez Andino, 1987).

Like the criminal statutes of a territory, the criminal statutes of the District of Columbia emanate from the same sovereign as the federal criminal code—the United States. Although Congress has granted "home rule" to the District of Columbia, it still retains ultimate authority over the District. Consequently, the Double Jeopardy Clause bars successive prosecutions in federal and local District of Columbia courts (United States v. Weathers, 1999; United States v. Alston, 1979).

An exception to the dual sovereignty doctrine *may* exist when one sovereign acts merely as a "tool" (Bartkus v. Illinois, 1959) or "puppet" (United States v. Tirrell, 1998) of another sovereign in bringing a second prosecution that would otherwise be barred by the Double Jeopardy Clause, that is, when collusion between two sovereign entities blurs the distinction between them so that prosecution by the second sovereign is merely a "sham" and a "cover" for a prohibited prosecution by the first sovereign (Bartkus v. Illinois, 1959). The United States Supreme Court hinted at such an exception in *Bartkus v. Illinois* (1959), but has never expressly stated that such an exception exists.

Though some lower courts have questioned whether *Bartkus* actually created an exception to the dual sovereignty doctrine (*e.g.*, United States v. Tirrell, 1997; United States v. Harrison, 1990), others have concluded that it did (*e.g.*, United States v. Solis, 2002; United States v. Nelson, 2002; United States v. Arena, 1999; United States v. Trammell, 1998; Hale v. State, 1999). Nevertheless, those courts recognizing such an exception place a "substantial burden" on the accused to show that the second prosecution was a "sham" (*e.g.*, United States v. Trammell, 1998). It is not enough for the accused merely to show that one of the sovereigns coordinated the investigation of him or that the two sovereigns cooperated with one another in that investigation; rather, the accused must show either that the sovereign bringing the second prosecution was acting at the behest of the other sovereign, or that the sovereign that brought the first prosecution acted as an agent of the sovereign bringing the second prosecution (*e.g.*, United States v. Arena, 1999).

As a result of this heavy burden on the accused, apparently only two courts since 1959 (when the Supreme Court decided *Bartkus*) have found that a prosecution brought by one sovereign was merely a sham for a prosecution by a separate sovereign (United States v. Scholz, 1995; United States v. Belcher, 1991). The overwhelming majority of courts that have recognized the so-called "*Bartkus* exception" have held that the particular defendant failed to show that the second prosecution was in fact a sham (*e.g.*, United States v. Arena, 1999; United States v. Trammell, 1998; Hale v. State, 1999).

Although long recognized, the dual sovereignty doctrine has been strongly criticized.[18] Critics of the doctrine emphasize the interests of the accused, rather than those of the sovereign entities involved. For example, United States Supreme Court Justice Hugo L. Black, in his dissenting opinion in *Abbate v. United States* (1959), wrote that a state and the United States cannot be deemed separate sovereigns "for the purpose of allowing them to do together what, generally, neither can do separately." Justice Black argued that "[i]t is just as much an affront to human dignity and just as dangerous to human freedom for a man to be punished twice for the same offense, once by a [s]tate and once by the United States, as it would be for one of these two [g]overnments to throw him in prison twice for the offense."

Justice Black expounded on this theme in his dissenting opinion in *Bartkus*, where he stated:

> Looked at from the standpoint of the individual who is being prosecuted, [the] notion [that a second trial for the same act is somehow less offensive if one of the trials is conducted by

> the federal government and the other by a state] is too subtle for me to grasp. If double punishment is what is feared, it hurts no less for two "sovereigns" to inflict it than for one. If danger to the innocent is emphasized, that danger is surely no less when the power of [s]tate and [f]ederal [g]overnments is brought to bear on one man in two trials, than when one of these "sovereigns" proceeds alone. In each case, inescapably, a man is forced to face danger twice for the same conduct.[19]

Justice Black contended that the dual sovereignty doctrine amounted to nothing more than the "dangerous fiction" that, "somehow, one act becomes two because two jurisdictions are involved." In response to the majority opinion in *Bartkus*, he attacked the notion that "federalism" requires that successive state-federal prosecutions be allowed. Rejecting the argument that one jurisdiction might provide minor sanctions for conduct severely punished by the other and by accepting a guilty plea insulate the wrongdoer from justice, he noted that it is unlikely that the states and the federal government would seek to subvert each other's laws, and that even if the states were to subvert federal laws, Congress could protect the national interest—either by enacting legislation giving the federal government exclusive jurisdiction over the crime in question, or by defining the crime to be punished and establishing minimum penalties applicable in both state and federal courts.

Supreme Court Justice Thurgood Marshall did not go quite so far as Justice Black in his criticism of the dual sovereignty doctrine. In his dissenting opinion in *Heath v. Alabama* (1985), Justice Marshall recognized that successive state and federal prosecutions for the same offense must be allowed because of the need to accommodate "complementary state and federal concerns within our system of concurrent territorial jurisdictions." He nonetheless argued that the doctrine should not be extended to cover successive prosecutions by different states. Justice Marshall wrote:

> Where two states seek to prosecute the same defendant for the same crime in two separate proceedings, the justifications found in the federal-state context for an exemption from double jeopardy constraints simply do not hold. Although the two [s]tates may have opted for different policies within their assigned territorial jurisdictions, the sovereign concerns with whose vindication each state has been charged are identical. Thus, in contrast to the federal-state context, barring the second prosecution would still permit one government to act upon the broad range of sovereign concerns that have been reserved to the States by the Constitution. The compelling need in the federal-state context to subordinate double jeopardy concerns is thus considerably diminished in cases involving successive prosecutions by different [s]tates....

Justice Marshall acknowledged that refusing to extend the dual sovereignty doctrine to state-state prosecutions would "preclude the [s]tate that has lost the 'race to the courthouse' from vindicating legitimate policies distinct from those underlying its sister [s]tate's prosecution," but concluded that "a [s]tate's desire to further a particular policy should [not] be permitted to deprive a defendant of his constitutionally protected right not to be brought to bar more than once to answer essentially the same charges."

More recent critics of the dual sovereignty doctrine point to the dramatic changes that occurred in the relationship between the federal government and the states in the last part of the twentieth century. They argue that these changes make what was perhaps acceptable—or at least tolerable—forty years ago no longer acceptable. First, critics note that the considerable expansion in the scope of federal criminal law during this period means that an enormous number of individuals today can be subjected to dual prosecutions, thereby posing a much greater risk to individual rights than existed years ago when the scope of federal criminal law was very narrow and the overlap of state and federal jurisdiction was quite small. Second, critics maintain that the dramatic increase in the degree of cooperation between state and federal law enforcement agencies means that it no longer "makes much sense to maintain the fiction that federal and state governments are so separate in their interests that the dual sovereignty doctrine is universally needed to protect one from the other" (United States v. All Assets of G.P.S. Automotive Corp., 1995 (Calabresi, J., concurring separately in part)).[20]

SUCCESSIVE PROSECUTIONS

The prohibition against multiple prosecutions for the same offense lies at the heart of the Double Jeopardy Clause (Jeffers v. United States, 1977; Sanabria v. United States, 1978; United States v. Martin Linen Supply Co., 1977). The Clause "protects against a second prosecution for the same offense after acquittal [and] against a second prosecution for the same offense after conviction" (North Carolina v. Pearce, 1969). This bar to reprosecution following either an acquittal or a conviction "ensures that the State does not make repeated attempts to convict an individual, thereby exposing him to continued embarrassment, anxiety, and expense, while increasing the risk of an erroneous conviction or an impermissibly enhanced sentence" (Ohio v. Johnson, 1978). As the United States Supreme Court stated in *United States v. Martin Linen Supply Co.* (1977), "'[s]ociety's awareness of the heavy personal strain which a criminal trial represents for the individual defendant is manifested in the willingness to limit the [g]overnment to a single criminal proceeding to vindicate its very vital interest in enforcement of criminal laws.'"

Even when a trial ends before the fact finder makes a final determination of guilt or innocence—that is, when the trial judge declares a mistrial, or when he dismisses the charge against the accused—the Double Jeopardy Clause protects the interest of the accused in avoiding multiple prosecutions (United States v. Scott, 1978).

Nonetheless, the double jeopardy provision does not stand as an *absolute* bar to successive trials (Justices of Boston Municipal Court v. Lydon, 1984). In limited circumstances, a second trial for the same offense is constitutionally permissible (Sanabria v. United States, 1978).

Reprosecution Following a Conviction

The Double Jeopardy Clause ordinarily accords finality to a judgment of conviction (Brown v. Ohio, 1977; United States v. Martin Linen Supply Co., 1977) and prohibits the government from prosecuting the convicted individual a second time for the same offense (United States v. Dixon, 1993; Harris v. Oklahoma, 1977; Brown v. Ohio, 1977; *In re* Nielsen, 1889). In such circumstances, it does not matter whether the judgment of conviction was based upon a verdict of guilty returned by a jury (Harris v. Oklahoma, 1977); a finding of guilty rendered by a judge in a bench trial (United States v. Dixon, 1993); or a plea of guilty or *nolo contendere* (no contest) entered by the accused (Brown v. Ohio, 1977; *In re* Nielsen, 1889). The finality accorded a conviction protects a convicted person against attempts by the government to secure additional punishment for the same offense (Justices of Boston Municipal Court v. Lydon, 1984; Brown v. Ohio, 1977; United States v. Martin Linen Supply Co., 1977; United States v. Wilson, 1975). It also protects him from "the burden of two trials for the same offense," that is, from being "twice put to the task of marshaling his resources against those of the State [and] twice subjected to the 'heavy personal strain' [of a criminal trial]" (Breed v. Jones, 1975). There are, however, circumstances when the government can prosecute an individual for the same offense for which he previously was convicted.

Conviction of a Greater-Inclusive Offense or a Lesser-Included Offense

As discussed previously in this Analysis, a greater offense constitutes the same offense for double jeopardy purposes as any lesser offense included within it. The guarantee against double jeopardy thus bars the government from prosecuting an individual for a lesser-included offense following his prosecution and conviction for the greater offense. For example, in *In re Nielsen* (1889), a grand jury in the Territory of Utah returned two indictments against Hans Nielsen. One indictment charged him with unlawfully cohabiting with two women during a specified period; the other indictment alleged that during that same period he committed adultery with one of the two women with whom he allegedly cohabited. Nielsen pleaded guilty to the unlawful cohabitation charge and received a sentence of three months' imprisonment and a fine of $100. The United States Supreme Court concluded that the material part of the adultery charge, sexual intercourse, was contained within the unlawful cohabitation charge. The Supreme Court therefore held that Nielsen's conviction for the crime of unlawful cohabitation barred his subsequent trial for the lesser-included offense of adultery.

So too, in *Harris v. Oklahoma* (1977), in which the State of Oklahoma tried and convicted Thomas Harris for felony-murder (*i.e.*, an unlawful killing during the commission of a felony), based upon his participation in the armed robbery (robbery with firearms) of a grocery store during which his accomplice shot and killed a clerk. The State of Oklahoma then brought Harris to trial on a separate information charging him with the offense of robbery with firearms. The United States Supreme Court, relying upon *Nielsen*, held that because the same robbery with firearms constituted the underlying felony for Harris's conviction of felony-murder and established the "intent" required for that offense, the State could not subsequently try Harris for the lesser-included offense, under the facts, of robbery with firearms.

Similarly, the Double Jeopardy Clause forbids the government from prosecuting an individual for a greater offense following his prosecution and conviction for a lesser-included offense. *Brown v. Ohio* (1977) provides an excellent illustration. Police in Wickliffe, Ohio, caught Nathaniel Brown driving a car that had been stolen nine days earlier in East Cleveland, Ohio. The Wickliffe police filed a complaint charging Brown with the misdemeanor of "joyriding," which a state statute defined as taking or operating a motor vehicle without the consent of the owner. Brown pleaded guilty to the charge and was sentenced to thirty days in jail and a $100 fine. Following Brown's release from jail, a grand jury in Cuyahoga County, Ohio, returned an indictment charging Brown with the felony of "auto theft" for stealing the car in which he had been caught joyriding.

Under Ohio law, the misdemeanor of joyriding was included in the felony of auto theft, the latter requiring not only the taking or operating of a motor vehicle without the consent of the owner ("joyriding"), but also the additional element of an intent on the part of the thief permanently to deprive the owner of possession of the vehicle. A prosecuting attorney who established the crime of auto theft necessarily established the crime of joyriding as well. The two statutory offenses therefore constituted the same offense for double jeopardy purposes. Moreover, under the joyriding statute, the taking and operating of a single car, even if operated on different days, constituted only one offense. Accordingly, the United States Supreme Court held that Brown's conviction for joyriding barred his subsequent prosecution for auto theft.

It could be argued, of course, that the proper remedy in a situation such as that in *Brown*, in which the government attempts to try an individual for a greater offense following his previous conviction for a lesser-included offense, is to allow the prosecution for the greater offense and, if the individual is convicted, to adjust the punishment for that offense to take into account the punishment already imposed for the lesser-included offense. As a plurality of the United States Supreme Court explained in *Jeffers v. United States* (1977), however, such a remedy would not cure the injury suffered as a result of multiple prosecutions, because "the double jeopardy problem inheres in the very fact of a second trial for the 'same' offense."

A number of exceptions exist to the general rule that, whatever the sequence may be, the guarantee against double jeopardy prohibits successive prosecutions for a greater and lesser-included offense. These exceptions are intended to ensure that the government has one full and fair opportunity to convict an individual of the greater offense.

One exception allows the government to prosecute an individual for a greater offense, despite his prior conviction for a lesser-included offense, "where the State [was] unable to proceed on the more serious charge at the outset because the additional facts necessary to sustain that charge [had] not occurred or [had] not been discovered despite the exercise of due diligence" (Brown v. Ohio, 1977; *accord* Illinois v. Vitale, 1980; Jeffers v. United States, 1977). Such was the case in *Diaz v. United States* (1912). Gabriel Diaz hit and kicked Cornelio Alcanzaren, inflicting bodily injuries upon him. The day after the incident, Diaz was charged with assault and battery. A justice of the peace found Diaz guilty of a misdemeanor and sentenced him to pay a fine. Nearly a month after the attack, Alcanzaren died, allegedly from the injuries inflicted by Diaz. The United States then charged Diaz with homicide. Diaz raised a double jeopardy claim, but the trial court rejected it; Diaz was tried, convicted, and sentenced to a term of imprisonment for the homicide. In holding that the trial court had properly rejected Diaz's plea of former jeopardy, the United States Supreme Court stated: "At the time of the trial for [assault and battery] the death had not ensued, and not until it did ensue was the homicide committed. Then, and not before, was it possible to put the accused in jeopardy for that offense."

Absent such an exception to the general rule, the government would be placed in an untenable position. On one hand, it could choose to prosecute the individual immediately for a particular offense based upon the facts known to it at that time, as it did in *Diaz*. The cost to the government of electing to do so, however, might be significant. It would forfeit its right to prosecute the individual for any greater-inclusive offense if more serious harm subsequently resulted from the individual's conduct or if the government later discovered new facts concerning the scope of the individual's liability. Alternatively, the government could decide to postpone prosecuting the individual for *any* offense until the ultimate result of his conduct became known or until it investigated the facts surrounding the event to the fullest extent possible. It might be weeks or months—or in some cases even years—before the individual's conduct has its full effect, and it might take just as long before all the facts come to light. During that period the individual might flee the jurisdiction; crucial evidence might be lost or destroyed; key government witnesses might die or otherwise become unavailable to testify; and the memories of those witnesses who are ultimately available to testify almost certainly will have faded. As a consequence, the prosecution might not be able to, or because of a weak case decide not to, bring the individual to trial at all, resulting in his avoiding all criminal liability for his illegal conduct.

A second exception to the general rule that conviction for an offense bars a subsequent prosecution for either a greater-inclusive or lesser-included offense exists when the accused "elect[ed] to have the two offenses tried separately and persuade[d] the trial court to honor his election" (Jeffers v. United States, 1977 (plurality opinion)). This can occur, for example, if the government obtained a single indictment charging an individual with both the greater and lesser offenses, but the individual expressly requested a severance and obtained separate trials for the two offenses. It also can occur if the grand jury charged the accused with the greater offense in one indictment and the lesser-included offense in a separate indictment, after which the accused successfully opposed an attempt by the government to join the two charges for trial in a single proceeding and, in doing so, failed to point out that one of the offenses might be a lesser-included offense of the other. In each of these situations the accused bears sole responsibility for the successive prosecutions. He could have avoided consecutive trials, but either by seeking a severance of the charges or opposing a joinder of the charges he chose not do so; he, therefore, cannot be heard to complain. Of course, if any action by the government contributed to the separate prosecutions on the greater and lesser charges, the considerations relating to the propriety of the second trial would be different, and the exception should not apply (Jeffers v. United States, 1977 (plurality opinion)).

A third exception to the general rule allows the government to continue the prosecution of an accused for a greater offense when, over the government's objection, he enters a plea of guilty to a lesser-included offense in a proceeding in which he is charged with both the greater and lesser offenses. The United States Supreme Court reached this conclusion in *Ohio v. Johnson* (1984). There, in a four-count indictment, a grand jury charged Kenneth Johnson with murder, involuntary manslaughter, aggravated robbery, and grand theft stemming from the killing of Thomas Hill and the theft of property from Hill's apartment. At his arraignment, Johnson offered to plead guilty to involuntary manslaughter and grand theft, while pleading not guilty to the more serious charges of murder and aggravated robbery. The government objected, but the trial court nonetheless accepted the guilty pleas and sentenced Johnson to a term of imprisonment. Johnson then moved to dismiss the murder and aggravated robbery charges. He contended that following the trial court's acceptance of his guilty pleas to involuntary manslaughter and grand theft, the guarantee against double jeopardy barred continued prosecution of the remaining charges because involuntary manslaughter and grand theft, respectively, constituted lesser-included offenses of murder and aggravated robbery. The trial court granted the motion, but the Supreme Court reversed the decision.

The Supreme Court concluded that the principles of finality and prevention of prosecutorial overreaching applicable in *Brown* did not apply to the situation in *Johnson,* and that an accused should not be entitled to use the Double Jeopardy

Clause as a sword to prevent the government from completing its prosecution on the remaining charges. The Court reasoned:

> No interest of [Johnson] protected by the Double Jeopardy Clause is implicated by continuing prosecution on the remaining charges brought in the indictment. Here [Johnson] offered only to resolve part of the charges against him, while the State objected to disposing of any of the counts against [him] without a trial. [Johnson] has not been exposed to conviction on the charges to which he pleaded not guilty, nor has the State had the opportunity to marshal its evidence and resources more than once or to hone its presentation of its case through a trial.... There simply has been none of the governmental overreaching that double jeopardy is supposed to prevent. On the other hand, ending prosecution now would deny the State its right to one full and fair opportunity to convict those who have violated its laws.

A final exception to the general rule governing greater and lesser-included offenses may exist when an individual breaches a plea agreement he entered into with the government under which he pleaded guilty to a lesser-included offense of the crime charged and undertook certain other obligations—such as testifying against an alleged accomplice—in exchange for the dismissal of the greater charge. Under such circumstances the Double Jeopardy Clause does not bar the government from reinstating the original charge and prosecuting the individual for that greater offense, at least when the plea agreement provided that the original charge could be reinstated if the accused did not fulfill his obligations under the agreement.

For example, in *Ricketts v. Adamson* (1987), the State of Arizona charged James Adamson with first-degree murder for killing Donald Bolles, an investigative reporter for the Arizona Republic newspaper. Following plea negotiations, Adamson entered into an agreement under which the State allowed him to plead guilty to second-degree murder in exchange for his testifying against two other individuals allegedly involved in the killing. Adamson pleaded guilty to second-degree murder and testified against the two men at a trial that resulted in their convictions. He subsequently breached the plea agreement, however, by refusing to testify at a retrial of the alleged accomplices following an appellate court's reversal of their initial convictions. Responding to the breach, the State of Arizona reinstated the first-degree murder charge against Adamson.

The United States Supreme Court held that under the terms of the plea agreement, the Double Jeopardy Clause did not prohibit the State from reinstating the more serious charge. The Supreme Court relied heavily upon a provision of the plea agreement that stated that "[s]hould [Adamson] refuse to testify ... then this entire agreement is null and void and the original charge [of first-degree murder] will be automatically reinstated." The Court concluded that this provision constituted the precise equivalent of an agreement waiving a double jeopardy defense. Because of the Court's emphasis in *Ricketts* on the specific terms of the plea agreement, it remains unclear whether the Double Jeopardy Clause allows reinstatement of the greater charge in the absence of such a provision in the plea agreement.

After a Conviction is Set Aside at the Behest of the Accused

Although the Double Jeopardy Clause normally prohibits prosecution of an individual for an offense for which he already has been convicted, the United States Supreme Court has stated that it imposes "no limitations whatever" (North Carolina v. Pearce, 1969) upon the government's power to retry an individual who succeeds in having his conviction set aside on appeal, or through some other procedure, because of what is known as "trial error" (Lockhart v. Nelson, 1988; Montana v. Hall, 1987; Price v. Georgia, 1970; Forman v. United States, 1960; United States v. Ball, 1896). "Trial error" comprises errors made in the proceedings leading to the defendant's conviction that are unrelated to his guilt or innocence. Examples of "trial error" include a defect in the instrument charging the defendant with the crime (Montana v. Hall, 1987; United States v. Ball, 1896); the erroneous admission or exclusion of evidence at trial (Lockhart v. Nelson, 1988); prejudicial comments or conduct by the prosecuting attorney at the trial (Burks v. United States, 1978; United States v. Tateo, 1964 (Goldberg, J., dissenting)); improper instructions concerning the applicable law given to the jury by the trial judge (Price v. Georgia, 1970; Forman v. United States, 1960); and the acceptance by the trial judge of an involuntary (*i.e.*, coerced) plea of guilty tendered by the accused (United States v. Tateo, 1964).

The Supreme Court originally indicated that a convicted individual can be retried following the reversal of his conviction on appeal because, in filing the appeal and seeking a new trial, he "waives" the protection of the Double Jeopardy Clause and consents to a second trial (Trono v. United States, 1905). The Court later relied upon the concept of "continuing jeopardy" to justify allowing the government to retry an individual following his successful appeal. It reasoned that because of the reversal at the individual's behest, "criminal proceedings against [him had] not run their full course," so his initial jeopardy had never ended and a new trial would be merely a continuation of that initial jeopardy (Price v. Georgia, 1970; *see also* Justices of Boston Municipal Court v. Lydon, 1984).

More recently, however, the Supreme Court has focused upon society's interest in the orderly administration of justice as "the most reasonable justification" (Burks v. United States, 1978) for allowing a retrial in these circumstances (Lockhart v. Nelson, 1988; Montana v. Hall, 1987; Justices of Boston Municipal Court v. Lydon, 1984; Tibbs v. Florida, 1982; United States v. DiFrancesco, 1980; Burks v. United States, 1978). The Court first articulated this rationale in *United States v. Tateo* (1964), where it said:

> While different theories have been advanced to support the permissibility of retrial, of greater importance than the conceptual abstractions employed to explain the ... principle

> [allowing retrial] are the implications of that principle for the sound administration of justice. Corresponding to the right of an accused to be given a fair trial is the societal interest in punishing one whose guilt is clear after he has obtained such a trial. It would be a high price indeed for society to pay were every accused granted immunity from punishment because of any defect sufficient to constitute reversible error in the proceedings leading to conviction. From the standpoint of a defendant, it is at least doubtful that appellate courts would be as zealous as they now are in protecting against the effects of improprieties at the trial or pretrial stage if they knew that reversal of a conviction would put the accused irrevocably beyond the reach of further prosecution. In reality, therefore, the practice of retrial serves defendants' rights as well as society's interest.

The Court also has reasoned that requiring an individual to stand trial again after he has successfully invoked a statutory right of appeal to overturn his first conviction is "not an act of governmental oppression of the sort against which the Double Jeopardy Clause was intended to protect" (United States v. Scott, 1978; *accord* Tibbs v. Florida, 1982; United States v. DiFrancesco, 1980).

The drafters of the Double Jeopardy Clause appear to have intended to allow the retrial of an individual in these circumstances. James Madison's initial proposal in the House of Representatives stated that "[n]o person shall be subject, except in cases of impeachment, to more than one punishment or one trial for the same offence." When several representatives objected that this language might prevent a convicted defendant from seeking a new trial, Representative Samuel Livermore of New Hampshire spoke in favor of Madison's proposal, explaining that the language would not prevent an individual from doing so. The House ultimately approved Madison's proposal, with the Senate subsequently substituting the language appearing in the present Clause.[21]

A number of lower courts recognize an exception to the general rule that the Double Jeopardy Clause permits retrial of a defendant who succeeds in having his conviction set aside because of "trial error." Some of these courts hold that the guarantee against double jeopardy bars retrial when the prosecuting attorney engaged in improper conduct for the purpose of provoking the defendant into moving for a mistrial, the defendant unsuccessfully moved for a mistrial and was convicted, and the appellate court reversed that conviction on the basis of the prosecutorial misconduct that precipitated the motion for a mistrial (*e.g.*, Lackes v. State, 2001; People v. Walker, 1999; Collier v. State, 1987; Robinson v. Commonwealth, 1994; *see also* Greyson v. Kellam, 1991; Dinning v. State, 1997; State v. Cochran, 1988; *but see* United States v. Singleterry, 1982).

As will be discussed later in this analysis, the Double Jeopardy Clause bars retrial of a defendant following a mistrial declared because of misconduct by the prosecuting attorney intended to "goad" the defendant into moving for a mistrial so the government can obtain a second, more favorable, opportunity to obtain a conviction (*see* Oregon v. Kennedy, 1982; United States v. Scott, 1978; Lee v. United States, 1977). The result should be no different, reason some courts, when the misconduct leads to the reversal of a conviction rather than the declaration of a mistrial. As one judge explained:

> If the requested mistrial was erroneously denied and that error is found on appeal, why should the defendant be subjected to retrial? Why should a defendant, due to an *incorrect* ruling by the trial judge, lose his constitutional protection? It is simply inconceivable that the valuable double jeopardy protections suddenly vanish when the case enters the appellate process. The right of a defendant to be free from double jeopardy should not be determined by which court *correctly* determines that misconduct infected the trial. A constitutional *guarantee* should not morph into a "non-right" depending upon the point in the judicial process an individual finds himself. The trial judge, through an erroneous ruling, should not be allowed to forfeit an individual's valuable constitutional right. (*Ex parte* Davis, 1997 (Baird, J., dissenting)).

Moreover, as the Supreme Court of Arizona concluded in *State v. Jorgenson* (2000), pragmatic considerations may require recognition of such an exception. That court reasoned:

> Any other result would be an invitation to the occasional unscrupulous or overzealous prosecutor to try any tactic, no matter how improper, knowing that there is little to lose if he or she can talk an indulgent judge out of a mistrial. The worst that could then happen is reversal for a new trial and another shot at conviction. This, of course, is exactly the type of governmental abuse at which the double jeopardy clause was aimed.

Such an exception, of course, would not bar retrial in those situations in which the prosecuting attorney's misconduct did not come to light until after the defendant had been tried and convicted, and thus could not move for a mistrial. Accordingly, some courts have adopted an even broader exception to the general rule allowing retrial following the reversal of a conviction for trial error. They have held that retrial is prohibited when the prosecutor engaged in serious misconduct for the purpose of preventing an acquittal that he believed at the time was likely to occur in the absence of his misconduct (*e.g.*, United States v. Pavloyianis, 1993; United States v. Wallach, 1992; State v. Colton, 1995; *but see* United States v. Doyle, 1997). Like those courts recognizing the narrower exception, these courts analogize to the situation in which the prosecuting attorney goaded the defendant into obtaining a mistrial.

For example, in *United States v. Wallach* (1992), the United States Court of Appeals for the Second Circuit reasoned that if, under the United States Supreme Court's decision in *Oregon v. Kennedy* (1982), the Double Jeopardy Clause bars retrial when a prosecuting attorney committed an act of misconduct with the intention of provoking the accused to move for a mistrial, the same result should obtain when he did so with the intent to avoid an acquittal he then believed likely. It continued:

The prosecutor who acts with the intention of goading the defendant into making a mistrial motion presumably does so because he believes that completion of the trial will likely result in an acquittal. That aspect of the *Kennedy* rationale suggests precluding retrial where a prosecutor apprehends an acquittal and, instead of provoking a mistrial, avoids the acquittal by an act of deliberate misconduct. Indeed, if *Kennedy* is not extended to this limited degree, a prosecutor apprehending an acquittal encounters the jeopardy bar to retrial when he engages in misconduct of sufficient visibility to precipitate a mistrial motion, but not when he fends off the anticipated acquittal by misconduct of which the defendant is unaware until after the verdict. There is no justification for that distinction.

Despite the strong arguments in favor of these purported exceptions to the general rule permitting retrial, it is unlikely that the United States Supreme Court will recognize either of them. On numerous occasions the Supreme Court has stated that the Double Jeopardy Clause imposes "no limitations whatever" upon the government's power to retry a defendant who succeeds in having his conviction set aside because of trial error (North Carolina v. Pearce, 1969; *accord* Tibbs v. Florida, 1982; Oregon v. Kennedy, 1982; United States v. DiFrancesco, 1980; Ludwig v. Massachusetts, 1976).

A reversal on appeal, or through some other procedure, for "trial error" must be distinguished from a reversal for insufficiency of the evidence. In *Burks v. United States* (1978), the United States Supreme Court overruled a number of prior cases and held that the Double Jeopardy Clause prohibits retrial of a defendant for the same offense when a reviewing court reverses a conviction at the defendant's behest solely because it finds that the evidence introduced by the government at his trial was insufficient to sustain the jury's verdict of guilty (*accord* Greene v. Massey, 1978).

The Supreme Court in *Burks* reasoned that when a reviewing court reverses a conviction because of insufficient evidence, it determines that the government failed to meet its constitutional burden of proving the defendant's guilt beyond a reasonable doubt and that the trial court erred in failing to grant a judgment of acquittal. As discussed later in this Analysis, if the trial court had *correctly* concluded that the government failed to satisfy its burden of proof and had entered a judgment of not guilty, the Double Jeopardy Clause would have barred the government from retrying the defendant for the same offense. It should make no difference, though, reasoned the Court in *Burks*, whether the *trial court* initially found the evidence insufficient to convict the accused or whether a *reviewing court* did so. Not prohibiting a retrial in the latter situation would create "a purely arbitrary distinction" between those defendants who obtain redress on appeal from the trial court's erroneous decision not to enter a judgment of acquittal and those defendants who enjoy the benefit of a correct decision by the trial court. Moreover, reasoned the Supreme Court, allowing a retrial of an accused following the reversal of his conviction because of insufficient evidence would "afford the government an opportunity for the proverbial 'second bite at the apple,'" thereby frustrating the Double Jeopardy Clause's purpose of precluding "the prosecution another opportunity to supply evidence which it failed to muster in the first proceeding."

The United States Supreme Court subsequently extended the rule announced in *Burks* to the situation in which a trial judge, following the jury's return of a verdict of guilty, finds that the evidence introduced at trial was insufficient to support the jury's verdict and overrules that verdict by entering a judgment of acquittal (Hudson v. Louisiana, 1981). Lower courts have quite properly applied the rule from *Burks* to the reversal by a reviewing court of a judgment of conviction based upon a finding of guilty by a judge in a bench trial (*e.g.*, United States v. Gedraitis, 1982; People v. Cooper, 2000; Manley v. State, 1982; Commonwealth v. Smith, 2000; *see also* United States v. DiFrancesco, 1980).

A convicted defendant sometimes may claim on appeal or in a post-verdict motion for a new trial both that trial error infected his trial, and that the evidence introduced against him at trial failed to prove his guilt beyond a reasonable doubt. For instance, he may claim that the trial court erroneously excluded evidence offered in his defense and that, in addition, the total evidence introduced by the government against him failed to prove his guilt beyond a reasonable doubt. In such circumstances, the prevailing view in the lower courts is that the reviewing court cannot ignore the defendant's sufficiency-of-the-evidence claim, reverse the conviction on the basis of trial error, and then remand for a new trial; rather, the reviewing court *must* consider the defendant's challenge to the sufficiency of the evidence, and, if it agrees with the defendant that the evidence was legally insufficient, must reverse the defendant's conviction on that ground and cannot order a new trial (*e.g.*, United States v. Wiles, 1997; United States v. Weems, 1996; Rankin v. State, 1997; People v. Williams, 1998; *contra* United States v. Adkinson, 1998; United States v. Douglas, 1989). This result is theoretically sound. Any other result would undermine the rule set forth in *Burks* and allow the government a second opportunity to try a convicted defendant who should have been acquitted at trial, but who, because of the trial court's error, was not (*see* Justices of Boston Municipal Court v. Lydon, 1984 (Brennan, J., concurring in part and concurring in the judgment)).

When, however, a reviewing court sets aside a defendant's conviction because the trial court erroneously *admitted* certain evidence against him, the Double Jeopardy Clause does not bar retrial—even though the reviewing court also concludes that without the inadmissible evidence, there was insufficient evidence to support a conviction, at least when the prosecuting attorney did not engage in any misconduct in submitting the inadmissible evidence (Lockhart v. Nelson, 1988). In such circumstances the reversal of the defendant's conviction is for trial error—"the trial court erred in admitting a particular piece of evidence"—not for insufficiency of the evidence, because "clearly *with* that evidence, there was enough to support the [conviction]." Moreover, the Supreme Court in *Burks* reasoned that a reversal for insufficiency of the evidence should be treated the same as a trial court's granting a judgment of acquittal at the close of all the evidence. When a trial court passes on a defendant's motion for a judgment of acquittal, it considers *all* the evidence it has admitted. A reviewing court should consider precisely the same evidence. In addition, permitting a retrial in such circumstances does not constitute the type of governmental oppression at which the double jeopardy provision is aimed; rather, it serves the defendant's interest "by affording him an opportunity to 'obtai[n] a fair adjudication of his guilt free from error'" (Lockhart v. Nelson, 1988).

The Double Jeopardy Clause also does not bar retrial of a defendant when a reviewing court, or a trial judge ruling on a post-verdict motion for a new trial, sets aside the defendant's conviction on the ground that the jury's verdict was against the *weight* of the evidence. This ground for reversal differs in a number of respects from a reversal based upon the *insufficiency* of the evidence. A court reviewing the sufficiency of the evidence in a particular case must view the evidence introduced at trial in the light most favorable to the verdict of guilty, giving the government the benefit of all reasonable inferences that can be drawn from that evidence and crediting the testimony of the government's witnesses. Only if it finds that no rational fact finder could have found the defendant guilty beyond a reasonable doubt can a reviewing court conclude that the conviction rests upon insufficient evidence. In contrast, a court reviewing a claim that the conviction is contrary to the weight of the evidence need not view the evidence in the light most favorable to the verdict of guilty; rather, it may weigh the evidence and, in doing so, evaluate for itself the credibility of the witnesses. If it concludes that the evidence, though legally sufficient to convict, preponderates sufficiently heavily against the verdict of guilty that a miscarriage of justice may have occurred, the reviewing court may set aside the verdict, order a new trial, and allow another jury to decide the case.

The United States Supreme Court in *Tibbs v. Florida* (1982) explained why the double jeopardy consequences of these two bases for reversal of a conviction differ. It stated:

> A reversal [resting on the weight of the evidence], unlike a reversal based on insufficient evidence, does not mean that acquittal was the only proper verdict. Instead, the appellate court sits as a "thirteenth juror" and disagrees with the jury's resolution of the conflicting testimony. This difference of opinion no more signifies acquittal than does a disagreement among the jurors themselves. A deadlocked jury, we consistently have recognized, does not result in an acquittal barring retrial under the Double Jeopardy Clause. Similarly, an appellate court's disagreement with the jurors' weighing of the evidence does not require the special deference accorded verdicts of acquittal.
>
> A reversal based on the weight of the evidence, moreover, can occur only after the State both has presented sufficient evidence to support conviction and has persuaded the jury to

convict. The reversal simply affords the defendant a second opportunity to seek a favorable judgment. An appellate court's decision to give the defendant this second chance does not create "an unacceptably high risk that the [g]overnment, with its superior resources, [will] wear down [the] defendant" and obtain conviction solely through its persistence.

[In addition,] an appellate ruling based on the weight of the evidence ... involve[s] the usual principles permitting retrial after a defendant's successful appeal. Just as the Double Jeopardy Clause does not require society to pay the high price of freeing every defendant whose first trial was tainted by prosecutorial error, it should not exact the price of immunity for every defendant who persuades an appellate panel to overturn an error-free conviction and give him a second chance at acquittal. Giving the defendant this second opportunity, when the evidence is sufficient to support the first verdict, hardly amounts to "governmental oppression of the sort against which the Double Jeopardy Clause was intended to protect."

Sometimes a reviewing court, or a trial court ruling on a post-verdict motion for a new trial, will find that the government failed to prove the defendant guilty beyond a reasonable doubt of the offense for which he was convicted, but that the insufficiency in the evidence went *only* to an element that distinguishes that offense from a lesser-included one. For example, in *United States v. Skipper* (1996), the United States Court of Appeals for the Fifth Circuit concluded that the evidence introduced by the government at John Skipper's trial was insufficient to support his conviction for possession of crack cocaine with intent to distribute, but did prove beyond a reasonable doubt that he knowingly possessed crack cocaine, a lesser-included offense of possession with intent to distribute.

In such circumstances, the trier of fact's actual finding of guilt on all elements of the greater offense necessarily includes a finding of guilt on all elements of the lesser-included offense, because a lesser-included offense consists of some of the elements of the greater offense and does not require the proof of any element not present in the greater offense. As a result, an appellate court, or a trial court acting upon a post-verdict motion for a new trial, can vacate the conviction for the greater offense and enter a judgment of conviction for the lesser-included offense (*see, e.g.*, United States v. Hunt, 1997; United States v. Skipper, 1996; Shields v. State, 1998; State v. Whalen, 2001; State v. Muldrow, 2002; *see also* Rutledge v. United States, 1996), at least, in a jury trial, when the trial court instructed the jury concerning the lesser-included offense (*see, e.g.*, United States v. Dhinsa, 2001; United States v. Dinkane, 1994; United States v. Dickinson, 1983; Dickenson v. Israel, 1981; *Ex parte* Roberts, 1995; Logan v. State, 2001).

Lower courts have concluded that the Double Jeopardy Clause allows such a practice (*e.g.*, United States v. Silvers, 1996; Dickenson v. Israel, 1981; *Ex parte* Edwards, 1984). Although the United States Supreme Court has never considered the precise issue, its decision in *Morris v. Mathews* (1986) strongly supports the conclusion that the practice is constitutionally permissible. In *Morris*, James Mathews appealed his conviction in the State of Ohio for aggravated murder. He contended that under the Double Jeopardy Clause, his previous plea of guilty to the aggravated robbery of a bank barred his trial and conviction for aggravated murder because it was based upon his purposely causing the death of another while committing the same bank robbery to which he had pleaded guilty. The Ohio Court of Appeals agreed, but instead of reversing the conviction, modified it to one for murder, a lesser-included offense of aggravated murder. Under Ohio law, murder, unlike aggravated murder, required proof only that the defendant purposely killed another and thus was not barred by the Double Jeopardy Clause. Moreover, the judge in Mathews's trial for aggravated murder had instructed the jury on the elements of murder and told the jurors that if they found that the government proved all the elements of aggravated murder, they were not to consider the lesser-included offense of murder.

The Supreme Court held that reducing the conviction to murder could provide an adequate remedy for the double jeopardy violation. It reasoned:

> [O]ne of the purposes of the Double Jeopardy Clause is to prevent multiple prosecutions and to protect an individual from suffering the embarrassment, anxiety, and expense of another trial for the same offense. In cases like this, therefore, where it is clear that the jury necessarily found that the defendant's conduct satisfies the elements of the lesser included offense, it would be incongruous always to order yet another trial as a means of curing a violation of the Double Jeopardy Clause.

This reasoning applies equally to the situation in which an appellate court, or a trial court ruling on a post-verdict motion for a new trial, enters a judgment of conviction for a lesser-included offense after finding the evidence insufficient to sustain a conviction for the greater offense.

As an alternative to entering a judgment of conviction for the lesser-included offense in such circumstances, many courts have vacated the conviction for the greater offense and allowed the government to try the defendant for the lesser-included offense (*e.g.*. Shute v. Texas, 1997; State v. Malufau, 1995), at least if the judge in the defendant's original trial actually instructed the jury, if any, on the lesser-included offense (*e.g.*, Beverly v. Jones, 1988; *Ex parte* Roberts, 1995; Webster v. State, 1989; State v. O'Brien, 1993; People v. Sanchez, 2000; People v. Owens, 1996).

The United States Supreme Court has not yet ruled on the constitutionality of trying the defendant for the lesser-included offense under such circumstances, expressly declining to address the issue in *Greene v. Massey* (1978). Lower courts, however, agree that such a trial would not violate the Double Jeopardy Clause (*e.g.*, Shute v. Texas, 1997; Beverly v. Jones, 1988; *Ex parte* Beverly, 1986; State v. Malufau, 1995; People v. Sanchez, 2000; State v. O'Brien, 1993), because it does not present the government with a second opportunity to convict and punish an individual for a single offense, but rather permits the individual a second chance to obtain an acquittal for the lesser-included offense after the government has already proved his guilt of that offense in the trial for the greater offense (Shute v. Texas, 1997; Beverly v. Jones, 1988).

Conviction in the First Tier of a Two-Tier System of Trial Courts

Nearly half the states have established a two-tier system of trial courts for certain criminal offenses, generally relatively minor ones, such as municipal ordinance violations and misdemeanors. An individual accused of such an offense is tried in the first instance in the lower tier, the so-called inferior court, which may be known as the county, district, municipal, police, or justice of the peace court. These inferior courts are designed to provide speedier and less costly adjudications than trials in the criminal courts of general jurisdiction. For example, some states do not provide for a jury trial in the inferior court, some do not record the proceedings, and in some, the judge need not be a trained professional. If an individual is convicted after trial or on a plea of guilty in the inferior court, he may not seek ordinary appellate review of his conviction. Instead, he has an absolute right to "appeal" to a superior court, such as a criminal court of general jurisdiction, where he is entitled to a trial *de novo* (a new trial on both questions of fact and issues of law) by a jury. An individual need not allege error in the inferior court trial to be entitled to a trial *de novo*. In the trial *de novo*, the prosecution and defense begin anew, and the inferior court's findings and judgment in no way bind the judge and jury in the trial *de novo*; rather, the case is regarded exactly as if it originally had been brought in the superior court. If the individual is convicted in the trial *de novo*, he may seek appellate review in the same manner as a person tried initially in the superior court.

For purposes of double jeopardy analysis, an individual convicted in a first-tier court who elects to be tried *de novo* in the second tier occupies the same position as a convicted defendant in a single-tier system who obtains a new trial after successfully appealing his conviction to an appellate court on the basis of trial error. Accordingly, the trial *de novo* does not violate the Double Jeopardy Clause (Ludwig v. Massachusetts, 1976).

Moreover, although the Double Jeopardy Clause prohibits retrial of a defendant whose conviction was reversed by an appellate court because of insufficient evidence (Burks v. United States, 1978), it allows a trial *de novo* of an individual convicted in a first-tier trial despite the individual's claim in the superior court that the evidence introduced in the inferior court failed to prove him guilty beyond a reasonable doubt. The United States Supreme Court in *Justices of Boston Municipal Court v. Lydon* (1984) distinguished the two situations. The Supreme Court pointed out that an appellate court's reversal of a conviction because of insufficient evidence terminates the defendant's initial jeopardy, so that a retrial would place him in jeopardy a second time. In the situation of a trial *de novo*, on the other hand, the initial jeopardy that attached in the inferior court has never been terminated by a judicial determination that the evidence was insufficient, which means that the trial *de novo* involves no new jeopardy. The

Supreme Court explained: "'While technically [the defendant] is "tried again," the second stage proceeding can be regarded as but an enlarged, fact-sensitive part of a single, continuous course of judicial proceedings....'"

The Court in *Lydon* also concluded that even when a defendant convicted in the first tier claims insufficiency of the evidence, the typical two-tier system does not involve "'governmental oppression of the sort against which the Double Jeopardy Clause was intended to protect.'" First, the defendant's absolute right to obtain a trial *de novo* allows him to "wipe out" the judgment of the inferior court and ensures that virtually nothing can happen to him in the inferior court that he cannot avoid. Second, because the defendant can obtain a trial *de novo* without alleging error in the first-tier trial, he need not identify to the prosecution in advance of the trial *de novo* the precise area of evidentiary insufficiency in his first-tier trial. Finally, although the trial in the inferior court allows the prosecution an opportunity to see and assess the defendant's case prior to the trial *de novo*, it likewise allows the defendant a preview of the prosecution's case.

Conviction in a Court Lacking Jurisdiction

A court can render a valid judgment in a criminal case only when it has jurisdiction of the defendant and jurisdiction of the offense charged. That is to say, the court must have the power to exercise authority over the accused, as well as the power to hear and decide a case involving the particular offense in question. For example, a municipal court vested by a state statute with jurisdiction to try only misdemeanors and ordinance violations lacks subject matter jurisdiction over more serious offenses and therefore cannot try a person charged with a felony. Similarly, a state statute or constitutional provision may require that a criminal trial be held in the county where the crime occurred. Under such a provision, only a criminal court in that county has jurisdiction to try the case; absent a valid waiver by the accused, the criminal courts in other counties of the state lack jurisdiction to handle the case.

The United States Supreme Court stated in *United States v. Ball* (1896) that all proceedings in a case before a court having no jurisdiction over either the accused or the offense are "absolutely void, and therefore no bar to subsequent indictment and trial in a court which has jurisdiction ...." Although the Court in *Ball* was discussing the effect of an *acquittal* rendered in a court lacking jurisdiction, the principle it articulated also applies to a *conviction* rendered in a court lacking jurisdiction (Woodring v. United States, 1964; Bradley v. State, 2000; People v. Brancoccio, 1994; State v. Hazzard, 1987; Hoang v. State, 1993), at least when the government did not intentionally prosecute the defendant in a court it knew or had reason to know lacked jurisdiction (Commonwealth v. Keenan, 1987). The underlying rationale is that because that court lacked jurisdiction and therefore did not have the power to try the question of the defendant's guilt or innocence, the defendant was never placed in jeopardy in the trial court (Woodring v. United States, 1964; Bradley v. State, 2000; Commonwealth v. Keenan, 1987).

To illustrate, in many states the Juvenile Court (sometimes known as the Family Court) initially possesses exclusive jurisdiction of a child under a specified age who is charged with committing a crime. The Juvenile Court typically can waive its jurisdiction and transfer jurisdiction to an adult criminal court if, after an adversary hearing, it concludes that the welfare of the community requires criminal proceedings against the youth. Absent a valid waiver of jurisdiction by the Juvenile Court, however, an adult criminal court does not have jurisdiction of the child and therefore lacks the authority to try him. If the government erroneously brings charges against a youth in an adult criminal court, perhaps because it is mistaken about the child's age, that court lacks jurisdiction of the youth and any proceedings against him in that court are void. A conviction in that court, whether following a jury trial or upon a plea of guilty, thus will not bar subsequent proceedings against the youth in Juvenile Court, or following a valid waiver of jurisdiction, a subsequent prosecution of him in an adult criminal court (Hoang v. State, 1993).

Conviction Procured Through Fraud or Collusion

If an accused procures a conviction against himself through fraud or by collusion for the purpose of protecting himself from future prosecution and a more severe punishment, that conviction does not bar the government from trying him a second time for the same or a greater-inclusive offense (People v. Malveaux, 1996; State v. Bell, 1970; People *ex rel.* Leventhal on Behalf of Agosta v. Warden, 1984; State v. Hazzard, 1987; Benard v. State, 1972). This exception to the general rule that a prior conviction bars a subsequent prosecution for the same offense is "just and necessary to the proper administration of public justice" (State v. Simpson, 1881). It "is basically an offshoot of the rule that, if the accused's fate rests in his own hands, then he has not been in jeopardy and is, therefore, subject to reprosecution" (Rivera v. State, 1986). The exception prevents an individual who has engaged in criminal conduct from causing a complaint to be filed against him by a friend or relative, pleading guilty to the offense charged in that complaint in a proceeding conducted in an inferior court presided over by a magistrate or justice of the peace without the presence and participation of the public prosecutor, and then claiming the protection of the Double Jeopardy Clause in a subsequent prosecution against him by the government for the same or a greater-inclusive offense (Toney v. State, 1916; Richards v. State, 1913; Smith v. State, 1954; State v. Simpson, 1881; Halbert v. State, 1921; Richardson v. State, 1928; State v. Smith, 1947; *see also* Edwards v. Commonwealth, 1930).

Richardson v. State (1928), though an old case dealing with a claim of "former conviction" under state law rather than one based on the Double Jeopardy Clause of the Fifth Amendment, provides an excellent example of the exception. In that case, witnesses observed Richardson driving his automobile in an erratic manner, weaving from one side of the road to another. After stopping his vehicle in front of a store, Richardson fell asleep in an apparent drunken stupor. Thirty-five minutes to an hour later, witnesses observed Richardson get out of the car, stumble, and fall down, before a friend finally took him home. Thereafter, a private attorney prepared a complaint charging Richardson with being drunk in a public place. A friend of Richardson signed the complaint under oath before a justice of the peace and in Richardson's presence. Richardson immediately pleaded guilty to the offense, without a warrant being issued and without any evidence being heard. The justice court convicted Richardson of being drunk in a public place and sentenced him to pay a fine of $1.00. Two months later, a grand jury returned an indictment charging Richardson with driving while intoxicated. The indictment was based upon the same incident as the public drunkenness charge to which Richardson previously had pleaded guilty. In a trial at which he was represented by the same attorney who had filed the public drunkenness complaint, Richardson was convicted of drunken driving.

The Texas Court of Criminal Appeals upheld Richardson's conviction for drunken driving, concluding that the conviction for public drunkenness "engineered" by him did not bar the subsequent prosecution for driving while intoxicated. It reasoned:

> "[S]ometimes a man, conscious of guilt, procures a proceeding against himself, and suffers a slight punishment, thinking thereby to bar a prosecution carried on in good faith. In such a case, if the first prosecution is really managed by himself, either directly or through the agency of another, he is, while thus holding his fate in his own hand, in no jeopardy; the plaintiff state is no party in fact, but only such in name; the judge is imposed on, indeed, yet in point of law he adjudicates nothing. 'All is a mere puppet-show, and every wire moved by the defendant himself.' The judgment, therefore, is a nullity, and is no bar to a real prosecution."

This exception to the general rule that a prior conviction bars a subsequent prosecution for the same offense also prevents an adult who misrepresents his age and secures his adjudication of delinquency in Juvenile Court from raising that conviction as a bar to his subsequent trial and punishment for the same offense in an adult criminal court (People v. Malveaux, 1996; People v. Haynes, 1985).

For example, in *People v. Malveaux* (1996), a complainant filed a juvenile delinquency petition alleging that Craig Malveaux committed the crimes of armed robbery of an inhabited dwelling and possession of cocaine. At the outset of the proceedings in the Juvenile Department of the Los Angeles Superior Court, Malveaux informed the judge that he was seventeen years of age, a position he adamantly maintained throughout those proceedings. Only after finding that Malveaux had committed the crimes in question and sentencing him to the California Youth Authority for a period of ten years did the Juvenile Court judge learn that Malveaux was actually twenty-six years of age and therefore not properly the subject of a delinquency petition.

The State of California proceeded to prosecute Malveaux in the adult Criminal Department of the Los Angeles Superior Court for several offenses, including one for which he had been adjudicated delinquent in the Juvenile Department. Following Malveaux's conviction of that crime, the California Court of Appeals rejected his claim that the Double Jeopardy Clause precluded his criminal trial for that offense. It first concluded that the Juvenile Court, as a department of the Superior Court, had jurisdiction over the case, but that because the accused was over the age of eighteen years, it acted in excess of its authority. It then stated:

> [T]his is not a case where the [J]uvenile [C]ourt erroneously assumed a youthful looking person haled into that court was a minor when he actually was an adult. Rather, it is a case where an accused affirmatively misstated his true age in an attempt to be treated as a juvenile offender rather than an adult criminal defendant. That is a clear "fraud on the court." Thus, ... the [J]uvenile [C]ourt adjudication does not act as a double jeopardy bar against a retrial in the proper court, the adult criminal department, for [the] identical crime.

As the court in *Malveaux* made clear, this exception to normal double jeopardy principles applies only when the accused, or someone acting on his behalf, engaged in an affirmative act of fraud or collusion, such as misrepresenting his age, as in *Malveaux*, or by having a friend file a complaint against him for a relatively minor offense, as in *Richardson*. It is not enough that an accused or his attorney failed to volunteer certain information to the court in the accused's first trial and thereby allowed that court to proceed under a misapprehension, as in *People v. Correa,* (1993). There, while entering a guilty plea to four traffic violations on behalf of his client, Jose Correa's attorney did not inform the traffic court judge that a fatality had resulted from those violations and that felony charges for reckless homicide and driving while intoxicated were pending against Correa.

Reprosecution Following an Acquittal

The General Rule: The Absolute Finality of an Acquittal

Time and again the United States Supreme Court has asserted that the Double Jeopardy Clause accords absolute finality to an acquittal (Bullington v. Missouri, 1981; Sanabria v. United States, 1978; Burks v. United States, 1978; Arizona v. Washington, 1978; Green v. United States, 1957; United States v. Ball, 1896) and consequently bars the government from appealing or otherwise seeking review of an acquittal (Smalis v. Pennsylvania, 1986; Sanabria v. United States, 1978; United States v. Martin Linen Supply Co., 1977; United States v. Sisson, 1970; Fong Foo v. United States, 1962; Kepner v. United States, 1904; United States v. Ball, 1896) and from trying the defendant a second time for the same offense (United States v. DiFrancesco, 1980; Sanabria v. United States, 1978; United States v. Sisson, 1970; Benton v. Maryland, 1969; Green v. United States, 1957; Kepner v. United States, 1904; United States v. Ball, 1896). Indeed, the Supreme

Court has described the rule that an acquittal may not be reviewed on appeal, or otherwise, without putting the defendant twice in jeopardy as "[p]erhaps the most fundamental rule in the history of double jeopardy jurisprudence" (United States v. Martin Linen Supply Co., 1977; *accord* Sanabria v. United States, 1978).

In *United States v. Scott* (1978), the Supreme Court explained that the Double Jeopardy Clause "attaches particular significance to an acquittal. To permit a second trial after an acquittal, however mistaken the acquittal may have been, would present an unacceptably high risk that the [g]overnment, with its vastly superior resources, might wear down the defendant so that 'even though innocent, he may be found guilty'" (*see also* Justices of Boston Municipal Court v. Lydon, 1984). And in *Tibbs v. Florida* (1982), the Court stated:

> [T]he Double Jeopardy Clause attaches special weight to judgments of acquittal ....
>
> "[It] forbids a second trial for the purpose of affording the prosecution another opportunity to supply evidence which it failed to muster in the first proceeding." This prohibition, lying at the core of the Clause's protections, prevents the State from honing its trial strategies and perfecting its evidence through successive attempts at conviction. Repeated prosecutorial sallies would unfairly burden the defendant and create a risk of conviction through sheer governmental perseverance.

According finality to an acquittal also protects an individual against being compelled "to live in a continuous state of anxiety and insecurity" about whether the government will retry him and from the "embarrassment, expense and ordeal" of an actual reprosecution (Green v. United States, 1957).

The finality accorded an acquittal applies to verdicts of not guilty returned by a jury (Benton v. Maryland, 1969; United States v. Ball, 1896); to findings of not guilty rendered by a judge in a bench trial (Smalis v. Pennsylvania, 1986; United States v. Martin Linen Supply Co., 1977; Kepner v. United States, 1904); as well as to directed verdicts of not guilty (*i.e.*, when the trial judge in a jury trial directs the jury to return a verdict of acquittal) (United States v. Sisson, 1970; Fong Foo v. United States, 1962) and their functional equivalents, such as a judgment of acquittal entered by the trial judge in a jury trial (Sanabria v. United States, 1978; United States v. Martin Linen Supply Co., 1977).

For purposes of the Double Jeopardy Clause, what constitutes an "acquittal" by a trial judge (as opposed to a jury's verdict of not guilty) is not controlled by the form of the judge's action (Smalis v. Pennsylvania, 1986; United States v. Martin Linen Supply Co., 1977; United States v. Sisson, 1970); rather, a defendant is "acquitted" "when 'the ruling of the judge, whatever its label, actually represents a resolution [in the defendant's favor], correct or not, of some or all of the factual elements of the offense charged'" (United States v. Scott, 1978). An acquittal includes a "'judgment[] ... by the court that the evidence is insufficient to convict'" (Smalis v. Pennsylvania, 1986). For example, in *Smalis v. Pennsylvania* (1986), the United States Supreme Court held that the trial judge's action of granting a demurrer—the equivalent of a motion to dismiss the charge—filed by the defendants at the close of the government's case-in-chief constituted an "acquittal" for purposes of double jeopardy analysis because the judge based his ruling on his conclusion that, as a matter of the law, the prosecution's evidence was "insufficient to establish [the defendants'] factual guilt."

An acquittal is final "no matter how erroneous [the fact finder's] decision" (Burks v. United States, 1978), and "even if the legal rulings underlying the acquittal were erroneous" (Sanabria v. United States, 1978). As the Supreme Court explained in *Smalis*, "[t]he fact that the acquittal may result from erroneous evidentiary rulings or erroneous interpretations of governing legal principles ... affects the accuracy of that determination but it does not alter its essential character" (internal quotation marks omitted).

In *Fong Foo v. United States* (1962), for example, the trial judge, during the testimony of the fourth witness called by the government, directed the jury to enter a verdict of not guilty as to the defendants and subsequently entered a formal judgment of acquittal on that verdict. The judge based his actions upon one or both of two grounds: his belief that the prosecuting attorney had engaged in improper conduct by talking with a government witness during an overnight recess called while the witness was testifying on direct examination, and his belief that two of the government witnesses who had testified up to that point lacked credibility. The government petitioned the Court of Appeals to vacate the judgment of acquittal and order a new trial. That court granted the petition, holding that the trial judge had no power to halt the presentation of the government's case in mid-course by directing a verdict of not guilty (*In re* United States, 1961). The United States Supreme Court reversed that decision. While acknowledging that the acquittal may well have been based upon an "egregiously erroneous foundation," the Supreme Court nevertheless concluded that "'[t]he verdict of acquittal was final, and could not be reviewed ... without putting [the defendants] twice in jeopardy, and thereby violating the Constitution.'"

The Double Jeopardy Clause prohibits a subsequent prosecution for the same offense following an acquittal, even if the judge in a jury trial did not enter a formal judgment of acquittal upon the jury's verdict of not guilty (United States v. Ball, 1896; Green v. United States, 1957). It also bars a subsequent prosecution when the indictment or information in the individual's first trial was defective and could have been successfully challenged by him at that trial or, if he had been convicted, either in a post-trial motion to arrest the judgment or on appeal. For a fatally defective charging instrument does not render the judgment of the court *void*, but only *voidable* at the behest of the defendant (Benton v. Maryland, 1969; United States v. Ball, 1896).

When a defendant is tried for two different offenses in a single trial and is convicted of one of those offenses, but *expressly* acquitted of the other, the guarantee against double jeopardy precludes the government from trying him again for the offense for which he was acquitted, even if he successfully appeals the conviction and obtains a new trial. The government cannot condition a defendant's appeal of a conviction for one offense upon his surrender of a valid plea of double jeopardy on another offense (Benton v. Maryland, 1969). Thus, in *Benton v. Maryland* (1969), where the State of Maryland initially tried John Benton on charges of burglary and larceny and the jury convicted him of burglary, but acquitted him of larceny, the Double Jeopardy Clause barred the State from retrying him for larceny after he succeeded in having the burglary conviction set aside on appeal.

Implied Acquittal

An "acquittal" need not be express to bar the government from appealing the judgment or from subsequently prosecuting the accused anew for the same offense; rather, it may be implied from a conviction for one offense when the fact finder was given a full opportunity to find the accused guilty of a greater-inclusive offense (Price v. Georgia, 1970; Green v. United States, 1957).

The United States Supreme Court reached this result in *Green v. United States* (1957). In that case, the United States tried Everett Green for murder in the first degree (killing while perpetrating a felony), for allegedly causing the death of a woman while committing arson by maliciously setting fire to a house. At the close of evidence, the trial judge instructed the jury that it could find Green guilty of either first-degree murder, which was punishable by death, or the lesser-included offense of murder in the second degree (killing with malice aforethought), which was punishable by imprisonment for a term of years or for life. The jury convicted Green of second-degree murder; its verdict was silent on the charge of first-degree murder. Green appealed the second-degree murder conviction, and the appellate court reversed that conviction and remanded the case for a new trial. On remand, over Green's double jeopardy objection, the United States tried Green again for first-degree murder under the original indictment. This time the jury found him guilty of murder in the first degree, and the trial judge imposed the mandatory death sentence.

The Supreme Court, however, held that the Double Jeopardy Clause barred the second prosecution for first-degree murder because Green's conviction of second-degree murder in his first trial constituted an "implicit acquittal" on the charge of first-degree murder. The Court explained:

> Green was in direct peril of being convicted and punished for first degree murder at his first trial. He was forced to run the gauntlet once on that charge and the jury refused to convict him. When given the choice between finding him guilty of either first or second degree murder it chose the latter. In this situation ... the jury's verdict [constitutes] an implicit acquittal on the charge of first degree murder.... [W]e believe this case can be treated no differently, for purposes of former jeopardy, than if the jury had returned a verdict which expressly read: "We find the defendant not guilty of murder in the first degree but guilty of murder in the second degree."

The Supreme Court reached a similar conclusion in *Price v. Georgia* (1970). There, the Court held that the jury implicitly acquitted the accused of murder when, following his trial for that offense, it returned a verdict convicting him of the lesser-included offense of voluntary manslaughter and making no reference to the charge of murder.

On the other hand, a trial judge's acceptance of a guilty plea to a lesser offense (*e.g.*, second-degree murder) and dismissal of the original charge (*e.g.*, first-degree murder) as part of a negotiated plea agreement between the defendant and the government does not constitute an "implied acquittal" of the defendant on the original, more serious, charge (*i.e.*, first-degree murder). For in reviewing the plea agreement and deciding whether to accept the tendered guilty plea to the lesser offense, the trial judge is not free to consider conviction or acquittal on the original charge. The judge's acceptance of the guilty plea to the lesser offense in no way implies or determines that the defendant is not guilty of the original, more serious, offense (United States v. Barker, 1982; Klobuchir v. Pennsylvania, 1981; United States v. Williams, 1976; State v. Belmarez, 1998). The same is true when, as part of a plea bargain, a trial judge accepts a plea of guilty to one count in an indictment or information in exchange for his dismissing the remaining counts (*e.g.*, accepting a plea of guilty to burglary and dismissing charges of sexual assault and armed violence). Acceptance of the guilty plea does not constitute an "implied acquittal" of the dismissed charges (*i.e.*, sexual assault and armed violence) (United States v. Green, 1998; United States v. Johnson, 1976; Williams v. State, 1986). Consequently, in either situation, if the defendant subsequently challenges the validity of his guilty plea and succeeds in having it set aside, the Double Jeopardy Clause does not bar the government from prosecuting him for any charges that were dismissed in connection with that guilty plea (United States v. Green, 1998; Williams v. State, 1986; United States v. Barker, 1982; Klobuchir v. Pennsylvania, 1981; United States v. Johnson, 1976; United States v. Williams, 1976; State v. Belmarez, 1998).

A fortiori, when an indictment or information charges a defendant with both a greater offense and a lesser-included offense (*e.g.*, murder and involuntary manslaughter), the trial judge's acceptance of a guilty plea to the lesser-included offense, over the objection of the government and while charges on the greater offense remain pending, "has none of the implications of an 'implied acquittal'" (Ohio v. Johnson, 1984). Thus, as discussed earlier in this analysis, the government can continue to prosecute the accused for the greater offense, despite his conviction of the lesser-included offense (Ohio v. Johnson, 1984).

In cases such as *Green v. United States* (1957) and *Price v. Georgia* (1970), in which the fact finder *implicitly* acquits an accused of an offense by convicting him of a lesser-included offense, the accused does not "waive" his constitutional protection against double jeopardy by appealing the conviction of the lesser-included offense (Green v. United States, 1957; Price v. Georgia, 1970). A valid waiver of a constitutional right requires that the individual voluntarily, knowingly, and intentionally relinquish or abandon the right in question (Johnson v. Zerbst, 1938). It is "wholly fictional," however, to say that an individual convicted of one offense, and perhaps sentenced to a long term of imprisonment, "chooses" to forgo his constitutional defense of former acquittal on a greater offense so he can obtain a reversal of an erroneous conviction of the lesser offense. Such a defendant has "no meaningful choice" (Green v. United States, 1957). Nor does a defendant prolong his original jeopardy on the greater offense by appealing his conviction of the lesser-included offense (Green v. United States, 1957; Price v. Georgia, 1970). As the Supreme Court explained in *Price*, "[the defendant's] jeopardy on the greater charge ... ended when the first jury 'was given a full and fair opportunity to return a verdict' on that charge and instead reached a verdict on the lesser charge."

If the government erroneously tries the accused a second time for the greater, jeopardy-barred offense and the fact finder convicts the accused of that offense (as in *Green*), the appropriate remedy is not necessarily a third trial, this time for the lesser-included offense. Instead, the appellate court can, consistent with the double jeopardy provision, vacate the conviction for the greater offense and enter a judgment of conviction for the lesser-included offense.

As previously discussed in this Analysis, the United States Supreme Court considered a similar issue in *Morris v. Mathews* (1986). In that case, the State of Ohio tried Mathews for aggravated murder for purposely causing the death of another while committing bank robbery. The judge instructed the jury on the elements of both aggravated murder and the lesser-included offense of murder and told the jurors that they were not to consider the offense of murder if they found that the State proved all the elements of aggravated murder. The jury convicted Mathews of aggravated murder. On appeal, the Ohio Court of Appeals concluded that the Double Jeopardy Clause barred Mathews' trial for aggravated murder, because he previously had pleaded guilty to the offense of aggravated robbery of a bank—a lesser-included offense of aggravated murder during the commission of a bank robbery. Instead of remanding the case for a new trial on a charge of murder—another lesser-included offense of aggravated murder, but one that was not jeopardy-barred by the guilty plea to aggravated bank robbery, the Ohio Court of Appeals modified the conviction of aggravated murder to one of murder.

The Supreme Court held that in the absence of any prejudice to the defendant from trying him for the jeopardy-barred greater offense, the appellate court's entry of a judgment of conviction for the lesser-included offense could provide an adequate remedy for the double jeopardy violation. It reasoned that the jury, by its verdict of guilty of the greater offense, necessarily found that the conduct of the defendant satisfied the elements of the lesser-included offense and therefore "it would be incongruous always to order yet another trial as a means of curing a violation of the Double Jeopardy Clause." Of course, because the jury in *Morris* convicted Mathews of the greater offense (unlike in *Price*), there was no possibility (as existed in *Price*) that the jury had convicted as a result of a compromise between those favoring conviction on the jeopardy-barred greater offense and those favoring acquittal, and thus no chance of prejudice to Mathews from entering a judgment of conviction for the lesser-included offense.

If, on the other hand, the government, following the defendant's successful appeal of his conviction of the lesser-included offense, erroneously tries the defendant a second time for the greater, jeopardy-barred offense, but the accused is again convicted of only the lesser-included offense (as in *Price*), that conviction must be reversed. Faced with this situation in *Price*, the United States Supreme Court rejected the State's argument that the second jeopardy was harmless error and that Price's conviction of the lesser-included offense should be affirmed because Price was convicted of the same crime at both of his trials and suffered no greater punishment on the subsequent conviction. The Court reasoned:

> The Double Jeopardy Clause ... is cast in terms of the risk or hazard of trial and conviction, not of the ultimate consequences of the verdict. To be charged and to be subjected to a second trial for first-degree murder is an ordeal not to be viewed lightly. Further, and perhaps of more importance, we cannot determine whether or not the murder charge against [Price] induced the jury to find him guilty of the less serious offense of voluntary manslaughter rather than to continue to debate his innocence.

Exceptions to the General Rule that an Acquittal is Absolutely Final

There are several situations in which the Double Jeopardy Clause does not grant absolute finality to a purported acquittal. First, it does not prohibit an appeal by the government when the jury returns a verdict of guilty, but the trial judge overrules that decision and enters a judgment of acquittal on the ground that, as a matter of law, the evidence introduced at trial was insufficient to prove the defendant's guilt. An appeal by the government is constitutionally permissible in such circumstances because a conclusion by an appellate court that the trial judge erred in entering the judgment of acquittal would not require the defendant to submit to a second trial; rather, the error could be corrected on remand by the trial court's entering a judgment on the jury's original verdict of guilty (United States v. Jenkins, 1975; United States v. Baggett, 2001; United States v. Guadagna, 1999; United States v. Martinez, 1997; People v. Salgado, 2001; State v. Rincon, 1997).

For the same reason, the Double Jeopardy Clause does not bar an appeal by the government when the judge in a bench trial finds the defendant guilty, but then sets aside that finding and enters a judgment of acquittal after concluding that some of the evidence on which he based his initial finding of guilt should not have been admitted into evidence, perhaps because the government illegally obtained the evidence or because a rule of evidence barred its admission, and that without that evidence, the government failed to prove the defendant's guilt beyond a reasonable doubt. In such a situation, if an appellate court concludes that the trial judge erred in excluding the evidence and entering the judgment of acquittal, the defendant would not have to undergo a second trial or any further factual proceedings in the trial court. The trial judge could merely reinstate his initial finding of guilt (United States v. Ceccolini, 1978).

Third, the Double Jeopardy Clause does not bar retrial of an accused when the "acquittal" was obtained in a court lacking jurisdiction over either the accused or the offense, that is, when the court lacked the power either to exercise authority over the accused or to try an individual charged with the offense in question (United States v. Ball, 1896; United States v. Kahn, 1987; B.D.T. v. State, 2000; State v. Mesman, 1986; State v. Hamilton, 1998; Commonwealth v. Simeone, 1972; State v. Kenney, 1987). As the Supreme Court stated in *United States v. Ball* (1896), "[a]n acquittal before a court having no jurisdiction is, ... like all proceedings in the case, absolutely void, and therefore no bar to subsequent indictment and trial in a court which has jurisdiction ..." In such circumstances, the defendant was never in "jeopardy" in the first trial because the proceeding was conducted in a court that did not "hav[e] jurisdiction to try the question of [his] guilt or innocence ..." (Kepner v. United States, 1904).

For example, in *Commonwealth v. Simeone* (1972), an individual stole a trailer from a loading dock in Philadelphia, Pennsylvania, drove it to Bucks County, Pennsylvania, and with the help of Anthony Simeone unloaded the contents of the trailer into a warehouse owned by Simeone. Simeone was tried in Philadelphia County for receiving stolen goods, but acquitted. Despite this acquittal, the Double Jeopardy Clause did not bar the State of Pennsylvania from prosecuting Simeone in Bucks County for the same offense, because the offense occurred in Bucks County and under state law only a criminal court in that county had jurisdiction to try an individual for an offense committed there.

Similarly, in *B.D.T. v. State* (2000), a sixteen-year-old implicitly acquitted in a Juvenile Court of committing criminal deviate conduct could not raise that acquittal as a bar to a subsequent prosecution for the same offense in an adult criminal court, because, by statute, the Juvenile Court lacked jurisdiction over a charge of criminal deviate conduct if the accused was at least sixteen years of age at the time of the crime.

Fourth, a line of cases in Illinois holds that an "acquittal" rendered following a "sham" trial constitutes an exception to the general rule that an acquittal bars a subsequent prosecution for the same offense (People v. Rudi, 1984; People v. Deems, 1980; People v. Hollan, 1986; People v. Verstat, 1983; People v. Edwards, 1981).

People v. Deems (1980), the progenitor of this line, is illustrative. On the date set for the trial of Donald Deems under an indictment charging him with knowingly receiving stolen property, the prosecuting attorney conceded in open court that Deems was not guilty of that offense and moved to dismiss the indictment so he could seek an indictment charging Deems with theft. Deems, however, demanded an immediate trial on the original charge. Likening the prosecutor's motion to a request for a continuance, the trial judge concluded that Deems was entitled to go to trial. The judge indicated he would have preferred to dismiss the case with prejudice (*i.e.*, a dismissal prohibiting the government from again bringing those charges against the accused) for want of prosecution, but under state law he lacked the power to do so. The judge therefore decided to call the case for trial and acquit Deems. Accordingly, Deems waived his right to a jury trial. Neither the prosecutor nor Deems presented an opening statement. When the judge called for the witnesses, only Deems was sworn, and he did not testify. After the prosecuting attorney stated he had no witnesses to call, the judge found Deems not guilty and entered a judgment of acquittal.

The State of Illinois subsequently indicted Deems for theft, but the trial court, relying upon Deems' previous acquittal of receiving stolen property, dismissed that charge on double jeopardy grounds. The State appealed both the dismissal and the earlier judgment of acquittal. The Supreme Court of Illinois reversed the dismissal of the theft indictment and vacated the judgment of "acquittal" on the receiving stolen property indictment, thereby allowing the State to go forward with its prosecution of Deems for theft. The Illinois Supreme Court concluded that despite the technical attachment of jeopardy when a witness was sworn, Deems in fact had not been subjected to jeopardy in his so-called "trial" for receiving stolen property.

The court reasoned that Deems' "trial" for receiving stolen property was a "sham," being merely an artifice employed by the trial judge to achieve the result he could not accomplish directly, namely, dismissal of the indictment with prejudice for want of prosecution. It reasoned further that while the trial judge labeled his action an "acquittal," it bore none of the characteristics of a true "acquittal." The court pointed out that the prosecutor made no attempt to convict Deems and that neither he nor Deems introduced any evidence in the "trial," so that Deems at no time in the proceedings faced the "danger of being found guilty of any offense." With respect to the rule that jeopardy attaches in a bench trial when the first witness is sworn, the court stated: "That rule is predicated upon the fact that the first witness is normally an individual whose testimony is part of the State's case—a prosecution witness whose appearance is a part of the incriminating presentation jeopardizing defendant."

Lower courts in Illinois have extended the holding in *Deems* to encompass cases in which the defendant actually testified, either, in response to a question from the trial judge, denying committing the offense charged (People v. Verstat, 1983) or, under questioning by defense counsel and without any cross-examination by the prosecuting attorney, testifying to her version of the events in question (People v. Edwards, 1981). They have even extended it to cases in which the prosecuting attorney asked the accused a question, albeit one that the trial court disallowed on objection by defense counsel (People v. Verstat, 1983).

Other courts, however, apparently do not recognize an exception to normal double jeopardy principles in situations such as those in *Deems* and its progeny (*e.g.*, Goolsby v. Huto, 1982; Daff v. Maryland, 1989; People v. Brower, 1987). The facts in *Goolsby v. Huto* (1982) were remarkably similar to those in *Deems*. The Commonwealth of Virginia charged Walter Goolsby with possession of marijuana, a misdemeanor. On the day set for trial, the prosecuting attorney moved for *nolle prosequi* of the misdemeanor charge (*i.e.*, to dismiss the charge while retaining the right to re-institute it) so he could obtain a grand jury indictment for possession of marijuana with intent to distribute, a felony. The trial judge, exercising the discretion granted him by state law, denied the motion, after which the prosecutor stated he would not present any evidence. Nevertheless, the judge called and swore in the investigating officer, who had been subpoenaed as a defense witness. When the prosecuting attorney refused to ask the witness any questions, the judge told the witness he could leave, stated that jeopardy had attached, and acquitted Goolsby because of lack of evidence.

The United States Court of Appeals for the Fourth Circuit held that Goolsby's acquittal at the misdemeanor trial barred a subsequent prosecution by the Commonwealth for possession of marijuana with intent to distribute. Rejecting the Commonwealth's argument that Goolsby was never in danger of conviction at his misdemeanor trial because no evidence was elicited from the only witness, the Court of Appeals held that jeopardy attached at that trial when the witness was sworn. It stated:

> [W]e think the Commonwealth is attempting to do what the Double Jeopardy Clause is designed to prevent; it is making repeated attempts to convict Goolsby. It is attempting to circumvent the Virginia statute which gives the court discretionary power to grant a motion for *nolle prosequi*, and because it does not agree with the Virginia court's disposition of the case, it has elected to subject Goolsby to another trial by further indictment.
>
> We also believe that Goolsby was put to trial before the trier of facts. When the general district court denied the motion for *nolle prosequi*, set the case for trial, and called and swore the first witness, Goolsby was then subjected either to conviction or acquittal. The fact that the witness gave no evidence required the acquittal of Goolsby by the general district court, just as his conviction would have been required had the witness given evidence sufficient to sustain his guilt.
>
> Since Goolsby was "put to trial before the trier of facts," we think it is reasonable to say that jeopardy attached when "the first witness ... [was] sworn," which was the point at which "the court began to hear evidence." Whether or not the witness in fact testified, we think is immaterial, for when the witness was sworn, we think the court began to hear the evidence....

At no point in its opinion did the Court of Appeals in *Goolsby* raise the possibility that an exception to normal double jeopardy principles might exist for an acquittal obtained in what the *Deems* court called a "sham" trial. Indeed, the Commonwealth apparently did not even make such an argument, conceding that "if jeopardy attached in the misdemeanor proceeding, the felony prosecution was barred by the double jeopardy clause."

Relying upon *Goolsby*, the Court of Appeals of Michigan reached the same result in *People v. Brower* (1987) on similar facts. Once again, the court did not discuss the possibility that the acquittal should not be given effect because it was obtained in a "sham" trial. Indeed, in *Daff v. State* (1989), the highest court of the State of

Maryland held that an acquittal barred further prosecution of the accused for the same offense even though the trial court entered the acquittal before any witnesses were called and without the accused having waived his right to a jury trial.

Even if these latter cases were wrongly decided, and *Deems* correctly decided, it is arguable that the Illinois Supreme Court's decision in *Deems* does not support the proposition that an acquittal does not bar a subsequent prosecution for the same offense whenever the trial resulting in that acquittal can be labeled a "sham" proceeding. As the Supreme Court of Illinois recognized in *Deems*, not even the semblance of a trial occurred in that case—the prosecutor made no attempt to convict the accused; neither party made opening statements; no witnesses testified; and no evidence was introduced. As a result, *Deems* can be read as holding that the ruling of the trial judge in Deems' "trial" for knowingly receiving stolen property did not constitute an "acquittal" for double jeopardy purposes because it did not even purport to "represent[] a resolution [in the defendant's favor], correct or not, of some or all of the factual elements of the offense charged" (United States v. Scott, 1978), but rather constituted a pretrial dismissal of the indictment for want of prosecution and should be treated as such for purposes of double jeopardy analysis—even though Deems was sworn as a witness. Indeed, in a subsequent case involving a "trial" similar to the one in *Deems*, the Illinois Supreme Court stated: "The 'trial' or 'acquittal' in this case was no more than a dismissal for want of prosecution, and as we held in *Deems* such dismissals do not put the defendant in jeopardy or bar retrial on a new indictment" (People v. Rudi, 1984).

Under this limited interpretation of *Deems*, an "acquittal" would not bar a subsequent prosecution for the same offense *only* when the prosecutor did not in any way participate in the proceedings leading to that "acquittal." If, in a bench trial, the prosecutor made any attempt to convict the accused after the first witness was sworn, such as by making an opening statement or calling or examining a witness, then "jeopardy" will have attached and the subsequent "acquittal" should bar a subsequent prosecution for the same offense.

Finally, an exception to the rule that an acquittal prohibits the government from trying an individual a second time for the same offense *may* exist when the individual's own fraud or collusion, such as bribery, blackmail, or intimidation of the fact finder, tainted the acquittal. While the United States Supreme Court frequently has stated that an acquittal "absolutely" (Tibbs v. Florida, 1982) or "unequivocally" (United States v. DiFrancesco, 1980; Arizona v. Washington, 1975) shields an individual from a second trial for the same offense, and has never stated—much less held—that an exception to this rule of "absolute finality" (Burks v. United States, 1978) exists when the accused obtained the acquittal through fraud or collusion, some text writers and legal encyclopedias have recognized such an exception.

For example, Joel Bishop, writing in the nineteenth century about the plea of *autrefoits acquit* (a former acquittal), asserted in his treatise on criminal law that "[a] judgment of acquittal upon a verdict procured by fraud will not bar a second trial for the same offense."[22] The legal encyclopedia *Corpus Juris Secundum* takes the same position, stating that "[a] verdict of acquittal procured by [the] accused by fraud and collusion is a nullity and does not put him in jeopardy; and consequently it is no bar to a second trial for the same offense."[23] In addition, several courts have made similar statements in *dicta* (*i.e.*, statements not essential to the decision in the case) (*e.g.*, State v. Lee, 1894; State v. Jones, 1849; Edwards v. Commonwealth, 1930; State v. Swepson, 1878; State v. Howell, 1951; McFarland v. State, 1887). Only a handful of cases, however, have actually *held* that a fraudulently-obtained acquittal does not bar a subsequent prosecution of the acquitted individual for the same offense (*e.g.*, Price v. State, 1913; State v. Johnson, 1966).

In *State v. Johnson* (1966), for example, a jury acquitted the three defendants of charges of rape and related offenses. The government subsequently filed a motion for a new trial, alleging that people acting on behalf of the defendants communicated with two jurors prior to trial and unduly influenced them. The defendants moved to dismiss the appeal on the ground that the government cannot appeal a judgment of acquittal. Although the Supreme Court of South Carolina ultimately concluded that the trial court did not abuse its discretion in finding that the two jurors had not been unduly influenced, it did consider the government's appeal on its merits. It held that an acquittal procured by an accused through fraud and collusion does not put him in jeopardy and therefore is no bar to a second trial for the same offense.

By far the most important case involving a fraudulently-obtained acquittal is that involving Harry Aleman, a reputed crime syndicate assassin.[24] In 1977, the State of Illinois tried Aleman for the murder of William Logan, a truck dispatcher and Teamsters union steward, who was shot to death outside his home in Chicago in 1972. Aleman waived his right to a jury trial and submitted to a trial before a judge sitting alone. At that trial, two eyewitnesses, including a friend of Aleman who claimed to have been an accomplice, identified Aleman as Logan's killer. Aleman presented an alibi defense, maintaining that at the time of the killing he had been at a driving range hitting golf balls. The trial judge, Frank Wilson, found Aleman not guilty of the murder and entered a judgment of acquittal.

Sixteen years later, the State of Illinois again prosecuted Aleman for the murder of Logan. After a pretrial evidentiary hearing, the trial court found that Aleman's previous acquittal of Logan's murder resulted from a $10,000 bribe paid to Judge Wilson by a corrupt lawyer acting on behalf of Aleman, and it concluded that that acquittal therefore did not bar the second prosecution of Aleman for murder. The Illinois Appellate Court affirmed the trial court's decision. It agreed with the trial court that "a judgment of acquittal procured by a defendant through fraud is a nullity and does not put him in jeopardy." The court concluded that "[g]iven his involvement in the bribery of Judge Wilson in order to procure an acquittal in his 1977 murder trial, ... Aleman clearly was not subject to the risk normally associated with a criminal prosecution" and "[t]he principles of double jeopardy do not bar [his] reindictment and reprosecution" (People v. Aleman, 1996).

Aleman then filed a petition for a writ of habeas corpus (a petition seeking his release from custody) in a federal district court seeking to block his second murder trial on double jeopardy grounds. The federal district court denied Aleman's petition (United States *ex rel.* Aleman v. Circuit Court of Cook County, 1997), after which the State of Illinois brought Aleman to trial for Logan's murder and obtained a conviction from a jury.

Meanwhile, Aleman appealed the federal district court's denial of his petition for a writ of habeas corpus. Under the applicable provisions of the recently-enacted Antiterrorism and Effective Death Penalty Act, Aleman could gain habeas corpus relief only if he demonstrated by clear and convincing evidence that the state trial court based its decision "on an unreasonable determination of the facts in light of the evidence presented" or, alternatively, if he showed that the state court's decision "was contrary to, or involved an unreasonable application of, clearly established Federal law, as determined by the Supreme Court of the United States."[25]

The United States Court of Appeals for the Seventh Circuit concluded that Aleman failed to establish either proposition and rejected his double jeopardy claims (Aleman v. Honorable Judges of the Circuit Court of Cook County, 1998). The court first dismissed Aleman's challenge to the trial court's factual findings in "short order," concluding that his efforts to rebut the strong evidence introduced by the State of Illinois at the evidentiary hearing was a "far cry" from the clear and convincing evidence of factual error necessary under the statute to invalidate the state trial court's findings of fact. With respect to Aleman's legal challenge, the court conceded that his claim that an acquittal absolutely bars a second prosecution for the same offense, no matter how it was obtained, "might not be an unreasonable application of Supreme Court precedent." The court nevertheless concluded that the contrary interpretation adopted by the Illinois state courts was "also not unreasonable." It stated:

> The Supreme Court has emphasized that "[j]eopardy denotes risk. In the constitutional sense, jeopardy describes the risk that is traditionally associated with criminal prosecution." Indeed, the Court has stated that preventing the hazards associated with risking conviction[, such as embarrassment, expense, and ordeal, as well as living in a continued state of anxiety and insecurity,] is the *raison d'etre* of the Double Jeopardy Clause....
>
> Aleman had to endure none of these risks because he "fixed" his case; the [state trial court] found that Aleman was so sanguine about the certainty of his acquittal that he went so far as to tell [one individual] before the trial that jail was "not an option". Aleman may be correct that some risk of conviction still existed after Judge Wilson agreed to fix the case, but it cannot be said that the risk was the sort "traditionally associated" with an impartial criminal justice system. It seems only appropriate that a defendant should not be allowed to escape punishment for murder because he bribed the judge. To allow Aleman to profit from his bribery and escape all punishment for the Logan murder would be a perversion of justice, as well as establish an unseemly and dangerous incentive for criminal defendants.

Although the decision of the Illinois courts that an acquittal obtained by bribing the trial judge in a bench trial does not bar a subsequent prosecution for the same offense may not be an "unreasonable" application of United States Supreme Court precedent, as the Seventh Circuit Court of Appeals held in *Aleman*, it is not necessarily the "correct" interpretation of Supreme Court precedent and the Double Jeopardy Clause. The policies underlying the Double Jeopardy Clause may well support the conclusion that that provision bars a second prosecution for the same offense following an acquittal even though that acquittal may have been the result of bribery, blackmail, intimidation, or other improper conduct by the defendant or others acting with his knowledge and acquiescence.[26]

When an individual undergoes a trial and succeeds in obtaining a judgment of acquittal, he has an interest in not having to defend himself a second time for the same offense. In addition, society has an interest in preserving the "finality" (Crist v. Bretz, 1978) or "integrity" (United States v. Scott, 1978) of that judgment. On at least one occasion the Supreme Court described this latter interest as "the primary purpose of the Double Jeopardy Clause" (United States v. Scott, 1978). In the context of an acquittal, the Supreme Court has never weighed the defendant's interest in avoiding a second trial against society's interest in affording the government one full and fair opportunity to convict the acquitted individual. In *Arizona v. Washington* (1978), the Supreme Court stated:

> The constitutional protection against double jeopardy unequivocally prohibits a second trial following an acquittal. *The public interest in the finality of criminal judgments is so strong that an acquitted defendant may not be retried even though "the acquittal was based upon an egregiously erroneous foundation."* If the innocence of the accused has been confirmed by a final judgment, the Constitution conclusively presumes that a second trial would be unfair. (Italics added.)

When an individual obtained a judgment of acquittal through fraud or other improper conduct, society's interest in retrying that individual outweighs the individual's interest in avoiding a second trial for the same offense. It also outweighs the individual's and society's interest in preserving the "finality" or "integrity" of the judgment of acquittal. Nevertheless, the Supreme Court has never engaged in such a balancing process. Moreover, the question whether to recognize an exception to normal double jeopardy principles for a fraudulently-obtained acquittal cannot be answered by narrowly focusing upon the competing interests involved when a *guilty* individual engaged in fraud to obtain an acquittal. One must examine the potential effect upon *all* acquitted defendants, whether in fact guilty or innocent of the offense charged, because *any* individual acquitted of a crime potentially could face the allegation that he fraudulently obtained the acquittal and should be retried for the same offense.

When a prosecuting attorney believes that an acquitted individual fraudulently obtained an acquittal, and additionally concludes that the public interest requires that the individual be reprosecuted for the offense (as opposed to, or in addition to, being prosecuted for the fraudulent conduct itself), the prosecutor will most likely file a new charge against the individual for the original offense.[27] The individual, of course, will seek dismissal of the charge on double jeopardy grounds. The government will respond that the prior acquittal does not bar the second prosecution because it resulted from fraud on the part of the accused, such as the bribery of the judge in a bench trial. The accused, on the other hand, will insist that neither he nor anyone acting in his behalf engaged in fraudulent conduct and that the acquittal represented a decision by the fact finder based solely upon the evidence presented at his trial.

In such circumstances, the trial judge will conduct a hearing to resolve the factual dispute. At that hearing, at which both sides will call witnesses and present other evidence, the government will bear the burden of proving by a preponderance of the evidence that the defendant's prior acquittal resulted from fraud. Such an evidentiary hearing could be quite lengthy and involved, for it essentially will be a trial of the accused for bribery, blackmail, intimidation, or the like—albeit with a lower standard of proof than the "beyond a reasonable doubt" standard constitutionally mandated to find guilt in a criminal trial (*see In re* Winship, 1970). Moreover, the stakes for the defendant at this "trial" will be extremely high. If the trial judge finds that the defendant did fraudulently procure the acquittal in his first trial—whether he in fact did so or not—the government will be allowed to try him a second time for the same offense, and he will face the possibility of being convicted and punished in that trial. A defendant who can afford it probably will expend considerable resources to "defend" himself, and all defendants certainly will suffer from the anxiety caused by their realization that they face the possibility of trial, conviction, and punishment for a criminal offense. This will be true even if the defendant ultimately prevails at the evidentiary hearing and the trial judge prohibits the second prosecution.

Furthermore, regardless of the outcome of the evidentiary hearing, the losing party likely will seek review of the decision in a higher court. The accused therefore will be compelled to continue to "defend" himself, this time in the appellate courts. Even if he ultimately prevails, he will have been forced to endure significant additional personal strain and expense to vindicate his right against being twice placed in jeopardy for the same offense.

The Double Jeopardy Clause is intended, among other things, to prevent the government from subjecting an individual to the embarrassment, expense, and ordeal of multiple trials for the same offense and from compelling him to live in a continuing state of anxiety and insecurity concerning a criminal charge. Although the evidentiary hearing and any appeal therefrom is not itself a second "trial" for the same offense, it is part of the government's second prosecution of the defendant for the same offense, and the government's objective in that proceeding is to secure a second trial of the defendant for the same offense. Allowing the government to attack the legitimacy of a judgment of acquittal would frustrate this purpose of the double jeopardy provision, even if the defendant ultimately prevailed on his claim that he did not engage in fraudulent conduct to obtain the acquittal in the first trial.

Moreover, the Double Jeopardy Clause accords "special weight" (United States v. DiFrancesco, 1980) to an acquittal in order to reduce the possibility that an innocent defendant will be erroneously convicted at a second trial for the same offense. This purpose also would be frustrated if the government could attack the legitimacy of a judgment of acquittal. For if the government succeeded in convincing the trial judge that the defendant's acquittal resulted from his own fraud—which it would have to do by only a preponderance of the evidence—it could try the accused a second time and could hone its trial strategies and perfect its evidence, based upon what it learned at the defendant's first trial, thereby increasing its chances of convicting him even though he may in fact be innocent.

Perhaps most importantly, though, allowing the government to prosecute an already-acquitted defendant when the acquittal resulted from fraud would frustrate "the primary purpose of the Double Jeopardy Clause" (United States v. Scott, 1978), namely, "preserv[ing] the finality of judgments" (Crist v. Bretz, 1978), or "protect[ing] the integrity of a final judgment" (United States v. Scott, 1978). Recognizing an exception to normal double jeopardy principles when an acquittal resulted from fraud would open up *every* judgment of acquittal to subsequent challenge by the government. An individual who went to trial and was found not guilty—whether through fraud or on the basis of the evidence presented at his trial—could never be certain that the government would not at some point–perhaps even years later, as in *Aleman*—haul him into court a second time, alleging that his previous acquittal resulted from bribery, blackmail, intimidation, or the like and forcing him to defend himself, first, against the allegation of fraud and then, if he fails on that score, against the criminal charge of which he already has been acquitted. No criminal defendant could ever view his acquittal as final.

In addition, allowing the government to prosecute an individual following his acquittal for the same offense would grant the government an enormous power that could be misused. An unscrupulous prosecutor, upset by the acquittal of a particular individual and bent upon harassing him, could do so by bringing a second prosecution for the same offense and alleging that the prior acquittal resulted from fraud. Even if the government fails in its attempt to retry the defendant, it will have forced him to defend himself in what in essence is a trial for bribery, blackmail, or intimidation; and, if the defendant prevails at that "trial," on appeal. No acquitted defendant would be safe from such a misuse of prosecutorial power.

Any exception to normal double jeopardy principles thus entails significant costs. These costs might be worth incurring if the exception allowed the government to prosecute and convict a large number of individuals who otherwise might avoid punishment for their criminal conduct; however, it does not seem that an exception to normal double jeopardy principles for a fraudulently obtained acquittal would do so. Although the precise number of acquittals obtained through fraud cannot be calculated, it seems reasonable to conclude that there are relatively few such acquittals in this country.

Tinkering with the protections of the Double Jeopardy Clause to create an exception covering those relatively rare situations in which a defendant procured his acquittal through fraud hardly seems worth the cost. Preserving the finality of *all* judgments of acquittal and allowing a few guilty defendants to avoid conviction seems preferable to allowing the government to pursue those defendants a second time at the cost of opening up every judgment of acquittal to re-examination and requiring some innocent individuals to defend themselves a second time, perhaps convicting and punishing some of them despite their innocence. Refusing to recognize an exception to normal double jeopardy principles would not leave the government without a remedy against a defendant who obtained an acquittal through improper conduct, nor would it encourage defendants to engage in such conduct in an attempt to procure their acquittal. The government certainly could prosecute a defendant for bribery, intimidation, or some other relevant offense dealing with the fraudulently-obtained acquittal, and, if successful, punish him for his misdeeds.

Collateral Estoppel

The Double Jeopardy Clause embodies the principle of collateral estoppel (Turner v. Arkansas, 1972; Harris v. Washington, 1971; Simpson v. Florida, 1971; Ashe v. Swenson, 1970), "or, in modern usage, issue preclusion" (Schiro v. Farley, 1994). Collateral estoppel means that "when an issue of ultimate fact has once been determined by a valid and final judgment, that issue cannot again be litigated between the same parties in any future lawsuit" (Ashe v. Swenson, 1970; *accord* Schiro v. Farley, 1994; Dowling v. United States, 1990; Harris v. Washington, 1971). An acquittal therefore bars not only a subsequent prosecution for the "same offense," but also a subsequent prosecution for a *different* offense if "the second prosecution requires the relitigation of factual issues already resolved [in the defendant's favor] by the first [trial]" (Brown v. Ohio, 1977).

For example, in *Ashe v. Swenson* (1970), discussed earlier in this Analysis, the United States Supreme Court held that Bob Fred Ashe's acquittal in a trial for robbing one participant in a late-night poker game, Donald Knight, precluded the State of Missouri from subsequently trying him for robbing Ray Roberts, another of the six participants in the poker game. The Supreme Court reasoned:

> Straightforward application of the [constitutional principle of collateral estoppel] to the present case can lead to but one conclusion. For the record is utterly devoid of any indication that the first jury could rationally have found that an armed robbery had not occurred, or that Knight had not been a victim of that robbery. The single rationally conceivable issue in dispute before the jury was whether [Ashe] had been one of the robbers. And the jury by its ver-

dict found that he had not. The [constitutional principle of collateral estoppel], therefore ... make[s] a second prosecution for the robbery of Roberts wholly impermissible.

The Court noted that it was not holding that the State of Missouri could not charge Ashe with six separate offenses for the robbery of the six poker players, or that it could not impose a total of six punishments if the fact finder convicted him in a single trial of robbing the six victims; rather, it stated it was simply holding that after a jury determined by its verdict that Ashe was not one of the robbers, the State could not, consistent with the guarantee against double jeopardy, "hale him before a new jury to litigate that issue again."

The Supreme Court in *Ashe* explained why the principle of collateral estoppel constitutes an integral part of the guarantee against double jeopardy. It stated:

After the first jury had acquitted [Ashe] of robbing Knight, Missouri could certainly not have brought him to trial again upon that charge. Once a jury had determined upon conflicting testimony that there was at least a reasonable doubt that [Ashe] was one of the robbers, the State could not present the same or different identification evidence in a second prosecution for the robbery of Knight in the hope that a different jury might find that evidence more convincing. The situation is constitutionally no different here, even though the second trial related to another victim of the same robbery. For the name of the victim, in the circumstances of this case, had no bearing whatever upon the issue of whether [Ashe] was one of the robbers.

In this case the State ... has frankly conceded that following [Ashe's] acquittal, it treated the first trial as no more than a dry run for the second prosecution: "No doubt the prosecutor felt the State had a provable case on the first charge and, when he lost, he did what every good attorney would do—he refined his presentation in light of the turn of events at the first trial." But this is precisely what the constitutional guarantee [against double jeopardy] forbids.

The principle of collateral estoppel applies not only to express acquittals, but also to "implicit acquittals" (*see* Green v. United States, 1957; Price v. Georgia, 1970), that is, when the fact finder was given a full opportunity to find the accused guilty of an offense, but found him guilty only of a lesser-included offense (Schiro v. Farley, 1994; State v. Bradshaw, 1979; State v. Rodriguez, 2000; State v. Conway, 1983; *Ex parte* Green, 1977). It also applies regardless of whether the fact finder in the accused's first trial considered all relevant evidence and irrespective of the government's good faith in bringing successive prosecutions (Harris v. Washington, 1971). Thus, in *Harris v. Washington* (1971), Arnold Harris' previous acquittal for the murder of one victim of a mail bombing, Ralph Burdick, conclusively established that he was not the one who mailed the bomb. That acquittal barred his subsequent prosecution for the murder of a second victim of the same bombing, Harris' infant son, and the assault of a third victim, Harris' estranged wife, even though the judge at Harris' first trial erroneously excluded from evidence a letter allegedly written by Harris containing threats against the lives of Burdick and Mrs. Harris, and even though a statute precluded the State from trying Harris for murder and robbery in a single trial.

On the other hand, the principle of collateral estoppel does not apply when the acquittal in the previous action did not resolve an issue of ultimate fact involved in the subsequent action. For example, in *Dowling v. United States* (1990), the United States Supreme Court concluded that Reuben Dowling's previous acquittal on charges of burglary, attempted robbery, and assault did not represent a jury determination that he was not one of two men who entered a home, struggled with its occupant, and took money from her. The Supreme Court reasoned that the question of identity, that is, of Dowling's being one of the men who entered the house, was not at issue in the first trial, for Dowling apparently claimed that a robbery did not occur because he and another "merely came to retrieve ... money from an individual in the house," and therefore was not determined in Dowling's favor at that trial.

One Lot Emerald Cut Stones v. United States (1972), though not dealing with the Double Jeopardy Clause, also illustrates this point. In that case, Francisco Klementova entered the United States without declaring to customs officials one lot of emerald cut stones and a ring. The United States tried Klementova for smuggling the articles into the country with the intent to defraud the United States. He was acquitted following a bench trial at which the trial judge specifically found that the United States had failed to establish his intent to defraud. The United States then instituted an action against the emeralds and the ring, seeking their forfeiture under a statute requiring the government to prove only that the articles had been brought into the country without the required customs declaration. Klementova intervened in the forfeiture proceeding and argued that under the nonconstitutional principle of collateral estoppel, his previous acquittal of the smuggling charge barred the forfeiture.

The United States Supreme Court rejected this argument. The Supreme Court concluded that Klementova's acquittal did not necessarily resolve the issues in the forfeiture proceeding. It reasoned that, given the trial judge's specific finding that the United States failed to establish the intent to defraud, the acquittal on the criminal charge may have involved a finding that Klementova unlawfully imported the goods, but that he lacked the requisite intent to defraud. Consequently, the criminal acquittal did not determine that Klementova did not unlawfully bring the goods into the country—the issue involved in the forfeiture action. Thus, the forfeiture proceeding did not involve an issue previously litigated and finally determined between Klementova and the United States.

Nor does the principle of collateral estoppel apply when the defendant, rather than the government, is responsible for various related charges not being tried together in a single trial (Ohio v. Johnson, 1984; United States v. Ashley Transfer & Storage Co., 1988; State v. Alston, 1986). In *Ohio v. Johnson* (1984), a grand jury charged Kenneth Johnson in a four-count indictment with the crimes of murder, involuntary manslaughter, aggravated robbery, and grand theft. All the charges stemmed from a single criminal transaction involving the killing of an individual and the theft of property from his home. Over the prosecutor's objection, Johnson pleaded guilty to involuntary manslaughter and grand theft. Johnson then moved to dismiss the murder and aggravated robbery charges on the ground, *inter alia,* that the principle of collateral estoppel barred continued prosecution of those charges because involuntary manslaughter and grand theft were mutually exclusive of the murder and aggravated robbery charges, respectively. The United States Supreme Court rejected this argument, stating that when it is not the government that is responsible for trying charges successively, "the considerations of double jeopardy protection implicit in the application of collateral estoppel are inapplicable."

The Supreme Court's rationale in *Johnson* extends beyond the situation present in that case and applies, for example, when an individual successfully moves for a severance of two or more charges, is tried and acquitted of one of those offenses in a separate proceeding, and then seeks to invoke the doctrine of collateral estoppel to preclude his trial on one or more of the remaining charges (State v. Alston, 1986).

When an accused seeks to foreclose relitigation of an issue of ultimate fact on the basis of collateral estoppel, he bears the burden of demonstrating that the fact finder in the previous trial "actually and necessarily" (Schiro v. Farley, 1994) decided that issue in his favor (Schiro v. Farley, 1994; Dowling v. United States, 1990). This allocation of the burden of proof has been criticized. United States Supreme Court Justice William J. Brennan, Jr., argued in his dissenting opinion in *Dowling* that because the doctrine of collateral estoppel serves to protect individuals against governmental overreaching, the *government* should have to prove that the issue it seeks to relitigate was *not* decided in favor of the accused. Justice Brennan further contended that because it usually is difficult to determine the basis for a jury's verdict of not guilty, placing the burden on the accused to prove what issues were actually decided in his first trial "essentially denies the protection of collateral estoppel to those defendants who affirmatively contest more than one issue or who put the [g]overnment to its burden of proof with respect to all elements of the offense." Despite the persuasiveness of Justice Brennan's argument, a majority of the Supreme Court refused to accept his position.

When the judgment of acquittal in the previous trial was based upon a finding of not guilty by a judge in a bench trial, it may be relatively easy to determine whether that trial actually resolved the particular issue of ultimate fact in favor of the accused. The judge may have made written findings of fact to support his conclusion that the defendant was not guilty of the offense charged, or, at a minimum, he may have articulated on the record the reason he found the defendant not guilty. For instance, in *One Lot Emerald Cut Stones*, the judge in Klementova's criminal trial for smuggling goods into the country stated "I'm not persuaded beyond a reasonable doubt that [Klementova] did what he did with the intent to defraud the United States."

On the other hand, when the judgment of acquittal in the previous trial was based upon a jury's verdict, the task will be more difficult. Ordinarily, a jury in a criminal trial returns a general verdict, that is, a verdict merely finding the defendant "guilty" or "not guilty," without any findings of fact or explanation of the reasons for its decision. In such circumstances, a court faced with a defendant's collateral estoppel claim should not apply the principle with the "hypertechnical and archaic approach of a 19th century pleading book," but rather with "realism and rationality." This requires that it "'examine the record of [the] prior proceeding, taking into account the pleadings, evidence, charge, and other relevant matter, and conclude whether a rational jury could have grounded its verdict upon an issue other than that which the defendant seeks to foreclose from consideration'" (Ashe v. Swenson, 1970; *accord* Schiro v. Farley, 1994; Dowling v. United States, 1990).

For example, in *Turner v. Arkansas* (1972), the United States Supreme Court examined the instructions given by the judge to the jury in Dennis Turner's trial for the murder of Larry Wayne Yates during a robbery. Those instructions obligated the jury to convict Turner of murder if it found that he killed Yates either with premeditation or unintentionally while perpetrating a robbery, or if it found that he and an accomplice robbed Yates and that the accomplice, rather than Turner, fired the shot that killed Yates. The Supreme Court determined that "[t]he only logical conclusion [that can be drawn from Turner's acquittal of murder] is that the jury found him not present at the scene of the murder and robbery." It therefore held that Turner's acquittal of the murder of Yates precluded his subsequent prosecution for the robbery of Yates.

As *Turner*, as well as *Ashe* and *Harris*, indicate, if the court in the second proceeding, after engaging in the requisite analysis, concludes that the accused met his burden of proof on the issue of collateral estoppel, it should bar the government from relitigating the issue of ultimate fact decided in the accused's first trial and dismiss the new charges against him. If, however, the court concludes that the accused did not meet his burden of proof, it should allow the government to proceed with the second prosecution.

When the collateral estoppel component of the Double Jeopardy Clause does not bar the government from prosecuting an individual for a particular offense, despite his previous acquittal for a *different* offense, it also does not preclude the government from using in that trial otherwise relevant and admissible evidence relating to the offense for which he was acquitted. Two justifications support this result. First, the acquittal in the first trial did not determine an ultimate issue of fact in the subsequent proceeding. Second, the standard of proof governing the admissibility of such evidence generally is lower than the standard of proof that was necessary to prove the individual's guilt in the prior criminal trial (Dowling v. United States, 1990). Under a generally-accepted rule of evidence, such as that contained in Federal Rule of Evidence 404(b), the government can introduce in a criminal case evidence of other crimes, wrongs, or acts committed by the defendant in an attempt to prove such things as the defendant's motive for, opportunity to commit, or identity as the perpetrator of the crime currently being tried. To introduce such "other crimes" evidence, the government need not demonstrate beyond a reasonable doubt that the defendant committed the other act; rather, to show the relevance of that evidence, it typically needs to show only that the fact finder could "reasonably conclude that the act occurred and that the defendant was the actor" (Huddleston v. United States, 1988). The acquittal of the defendant in the criminal trial for that same act, however, established only that a reasonable doubt existed about whether the defendant committed the act. The fact finder in the subsequent trial might reasonably conclude that the defendant committed the act in question even if it did not believe beyond a reasonable doubt that he did so (Dowling v. United States, 1990).

In *Dowling*, for example, the government alleged that Reuben Dowling was the man wearing a ski mask and armed with a small pistol who robbed a bank in the Virgin Islands. To help strengthen its identification of Dowling as the bank robber, the government—over Dowling's objection—introduced into evidence the testimony of Vena Henry. She identified Dowling as the man who, approximately two weeks after the bank robbery in question, entered her home wearing a knitted mask with cutout eyes and carrying a small handgun. The United States Supreme Court held that the collateral estoppel component of the Double Jeopardy Clause did not bar the government from introducing such evidence, despite Dowling's previously having been tried and acquitted of burglary, attempted robbery, assault, and weapons offenses in connection with the invasion of Ms. Henry's home.

The Supreme Court's refusal to extend the collateral estoppel component of the Double Jeopardy Clause to exclude otherwise relevant and admissible evidence relating to an offense for which the accused previously has been acquitted is consistent with its holdings that an acquittal in a criminal case does not collaterally estop the government from relitigating an issue of ultimate fact when it is presented in a subsequent proceeding requiring a lower standard of proof than "beyond a reasonable doubt," such as a civil *in rem* forfeiture proceeding against certain goods (*i.e.*, an action against the goods themselves to determine title to them), in which the standard of proof is only a "preponderance of the evidence"[28] (United States v. One Assortment of 89 Firearms, 1984; One Lot Emerald Cut Stones v. United States, 1972). Collateral estoppel does not apply in such situations because "an acquittal on criminal charges does not prove that the defendant is innocent; it merely proves the existence of a reasonable doubt as to his guilt" (United States v. One Assortment of 89 Firearms, 1984). The judgment of acquittal in the criminal trial does not negate the possibility that the government's evidence could show the existence of the fact in issue under the lesser standard of proof applicable in the subsequent civil proceeding.

The collateral estoppel component of the Double Jeopardy Clause applies only when the previous acquittal occurred in a trial involving the "same parties." This means that the acquittal of one defendant does not bar the government from subsequently prosecuting another individual, even though the government will have the opportunity to relitigate an issue of ultimate fact decided against it in its prosecution of the first defendant (Standefer v. United States, 1980; Williams v. State, 1980; People v. Paige, 1983; Commonwealth v. Winter, 1984). In such circumstances, the government is not bringing successive prosecutions against the second individual, as he was not a party to the other person's trial; moreover, he was never in jeopardy at that other person's trial, and therefore his trial would not place him in *double* jeopardy.

The United States Supreme Court recognized these principles in *Standefer v. United States* (1980). There, the United States charged F.W. Standefer, the head of the tax department of Gulf Oil Corporation, with aiding and abetting a federal revenue agent in accepting compensation in addition to that authorized by law. The government alleged that Standefer authorized payments for several vacation trips to Cyril Niederberger, the Internal Revenue Service agent in charge of the audits of Gulf's income tax returns. The government separately charged Niederberger with accepting compensation in addition to that provided by law for accepting payments from Gulf Oil for the vacation trips. Prior to Standefer's trial, a jury acquitted Niederberger. In holding that Standefer could be prosecuted for aiding and abetting Niederberger, despite Niederberger's prior acquittal, the Supreme Court stated that "[n]othing in the Double Jeopardy Clause ... forecloses putting [Standefer] on trial as an aider and abettor simply because another jury has determined that his principal [Niederberger] was not guilty of the offenses charged."

Reprosecution Following a Mistrial

Some criminal trials end without a final judgment of acquittal or conviction. A "mistrial" occurs when a judge terminates a trial without a determination of the factual guilt or innocence of the accused, either because of a procedural error, serious misconduct, or some other event making it impossible or impracticable to complete the trial, such as the jury's inability to reach a verdict. When a trial judge declares a mistrial, he all but invariably contemplates that the government will be permitted to proceed anew with the prosecution of the defendant for the same offense, notwithstanding a plea of double jeopardy by the accused (United States v. Scott, 1978).

A mistrial must be distinguished from the midtrial "dismissal" of the charge against an accused. Ordinarily, a midtrial dismissal occurs because of an error or defect thought by the trial judge completely to preclude the conviction of the defendant on the offense charged. Such an order of dismissal terminates the proceedings in favor of the accused and, unlike a mistrial order, "contemplates an end to all prosecution of the defendant for the offense charged" (Lee v. United

States, 1977; *accord* United States v. Scott, 1978). Sometimes, however, a mid-trial dismissal is based upon an error or defect that, like any prosecutorial or judicial error necessitating a mistrial, could be avoided, absent any double jeopardy bar, by commencing anew the prosecution of the defendant. Such an order of dismissal contemplates a second prosecution of the defendant for the same offense that had been dismissed (Lee v. United States, 1977).

As discussed earlier in this Analysis, an individual is placed in "jeopardy" in a trial well before a final judgment of guilty or not guilty. Consequently, in addition to protecting the integrity of a final judgment, the Double Jeopardy Clause safeguards a defendant's "valued right" to have his trial completed by the particular fact finder that began hearing the evidence in the case (Wade v. Hunter, 1949; *accord* Oregon v. Kennedy, 1982; United States v. Dinitz, 1976). This valued right merits constitutional protection for at least two reasons. First, the defendant possesses an interest in "being able, once and for all, to conclude his confrontation with society through the verdict of a tribunal he might believe to be favorably disposed to his fate" (United States v. Jorn, 1971 (plurality opinion)). In addition, "[e]ven if the [defendant's] first trial is not completed, a second prosecution may be grossly unfair. It increases the financial and emotional burden on the accused, prolongs the period in which he is stigmatized by an unresolved accusation of wrongdoing, and may even enhance the risk that an innocent defendant may be convicted" (Arizona v. Washington, 1978).

Under certain circumstances, the Double Jeopardy Clause gives dispositive weight to this valued right of the accused and bars his retrial for the same offense when his first trial ends prematurely by the declaration of a mistrial (*e.g.*, United States v. Jorn, 1971; Downum v. United States, 1963); however, "because of the variety of circumstances that may make it necessary to discharge a jury before a trial is concluded, and because those circumstances do not invariably create unfairness to the accused" (Arizona v. Washington, 1978), that weighty interest "does not mean that every time a defendant is put to trial before a competent tribunal he is entitled to go free if the trial fails to end in a final judgment" (Wade v. Hunter, 1949). For, as the United States Supreme Court stated in *Oregon v. Kennedy* (1982), "[t]he Double Jeopardy Clause ... does not offer a guarantee to the defendant that the State will vindicate its societal interest in the enforcement of the criminal laws in one proceeding." Denying the government the right to put the defendant to trial again following a mistrial frequently would frustrate the law's purpose of protecting society from those guilty of committing crimes.

As a general matter, the government may retry a defendant for the same offense following a mistrial when the defendant requested or consented to the mistrial (United States v. Dinitz, 1976), or when, regardless of the defendant's consent, either a "manifest necessity" existed for the declaration of the mistrial or the "ends of public justice" would otherwise have been defeated (United States v. Perez, 1824; *accord* United States v. Dinitz, 1976).

Mistrial Declared at the Request of the Defendant or With the Defendant's Consent

The Double Jeopardy Clause ordinarily does not bar retrial of a defendant when a trial judge declares a mistrial at the request of the defendant or with his consent, even if prosecutorial or judicial error necessitated his request (Oregon v. Kennedy, 1982; Lee v. United States, 1977; United States v. Dinitz, 1976). A defendant's motion for a mistrial, or his consent to the declaration of a mistrial, constitutes "a deliberate election on his part to forgo his valued right to have his guilt or innocence determined before the first trier of fact" (United States v. Scott, 1978). The United States Supreme Court explained in *United States v. Dinitz* (1976):

> Even when judicial or prosecutorial error prejudices a defendant's prospects of securing an acquittal, he may nonetheless desire "to go to the first jury and, perhaps, end the dispute then and there with an acquittal." Our prior decisions recognize the defendant's right to pursue this course in the absence of circumstances of manifest necessity requiring a *sua sponte* [on the court's own motion] judicial declaration of a mistrial. But it is evident that when judicial or prosecutorial error seriously prejudices a defendant, he may have little interest in completing the trial and obtaining a verdict from the first jury. The defendant may reasonably conclude that a continuation of the tainted proceeding would result in a conviction followed by a lengthy appeal and, if a reversal is secured, by a second prosecution. In such circumstances, a defendant's mistrial request has objectives not unlike the interests served by the Double Jeopardy Clause—the avoidance of the anxiety, expense, and delay occasioned by multiple prosecutions.

Consequently, if prosecutorial or judicial error of a magnitude sufficient to warrant a mistrial has occurred, "[t]he important consideration, for purposes of the Double Jeopardy Clause, is that the defendant retain primary control over the course to be followed ..." (United States v. Dinitz, 1976).

In *Dinitz*, for example, the trial judge excluded Dinitz's lead attorney from the trial for engaging in improper conduct during his opening statement to the jury. When another of Dinitz's attorneys informed the judge that his client wanted time to obtain a new lawyer to try the case, the judge presented Dinitz with three alternatives: (1) declaring a recess in the trial pending an appellate court's review of the propriety of the banishment of Dinitz's lead attorney from the proceedings; (2) continuing the trial with the assistant defense attorney; or (3) declaring a mistrial so Dinitz could obtain a new attorney. After considering the alternatives, Dinitz moved for a mistrial, which the trial judge granted. The United States Supreme Court held that even if the trial judge overreacted in expelling Dinitz's lead attorney from the courtroom, the Double Jeopardy Clause did not bar the government from retrying Dinitz, because, despite being given the opportunity to continue the trial before the jury that had already been selected, Dinitz *requested* the trial judge to declare the mistrial.

A mistrial may be deemed to have been declared at the defendant's request even though he did not expressly move for one. For instance, if a defendant files a motion he knows will force a mistrial if granted, and the trial court indeed grants the motion, the resultant declaration of a mistrial will be regarded as having been at the defendant's request.

United States v. LaRouche Campaign (1989) illustrates this point. In that case, several months after their trial began, the defendants moved to excuse five of the fifteen jurors (twelve regular jurors plus three alternates) because they believed the past and future length of the trial would cause these jurors severe hardship. The government objected to excusing four of the five and pointed out that, should the defendants' motion be granted, the trial could not continue with the remaining ten jurors unless the defendants agreed. After questioning the five jurors about the hardship they would suffer if they continued to serve, the trial judge excused them. When the defendants then refused to agree to proceed with fewer than twelve jurors, the trial judge declared a mistrial. Agreeing with the trial court, the United States Court of Appeals for the First Circuit held that the Double Jeopardy Clause did not bar a second trial of the defendants. It found the defendants' argument that they themselves did not request a mistrial "not convincing as a matter of logic." The court pointed out that the defendants' attorneys knew that the trial judge would be forced to declare a mistrial if he granted their request to excuse the five jurors. It concluded that because the defendants' motion to excuse the five jurors caused the mistrial and the defendants knew the inevitable consequences of their motion, the case differed in no significant way from one in which the defendant says the words "I want a mistrial," and must be treated in the same way.

On the other hand, the fact that the defendant objected to, or informed the trial judge of, certain conduct by the prosecuting attorney that ultimately resulted in the declaration of a mistrial should not, by itself, be construed as a request for, or consent to, a mistrial. In such circumstances, the defendant might believe that, far from being damaged by the allegedly improper conduct, he gained a benefit from it. Such may have been the case in *Lovinger v. Circuit Court* (1988). There, defense counsel told the judge in a bench trial that he had observed the prosecutor discussing the case with a government witness during a recess while the witness was in the midst of testifying. By reporting the conversation to the trial judge, defense counsel might have raised a question about the witness' credibility and, far from desiring a mistrial, might have wished to proceed to a verdict before the particular judge trying the case.

More broadly, however, construing an objection or complaint by defense counsel about the fairness of the proceedings as a motion for a mistrial would routinely give the government a second chance to prosecute an individual without meeting the more rigorous "manifest necessity" standard applicable when the trial court declares a mistrial on its own motion, or in response to a motion by the prosecuting attorney, and without the consent of the accused (Lovinger v. Circuit Court, 1988).

A mistrial should not always be considered to have been at the request of the defendant, or with his consent, merely because he moved for a mistrial at some earlier point in the proceedings. Specifically, a defendant should not be deemed to have requested or consented to a mistrial if he originally moved for a mistrial, but later withdrew his motion, either before the trial court acted upon it (United States v. Crotwell, 1990), or after the trial court initially denied it (United States v. Kwang Fu Peng, 1985; United States v. Mastrangelo, 1981).

The picture constantly changes during the course of a trial, and concerns that led a defendant to file a motion for a mistrial may have dissipated in light of later events. At that point, the defendant may no longer desire to end the trial and start the proceedings anew, but instead may prefer to continue the trial before the particular fact finder that began hearing the evidence in the case. To protect the defendant's "valued right to have his trial completed by a particular tribunal" (Wade v. Hunter, 1949), he must be entitled to resume control over the course of the proceedings after the trial judge denies his motion for a mistrial or takes it under consideration. Such control would be meaningless if it were subject to defeasance through a purported grant of a request for a mistrial made prior to the resumption of control (Braxton v. United States, 1978). Accordingly, if the trial judge does not immediately rule upon a defendant's motion for a mistrial and continues with the proceedings while he considers the motion, or if he initially denies the defendant's motion for a mistrial, but subsequently revives it on his own, the judge should not grant the motion without first inquiring whether the defendant wishes to maintain it (Jones v. Commonwealth, 1980). If the judge grants it without consulting the defendant, the mistrial should not be deemed to have been at the defendant's request or with his consent.

By like reasoning, a defendant should not be deemed to have requested the mistrial when he moved for a mistrial *with prejudice* (*i.e.*, a ruling barring the government from retrying the accused) because of judicial or prosecutorial error, but the trial judge declared a mistrial *without prejudice* (*i.e.*, a ruling allowing the government to retry the accused) (Weston v. Kernan, 1995; Davis v. Brown, 1986; Romero v. Justices of the Supreme Court, 1997), unless the judge gave the defendant an opportunity to withdraw his request for a mistrial before the judge granted the motion without prejudice (United States v. Huang, 1992; People v. Jefferson, 1998).

For a defendant to be deemed to have requested or consented to a mistrial, he need not personally have requested a mistrial or consented to one. It is sufficient if his attorney did so (Camden v. Circuit Court, 1989; United States v. Smith, 1980; People v. Brandon, 1995; People v. Echavarria, 1999; People v. Ferguson, 1986). By choosing professional representation, the accused relegates to his attorney "'full authority to manage the conduct of the trial'" (New York v. Hill, 2000), including the power to make such tactical decisions as whether to move for a mistrial or to consent to one (People v. Brandon, 1995; State v. Fitzpatrick, 1984;

People v. Ferguson, 1986; Rios v. State, 1977). As the New York Court of Appeals explained in *People v. Ferguson* (1986):

> There is an inherent duality in requesting or consenting to a mistrial: the defendant gives up his right to be tried by a particular tribunal, and subjects himself to a second trial, yet also avoids a verdict in a trial which may have been proceeding very poorly for him. Whether a mistrial is in a defendant's best interest requires an evaluation of the case, analysis of the evidence, recognition of potential harm to defendant's case from any errors or inappropriate remarks which may have occurred, and consideration of whether a more favorable jury is likely at a retrial and whether delay is likely to help or harm the defendant's case .... [S]uch factors make the decision as to a mistrial an appropriate one for the lawyer, not the client.

Consent to a mistrial need not be express; it may be inferred from the totality of the circumstances surrounding the declaration of the mistrial (United States v. Gantley, 1999; United States v. Nichols, 1992; State v. Tolliver, 1992; Harrison v. State, 1989). For example, many courts conclude that a defendant implicitly consented to a mistrial when his attorney, despite having a meaningful opportunity to do so, failed to object either when the trial judge indicated he was contemplating declaring a mistrial (United States v. Gantley, 1999; United States v. Nichols, 1992; United States v. Aguilar-Aranceta, 1992; People v. Ferguson, 1986), or immediately after the judge declared a mistrial, but before he discharged the jury (Camden v. Circuit Court, 1989; United States v. Smith, 1980). Statements by defense counsel before the judge discharged the jury also might indicate acquiescence to the declaration of a mistrial, as in one case in which the defendant's attorney affirmatively indicated his understanding that there could and would be a retrial (United States v. Smith, 1980).

On the other hand, consent should not be inferred from the failure to object to the declaration of a mistrial if the defendant and his attorney had no opportunity to object before the trial judge declared the mistrial (Love v. Morton, 1997; Glover v. McMackin, 1991; United States v. Bates, 1991; Torres v. State, 1981). Similarly, the fact that the defendant previously, yet unsuccessfully, moved for a mistrial on a particular ground does not mean that he consented to a subsequent mistrial declared on a different ground (Lovinger v. Circuit Court, 1988; Anderson v. United States, 1984; State v. Stevens, 1995; Torres v. State, 1981).

Although the Double Jeopardy Clause generally permits retrial of a defendant following the declaration of a mistrial at his behest, it does not allow a retrial when the conduct of the prosecuting attorney giving rise to the defendant's request was intended to "goad" the defendant into moving for a mistrial (Oregon v. Kennedy, 1982; *accord* United States v. Scott, 1978; Lee v. United States, 1977). The United States Supreme Court in *Oregon v. Kennedy* (1982) explained that in such circumstances, the defendant's valued right to complete his trial before the first tribunal would be a "hollow shell" if his inevitable motion for a mistrial precluded him from later invoking the bar of the double jeopardy provision.

This exception to the general rule allowing a retrial following the declaration of a mistrial at the request of the defendant is "intended to prevent the prosecution from forcing a mistrial when things are going badly for it, in the hope of improving its position in a new trial" (United States v. GAF Corporation, 1989). The exception, however, is a "narrow" one. A mistrial declared because of prosecutorial conduct that could be viewed as "harassment" or "overreaching" does not bar a retrial, even though that conduct was sufficient to justify a mistrial on motion of the defendant (Oregon v. Kennedy, 1982). For example, in *Kennedy*, the defendant successfully moved for a mistrial after the prosecuting attorney asked an expert witness on redirect examination whether the reason he had never done business with the defendant was "because [the defendant] is a crook." The Supreme Court concluded that even though the prosecuting attorney's conduct may have constituted "overreaching," the defendant could be retried because the prosecutor did not *intend* his conduct to cause a mistrial.

The Supreme Court in *Kennedy* articulated its reasons for rejecting the more general standards of prosecutorial "overreaching" or "harassment" as the standard for determining whether the double jeopardy provision bars the government from retrying a defendant following the declaration of a mistrial at his request, and instead, adopting a standard based upon the intent of the prosecutor. It explained that the more general standards offer virtually no criteria for their application, whereas a standard focusing upon the intent of the prosecuting attorney is a manageable one to apply, merely calling for the court to make a finding of fact. In addition, the Court reasoned:

> Were we to embrace the broad and somewhat amorphous standard [of prosecutorial "overreaching"], we are not sure that criminal defendants as a class would be aided. Knowing that the granting of the defendant's motion for mistrial would all but inevitably bring with it an attempt to bar a second trial on grounds of double jeopardy, the judge presiding over the first trial might well be more loath to grant a defendant's motion for mistrial. If a mistrial were in fact warranted under the applicable law, of course, the defendant could in many instances successfully appeal a judgment of conviction on the same grounds that he urged a mistrial, and the Double Jeopardy Clause would present no bar to retrial. But some of the advantages secured to him by the Double Jeopardy Clause—the freedom from extended anxiety, and the necessity to confront the government's case only once—would be to a large extent lost in the process of trial to verdict, reversal on appeal, and subsequent retrial.

Mistrial Declared Without the Defendant's Consent: The "Manifest Necessity" Standard

Under certain circumstances, the Double Jeopardy Clause allows the retrial of an accused when the trial court, acting without the consent of the accused, declares a mistrial upon its own motion (*sua sponte*) or in response to a motion by the prosecuting attorney. The United States Supreme Court explained in *Wade v.*

Hunter (1949) that a rule allowing a defendant to go free whenever his trial fails to end in a final judgment

> would create an insuperable obstacle to the administration of justice in many cases in which there is no semblance of the type of oppressive practices at which the double-jeopardy prohibition is aimed. There may be unforeseeable circumstances that arise during a trial making its completion impossible, such as the failure of a jury to agree on a verdict. In such event the purpose of law to protect society from those guilty of crimes frequently would be frustrated by denying courts power to put the defendant to trial again.

The Supreme Court has attempted to resolve the competing interests of the defendant and society by adopting a standard that "provides sufficient protection to the defendant's interests in having his case finally decided by the jury first selected while at the same time maintaining 'the public's interest in fair trials designed to end in just judgments'" (Oregon v. Kennedy, 1982). It first announced the rule for determining whether the Double Jeopardy Clause prohibits reprosecution following the declaration of a mistrial without the defendant's consent in 1824 in the case of *United States v. Perez*. The Court in *Perez* held that the double jeopardy provision does not bar reprosecution of a defendant when a trial court, in the exercise of its sound discretion, terminates a trial before verdict because it concludes that under all the circumstances "there is a manifest necessity for the act, or the ends of public justice would otherwise be defeated." The Supreme Court has consistently adhered to this formulation for over 180 years.

The "manifest necessity" standard places a "heavy" burden on the government if it is to avoid the bar of the double jeopardy provision following the declaration of a mistrial over the objection of the defendant. Nonetheless, the Supreme Court has stated that "the key word 'necessity' cannot be interpreted literally ...." Rather, the Court has assumed that "there are degrees of necessity," and has held that a mistrial is appropriate—and retrial not barred by the Double Jeopardy Clause—if there exists a "high degree" of need for the declaration of the mistrial (Arizona v. Washington, 1978).

The "manifest necessity" rule requires that the trial judge "tak[e] all the circumstances into consideration" (United States v. Perez, 1824). It does not attempt to lay down a rigid formula (Wade v. Hunter, 1949) or prescribe "a standard that can be applied mechanically or without attention to the particular problem confronting the trial judge" (Arizona v. Washington, 1978; *see also* Illinois v. Somerville, 1973). For the most part, the Supreme Court has "explicitly declined ... to formulate rules based on categories of circumstances which will permit or preclude retrial" (United States v. Jorn, 1971 (plurality opinion)). Instead, because a trial judge "is best situated intelligently to make [the] decision" that the "ends of substantial justice cannot be attained without discontinuing the trial" (Gori v. United States, 1961), the Court has declared that a trial judge has "broad discretion" in determining whether either "manifest necessity" or the "ends of public justice" dictate the declaration of a mistrial (Illinois v. Somerville, 1973).

In exercising this discretion, a trial judge should consider "'the importance to the defendant of being able, once and for all, to conclude his confrontation with society through the verdict of a tribunal he might believe to be favorably disposed to his fate'" (Arizona v. Washington, 1978). A judge should not act hastily in declaring a mistrial, either on his own motion or in response to a request by the prosecutor, and should give the attorneys a full opportunity to explain their positions on the propriety of a mistrial. Although an explicit finding by the trial judge of "manifest necessity" facilitates appellate review of his decision to declare a mistrial, the Constitution does not mandate such a finding; nor does it require that the trial judge give an explanation of the reasons supporting his decision to declare a mistrial, so long as the record of the proceedings adequately discloses the basis for his mistrial order (Arizona v. Washington, 1978).

At one extreme, it has been established since the United States Supreme Court's decision in *Perez* that a genuinely deadlocked jury, *i.e.*, one that after hearing all the evidence is unable to agree upon a verdict, is an instance of "manifest necessity" allowing a judge to terminate a trial—even without the defendant's consent—and to require the accused to undergo a second trial (Richardson v. United States, 1984; United States v. Sanford, 1976; Keerl v. Montana, 1909; Dreyer v. Illinois, 1902; Logan v. United States, 1892). This rule permitting a retrial following a "hung jury" "accords recognition to society's interest in giving the prosecution one complete opportunity to convict those who have violated its laws" (Arizona v. Washington, 1978; *accord* Richardson v. United States, 1984).

A trial judge necessarily must be granted broad discretion in determining whether "manifest necessity" justifies discharging the jury when it reports to him that it cannot reach a verdict, for he is in the best position to assess all the factors that must be considered in deciding whether the jury will be able to reach a just verdict if it continues to deliberate. Moreover, if the trial judge discharges the jury when further deliberations might produce a fair verdict, his action will deprive the defendant of his "valued right to have his trial completed by a particular tribunal." On the other hand, failing to discharge a jury that is unable to reach a verdict after prolonged deliberations creates a significant risk that a verdict may result from pressures inherent in the situation instead of the considered judgment of all the jurors. If the retrial of an individual were prohibited whenever an appellate court viewed the "necessity" for a mistrial differently than the trial judge, there would be a danger that a trial judge—aware of the serious consequences to society of an erroneous decision to declare a mistrial—would use coercive means to break the apparent deadlock, thereby frustrating the public interest in just judgments. For these reasons, an appellate court must accord great deference to a trial judge's decision to declare a mistrial when he considers the jury deadlocked; however, if the record of the proceedings reveals that the trial judge failed to exercise the discretion entrusted to him, an appellate court must closely scrutinize his decision to discharge the jury and declare a mistrial (Arizona v. Washington, 1978).

As previously discussed in this Analysis, the Double Jeopardy Clause bars the government from reprosecuting a defendant following an appellate court's reversal of his conviction on the ground that the government failed to introduce sufficient evidence to convict him at his original trial (Burks v. United States, 1978). Nevertheless, the rule permitting a retrial following a mistrial declared because of a hung jury applies even though the government may have failed to introduce sufficient evidence to prove the defendant's guilt beyond a reasonable doubt at his first trial (Richardson v. United States, 1984).

In *Richardson v. United States* (1984), a federal grand jury indicted Robert Richardson on two counts of distributing, and one count of conspiring to distribute, illegal drugs. At the close of the government's case and again after all the evidence had been presented, Richardson moved unsuccessfully for a judgment of acquittal, claiming that the government had failed to introduce sufficient evidence to permit the jury to find him guilty beyond a reasonable doubt. The jury acquitted Richardson of one of the drug charges, but could not reach a verdict on the two remaining counts. With respect to those counts, the trial judge declared a mistrial and, over Richardson's objection on double jeopardy grounds, scheduled a retrial.

The United States Supreme Court rejected Richardson's double jeopardy claim. The Supreme Court explained that the protection of the Double Jeopardy Clause comes into play only when some event, such as an acquittal, terminates the accused's original jeopardy. The failure of the jury to reach a verdict, reasoned the Court, is not the equivalent of an acquittal and is not an event that terminates the original jeopardy to which the defendant was subjected. The Court concluded that regardless of the sufficiency of the evidence at Richardson's first trial, his retrial would not place him twice in jeopardy for the same offense.

The rule allowing a retrial following a mistrial declared because of a hung jury also applies when the trial court subsequently dismissed the charge against the accused prior to his scheduled second trial (United States v. Sanford, 1976). For example, in *United States v. Sanford* (1976), the judge in the defendants' trial for illegal game hunting in Yellowstone National Park declared a mistrial after the jury could not reach a verdict. Four months later, while the government was preparing to retry the defendants, the trial judge granted the defendants' motion to dismiss the indictment on the ground that the government had consented to the activities forming the basis of the indictment. The government sought to appeal that ruling, but the Court of Appeals for the Ninth Circuit dismissed the appeal. It concluded that the Double Jeopardy Clause barred reprosecution of the defendants and therefore the statute governing appeals by the government did not authorize an appeal of the dismissal of the indictment.

The United States Supreme Court reversed that decision. The Supreme Court held that, under *Perez*, the government could retry the defendants following a mistrial based on a hung jury. Moreover, because the dismissal of the indictment occurred several months after the first trial ended in a mistrial, but before the retrial of the defendants, the Court treated the dismissal as a *pretrial* order. It then concluded that because the Double Jeopardy Clause does not prohibit the government from retrying a defendant following the government's successful appeal of a pretrial dismissal of an indictment, the government was statutorily authorized to appeal the dismissal.

The situation presented in *Sanford* must be distinguished, however, from that involved in *United States v. Martin Linen Supply Co.* (1977). In *Martin Linen Supply Co.*, the judge in a trial for criminal contempt discharged a "hopelessly deadlocked" jury and declared a mistrial. After doing so, the judge informed the attorneys that he would be inclined "to enter a judgment of acquittal ... if an appropriate motion was made." He told the attorneys that he had "almost instructed a verdict for all [d]efendants" because the government's case was "without doubt the weakest [contempt case that] [he'd] ever seen." Six days after the judge declared the mistrial, the defendants moved for a judgment of acquittal pursuant to Federal Rule of Criminal Procedure 29(c). That rule provides that "[i]f the jury ... is discharged without having returned a verdict, a motion for judgment of acquittal may be made ... within 7 days after the jury is discharged [and] the court may enter judgment of acquittal." Two months later, the trial judge entered judgments of acquittal.

The government sought to appeal those judgments, but the United States Supreme Court held it could not, because the Double Jeopardy Clause barred a retrial of the accused. The Supreme Court explained that the normal rule allowing the government to retry a defendant after a mistrial declared on the basis of a "hung jury" does not apply if the trial judge enters a valid judgment of acquittal following the discharge of the jury. Such a judgment, reasoned the Court, acts to terminate a trial in which jeopardy had long since attached. The Court distinguished *Sanford* on the ground that the trial judge in *Sanford* entered a pretrial order dismissing the indictment against the accused, not a judgment of acquittal.

Possible bias on the part of a juror may be another instance of "manifest necessity" for the declaration of a mistrial. As the United States Supreme Court remarked in *Simmons v. United States* (1891):

> There can be no condition of things in which the necessity for the exercise of [the] power [to discharge the jury] is more manifest, in order to prevent the defeat of the ends of public justice, than when it is made to appear to the court that, either by reason of facts existing when the jurors were sworn, but not then disclosed or known to the court, or by reason of outside influences brought to bear on the jury pending the trial, the jurors, or any of them, are subject to such bias or prejudice as not to stand impartial between the government and the accused.

As with the decision to declare a mistrial because of a hung jury, an appellate court must accord great deference to the trial judge's decision to declare a mistrial based upon possible juror bias. Such deference is appropriate because the trial judge is in the best position to assess the likelihood that certain conduct or events affected the impartiality of one or more jurors. The trial judge observed and heard the jurors during the jury-selection process. Moreover, he is the judge most familiar with the evidence and the background of the particular case. "In short," stated the United States Supreme Court in *Arizona v. Washington* (1978), "he is far more 'conversant with the factors relevant to the determination' than any reviewing court can possibly be."

Of course, because the decision to declare a mistrial inevitably affects a constitutionally protected interest of the defendant, an appellate court faced with a mistrial declared on the basis of possible juror bias has an obligation to investigate whether "the trial court exercised 'sound discretion' in declaring a mistrial." Should it find that the trial judge acted "irrationally" or "irresponsibly," it should not find manifest necessity for the mistrial and should bar retrial of the defendant (Arizona v. Washington, 1978).

Applying these principles in *Washington*, the United States Supreme Court held that there existed a "high degree" of necessity for the trial judge's decision to declare a mistrial after George Washington's lawyer improperly told the jury during his opening statement that Washington, who previously had been convicted of the offense charged, had been granted a new trial because the prosecuting attorney had purposely withheld exculpatory evidence from the defense in Washington's first trial. The Supreme Court noted that the trial judge did not act precipitately in response to the prosecutor's request for a mistrial, but rather showed a concern for the possible double jeopardy consequences of an erroneous decision by giving both Washington's attorney and the prosecutor a full opportunity to explain their positions on the propriety of a mistrial. The Court then concluded that the trial judge acted "responsibly and deliberately" and accorded careful consideration to the Washington's interest in having the trial completed in a single proceeding.

Similarly, in *Simmons v. United States* (1891), the United States Supreme Court held that the trial judge was justified in declaring a mistrial because of possible juror bias after learning that several jurors had read a newspaper story describing a letter written by Simmons' attorney denying an allegation by a third person that one of the jurors was acquainted with Simmons. The Supreme Court reached the same result in *Thompson v. United States* (1894), in which the trial judge declared a mistrial because of possible juror bias after discovering that one of the jurors trying the case had been a member of the grand jury that indicted Thomas Thompson and therefore was disqualified to sit on the trial jury.

"Manifest necessity" for the declaration of a mistrial also ordinarily exists when "a verdict of conviction could be reached but would have to be reversed on appeal due to an obvious procedural error in the trial." In such circumstances, "it would not serve 'the ends of public justice' to require that the [g]overnment proceed with its proof when, if it succeeded before the jury, it would automatically be stripped of that success by an appellate court" (Illinois v. Somerville, 1973).

In *Illinois v. Somerville* (1973), for example, a grand jury in the State of Illinois indicted David Somerville for the crime of theft. The day after the jury was impaneled and sworn, and before the government presented any evidence, the prosecuting attorney realized that the indictment was insufficient to charge an offense because it did not allege that Somerville intended permanently to deprive the owner of his property. Under Illinois law, this defect could not be cured by amending the indictment; it could not be waived by the defendant's failure to object; and, if the defendant were convicted at trial, he could raise the defect on appeal to overturn that conviction. The prosecuting attorney moved for a mistrial so he could obtain a new indictment. After concluding that further proceedings under the defective indictment would be useless, the trial judge granted the motion and discharged the jury.

The United States Supreme Court held that the trial judge did not abuse his discretion in declaring a mistrial and that the Double Jeopardy Clause therefore did not bar the State of Illinois from subsequently trying Somerville for the same offense under a valid indictment. The Supreme Court reasoned that if a mistrial were not constitutionally available in such circumstances, the state's policy of preserving the right of each defendant to insist that a criminal prosecution against him be commenced by the action of a grand jury "could only be implemented by conducting a second trial after verdict and reversal on appeal thus wasting time, energy, and money for all concerned." The Court in *Somerville* warned, however, that "the declaration of a mistrial on the basis of a rule or a defective procedure that would lend itself to prosecutorial manipulation would involve an entirely different question."

At the other extreme from a mistrial based upon either the jury's inability to reach a verdict, possible juror bias, or an obvious procedural error or defect in the trial that would necessitate reversal of a conviction on appeal are cases in which the trial judge—realizing that the government's case is going badly and fearing that the jury is likely to acquit the accused—declares a mistrial at the request of the prosecuting attorney, or *sua sponte*, to allow the prosecuting attorney "to buttress weaknesses in his evidence" (Arizona v. Washington,1978), or otherwise "afford the [government] a more favorable opportunity to convict" (Downum v. United States, 1963). Also at this end of the spectrum are cases in which the trial judge declares a mistrial at the request of the prosecuting attorney, or *sua sponte*, to allow the prosecuting attorney to use the superior resources of the state to harass the accused or achieve a tactical advantage over him (Arizona v. Washington, 1978). In none of these cases does "manifest necessity" exist for the trial judge's declaration of a mistrial and, as a result, the Double Jeopardy Clause prohibits the government from retrying the accused (Arizona v. Washington, 1978; Downum v. United States, 1963; Gori v. United States, 1961).

Downum v. United States (1963) provides an excellent example. There, a grand jury returned a multi-count indictment charging Robert Downum and three others with stealing from the mail and forging and uttering checks so stolen. On the day before the case was called for trial, the prosecuting attorney's assistant checked with the United States Marshal who had been given a subpoena to deliver to one Rutledge, the payee on the checks involved in two of the six counts involving Downum. The prosecuting attorney's assistant learned that Rutledge's wife had told the marshal that she did not know the whereabouts of her husband, but would notify the marshal if she located him. The marshal did not hear from Mrs. Rutledge and did not follow-up on his initial conversation with her. Nevertheless, the next morning, when Downum's case was called for trial, both the prosecuting attorney and defense counsel announced they were ready to proceed. The trial judge impaneled a jury and instructed it to return that afternoon. When the jury returned, the prosecuting attorney asked the trial judge to discharge the jury because of Rutledge's absence. Defense counsel responded by moving to dismiss for want of prosecution the two counts involving the checks made out to Rutledge and asking that the trial proceed on the other four counts involving Downum. The trial judge denied the motion and, over Downum's objection, declared a mistrial.

The United States Supreme Court held that the trial judge abused his discretion in discharging the jury. The Supreme Court acknowledged that the absence of a prosecution witness sometimes might justify the declaration of a mistrial without the defendant's consent and later retrial of the accused, but concluded that the double jeopardy provision barred retrial of Downum. The Court reasoned that in Downum's case, the prosecuting attorney knew of the unavailability of one of its key witnesses before the jury had been selected and sworn and jeopardy had attached. Moreover, the Court noted, the absent witness was essential for only two of the six counts concerning Downum, yet the government opposed defense counsel's motion to dismiss those two counts and to proceed with a trial on the other four counts. The Court declared that the following statement of the Court of Appeals for the Ninth Circuit in *Cornero v. United States* (1931) set forth the governing principle:

> The fact is that, when the district attorney impaneled the jury without first ascertaining whether or not his witnesses were present, he took a chance. While their absence might have justified a continuance of the case in view of the fact that they were under bond to appear at that time and place, the question presented here is entirely different from that involved in the exercise of the sound discretion of the trial court in granting a continuance in furtherance of justice. The situation presented is simply one where the district attorney entered upon the trial of the case without sufficient evidence to convict. This does not take the case out of the rule with reference to former jeopardy. There is no difference in principle between a discovery by the district attorney immediately after the jury was impaneled that his evidence was insufficient and a discovery after he had called some or all of his witnesses.

As discussed earlier in this Analysis, the Double Jeopardy Clause prohibits the government from retrying a defendant following the trial court's declaration of a mistrial at the defendant's request when that request was precipitated by conduct of the prosecuting attorney that was intended to "goad" the defendant into moving for a mistrial (Oregon v. Kennedy, 1982; *accord* United States v. Scott, 1978; Lee v. United States, 1977). In such circumstances, the defendant's valued right to complete his trial before the fact finder that began hearing evidence in the case would be a "hollow shell" if his inevitable motion for a mistrial prevented him from later invoking the bar of the Double Jeopardy Clause (Oregon v. Kennedy, 1982). Moreover, if reprosecution were allowed in such situations, the government could force a mistrial when its case was going badly, in the hope that it could improve its position in a new trial. By like reasoning, the Double Jeopardy Clause must be read to bar reprosecution of a defendant following the trial court's declaration of a mistrial on its own motion when, regardless of whether a manifest necessity existed for the mistrial, the cause of the mistrial was conduct of the prosecuting attorney intended either to "goad" the trial judge into declaring a mistrial, or to "goad" the defendant into moving for a mistrial (but the defendant failed to move for a mistrial before the trial judge acted on his own).

Between the two extremes are a myriad of situations in which a trial judge might declare a mistrial without the consent of the accused. In each one, the trial judge must examine the facts of the particular case and determine whether "manifest necessity" or the "ends of public justice" require that he terminate the trial before verdict.

In United States v. Jorn (1971), for example, the trial judge learned after the commencement of trial that five taxpayers whom the defendant, Milton Jorn, allegedly assisted in preparing fraudulent income tax returns and whom the government intended to call as witnesses had been warned of their constitutional rights only by Internal Revenue Service agents when the agents first contacted them about the case. Believing that these warnings were probably inadequate, the trial judge, on his own motion, declared a mistrial so these witnesses could consult with their own attorneys about their privilege against self-incrimination and their constitutional right to the assistance of counsel.

In an earlier case, *Wade v. Hunter* (1949), the commanding general of the 76th Infantry Division of the United States Army ordered a general court-martial convened in Germany during World War II to try two soldiers for the rape of a German woman. After hearing some evidence, the court-martial continued the case so it could hear the testimony of the rape victim's parents who, because of illness, were not then available. Before these additional witnesses could be heard, the commanding general withdrew the charges from the court-martial and directed it to take no further action—the functional equivalent of a mistrial. He then transmitted the charges to the commanding general of the Third Army with a recommendation that they be tried by a new court-martial. He explained that he was transferring the charges because, in the three weeks since the alleged rape, his troops had advanced farther into Germany and "[d]ue to the tactical situation the distance to the residence of [the victim's parents had] become so great that the case [could] not be completed within a reasonable time."

The United States Supreme Court in *Wade* concluded that "the tactical situation brought about by a rapidly advancing army" constituted a manifest necessity for withdrawing the charges from the court-martial. The Supreme Court reasoned:

> [T]he ... order of transmittal of the charges ... was made by the Commanding General of the 76th Division who was responsible for convening the court-martial and who was also responsible for the most effective military employment of that Division in carrying out the plan for the invasion of Germany. There is no intimation in the record that the tactical situation did not require the transfer order. The court-martial was composed of officers of the invading Army Division. Momentous issues hung on the invasion and we cannot assume that these court-martial officers were not needed to perform their military functions.... This case presents extraordinary reasons why the judgment of the Commanding General should be accepted by the courts. At least in the absence of charges of bad faith on the part of the Commanding General, courts should not attempt to review his on-the-spot decision that the tactical situation required transfer of the charges.

In *Jorn*, on the other hand, four of the seven Justices who reached the merits of Jorn's claim[29] that the Double Jeopardy Clause precluded his retrial concluded that the trial judge abused his discretion in declaring a mistrial and that the double jeopardy provision therefore barred the government from retrying Jorn for the same offenses. The plurality in *Jorn* reasoned that the trial judge did not consider the possibility of a continuance of the trial and, indeed, acted so abruptly in discharging the jury that it was "abundantly apparent that [he] made no effort to exercise a sound discretion to assure that, taking all the circumstances into account, there was a manifest necessity for the *sua sponte* declaration of [the] mistrial."

Mention should be made at this point of the United States Supreme Court's decision in *Gori v. United States* (1961). In that case, the judge at Dante Gori's first trial apparently feared that the prosecuting attorney's questioning of a witness might lead to the introduction of inadmissible evidence of other crimes committed by Gori. Acting with what might have been an "overeager solicitude" for Gori's rights, the trial judge declared a mistrial without first obtaining Gori's consent. The Supreme Court held that the trial judge did not abuse his discretion and that Gori's second trial was constitutionally permissible. The Court stated that it was "unwilling, where it clearly appears that a mistrial has been granted *in the sole interest of the defendant*, to hold that its necessary consequence is to bar all retrial" (italics added).

If *Gori* held that the Double Jeopardy Clause does not bar the retrial of a defendant when the trial judge, acting without the defendant's consent, terminates the proceedings before verdict "in the sole interest of the defendant," that holding probably does not remain good law. The government relied heavily upon *Gori* in *Jorn*. It argued that even if the trial judge in that case abused his discretion when he declared a mistrial on his own motion in order to give several of the government's witnesses an opportunity to consult with their own attorneys about their constitutional rights, reprosecution of Jorn should be permitted because the judge's ruling "benefited" Jorn and was not compelled by bad-faith conduct on the part of the prosecuting attorney aimed at triggering a mistrial. The plurality in *Jorn* acknowledged that *Gori* "*suggest[s] the possibility* of a variation on [the *Perez*] theme [of a 'manifest necessity'] according to a determination by the appellate court as to which party to the case was the beneficiary of the mistrial ruling" (italics added); however, after concluding that the mistrial in *Jorn* was motivated by the trial judge's desire to protect the prosecution's witnesses and was not declared "in the sole interest of the defendant," the plurality said:

> Further, we think that a limitation on the abuse-of-discretion principle based on an appellate court's assessment of which side benefitted from the mistrial ruling does not adequately satisfy the policies underpinning the double jeopardy provision. Reprosecution after a mistrial has unnecessarily been declared by the trial court obviously subjects the defendant to the same personal strain and insecurity regardless of the motivation underlying the trial judge's action ....
>
> [B]right-line rules based on ... the intended beneficiary of the [mistrial] ruling would only disserve the vital competing interests of the [g]overnment and the defendant.

This language in *Jorn* seems to repudiate the reasoning in *Gori*. And, although only a plurality of the Court in *Jorn* subscribed to it, the United States Supreme Court has not relied upon the reasoning in *Gori* since *Jorn*.

Reprosecution Following the Dismissal of a Charge

The Double Jeopardy Clause generally accords absolute finality to a judgment of acquittal. As a result, the government ordinarily can neither appeal an acquittal nor prosecute the accused a second time for the same offense. In contrast, the double jeopardy provision does not grant such finality to a trial judge's order dismissing a charge against an accused. In some circumstances following a dismissal, the government can attempt to remedy the defect or error that led to the dismissal and then prosecute the accused a second time for the same offense, while in others it can appeal the order of dismissal and, if successful in obtaining a reversal of that order, try the accused on the charge that had been erroneously dismissed.

Distinguishing an Acquittal from a Dismissal

Because the double jeopardy ramifications of a "dismissal" may differ from those of an "acquittal," it is essential to distinguish between the two. As discussed earlier in this Analysis, a trial judge's action constitutes an "acquittal" "when '[his] ruling ..., whatever its label, actually represents a resolution [in favor of the defendant], correct or not, of some or all of the factual elements of the offense charged'" (United States v. Scott, 1978). A dismissal, on the other hand,

terminates the proceedings against the accused on a basis unrelated to his factual guilt or innocence.

Some dismissals are predicated upon an error or defect thought by the trial judge to preclude completely the conviction of the defendant for the offense charged. This type of dismissal terminates the proceedings in favor of the accused and contemplates an end to all prosecution of him for that offense (United States v. Scott, 1978). In *United States v. Scott* (1978), for example, after the jury had heard all the evidence in the case, the trial judge granted John Scott's motion to dismiss two counts of a three-count indictment on the ground that the government's delay in charging him with the narcotics transactions alleged in those counts prejudiced his defense and thereby deprived him of his constitutional right to due process of law. The trial judge's action in *Scott* constituted a "dismissal," rather than an "acquittal," because he based his resolution of the case in the defendant's favor on a ground not related to the defendant's factual guilt or innocence of the offense charged.

Other dismissals, however, are based upon an error or defect that could be cured—absent any double jeopardy bar—by beginning anew the prosecution of the accused. A dismissal of this type contemplates a second prosecution of the defendant for the same offense charged in the indictment or information that the judge dismissed (Lee v. United States, 1977). In *Lee v. United States* (1977), for example, after hearing the evidence in the case, the judge in a bench trial for the theft of two billfolds granted Phillip Lee's motion to dismiss the information on the ground that it did not provide adequate notice of the crime charge because it failed to allege that he took the billfolds knowingly and with the intent to deprive the victim of his property. The trial judge's action in *Lee* constituted a "dismissal," rather than an "acquittal," because he based his action upon the inadequacy of the charging instrument, a ground not related to the defendant's factual guilt or innocence. Unlike the trial judge in *Scott*, though, the trial judge in *Lee* did not predicate the dismissal on a determination that Lee could *never* be prosecuted or convicted for stealing the billfolds; rather, he anticipated that the government would commence a new prosecution of Lee for the theft of the wallets by filing a new information properly charging that offense.

Dismissal Before the Attachment of Jeopardy

When a trial judge dismisses an indictment or information against an accused before jeopardy has "attached," the Double Jeopardy Clause does not bar the government from appealing the order of dismissal and, if it succeeds in having the order reversed, prosecuting the individual anew on the charge the trial judge erroneously dismissed (Serfass v. United States, 1975; State v. Osborn, 2001; State v. Hellems, 2000; Commonwealth v. Wallace, 1996). This is true even if the trial judge based his ruling on evidentiary facts that were not contained in the charging instrument and that would constitute a defense on the merits at trial (Serfass v. United States, 1975).

The United States Supreme Court considered this issue in *Serfass v. United States* (1975). In that case, the government obtained an indictment charging David Serfass with willfully failing to report for and submit to induction in the Armed Services. Serfass pleaded not guilty and demanded a jury trial. Prior to his trial, he moved to dismiss the indictment on the ground that his local draft board did not state adequate reasons for its refusal to reopen his Selective Service file after he submitted a form requesting reclassification as a conscientious objector. Following its consideration of an affidavit Serfass had attached to his motion, as well as Serfass's Selective Service file and an oral stipulation by the prosecuting attorney and defense counsel that the information Serfass submitted to the draft board established a *prima facie* claim for conscientious objector status, the trial court granted the motion to dismiss.

The Supreme Court held that the Double Jeopardy Clause did not prohibit further prosecution of Serfass and that the applicable statute therefore authorized the government to appeal the dismissal of the indictment. The Court reasoned that because jeopardy had not yet attached when the trial judge granted the motion to dismiss, and Serfass never faced the risk of being convicted, the constitutional prohibition against double jeopardy did not apply. It explained that the policies underpinning the guarantee against double jeopardy "are not implicated before that point in the proceedings at which 'jeopardy attaches,'" because, when a criminal prosecution is terminated before trial, "an accused is often spared much of the expense, delay, strain, and embarrassment which attend a trial," he is not "'subjected to the hazards of trial and possible conviction,'" and "an appeal by the [government would not] 'allow the prosecutor to seek to persuade a second trier of fact of the defendant's guilt after having failed with the first.'" In addition, continued the Court, an action taken by a trial court—even if characterized by it as an "acquittal"—cannot bar a subsequent prosecution "unless jeopardy has once attached and [the] accused has been subjected to the risk of conviction," because a "fundamental principle" of double jeopardy jurisprudence provides that "an accused must suffer jeopardy before he can suffer double jeopardy."

For the same reasons articulated by the Supreme Court in *Serfass*, when a trial judge dismisses an indictment or information prior to the attachment of jeopardy because of some curable error or defect (such as the failure of the charging instrument to allege an element of the crime), the Double Jeopardy Clause does not bar the government from correcting the error or defect and reprosecuting the accused for the same offense in a new indictment or information (*e.g.*, United States v. Osteen, 2001; United States v. Gamble, 1998; Commonwealth v. Hunter, 1996; Neff v. Commonwealth, 2002). Had the trial judge in *Lee*, granted Lee's motion to dismiss the information at the time defense counsel filed the motion (immediately after the prosecuting attorney completed his opening statement to the judge in a bench trial), rather than waiting until after he had heard all the evidence in the case, there would have been no question but that the government could have filed a new information properly charging Lee with the same theft charged in the

information the trial judge dismissed. In such circumstances, Lee would not have been placed in "jeopardy" under the defective information because jeopardy does not "attach" in a bench trial until the judge begins hearing evidence. A trial under a properly-drafted information, therefore, would not constitute *double* jeopardy.

Sometimes the dismissal of an indictment or information occurs after the declaration of a mistrial in the defendant's first trial, but before the commencement of a constitutionally-permissible retrial. This is what transpired in *United States v. Sanford* (1926). There, the jury in the defendants' trial for illegal game hunting in a national park could not reach a verdict, and the judge declared a mistrial. Several months later, after the expiration of the time during which he could have entered a post-verdict judgment of acquittal, and while the government was preparing to retry the defendants, the trial judge granted the defendants' motion to dismiss the indictment on the ground that the government had consented to the activities forming the basis of the indictment. The United States Supreme Court concluded that the dismissal should be treated as a pretrial order and held that under the applicable statute the government could appeal that dismissal because, if it succeeded in its appeal, the Double Jeopardy Clause would not preclude it from retrying the defendants.

Dismissal After the Attachment of Jeopardy

Even when a trial judge dismisses a charge against an accused after jeopardy has attached, the Double Jeopardy Clause does not always bar the government from appealing the dismissal or from retrying the accused for the same offense. A trial court's midtrial dismissal of an information or indictment on a ground consistent with reprosecution of the accused for the offense charged (such as a procedural defect in the charging instrument) is "functionally indistinguishable from a declaration of a mistrial," and the double jeopardy principles governing the permissibility of retrial after a mistrial therefore apply to such dismissals. Accordingly, if the defendant requested or consented to the dismissal, the government can retry him—even if the dismissal was predicated upon prosecutorial or judicial error—unless that error was "intended to provoke" the defendant into seeking dismissal of the charge (Lee v. United States, 1977).

For instance, in *Lee*, the judge in a bench trial for the theft of two wallets heard all the evidence in the case and then granted Lee's motion to dismiss the information on the ground that it failed to allege that Lee took the wallets knowingly and with the intent to deprive the victim of his property. Reasoning that the government's error in drafting the information was one that, like any prosecutorial or judicial error necessitating a mistrial, could be avoided (absent any double jeopardy bar) by beginning the prosecution anew, and that the trial judge, in granting the motion to dismiss contemplated such a second prosecution, the United States Supreme Court concluded that the order of dismissal constituted the functional equivalent of a declaration of a mistrial. The Supreme Court held that the government did not violate Lee's protection against double jeopardy by prosecuting him a second time for the same theft; the trial judge terminated the first trial at Lee's request and the government's error in drafting the information was at most an act of negligence, not one intended to provoke a request for dismissal.

On the other hand, if the trial judge dismisses an indictment or information at the request of the prosecuting attorney or on his own motion (and without the consent of the accused), the government can retry the accused *only* if the trial judge—in the exercise of his sound discretion—terminated the first trial before verdict because a "manifest necessity" existed for the dismissal or the "ends of public justice" would otherwise have been defeated (*see* Lee v. United States, 1977; *see also* United States v. Perez, 1824; United States v. Dinitz, 1976). If such circumstances did not exist, the Double Jeopardy Clause bars retrial of the defendant (*e.g.*, Wilcox v. McGee, 2001). A comparison of a hypothetical case based upon a variation on the facts involved in the United States Supreme Court's decision in *Illinois v. Somerville* (1973) with the decision of the United States Court of Appeals for the Ninth Circuit in *Wilcox v. McGee* (2001) illustrates this principle.

After David Somerville had been placed in jeopardy in his trial upon an indictment charging him with theft, the prosecuting attorney discovered that the indictment was fatally deficient under state law because it failed to allege that Somerville intended permanently to deprive the owner of his property. State law prohibited the prosecuting attorney from curing the defect by amending the indictment. It allowed a convicted defendant to raise the defect in the indictment to overturn any conviction obtained under it. Upon discovering the error, the prosecutor in *Somerville* successfully moved for a mistrial so he could obtain a new indictment.

The United States Supreme Court held that the Double Jeopardy Clause did not bar reprosecution of Somerville for the same theft under a valid indictment. The Supreme Court reasoned that "manifest necessity" dictated termination of the first trial, because an appellate court would have been required to reverse any verdict of guilty obtained by the government under the defective indictment. As the Court put it, the defect in the indictment "would [have made] reversal on appeal a certainty" (Illinois v. Somerville, 1973).

Had the prosecutor in *Somerville* moved to *dismiss* the defective indictment instead of moving for a mistrial, the same manifest necessity for termination of the trial would have existed and, if the trial judge had *dismissed* the fatally deficient indictment, the double jeopardy provision would not have barred Somerville's retrial under a valid indictment. The Supreme Court made this clear in *Lee*, when, after discussing the holding in *Somerville*, it stated that "[t]here is no reason to believe that *Somerville* would have been analyzed differently if the trial judge ... had labeled his action a 'dismissal' rather than a mistrial."

In contrast, no manifest necessity existed in *Wilcox* for the dismissal of an indictment returned by a grand jury in the State of Oregon charging Robert Wilcox with burglary. In that case, the prosecuting attorney discovered during the testimony of the first witness that the indictment incorrectly listed the date and address of the alleged burglary. The prosecutor moved to amend the indictment to correct the error, or alternatively, to dismiss the indictment so he could seek a new one. Over the objection of Wilcox's lawyer, the trial judge dismissed the indictment. Following Wilcox's reindictment and conviction for the same burglary, the Court of Appeals for the Ninth Circuit concluded that under Oregon law the trial judge could have amended the first indictment because the variances in it were of form, rather than substance. The Court of Appeals acknowledged that a state appellate court in Oregon conceivably could have reached a different conclusion and reversed a conviction based upon an amended indictment. Nevertheless, it held that for manifest necessity to exist under *Somerville*, reversal of a conviction on appeal must be a "certainty." Accordingly, the court of appeals held that the Double Jeopardy Clause barred the State of Oregon from reprosecuting Wilcox for the burglary charged in the original indictment.

It should be noted that there may be one situation in which the Double Jeopardy Clause prohibits the government from reprosecuting an individual following a trial court's midtrial dismissal of the charge against him at his request, even though the dismissal was functionally indistinguishable from a declaration of a mistrial and was predicated upon prosecutorial or judicial error not "intended to provoke" the defendant into seeking the dismissal. If a defendant moves to dismiss the charge against him *before* he is placed in jeopardy, but the trial judge does not grant the motion until *after* jeopardy has attached, the double jeopardy provision *may* protect the defendant against reprosecution.

This sequence of events occurred in *Lee*. After the prosecuting attorney made his opening statement in a bench trial, a point before jeopardy had attached, Phillip Lee filed a motion to dismiss the information charging him with the theft of two billfolds. Lee contended that the information was defective because it failed to allege certain elements of the crime. The trial court tentatively denied the motion, but told defense counsel that it would give the motion further consideration. Defense counsel offered no objection to proceeding with the trial subject to the court's further study of the motion to dismiss. After a trial lasting less than two hours, the trial court granted Lee's motion and dismissed the charge without entering any formal finding concerning Lee's guilt or innocence.

The United States Supreme Court held that the government could retry Lee for the same theft. The Supreme Court stated that the trial court's failure to postpone the taking of evidence in the case until it could give full consideration to the motion to dismiss was "entirely reasonable," given the last-minute timing of the motion and the failure of Lee's attorney to request a continuance or otherwise impress upon the court the importance to Lee of not being placed in jeopardy on a defective information.

Justice William J. Brennan, Jr., joined the Court's opinion in *Lee*, but wrote a concurring opinion in which he emphasized that "an entirely different case would be presented if the [defendant] had afforded the trial judge ample opportunity to rule on his motion [to dismiss] prior to trial, and the court, in failing to take advantage of this opportunity, permitted the attachment of jeopardy before ordering the dismissal of the information." Justice Brennan believed that in such a situation, the trial judge's delay in ruling on the motion to dismiss "would effectively deprive [the defendant] of his 'valued right' to receive a factual determination from the first empaneled fact finder and would subject [him] to the 'embarrassment, expense and ordeal' of a needless trial." Justice Brennan also maintained that even if the defendant renewed his motion to dismiss after the commencement of trial, it could not be said that he made the choice to forgo the right of presenting his case to the first fact finder so he could attain a beneficial legal ruling. Justice Brennan wrote:

> On the contrary, the defendant placed in this predicament by the trial judge would have done everything in his power to receive a fair adjudication of his legal claims without compromising his right to proceed with the first factfinder. Honoring his double jeopardy claim thus not only is in keeping with the policies and interests served by the [Double Jeopardy] Clause, but also would further the cause of efficient judicial administration by encouraging defendants to present, and judges to rule on, legal claims prior to the clamor and heat of trial.

If a defendant successfully moves to terminate his trial on a ground unrelated to his factual guilt or innocence, and one that contemplates that the proceedings will end then and there in his favor (such as prejudicial delay in charging him with the offense), the government can—consistent with the double jeopardy provision—appeal the trial court's order dismissing the charge and, if it succeeds in obtaining a reversal of that order, prosecute the defendant anew for the charge that had been erroneously dismissed (United States v. Scott, 1978).

An order dismissing an indictment or information on a ground not related to the factual guilt or innocence of the accused does not constitute an "acquittal," even when the trial judge based his ruling upon facts outside the face of the charging instrument, or upon the ground that the accused simply could not be convicted of the offense charged. Moreover, the government's appeal of the midtrial dismissal of a charge, granted by the court at the request of the accused,

> scarcely [presents] a picture of an all-powerful state relentlessly pursuing a defendant who had either been found not guilty or who had at least insisted on having the issue of guilt submitted to the first trier of fact. It is instead a picture of a defendant who chooses to avoid conviction and imprisonment, not because of his assertion that the [g]overnment has failed to make out a case against him, but because of a legal claim that the [g]overnment's case against him must fail even though it might satisfy the trier of fact that he was guilty beyond a reasonable doubt. (United States v. Scott, 1978).

Furthermore, according to the Supreme Court in *United States v. Scott* (1978), a defendant who "deliberately choos[es]" to seek to terminate the proceedings against him on a ground unrelated to guilt or innocence is not deprived of his "valued right" to have his trial completed before the first fact finder; rather, "the public has been deprived of its valued right to 'one complete opportunity to convict those who have violated its laws.'"

Of course, if a trial court—on its own motion and without the defendant's consent—terminates the proceedings before a verdict on a ground unrelated to the defendant's factual guilt or innocence, the defendant does not "deliberately choos[e]" to seek to end the proceedings against him. In such circumstances, "the defendant has been deprived of his valued right to have his trial completed by a particular tribunal" (United States v. Scott, 1978 (internal quotation marks omitted)). Accordingly, even if the trial judge erred in dismissing the charge against the accused, the Double Jeopardy Clause bars the government from either appealing the dismissal or reprosecuting the defendant for the same offense (United States v. Gaytan, 1997; United States v. Govro, 1987; United States v. Dahlstrum, 1981; State v. Bell, 2000; People v. Wiley, 1979; State v. Vestal, 1998; *contra* State v. Calhoun, 1985).

Sentencing Proceeding Following Conviction

After a defendant is convicted at the guilt-innocence phase of his trial, the court holds a hearing at which it considers the appropriate sentence to impose. A sentencing hearing may involve the testimony of witnesses and the introduction of other evidence. Such a proceeding does not, however, constitute a successive prosecution for purposes of the Double Jeopardy Clause (Schiro v. Farley, 1994). In *Schiro v. Farley* (1994), the United States Supreme Court rejected Thomas Schiro's argument that a sentencing hearing following his conviction of murder for killing while committing the crime of rape constituted a second prosecution for intentional murder because the jury that convicted him at the guilt-innocence phase of the trial had left blank a verdict sheet concerning his guilt for intentional murder and the government, at the sentencing hearing, attempted to prove, as an aggravating factor necessary for imposition of the death penalty, that Schiro "committed the murder by intentionally killing the victim while committing or attempting to commit ... rape" or another enumerated felony.

MULTIPLE PUNISHMENTS

The Double Jeopardy Clause protects "against multiple punishments for the same offense" (North Carolina v. Pearce, 1969; *accord* Jones v. Thomas, 1989; United States v. Halper, 1989; Missouri v. Hunter, 1983; Albernaz v. United States, 1981; Whalen v. United States, 1980; Brown v. Ohio, 1977), thereby recognizing the injustice inherent in punishing an individual more than once for the same offense. The constitutionality of cumulative punishments can arise in two different contexts: first, when they are imposed in a single proceeding, and second, when they are imposed in separate proceedings.

In a Single Proceeding

In the context of multiple punishments in a single proceeding, the protection afforded by the double jeopardy provision "is designed to ensure that the sentencing discretion of courts is confined to the limits established by the legislature" (Ohio v. Johnson, 1984; *accord* Jones v. Thomas, 1989; United States v. Halper, 1989; Brown v. Ohio, 1977). The question whether punishments imposed by a sentencing court following an individual's conviction of criminal charges are unconstitutionally multiple therefore cannot be resolved without determining what punishment the legislature authorized (Whalen v. United States, 1980; *see also* Ohio v. Johnson, 1980).

In enacting statutes defining criminal offenses and their punishments, legislatures frequently provide that an offense may be punished by more than one sanction, such as by a monetary fine and a term of imprisonment. A sentencing court does not violate the Double Jeopardy Clause's prohibition against multiple punishments by imposing both sanctions upon an individual in accordance with such a provision (Whalen v. United States, 1980). Under such circumstances, the legislature clearly expressed its intent to allow the imposition of both punishments; however, if the applicable statute provides that the offense is punishable by *either* of two sanctions, for example, by a monetary fine *or* a term of imprisonment, imposition of both punishments would violate the Double Jeopardy Clause (Whalen v. United States, 1980), as the United States Supreme Court held in *Ex parte Lange* (1874). There, the trial court, through inadvertence, sentenced the defendant to serve one year in prison and to pay a fine of $200, under a statute providing a maximum penalty for the offense in question of imprisonment for not more than one year *or* a fine of up to $200.

As discussed earlier in this Analysis, the guarantee against double jeopardy generally prohibits multiple prosecutions of an individual for the same offense. It does not, however, preclude the government from charging an individual with two or more statutory offenses based upon the same act or transaction and prosecuting those charges in a single trial (Ohio v. Johnson, 1980; *accord* Ball v. United States, 1985). For example, in *Blockburger v. United States* (1932), the government alleged that Blockburger sold a quantity of morphine hydrochloride and, on the basis of that single act, charged him with the two statutory offenses—selling a narcotic drug not in or from the original stamped package and selling a narcotic drug not in pursuance of a written order of the purchaser (*see also* Gore v. United States, 1958). When the government charges an individual in a single proceeding with two or more offenses based upon the same act or transaction and the fact finder convicts the individual of more than one of the offenses in a single trial, as it did in *Blockburger*, the question arises whether the court may punish him separately for each offense or whether the Double Jeopardy Clause's protection against multiple punishments for the same offense allows the court to punish him for only one.

The United States Supreme Court held in *Blockburger* that, in such cases, so long as there are two offenses, the sentencing court can impose cumulative punishments (as it did in that case). The Supreme Court stated that "the test to be applied to determine whether there are two offenses or only one is whether each provision requires proof of a fact which the other does not." Applying this test in *Blockburger*, the Court concluded that the two offenses of which Blockburger was convicted were not the "same," so that the trial court did not err in sentencing him to consecutive terms of five years in prison for each of the offenses (*i.e.*, the sentence for the second offense would not commence until he finished serving his sentence for the first offense) (*see also* Gore v. United States, 1958).

Although the Supreme Court in *Blockburger* appeared to be establishing the constitutional standard for determining when cumulative punishments can be imposed in a single proceeding, it has since stated that in the context of multiple punishments in a single proceeding, the *Blockburger* test is merely "a rule of statutory construction" (Whalen v. United States, 1980; *accord* Ball v. United States, 1985; Albernaz v. United States, 1981). The underlying assumption of that rule is that the legislature "*ordinarily* does not intend to punish the same offense under two different statutes" (Whalen v. United States, 1980 (italics added); *accord* Ball v. United States, 1985). "Accordingly, where two statutory provisions proscribe the 'same offense,' they are construed not to authorize cumulative punishments *in the absence of a clear indication of contrary legislative intent*" (Whalen v. United States, 1980 (italics added)). When such a contrary legislative intent appears, however, a sentencing court may impose cumulative punishments for the same offense, without violating the Double Jeopardy Clause. For, in the context of multiple punishments in a single proceeding, "the Double Jeopardy Clause does no more than prevent the sentencing court from prescribing greater punishment than the legislature intended" (Missouri v. Hunter, 1983; *accord* Jones v. Thomas, 1989; *see also* Ohio v. Johnson, 1984; Brown v. Ohio, 1977).

To illustrate, in *Whalen v. United States* (1980), the United States Supreme Court held that cumulative punishments could not be imposed for the separate statutory offenses of rape and felony-murder (an unintentional killing during the commission of a felony) based upon the killing of the rape victim in the perpetration of the rape. The Supreme Court concluded that because proof of the rape was a necessary element of proof of the felony-murder, the two statutes proscribed the "same offense" under the *Blockburger* test, but it did not base its decision on that fact. It concluded that cumulative punishments could not be imposed because Congress did not authorize cumulative punishments.

The year after it decided *Whalen*, the Supreme Court held in *Albernaz v. United States* (1981) that separate punishments could be imposed for the offenses of conspiracy to import marijuana and conspiracy to distribute marijuana, even though both offenses were based upon the same agreement. The Court concluded that the offenses were not the "same" under the *Blockburger* test, but it nonetheless went on to say that because the *Blockburger* rule of statutory construction serves as a means of discerning congressional purpose, it "should not be controlling where, for example, there is a clear indication of contrary legislative intent." The Court discovered no such contrary intent and therefore held that Congress intended to allow the imposition of consecutive sentences for the violations of the two statutes. With respect to the Double Jeopardy Clause, the Court relied upon *Whalen* and held that "the question of what punishments are constitutionally permissible is not different from the question of what punishments the Legislative Branch intended to be imposed. Where Congress intended, as it did here, to impose multiple punishments, imposition of such sentences does not violate the Constitution."

Then, two years after it decided *Albernaz*, the Supreme Court held in *Missouri v. Hunter* (1983) that a defendant who was tried and convicted in a single trial of both first-degree robbery and "armed criminal action" based upon that robbery could constitutionally be convicted and sentenced for each offense, even though the two statutes at issue defined the same crime. The Court reasoned that the double jeopardy provision did not prohibit cumulative punishments for the same offense because the Missouri legislature intended to authorize the imposition of cumulative punishments for violations of the statutes. The Court explained:

> [S]imply because two criminal statutes may be construed to proscribe the same conduct under the *Blockburger* test does not mean that the Double Jeopardy Clause precludes the imposition, in a single trial, of cumulative punishments pursuant to those statutes. The [*Blockburger*] rule of statutory construction ... is not a constitutional rule requiring courts to negate clearly expressed legislative intent ....
>
> Where ... a legislature specifically authorizes cumulative punishment under two statutes, regardless of whether those two statutes proscribe the "same" conduct under *Blockburger*, a court's task of statutory construction is at an end and the prosecutor may seek and the trial court or jury may impose cumulative punishment under such statutes in a single trial. (*See also* Ohio v. Johnson, 1984.)

In Successive Proceedings

Following a Permissible Second Prosecution

As discussed previously in this Analysis, when a convicted defendant succeeds in having his conviction overturned on appeal because of trial error, the government can retry him for the same offense without violating the Double Jeopardy Clause. If the defendant is convicted at his retrial, however, the double jeopardy provision's protection against multiple punishments for the same offense requires that credit be given for punishment already endured by the defendant (North Carolina v. Pearce, 1969). The United States Supreme Court in *North Carolina v. Pearce* (1969), explained:

> We think it is clear that [the] basic constitutional guarantee [against being twice punished for the same offense] is violated when punishment already exacted for an offense is not fully "credited" in imposing sentence upon a new conviction for the same offense. The constitutional violation is flagrantly apparent in a case involving the imposition of a maximum sentence after reconviction. Suppose, for example, in a jurisdiction where the maximum allowable sentence for larceny is 10 years' imprisonment, a man succeeds in getting his larceny conviction set aside after serving three years in prison. If, upon reconviction, he is given a 10-year sentence, then, quite clearly, he will have received multiple punishments for the same offense. For he will have been compelled to serve separate prison terms of three years and 10 years, although the maximum single punishment for the offense is 10 years' imprisonment. Though not so dramatically evident, the same principle obviously holds true whenever punishment already endured is not fully subtracted from any new sentence imposed.

Although the Supreme Court in *Pearce* spoke primarily in terms of imprisonment, it noted that the same rule applies when the defendant paid a fine following his first conviction. That is, any new fine imposed by the trial court upon reconviction must be decreased by the amount previously paid by the defendant.

Under certain circumstances, the Double Jeopardy Clause does not bar the government from prosecuting an individual for an offense even though he previously was convicted of another offense constituting the "same offense" for purposes of multiple prosecutions. For example, in *Diaz v. United States* (1912), the double jeopardy provision permitted the government to try the defendant for homicide following his conviction for the lesser-included offense of assault and battery upon the same victim, because, at the time of the assault and battery trial, the victim had not yet died and therefore all the facts necessary for the greater offense of homicide had not occurred (*see also* Garrett v. United States, 1985). Similarly, in *Jeffers v. United States* (1977), the provision allowed the government to try an individual for a greater offense following his conviction for a lesser-included offense, because, according to a plurality of the Supreme Court, the individual elected to have the two offenses tried separately and persuaded the trial court to honor his election.

If an individual is convicted in a permissible second proceeding for the same offense, the question arises whether he may be punished separately for each of the two offenses, or whether the Double Jeopardy Clause limits his total punishment to the maximum provided for the more serious offense. Under the United States Supreme Court's decision in *Garrett v. United States* (1985), a court may impose a separate punishment for the second offense without violating the Double Jeopardy Clause, so long as the legislature intended to allow cumulative punishments (*see also* Jeffers v. United States, 1971 (plurality opinion)). As with multiple punishments in a single trial, the Double Jeopardy Clause in this context "'does no more than prevent the sentencing court from prescribing greater punishment than the legislature intended'" (Garrett v. United States, 1985).

Sanctions Imposed in Both a Criminal Prosecution and a Civil Proceeding

An individual against whom the government brings a civil action generally is not placed in "jeopardy" in such a proceeding because he does not face the risk "traditionally associated with 'actions intended to authorize criminal punishment to vindicate public justice" (Breed v. Jones, 1975). A legislature therefore "may impose both a criminal and a civil sanction in respect to the same act or omission" (Helvering v. Mitchell, 1938) without running afoul of the Double Jeopardy Clause. In *United States ex rel. Marcus v. Hess* (1943), for example, an action by private individuals in the name of the United States against a group of electrical contractors who allegedly defrauded the government, the United States Supreme Court concluded that a proceeding under a statute authorizing recovery of $2000 for each false claim against the government, double damages, and the costs of the lawsuit was remedial in character and imposed a civil sanction. The Supreme Court found that the primary purpose of the statute was "to provide for restitution to the government of money taken from it by fraud, and that the device of double damages plus a specific sum was chosen to make sure that the government would be made completely whole." The Court therefore held that the action was not barred by the defendants' previous plea of *nolo contendere* (no contest) and fine of $54,000 on an indictment for defrauding the government in connection with the same transactions.

Traditionally, determining whether the double jeopardy provision applied in a particular type of proceeding labeled "civil" in nature involved a two-step analysis. First, one first looked at whether the legislature intended the proceeding and its authorized sanctions to be civil in nature. If it did, one then examined whether the authorized sanction was "so punitive either in purpose or effect as to negate that intention'" (United States v. v. One Assortment of 89 Firearms, 1984). For the most part, the intent of the legislature was controlling, because "[o]nly the clearest proof that the purpose and effect of the [sanction were] punitive [would] suffice to override [the legislature's] manifest preference for a civil sanction" (internal quotation marks omitted).

However, the United States Supreme Court unanimously held in *United States v. Halper* (1989) that in any particular case a sanction imposed upon the defendant in a civil action brought by the government could be "so extreme and so divorced from the [g]overnment's damages and expenses as to constitute punishment" for purposes of double jeopardy analysis. It held further that because the Double Jeopardy Clause protects against multiple punishments for the same offense, an individual who already had been punished in a criminal prosecution could not be subjected to any additional civil sanction for the same conduct to the extent the sanction constituted "punishment," that is, to the extent that it could "not fairly be characterized as remedial, but only as a deterrent or retribution." The *Halper* Court concluded that "in determining whether a particular civil sanction constitutes criminal punishment, it is the purposes actually served by the sanction in question, not the underlying nature of the proceeding giving rise to the sanction, that must be evaluated."

In *Halper*, Irwin Halper, the manager of a company that provided medical services to patients eligible for benefits under the Medicare program, submitted to the federal government sixty-five separate false claims for reimbursement for services rendered. As a result, the government overpaid the company a total of $585. In a criminal prosecution brought by the United States, Halper was convicted for sixty-five separate violations of the criminal false-claims statute and he was sentenced to two years' imprisonment and to pay a fine of $5000. The government then brought a civil action against Halper under the *civil* False Claims Act, based upon the same conduct that led to Halper's criminal convictions. The False Claims Act provided that a person making a false statement to obtain payment of a fraudulent claim was "liable to the United States Government for a civil penalty of $2000, an amount equal to 2 times the amount of damages the Government sustains because of the act of that person, and costs of the civil action."[30]

The trial court found Halper liable for making false claims, which under the statute made him subject to a civil penalty of $130,000—$2000 for each of sixty-five separate violations; however, the United States Supreme Court held that under the facts of the particular case a penalty of that magnitude—even though civil in nature—would constitute "punishment" for double jeopardy purposes. The Supreme Court acknowledged that, as a general matter, "the [g]overnment is entitled to rough remedial justice, that is, it may demand compensation according to somewhat imprecise formulas, such as reasonable liquidated damages or a fixed sum plus double damages, without being deemed to have imposed a second punishment for the purpose of double jeopardy analysis." Nevertheless, the Court concluded that in a particular case one of these imprecise formulas can create a "clear injustice" by authorizing a supposedly remedial sanction that does not remotely approximate the government's damages and actual costs.

The Supreme Court in *Halper* reasoned that because of the "intrinsically personal" nature of the protection against double jeopardy, "[i]ts violation can be identified only by assessing the character of the actual sanctions imposed on the individual by the machinery of the state." The Court continued:

> In making this assessment, the labels "criminal" and "civil" are not of paramount importance. It is commonly understood that civil proceedings may advance punitive as well as remedial goals, and, conversely, that both punitive and remedial goals may be served by criminal penalties. The notion of punishment, as we commonly understand it, cuts across the division between the civil and the criminal law, and for the purposes of assessing whether a given sanction constitutes multiple punishment barred by the Double Jeopardy Clause, we must follow the notion where it leads. To that end, the determination whether a given civil sanction constitutes punishment in the relevant sense requires a particularized assessment of the penalty imposed and the purposes that the penalty may fairly be said to serve. Simply put, a civil as well as a criminal sanction constitutes punishment when the sanction as applied in the individual case serves the goals of punishment.

These goals are familiar. We have recognized in other contexts that punishment serves the twin aims of retribution and deterrence. Furthermore, "[r]etribution and deterrence are not legitimate nonpunitive governmental objectives." From these premises, it follows that a civil sanction that cannot fairly be said solely to serve a remedial purpose, but rather can be explained only as also serving either retributive or deterrent purposes, is punishment, as we have come to understand that term.

The Court emphasized, however, that cases in which a civil sanction constitutes "punishment" would not arise often. It stated:

What we announce now is a rule for the rare case ... where a fixed-penalty provision subjects a prolific but small-gauge offender to a sanction overwhelmingly disproportionate to the damages he has caused. The rule is one of reason: Where a defendant previously has sustained a criminal penalty and the civil penalty sought in the subsequent proceeding bears no rational relation to the goal of compensating the [g]overnment for its loss, but rather appears to qualify as "punishment" in the plain meaning of the word, then the defendant is entitled to an accounting of the [g]overnment's damages and costs to determine if the penalty sought in fact constitutes a second punishment. We must leave to the trial court the discretion to determine on the basis of such an accounting the size of the civil sanction the [g]overnment may receive without crossing the line between remedy and punishment.

Applying this standard to the facts in *Halper*, the Supreme Court concluded that the disparity between the civil penalty authorized by the statute, under which the defendant was subject to liability of $130,000 for false claims amounting to $585 made to the government, and the trial court's approximation of the government's expenses arising from the fraud, $16,000, was sufficiently disproportionate that the sanction constituted "punishment" for double jeopardy purposes. Imposition of such a sanction, held the Court, therefore would violate the Double Jeopardy Clause, because the defendant already had been convicted and punished in a criminal prosecution for the same conduct.

Several years after *Halper*, the United States Supreme Court, relying upon that case, recognized in *Department of Revenue of Montana v. Kurth Ranch* (1994) that a tax on the possession of illegal drugs can constitute "punishment" for purposes of double jeopardy analysis. After examining various features of the tax in question, including the high rate of taxation; its obvious deterrent purpose; its being conditional upon the commission of a crime; and the fact that it was levied on goods neither owned nor possessed by the taxpayer when the tax was imposed, the Supreme Court concluded that "[t]aken as a whole, this drug tax is a concoction of anomalies, too far removed in crucial respects from a standard tax assessment to escape characterization as punishment ...." The Court held that the Double Jeopardy Clause prohibited assessment of the tax upon one who, in a separate proceeding, already was convicted and punished for possession of the same drugs.

Two years after its decision in *Kurth Ranch*, however, the Supreme Court began retreating from its position in *Halper*. In *United States v. Ursery* (1996), the Court indicated that *Halper* did not have any application to sanctions other than monetary penalties. The Court in *Ursery* held that civil forfeitures of property or money, based upon its connection to criminal activity, do not constitute "punishment" for double jeopardy purposes. The Court stated that the rule of *Halper* was limited to the context of "civil penalties," in part, because of "the practical difficulty of applying *Halper* to a civil forfeiture." The Court reasoned:

> Civil penalties are designed as a rough form of "liquidated damages" for the harms suffered by the [g]overnment as a result of a defendant's conduct. The civil penalty involved in *Halper*, for example, provided for a fixed monetary penalty for each false claim count on which the defendant was convicted in the criminal proceeding. Whether a "fixed-penalty provision" that seeks to compensate the [g]overnment for harm that it has suffered is "so extreme" and "so divorced" from the penalty's nonpunitive purpose of compensating the [g]overnment as to be a punishment may be determined by balancing the [g]overnment's harm against the size of the penalty. Civil forfeitures, in contrast to civil penalties, are designed to do more than simply compensate the [g]overnment. Forfeitures serve a variety of purposes, but are designed primarily to confiscate property used in violation of the law, and to require disgorgement of the fruits of illegal conduct. Though it may be possible to quantify the value of the property forfeited, it is virtually impossible to quantify, even approximately, the nonpunitive purposes served by a particular civil forfeiture. Hence, it is practically difficult to determine whether a particular forfeiture bears no rational relationship to the nonpunitive purposes of that forfeiture. Quite simply, the case-by-case balancing test set forth in *Halper*, in which a court must compare the harm suffered by the [g]overnment against the size of the penalty imposed, is inapplicable to civil forfeiture.

The Supreme Court rejected Justice John Paul Stevens' view, expressed in a dissenting opinion, that *Halper* announced "a general rule, applicable to all civil sanctions, useful for determining whether a sanction is 'of punitive character.'" It said that the *Halper* Court's statement that a "civil sanction that cannot fairly be said solely to serve a remedial purpose, but rather can only be explained as also serving either retributive or deterrent purposes, is punishment," was a "dictum" and that the *Halper* Court did not intend to set forth a new rule for determining what constitutes "punishment" for purposes of the Double Jeopardy Clause.

The Court in *Ursery* then concluded that the traditional two-part test used in *United States v. One Assortment of 89 Firearms* (1984) provided a "useful analytical tool" to determine whether a civil forfeiture constitutes "punishment" for purposes of double jeopardy analysis. After examining the statutes in question, the Court found that "[t]here [was] little doubt that Congress intended [the] forfeitures [in question] to be civil proceedings." Moving to the second part of the two-part test, the Court concluded that "there is little evidence, much less the 'clearest proof,'" suggesting that the forfeiture statutes in question were so punitive in form and effect to render them criminal despite Congress' contrary intent.

Finally, one year after its decision in *Ursery*, the Supreme Court "in large part disavow[ed] the method of analysis used in *Halper* and reaffirm[ed] the previously established rule" for determining whether a sanction was criminal in nature and therefore constituted "punishment" for double jeopardy purposes (Hudson v. United States, 1997).

In *Hudson v. United States* (1997), the Office of the Comptroller of the Currency (OCC) administratively imposed monetary penalties ranging from $12,500 to $16,500 on three individuals who allegedly used their positions with two banks to arrange a series of loans to third parties, in violation of various federal banking statutes and regulations. In addition, the OCC barred the individuals from participating in the affairs of any banking institution without the written authorization of the OCC and all other relevant regulatory agencies. Nearly three years later, a grand jury indicted the individuals for conspiracy, misapplication of bank funds, and making false bank entries. All the charges in the indictment rested upon the same lending transactions that formed the basis for the prior administrative actions brought by the OCC. The individuals moved to dismiss the indictment on double jeopardy grounds. Relying upon *Halper*, they claimed that they had already been "punished" for the acts alleged in the indictment and that the Double Jeopardy Clause therefore barred criminal proceedings against them. The trial court granted the motions, holding that the monetary penalties imposed by the OCC—but not the occupational debarment—constituted "punishment" for double jeopardy purposes. The United States Supreme Court disagreed in part, and held that neither the monetary penalties nor the debarment sanctions constituted "punishment" under the Double Jeopardy Clause.

The Supreme Court began its analysis in *Hudson* by setting forth what it termed "traditional double jeopardy doctrine." First, it stated that the double jeopardy provision "protects only against the imposition of multiple *criminal* punishments for the same offense." It then explained:

> Whether a particular punishment is criminal or civil is, at least initially, a matter of statutory construction. A court must first ask whether the legislature, "in establishing the penalizing mechanism, indicated either expressly or impliedly a preference for one label or the other." Even in those cases where the legislature "has indicated an intention to establish a civil penalty, we have inquired further whether the statutory scheme was so punitive either in purpose or effect" as to transfor[m] what was clearly intended as a civil remedy into a criminal penalty."

The Court went on to say that in determining whether a sanction intended by the legislature to be a civil remedy was in fact a criminal penalty, the factors listed in *Kennedy v. Mendoza-Martinez* (1963) "provide useful guideposts":

> (1) "[w]hether the sanction involves an affirmative disability or restraint"; (2) "whether it has historically been regarded as a punishment"; (3) "whether it comes into play only on a finding of *scienter*"; (4) "whether its operation will promote the traditional aims of punishment–retribution and deterrence"; (5) "whether the behavior to which it applies is already a crime"; (6) "whether an alternative purpose to which it may rationally be connected is assignable for it"; (7) "whether it appears excessive in relation to the alternative purpose assigned."

The Court emphasized that "'these factors must be considered in relation to the statute on its face,' and 'only the clearest proof' will suffice to override legislative intent and transform what has been denominated a civil remedy into a criminal penalty."

Turning to *Halper*, the *Hudson* Court pointed out that the analysis applied by a unanimous Court in that case deviated from this traditional double jeopardy doctrine in two key respects: first, it bypassed the threshold question of whether the successive punishment at issue was a "criminal" punishment, focusing instead on "whether the sanction, regardless of whether it was civil or criminal, was so grossly disproportionate to the harm caused as to constitute 'punishment'"; and second, it assessed the character of the actual sanctions imposed, rather than "evaluating the 'statute on its face' to determine whether it provided for what amounted to a criminal sanction." The Court in *Hudson* concluded that "*Halper*'s deviation from longstanding double jeopardy principles was ill considered" and that "traditional double jeopardy principles," rather than the approach taken in *Halper*, should govern claims of multiple punishment for the same offense. *Hudson* thereby rendered *Halper* little more than a blip on the screen of double jeopardy analysis.

Since the United States Supreme Court's decision in *Hudson*, lower courts have held that various other monetary penalties (*e.g.*, United States v. Lippert, 1998; S.A. Healy Co. v. Occupational Safety and Health Review Comm'n, 1998; Grossfield v. Commodity Futures Trading Comm'n, 1998; SEC v. Palmisano, 1998; State v. Farricielli, 2002; State v. McKeeth, 2001; Commonwealth v. Lawson Mardon Flexible Packaging, Inc., 1999) and occupational debarments, including disbarment of an attorney (*In re* Chastain, 2000); a permanent ban on trading and revocation of an individual's trading license (*e.g.*, Vercillo v. Commodities Futures Trading Comm'n, 1998); revocation of an individual's insurance license (Burnett v. Commonwealth, 1999); suspension of an individual's optometry license (Consumer & Industry Services v. Greenberg, 1998); revocation of a general contractor's construction license (State v. Bowling, 1998); and revocation of an automobile dealer's salesperson's license and dealer's license (Nicoletti v. State Bd. of Vehicle Mfrs., Dealers & Salespersons, 1998), do not constitute "punishment" for purposes of double jeopardy analysis. Lower courts have reached the same conclusion about a variety of other nonmonetary sanctions, such as the revocation or suspension of an individual's driver's license (*e.g.*,

Rivera v. Pugh, 1999; Herbert v. Billy, 1998; State v. Isham, 2001; State v. Price, 1998); the disqualification from participation in the federal food stamp program (Traficanti v. United States, 2000); sanctions imposed upon an inmate in prison disciplinary proceedings (United States v. Mayes, 1998; State v. McKinney, 1998; State v. Thompson, 1999; Worthen v. State, 1998; Commonwealth v. McGee, 2000); suspension of a student from a public school (*In re* Phillips, 1998); registration requirements for certain sex offenders and/or community notification provisions dealing with registered sex offenders (Cutshall v. Sundquist, 1999; Lanni v. Engler, 1998; People v. Malchow, 2000; *see also* Smith v. Doe, 2002); ineligibility for benefits under government assistance programs (Turner v. Glickman, 2000); and the revocation of parole (Dantzler v. Travis, 1998) or bail (Wilcox v. State, 2001).

Enhancement of a Sentence Because of Previous Criminal Conduct

Following a defendant's conviction of a crime, the trial court conducts a sentencing hearing to determine the particular sentence to impose. At that sentencing hearing, the court considers, among other things, the nature of the crime committed by the defendant and the defendant's past criminal behavior. A sentencing court normally has discretion to consider a defendant's previous conviction in determining his sentence for the current offense. Indeed, in some jurisdictions, sentencing guidelines may *require* that the sentencing court take the previous conviction into account in calculating the defendant's offense level for the crime in question. In addition, statutes sometimes require a higher minimum sentence for a convicted defendant with a previous conviction for the same type of offense, such as a second-offense for driving under the influence of alcohol or drugs. Other statutes may require a mandatory minimum sentence for an individual with a certain number of previous convictions, such as a "three-strikes" law, under which a defendant convicted of a felony offense must be sentenced to a minimum of 25 years to life imprisonment if he previously was convicted of two serious felony offenses.

The Double Jeopardy Clause does not bar enhancement of a defendant's sentence on the basis of other criminal conduct for which he already has been convicted and punished (Gryger v. Burke, 1948). Such sentence enhancements have not been construed as additional punishment for the previous offense; "rather, they act to increase a sentence 'because of the manner in which [the defendant] committed the crime of conviction'" (Monge v. California, 1998). As the United States Supreme Court explained in *Monge v. California,* (1998), "[a]n enhanced sentence imposed on a persistent offender ... [is] 'a stiffened penalty for the latest crime, which is considered to be an aggravated offense because a repetitive one'" *see also* Moore v. Missouri, 1895).

For example, in *Williams v. Oklahoma* (1959), Edward Williams pleaded guilty in a Muskogee County court to a charge of committing murder in that county and was sentenced to life imprisonment. Shortly thereafter, Williams pleaded guilty in a Tulsa County court to a charge of kidnapping the murder victim in that county. In sentencing Williams to death for the kidnapping, the trial judge considered the fact that Williams had murdered the kidnapping victim. The United States Supreme Court rejected Williams' contention that in taking the murder into consideration in imposing sentence for kidnapping the sentencing court would punish him a second time for the same offense. The Supreme Court stated that upon Williams' plea of guilty to the charge of kidnapping,

> it became the duty of the trial judge to impose an appropriate sentence. The [kidnapping] statute made appropriate, and required the imposition of, a sentence within the range of imprisonment for a term of 10 years to the maximum of death, as determined by the sentencing judge in the exercise of his sound discretion. Necessarily, the exercise of a sound discretion in such a case required consideration of all the circumstances of the crime, for "[t]he belief no longer prevails that every offense in a like legal category calls for an identical punishment ...." In discharging his duty of imposing a proper sentence, the sentencing judge is authorized, if not required, to consider all of the mitigating and aggravating circumstances involved in the crime .... Certainly one of the aggravating circumstances involved in this kidnaping crime was the fact that [Williams] shot and killed the victim in the course of its commission. We cannot say that the sentencing judge was not entitled to consider that circumstance, along with all the other circumstances involved, in determining the proper sentence to be imposed for the kidnaping crime. And in view of the obvious fact that, under the law of Oklahoma, kidnaping is a separate crime, entirely distinct from the crime of murder, the court's consideration of the murder as a circumstance involved in the kidnaping crime cannot be said to have resulted in punishing [Williams] a second time for the same offense ....

Similarly, the double jeopardy provision does not bar a prosecution or punishment for criminal activity that previously was used to enhance the defendant's sentence for a separate offense. In such situations, the individual was punished in the first proceeding *only* for the offense for which he was convicted, regardless of whether the sentencing judge in the first proceeding took the conduct into account as an act of discretion, or whether the applicable sentencing guidelines required the sentencing judge to consider the conduct (Witte v. United States, 1995).

RESENTENCING

Resentencing by the Trial Judge in the Same Proceeding

Sometimes a trial judge imposes a sentence upon a convicted defendant, but shortly afterward learns of some error or deficiency in the sentence. The question arises whether the trial judge can at that point alter the original sentence without running afoul of the guarantee against double jeopardy.

The United States Supreme Court has dealt with this issue on several occasions. In *Ex parte Lange* (1874), a jury convicted Edward Lange of appropriating to his own use certain mailbags belonging to the Post Office Department. The applicable statute provided that the punishment for that offense was imprisonment for up to one year *or* a fine not to exceed $200; however, the trial judge, apparently through inadvertence, sentenced Lange to one year's imprisonment *and* a fine of $200. Lange immediately began serving his jail sentence. On the following day, he paid the $200 fine to the clerk of the court, who deposited the money into the Treasury of the United States where it was beyond the control of the court. Five days after he began serving his term of imprisonment, Lange petitioned the trial court for his immediate release. He contended that the applicable statute did not authorize the imposition of both a fine and a prison sentence. The trial judge, realizing his error, vacated the original sentence and imposed a new sentence of imprisonment for one year from that date.

The Supreme Court held that the new sentence violated the Double Jeopardy Clause because it imposed multiple punishments upon Lange for the same offense. The Court explained that if the second sentence were allowed to stand, Lange would end up paying a $200 fine and serving one year and five days' imprisonment, a greater sentence than authorized by statute. The Court concluded:

> We are of opinion that when the prisoner, as in this case, by reason of a valid judgment, had fully suffered one of the alternative punishments to which alone the law subjected him, the power of the court to punish further was gone. [The Double Jeopardy Clause] then interposed its shield, and forbid that he should be punished again for that offence. The record of the court's proceedings, at the moment the second sentence was rendered, showed that in that very case, and for that very offence, the prisoner had fully performed, completed, and endured one of the alternative punishments which the law prescribed for that offence, and had suffered five days' imprisonment on account of the other. It thus showed the court that its power to punish for that offence was at an end. [T]he authority of the court to punish the prisoner was gone. The power was exhausted; its further exercise was prohibited.

Because Lange, by paying the $200 fine, had fully satisfied one of the two alternative punishments authorized by the applicable statute, the Court held he was entitled to his release.

Similarly, in *In re Bradley* (1943), the trial judge sentenced the defendant to six months' imprisonment *and* a fine of $500 under a statute authorizing only a fine *or* imprisonment. Several days later, and after the defendant had paid the fine to the clerk of the court, the trial judge realized his error and amended the original sentence by eliminating the fine. Although the clerk attempted to return the fine, the defendant refused to receive it. Relying upon *Lange*, the United States Supreme Court held the amended sentence invalid and ordered the defendant's release. The Supreme Court reasoned that when the defendant paid the fine to the clerk, he fully satisfied one of the alternative penalties authorized by law and "the power of the court was at an end." The Court found it "unimportant" that at the time the judge amended the sentence, the clerk had not yet paid the fine to the treasury, because the clerk was the officer of the United States authorized to receive the fine.

In *Bozza v. United States* (1947), however, the United States Supreme Court held that the double jeopardy provision did not bar a trial judge from increasing the initial sentence he imposed on the defendant when that initial sentence failed to meet the mandatory minimum required by the applicable statute. In that case, the trial judge imposed a term of imprisonment upon an individual convicted of operating a distilling business with the intent to defraud the United States of taxes. The individual was then taken to the local federal detention center to await transportation to the penitentiary. Shortly thereafter, the judge learned that the applicable statute mandated a minimum sentence of a $100 fine in addition to a term of imprisonment. About five hours after announcing the original sentence, the judge recalled the defendant and imposed a fine of $100. The Supreme Court concluded that the judge did not err in doing so. The Court stated:

> It is well established that a sentence which does not comply with the letter of the criminal statute which authorizes it is so erroneous that it may be set aside on appeal .... But ... an excessive sentence should be corrected, even though the prisoner ha[s] already served part of his term, not by absolute discharge of the prisoner, but by an appropriate amendment of the invalid sentence by the court of original jurisdiction .... [T]he fact that [the defendant] has been twice before the judge for sentencing and in a federal place of detention during the five-hour interim cannot be said to constitute double jeopardy .... If this inadvertent error cannot be corrected in the manner used here by the trial court, no valid and enforceable sentence can be imposed at all. This Court has rejected the "doctrine that a prisoner, whose guilt is established by a regular verdict, is to escape punishment altogether, because the court committed an error in passing the sentence." The Constitution does not require that sentencing should be a game in which a wrong move by the judge means immunity for the prisoner. In this case the court "only set aside what it had no authority to do and substitute[d] directions required by the law to be done upon the conviction of the offender." It did not twice put [the defendant] in jeopardy for the same offense. The sentence, as corrected, imposes a valid punishment for an offense instead of an invalid punishment for that offense.

The Court distinguished *Lange* on the ground that at the time the trial judge in that case corrected the initial sentence, Lange had already fully satisfied one of the alternative penalties authorized by the applicable statute, whereas Bozza "had not suffered any lawful punishment until the court had announced the full mandatory sentence of imprisonment *and* fine."

Finally, in *Jones v. Thomas* (1989), the United States Supreme Court clarified the basis for its holding in *Lange*. In *Jones*, a jury convicted Larry Thomas of both attempted robbery and felony-murder (an unintentional killing during the commission of a felony) for shooting and killing a customer while attempting to rob an auto parts store. The trial judge sentenced Thomas to consecutive terms of 15 years' imprisonment for the attempted robbery and life imprisonment for the felony murder, with the 15-year sentence to run first. Following the commutation by the governor (and thus Thomas' completion) of the 15-year sentence, Thomas succeeded in having the attempted robbery conviction and sentence vacated on the ground that the trial court improperly imposed separate sentences for attempted robbery and felony-murder. He then sought his immediate release, arguing that because he had completed the sentence for attempted robbery through the governor's commutation of his sentence, *Lange* and *Bradley* precluded his further punishment.

The Supreme Court rejected Thomas' argument. The Court held that the Double Jeopardy Clause's protection against multiple punishments in a single proceeding "'does no more than prevent the sentencing court from prescribing a greater punishment than the legislature intended,'" and that Thomas' double jeopardy rights were fully vindicated when the trial court vacated the attempted robbery conviction and sentence and credited the time he had served under that conviction against the remaining sentence for felony-murder. His continued confinement at that point did not constitute double jeopardy, reasoned the Court, because he stood convicted only of felony-murder and was being confined under a single sentence for that crime.

The Court acknowledged that *Lange* and *Bradley* contain language "to the effect that once a defendant 'had fully suffered one of the alternative punishments to which alone the law subjected him, the power of the court to punish further was gone,'" but concluded that application of that language to the facts presented in *Jones* was "neither compelled by precedent nor supported by any double jeopardy principle." It stated that if the second sentence imposed in *Lange* had been enforced, Lange would have both paid a fine and served a prison term, a punishment that would have exceeded that authorized by the legislature. *Lange*, it said, merely stands for the proposition that the double jeopardy provision prohibits punishment in excess of that authorized by the legislature and "not for the broader rule suggested by its dictum."

The Court acknowledged that *Bradley* provided a "closer analogy," strict application of which would support Thomas' argument, because "satisfaction of one of two alternatives that could lawfully be imposed (*e.g.*, the fine in *Bradley* and the commuted sentence here) is dispositive, and any attempt to correct the erroneous sentence by repaying the fine or crediting time served would be futile." Nevertheless, the Court found "important differences" between *Jones* and *Bradley*. First, *Bradley* involved alternative punishments that were prescribed by the legislature for a single criminal act, whereas *Jones* involved "separate sentences imposed for what the sentencing court thought to be separately punishable offenses, one far more serious that the other." The Court reasoned that "[i]n a true alternative sentences case such as *Bradley*, it would be difficult to say that one punishment or the other was intended by the legislature, for the legislature viewed each alternative as appropriate for some cases," but that in cases such as *Jones* the legislature plainly intended one of two results for individuals who commit murder in the course of a felony: either they are to be convicted of felony-murder, or they are to be convicted separately of the felony and of nonfelony murder. "It could not be suggested seriously," said the Court, "that the legislature intended an attempted robbery conviction to suffice as an alternative sanction for murder." Second, *Bradley* involved alternative sentences of a different type—a fine and imprisonment. Although a fine cannot be "credited" against time in prison, reasoned the Court, "crediting time served under one sentence against the term of another has long been an accepted practice."

The Court in *Jones* recognized that, in addition to protecting against punishment in excess of legislative intent, the Double Jeopardy Clause protects "against additions to a sentence in a subsequent proceeding that upset a defendant's legitimate expectation of finality," such as when a trial judge imposes a sentence of fifteen years' imprisonment under a statute authorizing a sentence of from fifteen years to life and, upon having second thoughts after the defendant serves that sentence, imposes an additional ten years in prison. Nonetheless, the Court found that Thomas "plainly had no expectation of serving only an attempted robbery sentence when he was convicted" and sentenced initially. Indeed, at that time his expectation was to serve consecutive sentences for the two offenses.

The Court in *Jones* also reasoned that extension of *Bradley* would "lead to anomalous results," depending upon the order in which the trial court imposed the consecutive sentences. If the defendant had been sentenced to the life term first, he could not raise a double jeopardy claim, although he would be serving the very same term.

Resentencing Following Reconviction for the Same Offense

As discussed previously in this Analysis, a convicted defendant who succeeds in having his conviction overturned because of trial error can be tried a second time for the same offense. If he is convicted in his retrial, the Double Jeopardy Clause imposes no restrictions upon the severity of the sentence the appropriate sentencing authority can impose (North Carolina v. Pearce, 1969; Chaffin v. Stynchcombe, 1973). The United States Supreme Court explained in *North Carolina v. Pearce* (1969): "[A] corollary of the power to retry a defendant [following the setting aside of his conviction on the basis of trial error] is the power, upon the defendant's reconviction, to impose whatever sentence may be legally authorized, whether or not it is greater than the sentence imposed after the first conviction," because "so far as the [original] conviction itself goes, and that part of the sentence that has not yet been served, ... the slate has been wiped clean" (italics omitted) at the defendant's behest.

For example, in *Stroud v. United States* (1919), a jury convicted Robert Stroud, popularly known as the "Birdman of Alcatraz," of murder in the first degree and sentenced him to life imprisonment. The appellate court reversed the conviction and granted him a new trial. At his retrial, the jury again convicted him of first-degree murder. This time, however, the jury did not make a recommendation dispensing with capital punishment, and the trial judge imposed a sentence of death. The United States Supreme Court unanimously upheld the harsher sentence imposed upon retrial, rejecting Stroud's claim that it violated the guarantee against double jeopardy.

Nearly half the States have established a two-tier system of trial courts for certain minor criminal offenses. An individual charged with such an offense is tried in the first instance in the lower tier. If convicted, he may not seek ordinary appellate review of his conviction. Instead, he has an absolute right to "appeal" to a superior court, where he is entitled to a trial *de novo* (a new trial on both questions of fact and issues of law) by a jury. An individual need not allege error in the inferior court trial to be entitled to a trial *de novo*. In the trial *de novo*, the case is regarded exactly as if it originally had been brought in the superior court. For purposes of double jeopardy analysis, an individual convicted in a first-tier court who elects to be tried *de novo* in the second tier occupies the same position as a convicted defendant in a single-tier system who obtains a new trial after successfully appealing his conviction to an appellate court on the basis of trial error. Accordingly, if the defendant is again convicted following the trial *de novo*, the double jeopardy provision does not preclude the trial judge from imposing a harsher sentence than the defendant received following his initial conviction in the first-tier court (Colten v. Kentucky, 1972).

Whenever a defendant is validly convicted a second time for the same offense, the Double Jeopardy Clause's protection against multiple punishments requires that he receive full credit for time already served for the first conviction (North Carolina v. Pearce, 1969; *accord* Ohio v. Johnson, 1984). Such credit must include any credits he earned for good behavior or otherwise while serving the first prison sentence (North Carolina v. Pearce, 1969). By like reasoning, any new monetary fine imposed upon reconviction must be decreased by the amount previously paid by the defendant following his first conviction (North Carolina v. Pearce, 1969).

The general rule that the Double Jeopardy Clause does not prohibit a harsher sentence following reconviction does not apply, however, to capital sentencing proceedings in which the sentencing authority makes the sentencing decision in a separate proceeding that resembles a trial on the issue of guilt or innocence and in which the government has the burden of proving certain elements beyond a reasonable doubt before the death penalty can be imposed (Bullington v. Missouri, 1981; *accord* Arizona v. Rumsey, 1984).

In *Bullington v. Missouri* (1981), a jury convicted Robert Bullington of capital murder. Pursuant to the applicable statute, the trial court then held a separate presentence hearing at which the same jury considered which of two possible sentences to impose: death or life imprisonment without eligibility for probation or parole for fifty years. At that hearing, the government attempted to establish beyond a reasonable doubt that certain aggravating circumstances listed in the capital murder statute existed and that those aggravating circumstances outweighed any mitigating circumstances and warranted imposition of the death penalty. After considering the evidence, the jury fixed Bullington's punishment at life imprisonment without eligibility for probation or parole for fifty years. The trial court subsequently granted Bullington's posttrial motion for a new trial and set aside the conviction and sentence because of a constitutional defect in the jury-selection process. Prior to Bullington's retrial, the government filed a formal notice stating that it intended again to seek the death penalty. The United States Supreme Court held, however, that the Double Jeopardy Clause barred the imposition of the death penalty at the second trial.

The Supreme Court in *Bullington* reasoned that the Missouri capital sentencing proceeding was "itself a trial on the issue of punishment" at which the government "undertook the burden of establishing certain facts beyond a reasonable doubt in its quest to obtain the harsher of two alternative verdicts" and the jury, applying detailed substantive standards concerning aggravating and mitigating circumstances articulated in the capital murder statute, had to choose between two alternatives. The sentence of life imprisonment imposed upon the defendant at his first trial therefore meant that the jury concluded that the government had not "proved its case" and had "acquitted" the defendant of whatever was necessary to impose the death penalty. The Court distinguished *Stroud* on the two grounds. First, *Stroud* did not involve a separate sentencing proceeding at which the government was required to prove additional facts in order to justify the particular sentence. Second, the statute involved in *Stroud* did not contain standards to guide the jury's discretion concerning the sentence to impose.

The *Bullington* Court also concluded that the underlying policy reasons for affording absolute finality to a verdict of acquittal on the issue of guilt or innocence apply equally to an "acquittal" at the penalty phase of a Missouri capital murder trial. It stated:

> The "embarrassment, expense and ordeal" and the "anxiety and insecurity" faced by a defendant at the penalty phase of a Missouri capital murder trial surely are at least equivalent to that faced by any defendant at the guilt phase of a criminal trial. The "unacceptably high risk that the [prosecution], with its superior resources, would wear down a defendant," thereby leading to an erroneously imposed death sentence, would exist if the State were to have a further opportunity to convince a jury to impose the ultimate punishment.

In *Arizona v. Rumsey* (1984), the United States Supreme Court reached the same result as in *Bullington* with respect to a capital sentencing proceeding in which the trial judge, rather than a jury, made the sentencing decision. In finding *Bullington* controlling, the Court made it clear that the Double Jeopardy Clause prohibits the sentencer from imposing the death penalty at a defendant's retrial, even though the original sentencer relied upon an error of law in "acquitting" the accused of the death penalty and imposing the lesser sentence, as in *Rumsey*, where the trial judge found the nonexistence of a particular aggravating circumstance because of his misinterpretation of the scope of that circumstance.

On the other hand, the mere failure of the sentencer to find a particular aggravating circumstance alleged by the government does not constitute an "acquittal" of that circumstance for purposes of the double jeopardy guarantee. The *Bullington* principle therefore does not apply in cases in which, on appeal from a death sentence, the reviewing court finds that the evidence of aggravating circumstances the sentencer relied upon was insufficient to support the death penalty, but finds in the record of the sentencing hearing other evidence supporting the death penalty that the first sentencer erroneously rejected. In such situations, neither the sentencer nor the reviewing court concluded that the prosecution failed to prove its case that the death penalty is appropriate and therefore did not "acquit" the defendant (Poland v. Arizona, 1986).

In *Poland v. Arizona* (1986), at the conclusion of the defendants' capital sentencing hearing for first-degree murder, the trial judge found that one of the alleged aggravating circumstances—that the defendants committed the offense as consideration for pecuniary gain–was not present, but that the second alleged aggravating circumstance—that the defendants committed the offense in an "especially heinous, cruel, or depraved manner"—existed. On appeal, the Supreme Court of Arizona reversed the defendants' convictions and ordered a new trial because in the course of its deliberations the jury discussed evidence not admitted at trial. That court also found that the evidence at the capital sentencing hearing was insufficient to support a finding of the "especially heinous, cruel, or depraved" aggravating circumstance. It did, however, find that the trial court erred in not finding the existence of the "pecuniary gain" aggravating circumstance because that circumstance was not limited to situations involving contract killings—as the trial judge supposed—and held that if the defendants were convicted upon retrial, the trial judge could find the existence of that aggravating circumstance. At their retrial, the defendants were again convicted of first-degree murder and sentenced to death.

The United States Supreme Court held that the Double Jeopardy Clause did not bar the second capital sentencing proceeding. The Supreme Court concluded that "[a]t no point during [the defendants'] first capital sentencing hearing and appeal did either the sentencer or the reviewing court hold that the prosecution had 'failed to prove its case' that [the defendants] deserved the death penalty." The Court noted that the trial judge actually imposed the death sentence and that the Arizona Supreme Court clearly indicated that the government had proved the "pecuniary gain" aggravating circumstance. The Court rejected the defendants' argument that the Arizona Supreme Court "acquitted" them of the death penalty by finding the evidence insufficient to support the only aggravating circumstance found by the sentencing judge. Examining the policies underlying the double jeopardy protection, the Court concluded that the "concern with protecting the finality of acquittals is not implicated when ... a defendant is sentenced to death, *i.e.*, 'convicted.'" It explained:

> There is no cause to shield such a defendant from further litigation; further litigation is the only hope he has. The defendant may argue on appeal that the evidence presented at his sentencing hearing was as a matter of law insufficient to support the aggravating circumstances on which his death sentence was based, but the Double Jeopardy Clause does not

require the reviewing court, if it sustains that claim, to ignore evidence in the record supporting another aggravating circumstance which the sentencer has erroneously rejected. Such a rule would have the odd and unacceptable result of requiring a reviewing court to enter a death penalty "acquittal" even though that court is of the view that the [government] has "proved its case."

The failure of the jury in a capital sentencing proceeding to reach a decision on the issue of the death penalty also does not constitute an "acquittal" for purposes of the double jeopardy guarantee, even though the trial judge imposed a sentence of life imprisonment as required by the applicable statute when the jury does not reach a verdict on the death penalty (Sattazahn v. Pennsylvania, 2003). The United States Supreme Court explained in *Sattazahn v. Pennsylvania* (2003) that a deadlocked jury's inability to reach a decision "cannot fairly be called an acquittal 'based on findings sufficient to establish legal entitlement to the life sentence'" and that the entry of a life sentence by the trial judge, as mandated by the applicable statute when he finds the jury deadlocked, cannot be deemed an "acquittal" because "'[t]he judge makes no findings and resolves no factual matter.'" The Supreme Court also concluded that in such circumstances the prospect of a second capital-sentencing proceeding does not implicate any of "the 'perils against which the Double Jeopardy Clause seeks to protect.'" The Court explained:

> The dissent stresses that a defendant in such circumstances is "subject to the 'ordeal' of a second full-blown life or death trial," which "'compel[s] [him] to live in a continuing state of anxiety and insecurity.'" But ... we have not found this concern determinative of double jeopardy in all circumstances. And it should not be so here. This case hardly presents the specter of "an all-powerful state relentlessly pursuing a defendant who had either been found not guilty or who had at least insisted on having the issue of guilt submitted to the first trier of fact." Instead, we see here a state which, for any number of perfectly understandable reasons, has quite reasonably agreed to accept the default penalty of life imprisonment when the conviction is affirmed and the case is, except for that issue, at an end—but to pursue its not-yet-vindicated interest in "'one complete opportunity to convict those who have violated it laws'" where the case must be retried anyway.

Thus, the Supreme Court in *Sattazahn* held that the double jeopardy provision did not preclude the imposition of the death penalty upon a defendant who was convicted on retrial after successfully appealing his initial conviction for first-degree murder for which he had been sentenced to life imprisonment when the jury was unable to reach a unanimous verdict on the death penalty in his capital sentencing proceeding.

Finally, the *Bullington* rationale applies only to "the unique circumstances of capital sentencing" and does not extend to noncapital sentencing proceedings, such as repeat offender enhancement proceedings (Monge v. California, 1998). The United States Supreme Court held in *Monge v. California* (1998) that a defendant who received an enhanced sentence because of his prior conviction for a "serious felony" could be retried on the prior conviction allegations after the appellate court concluded that the government failed to introduce sufficient evidence to support those allegations at his initial repeat-offender sentencing proceeding. The Supreme Court rejected the defendant's argument that the rationale for imposing a double jeopardy bar in *Bullington* applies with equal force to proceedings to determine the truth of a prior conviction allegation because it has the "hallmarks of a trial on guilt or innocence." The Court stated:

> Even assuming ... that the proceedings on the prior conviction allegation has the "hallmarks" of a trial that we identified in *Bullington*, a critical component of our reasoning in that case was the capital sentencing context. The penalty phase of a capital trial is undertaken to assess the gravity of a particular offense and to determine whether it warrants the ultimate punishment; it is in many respects a continuation of the trial on guilt or innocence of capital murder. "It is of vital importance" that the decisions made in that context "be, and appear to be, based on reason rather than caprice or emotion." Because the death penalty is unique "in both its severity and its finality," we have recognized an acute need for reliability in capital sentencing proceedings.
>
> That need for reliability accords with one of the central concerns animating the constitutional prohibition against double jeopardy. [T]he Double Jeopardy Clause prevents states from "mak[ing] repeated attempts to convict an individual for an alleged offense, thereby subjecting him to embarrassment, expense and ordeal and compelling him to live in a continuing state of anxiety and insecurity, as well as enhancing the possibility that even though innocent he may be found guilty." Indeed, we cited the heightened interest in accuracy in the *Bullington* decision itself. We noted that in a capital sentencing proceeding, as in a criminal trial, "'the interests of the defendant [are] of such magnitude that ... they have been protected by standards of proof designed to exclude as nearly as possible the likelihood of an erroneous judgment.'"
>
> ... The holding of *Bullington* turns on *both* the trial-like proceedings at issue and the severity of the penalty at stake ....
>
> ... Where noncapital sentencing proceedings contain trial-like protections, that is a matter of legislative grace, not constitutional command. Many [s]tates have chosen to implement procedural safeguards to protect defendants who may face dramatic increases in their sentences as a result of recidivism enhancements. We do not believe that because the states have done so, we are compelled to extend the double jeopardy bar. Indeed, were we to apply double jeopardy here, we might create disincentives that would diminish these important procedural protections.

Resentencing Following an Appeal of the Initial Sentence

Statutes in many jurisdictions authorize the government to seek appellate review of a convicted defendant's sentence and allow the appellate court either to increase the sentence or remand the case to the trial court so it can impose a more severe sentence. As discussed later in this Analysis, the Double Jeopardy Clause does not absolutely prohibit the government from appealing a sentence because a criminal sentence, once pronounced, is not accorded the same constitutional finality and conclusiveness as a judgment of acquittal (United States v. DiFrancesco, 1980). Moreover, the increase of a sentence on appeal pursuant to the applicable statute does not run afoul of the multiple punishment component of the double jeopardy provision for, as discussed earlier in this Analysis, that protection merely guarantees a defendant that he will not receive a greater sentence than authorized by the legislature. Accordingly, if the government exercises a statutory right of appeal and succeeds in convincing the appellate court that the sentence imposed by the trial court was too lenient, the double jeopardy provision does not preclude either the appellate court or the trial court, upon remand, from imposing a harsher sentence than that originally imposed (United States v. DiFrancesco, 1980; *see also* North Carolina v. Pearce, 1969). It does, however, require that the defendant receive full credit for time already served under the original sentence (North Carolina v. Pearce, 1969; *accord* Ohio v. Johnson, 1984).

APPEALS

By the Accused

The United States Constitution does not guarantee a criminal defendant the right to an appeal (Abney v. United States, 1977; McKane v. Durston, 1894). The right of appeal is "purely a creature of statute," and a defendant in a criminal case can exercise a statutory right of appeal only if he comes within the terms of the applicable statute (Abney v. United States, 1977). As a general matter, federal and state statutes allow a defendant to appeal only a final judgment. This rule of finality is designed to avoid "'the delays and disruptions attendant upon intermediate appeal'" and their consequent inimical effects on the "'effective and fair administration of the criminal law'" (Abney v. United States, 1977). Under a rule against interlocutory or "piecemeal" appeals, an accused ordinarily cannot immediately appeal adverse rulings of the trial court, such as the denial of a motion to exclude evidence alleged to have been obtained through illegal means; rather, he must await the end of his trial and, if convicted, can appeal at that time.

In *Abney v. United States* (1977), the United States Supreme Court considered whether a pretrial order denying a motion to dismiss an indictment on double jeopardy grounds was a "final decision" within the meaning of the applicable federal statute and thus immediately appealable. Although such a pretrial order does not terminate the criminal proceedings in the trial court and therefore "lacks the finality traditionally considered indispensable to appellate review," the Supreme Court concluded that it nonetheless fits within a narrow exception to the final-judgment rule and can be appealed immediately. The Court first noted that "such orders constitute a complete, formal, and, in the trial court, final rejection of a criminal defendant's double jeopardy claim." It then found that a double jeopardy claim, by its very nature, is "collateral to, and separable from the principal issue at the accused's impending criminal trial," *i.e.*, whether the accused is guilty of the offense charged. The Court observed that in arguing that the Double Jeopardy Clause bars his prosecution, the defendant "makes no challenge whatsoever to the merits of the charge against him;" but instead "is contesting the very authority of the [g]overnment to hale him into court to face trial on the charge against him." Finally, the Court reasoned, "the rights conferred on a criminal accused by the Double Jeopardy Clause would be significantly undermined if appellate review of double jeopardy claims were postponed until after conviction and sentence." The Court recognized that the Double Jeopardy Clause's protection against a second conviction for the same offense could be fully vindicated on an appeal following a final judgment, but pointed out that the Clause protects an individual against more than being subjected to double punishments: "It is a guarantee against being twice put to *trial* for the same offense" and focuses upon "the risk that an accused for a second time will be convicted of the 'same offense' for which he was initially tried." The Court continued:

> Because of this focus on the "risk" of conviction, the guarantee against double jeopardy assures an individual that, among other things, he will not be forced, with certain exceptions, to endure the personal strain, public embarrassment, and expense of a criminal trial more than once for the same offense. It thus protects interests wholly unrelated to the propriety of any subsequent conviction.... Obviously, these aspects of the guarantee's protections would be lost if the accused were forced to "run the gauntlet" a second time before an appeal could be taken; even if the accused is acquitted, or, if convicted, has his conviction ultimately reversed on double jeopardy grounds, he has still been forced to endure a trial that the Double Jeopardy Clause was designed to prohibit. Consequently, if a criminal defendant is to avoid *exposure* to double jeopardy and thereby enjoy the full protection of the Clause, his double jeopardy challenge to the indictment must be reviewable before that subsequent exposure occurs.

In later cases, the Supreme Court refined its holding in *Abney*, explaining that a double jeopardy claim must be at least "colorable" for it to be appealable prior to trial (Richardson v. United States, 1984; United States v. MacDonald, 1978), that is, there must be "some possible validity to [the] claim" (Richardson v. United States, 1984).

The Supreme Court based its decision in *Abney* on its interpretation of the federal statute governing appeals. The Court did not hold that the Double Jeopardy Clause *requires* the States to provide a mechanism for an interlocutory appeal from a trial court's pretrial order denying a defendant's motion to dismiss the charge against him on double jeopardy grounds (People *ex rel.* Mosley v. Carey, 1979; State v. Hubbard, 1999). Nevertheless, most state courts have construed their own statutes and procedures governing appeals to allow immediate appellate review of such an order (*e.g.*, *Ex parte* Ziglar, 1995; Smith v. State, 1992; State v. Baranco, 1994; State v. Milenkovich, 1990; Stephens v. State, 1990).

By the Government

The Double Jeopardy Clause does not absolutely bar an appeal by the government in a criminal case (United States v. DiFrancesco, 1980). So long as the appeal presents neither a threat of successive prosecutions (United States v. Martin Linen Supply Co., 1977; *accord* United States v. DiFrancesco, 1980) nor a threat of multiple punishments (United States v. DiFrancesco, 1980), the government can seek appellate review of a trial court's judgment without running afoul of the double jeopardy provision. Like a criminal defendant, though, the government has the right to appeal an adverse ruling in a criminal case *only* when specifically authorized by statute to do so (United States v. Sanges, 1892; *accord* Arizona v. Manypenny, 1981; United States v. Martin Linen Supply Co., 1977; United States v. Wilson, 1975). In the absence of such statutory authorization, the government cannot appeal, even though such an appeal would not violate the double jeopardy guarantee (United States v. Sanges, 1892).

Appeal Before the Attachment of Jeopardy

The Double Jeopardy Clause does not prohibit the government from appealing a trial judge's order dismissing an indictment or information against an accused before jeopardy "attached" (Serfass v. United States, 1975). For, so long as jeopardy had not "attached," the accused did not face the risk of being convicted, and any subsequent trial of him for the offense in question would not violate the double jeopardy provision's protection against successive prosecutions. As the United States Supreme Court explained in *Serfass v. United States* (1975), when a trial judge terminates a criminal prosecution prior to trial, the defendant may be "spared much of the expense, delay, strain, and embarrassment" that attend a trial and an appeal of the dismissal would not allow the government to seek to persuade a second fact finder of the defendant's guilt after having failed to convince the first. Moreover, an action taken by a trial court—even if characterized by it as an "acquittal"—cannot bar a subsequent prosecution unless jeopardy has attached and the accused has faced the risk of conviction, because a "fundamental principle" of double jeopardy jurisprudence provides that "an accused must suffer jeopardy before he can suffer double jeopardy."

Sometimes the dismissal of an indictment or information occurs after the declaration of a mistrial in the defendant's first trial, but before the commencement of a constitutionally-permissible retrial. In such circumstances, the dismissal constitutes a pretrial order and the Double Jeopardy Clause does not prohibit the government from appealing that dismissal (United States v. Sanford, 1976).

Appeal After the Attachment of Jeopardy

The Double Jeopardy Clause generally affords absolute finality to an acquittal and prohibits the government from retrying a defendant following his acquittal, even if "the acquittal was based upon an egregiously erroneous foundation" (Fong Foo v. United States, 1962). Consequently, the double jeopardy guarantee ordinarily bars the government from appealing a judgment of acquittal (United States v. Wilson, 1975), whether entered upon a jury's verdict of not guilty (United States v. Ball, 1896); a finding of not guilty by a trial judge in a bench trial (Smalis v. Pennsylvania, 1986; Kepner v. United States, 1904); or a directed verdict of not guilty (*i.e.*, when the trial judge in a jury trial directs the jury to return a verdict of acquittal) (Fong Foo v. United States, 1962) or its functional equivalent, such as a judgment of acquittal entered by the trial judge in a jury trial (Sanabria v. United States, 1978; United States v. Martin Linen Supply Co., 1977). Allowing the government to appeal a judgment of acquittal "would allow the prosecutor to seek to persuade a second trier of fact of the defendant's guilt after having failed with the first; it would permit him to re-examine the weaknesses in his first presentation in order to strengthen the second; and it would disserve the defendant's legitimate interest in the finality of a verdict of acquittal" (United States v. Wilson, 1975).

Nevertheless, as discussed earlier in this Analysis, an exception to the general rule that an acquittal is final *may* exist when the defendant obtained the acquittal through fraud or collusion, such as bribery, blackmail, or intimidation of the fact finder. *If* such an exception exists, the government should be allowed to appeal an acquittal on the ground that it was fraudulently-obtained.[31] For, if the government wins its appeal, the Double Jeopardy Clause would not bar a second trial.

When a jury returns a verdict of guilty, but the trial judge disagrees with the jury's assessment of the evidence and enters a judgment of acquittal, the double jeopardy provision does not bar the government from appealing the judge's ruling (United States v. Mundt, 1988; White v. Wainwright, 1987; State v. Smith, 2002; Commonwealth v. Rawles, 1983; State v. Savage, 1996), because, if the government succeeds in overturning that ruling, a retrial would not be necessary. The appellate court could merely reinstate the jury's original verdict of guilty (*see* United States v. Wilson, 1975; United States v. Jenkins, 1975).

For essentially the same reason, the Double Jeopardy Clause does not bar the government from appealing to a higher court an intermediate appellate court's decision reversing a defendant's conviction on the ground that the evidence relied upon by the fact finder at trial was legally insufficient to prove the defendant's guilt beyond a reasonable doubt (Young v. Kemp, 1985; State v. Keehner, 1988; State v. Bowden, 1980). In such circumstances, if the higher court concludes that the intermediate appellate court erred in finding the evidence insufficient, it can merely reinstate the trial court's original judgment of conviction.

The Double Jeopardy Clause generally accords finality to a judgment of conviction and prohibits the government from prosecuting the convicted individual a second time for the same offense (United States v. Dixon, 1993; Harris v. Oklahoma, 1977; Brown v. Ohio, 1977; *In re* Nielsen, 1889), whether that conviction is based upon a verdict of guilty returned by a jury (Harris v. Oklahoma, 1977); a finding of guilty rendered by a judge in a bench trial (United States v. Dixon, 1993); or a plea of guilty or *nolo contendere* entered by the accused (Brown v. Ohio, 1977; *In re* Nielsen, 1889). Accordingly, the double jeopardy provision precludes the government from appealing a judgment of conviction in an attempt to obtain its reversal and the opportunity to retry the accused in the hope that it can obtain a conviction in a new trial and that the new sentencing authority will impose a greater sentence than the first (United States v. Martin Linen Supply Co., 1977).

Sometimes a criminal trial ends without a final judgment of acquittal or conviction. When faced with a procedural error, serious misconduct, or some other event making it impossible or impracticable to complete the trial, such as a "deadlocked" jury, the trial judge might declare a mistrial and terminate the trial without a determination of the defendant's factual guilt or innocence. Other cases may involve an error or defect thought by the trial judge completely to preclude the conviction of the accused on the offense charged. In such cases, the judge may enter an order dismissing the charge and terminating the trial in favor of the defendant.

The Double Jeopardy Clause bars retrial of a defendant following the declaration of a mistrial in two situations. First, when the defendant did not consent to the mistrial and a "manifest necessity" for the mistrial did not exist (United States v. Jorn, 1971 (plurality opinion); Downum v. United States, 1963), and second, when the defendant requested the mistrial in response to conduct by the prosecuting attorney intended to "goad" him into seeking the mistrial (Oregon v. Kennedy, 1982). If a trial court concludes that the double jeopardy provision bars retrial of an accused for either of these reasons, the Double Jeopardy does not bar the government from appealing that decision (United States v. Jorn, 1971 (plurality opinion and Stewart, J., dissenting)); for, if the appellate court disagrees with the trial judge, a second trial would be constitutionally permissible.

Similarly, when a trial judge dismisses an indictment or information at the request of the accused and terminates the trial on a ground unrelated to guilt or innocence, the double jeopardy guarantee does not bar the government from seeking appellate review of that decision because, if the government succeeds in its appeal, a second trial would not be barred the double jeopardy provision (United States v. Scott, 1978). On the other hand, if a trial judge dismisses a charge without the consent of the accused, the government can retry the accused only if the trial judge, in the exercise of his sound discretion, terminated the first trial because of a "manifest necessity" (*see* Lee v. United States, 1977; *see also* United States v. Perez, 1824; United States v. Dinitz, 1976). If a trial court concludes that the government cannot retry the accused because no manifest necessity existed for the dismissal, the government can appeal that ruling without violating the Constitution; for, if it is successful on appeal, the double jeopardy guarantee would not preclude it from trying the accused a second time.

Sometimes a trial judge dismisses a charge against an accused after the jury has returned a verdict of guilty on that charge. In such circumstances, the Double

Jeopardy Clause does not bar the government from appealing the trial court's ruling, so long as no further factual proceedings would be required if the order dismissing the charge were reversed. To illustrate, in *United States v. Wilson* (1975), the jury returned a verdict convicting George Wilson, the business manager of a local union, of converting union funds to his own use, in violation of a provision of the Labor-Management Reporting and Disclosure Act of 1959. The trial judge, however, granted Wilson's post-verdict motion to dismiss the indictment, concluding that the extensive delay between the commission of the alleged offense and the indictment had substantially prejudiced Wilson's right to a fair trial. The United States Supreme Court held that the protection against government appeals afforded by the double jeopardy provision attaches only when there exists a danger of subjecting the defendant to a second trial for the same offense and that therefore that provision did not bar the government from appealing the dismissal. For a reversal of the trial judge's order would not require a new trial or any further factual proceedings, but merely the reinstatement of the jury's verdict of guilty. The Supreme Court reasoned that correction of an error of law in a post-verdict ruling would not grant the government a new trial in which it could attempt to strengthen its case against the accused and seek to persuade a second fact finder of the defendant's guilt after its failure to convince the first. And while recognizing that appellate review of any ruling of law discharging an accused enhances the likelihood of conviction and subjects the individual to continuing anxiety, the Court nonetheless concluded that "a defendant has no legitimate claim to benefit from an error of law when that error could be corrected without subjecting him to a second trial before a second trier of fact" (United States v. Wilson, 1975).

Appeal of a Sentence

Although the Double Jeopardy Clause precludes the government from appealing a judgment of conviction, it does not prevent the government from seeking review of a convicted defendant's sentence (United States v. DiFrancesco, 1980). In *United States v. DiFrancesco* (1980), a jury convicted the defendant for several offenses. After a special hearing, the trial judge found the defendant to be a "dangerous special offender" as defined in the Organized Crime Control Act of 1970 and, under that Act, sentenced him to an increased term of imprisonment. The judge, however, specified that the dangerous special offender sentence run concurrently with the sentence for the underlying offenses, thereby resulting in additional punishment of only about a year. Acting pursuant to a provision of the Organized Crime Control Act, the United States appealed the dangerous special offender sentence, contending that imposition of a concurrent sentence constituted an abuse of discretion because it added only one year of imprisonment to the defendant's sentences for the underlying offenses.

The United States Supreme Court held that the Double Jeopardy Clause did not bar the government from appealing the dangerous special offender sentence. The Supreme Court concluded that neither the history of sentencing practices, its previous decisions, nor the policies underlying the double jeopardy guarantee supported the proposition that a criminal sentence, once pronounced, must be accorded the same constitutional finality and conclusiveness as a judgment of acquittal. The Court observed, for example, that in *North Carolina v. Pearce* (1969), it held that the double jeopardy provision did not bar the imposition of a harsher sentence on reconviction following the defendant's successful appeal of his original conviction. The Court reasoned that "[i]f any rule of finality had applied to the pronouncement of a sentence, the original sentence in *Pearce* would have served as a ceiling on the one imposed at retrial." It noted that *Pearce* rejected the notion that the imposition of a sentence of less than the maximum authorized by the applicable statute operates as an implied acquittal of any greater sentence. And, while the Court recognized that *Pearce* dealt with the imposition of a new sentence after retrial rather than after appeal, it remarked that "that difference is no more than a 'conceptual nicety.'"

With respect to the policies underlying the guarantee against double jeopardy, the Supreme Court in *DiFrancesco* first reasoned that the basic design of the double jeopardy provision is to serve "as a bar against repeated attempts to convict, with consequent subjection of the defendant to embarrassment, expense, anxiety, and insecurity, and the possibility that he may be found guilty even though innocent," but concluded that "[t]hese considerations ... have no significant application to the prosecution's statutorily granted right to review a sentence." The Court stated:

> This limited appeal [of the sentence] does not involve a retrial or approximate the ordeal of a trial on the basic issue of guilt or innocence. Under [the applicable statute], the appeal is to be taken promptly and is essentially on the record of the sentencing court. The defendant, of course, is charged with knowledge of the statute and its appeal provisions, and has no expectation of finality in his sentence until the appeal is concluded or the time to appeal has expired. To be sure, the appeal may prolong the period of any anxiety that may exist, but it does so only for the finite period provided by the statute. The appeal is no more of an ordeal than any [g]overnment appeal ... from the dismissal of an indictment or information. The defendant's primary concern and anxiety obviously relate to the determination of guilt or innocence, and that already is behind him. The defendant is subject to no risk of being harassed and then convicted, although innocent.

The Court next concluded that the Double Jeopardy Clause does not provide a defendant "with the right to know at any specific moment in time what the exact limit of his punishment will turn out to be." It noted that the defendant was aware that a dangerous special offender sentence is subject to increase on appeal, so that his legitimate expectations are not defeated if his sentence is increased on appeal.

Finally, the Supreme Court in *DiFrancesco* concluded that the increase of a sentence on appeal under the provision in question did not constitute multiple punishment, because the guarantee against multiple punishments contained in the double jeopardy provision merely protects a defendant against receiving a greater sentence than authorized by the legislature and Congress, in the Organized Crime Control Act of 1970, specifically authorized the government to appeal a sentence imposed upon a special dangerous offender.

Despite the United States Supreme Court's holding in *DiFrancesco*, its decision in *Bullington v. Missouri* (1981) must be read to preclude the government from appealing a sentence of imprisonment rendered after the fact finder in a separate capital sentencing proceeding that resembled a trial on the issue of guilt or innocence "acquitted" the convicted defendant of the death penalty because the government failed to meet its burden of proving certain elements beyond a reasonable doubt in its quest to obtain a penalty of death. In *Bullington*, the Supreme Court held that the general rule that the Double Jeopardy Clause does not prohibit a harsher sentence following reconviction does not apply to such capital sentencing proceedings (*accord* Arizona v. Rumsey, 1984). The Court equated the fact finder's decision to reject the death penalty in such a hearing to an "acquittal" at the guilt-innocence phase of a trial, concluding that the underlying policy reasons for affording absolute finality to a verdict of acquittal on the issue of guilt or innocence were equally applicable to an "acquittal" at the penalty phase of a capital murder trial. That "absolute finality" must preclude not only an increase in sentence following reconviction, as in *Bullington* and *Rumsey v. Arizona* (1984), but also an appeal by the government of a sentence of imprisonment imposed by the fact finder following such a capital sentencing proceeding. That is, the double jeopardy provision must bar the government from seeking to have the appellate court either impose the death penalty or remand the case to the trial court for a new sentencing hearing at which the death penalty could be imposed.

NOTES

1. The word "person," as used in the Double Jeopardy Clause, includes not only an individual human being, but also a corporation (United States v. Martin Linen Supply Co., 1977; Fong Foo v. United States, 1962). For the sake of convenience, I use the words "person" and "individual" interchangeably in the text, with each term encompassing both natural persons and corporations.

2. *See generally* Jack H. Friedenthal, Mary Kay Kane & Arthur R. Miller, *Civil Procedure*, 625–75 (West Group, 3rd ed. 1999).

3. Comment, *Twice in Jeopardy*, 75 Yale Law Journal 262, 278 n.74 (1965).

4. Akhil Reed Amar & Jonathan L. Marcus, *Double Jeopardy Law After Rodney King*, 95 Columbia Law Review 1, 31 n.158 (1995).

5. Peter Westen & Richard Drubel, *Toward a General Theory of Double Jeopardy*, The Supreme Court Review (1978) 81, 84, 129–32; Peter Westen, *The Three Faces of Double Jeopardy: Reflections on Government Appeals of Criminal Sentences*, 78 Michigan Law Review 1001–02, 1012–18 (1980).

6. The Sixth Amendment guarantees an indigent defendant charged with a felony the right to appointed counsel at the government's expense (Gideon v. Wainwright, 1963). In cases involving a misdemeanor or other petty offense, it prohibits the incarceration of an

indigent defendant convicted at a trial at which the defendant was not represented by appointed counsel (Alabama v. Shelton, 2002; Scott v. Illinois, 1979; Argersinger v. Hamlin, 1971).

7. *See generally* Special Project, *An Analysis of the Legal, Social, and Political Issues Raised by Asbestos Litigation*, 36 Vanderbilt Law Review 573 (1983).

8. 2 Matthew Hale, *The History of the Pleas of the Crown* (*Historia Placitorium Coronae*) *240–55; 11(1) *Halsbury's Laws of England* ¶ 970 (Lord Hailsham of St. Marylebone ed., Butterworth's 1990). *See also* 4 William Blackstone, *Commentaries* *335 (commenting that the pleas of *autrefoits acquit*, or a former acquittal, and *autrefoits convict*, or a former conviction, are based upon the "universal maxim ... that no man is to be brought into jeopardy of his life, more than once, for the same offence").

Early interpretations of the Double Jeopardy Clause of the Fifth Amendment also required a complete trial culminating in either a conviction or an acquittal before jeopardy attached (*see* Crist v. Bretz, 1978).

9. *E.g.*, 1 Joel P. Bishop, *New Commentaries on the Criminal Law* § 1009 (T.H. Flood, 8th ed.1892); Blackstone, *supra* note 8, at *335; 22 *Corpus Juris Secundum* 217 (West Publishing Co. 1989); 17 *The American and English Encyclopedia of Law* 593 (Edward Thompson Company, 2nd ed. 1900). *But see* 9 Matthew Bacon, *A New Abridgement of the Law* 628 (T. & J.O. Johnson 1854) ("[I]f the acquittal in an indictment have [sic] been procured by trick or fraud of the defendant, he may be punished for the trick or fraud; but ... the court cannot grant a new trial.").

10. As indicated later in this Analysis, the United States Supreme Court subsequently held that when the legislature clearly indicates its intent to authorize cumulative punishments for the same offense, a sentencing court may impose cumulative punishments without violating the Double Jeopardy Clause, because, in context of multiple punishments in a single proceeding, "the Double Jeopardy Clause does no more than prevent the sentencing court from prescribing greater punishment than the legislature intended" (Missouri v. Hunter, 1983; *accord* Jones v. Thomas, 1989; *see also* Ohio v. Johnson, 1984; Brown v. Ohio, 1977).

11. *E.g.*, 720 Illinois Compiled Statutes §§ 5/3–3, 5/3–4(b) (2002); New York Criminal Procedure Law § 40.20 (McKinney 2003); 18 Pennsylvania Consolidated Statutes Annotated §110(1) (Supp. 2003).

12. Interestingly, English common law apparently recognized the pleas of *autrefoits acquit* and *autrefoits convict* to preclude the prosecution of an individual in England for the same offense for which he previously had been prosecuted in a foreign country (*see* Blackstone, *supra* note 8 at *335; Beak v. Thyrwhit, 1688 (discussing Rex v. Hutchinson, in which an individual previously acquitted of murder in Portugal successfully raised his prior acquittal as a bar to his prosecution in England for the same killing); *see also* The King v. Roche, 1775; J.A.C. Grant, *The Lanza Rule of Successive Prosecutions*, 32 Columbia Law Review 1309, 1319–28 (1932); George C. Pontikes, *Dual Sovereignty and Double Jeopardy: A Critique of Bartkus v. Illinois* and *Abbate v. United States*, 14 Western Reserve Law Review 700, 704–05 (1963).

13. A state may, however, be barred by its own constitution (*e.g.*, Mont. Const. art. II, § 25; State v. Hogg, 1978; Commonwealth v. Mills, 1971), or by a local statute (*e.g.*, California Penal Code §656 (West 1999); 720 Illinois Compiled Statutes § 5/3–4(c)) (2002); New York Criminal Procedure Law § 40.20 (McKinney 2003)), from trying an individual following his prosecution by another state for the same conduct.

14. A state may, however, be barred by its own constitution (*e.g.*, State v. LeCoure, 1971; State v. Hogg, 1978; Commonwealth v. Mills, 1971), or by a local statute (*e.g.*, California Penal Code §656 (West 1999); 720 Illinois Compiled Statutes § 5/3–4(c) 2002); New York Criminal Procedure Law § 40.20 (McKinney 2003)), from trying an individual following his prosecution by the federal government for the same conduct.

15. The precise holding of the United States Supreme Court in *Bartkus* was that successive federal and state prosecutions of a person for the same act does not deprive that individual of due process of law, as guaranteed by the Fourteenth Amendment to the United States Constitution. At the time the Supreme Court decided *Bartkus*, it had not yet held the Double Jeopardy Clause applicable to the States. Nevertheless, in reaching its result in *Bartkus*, the Court relied upon its double jeopardy jurisprudence, particularly, the dual sovereignty doctrine.

16. For example, 15 United States Code § 80a-36 (2000) provides:

Whoever steals, unlawfully abstracts, unlawfully and willfully converts to his own use or to the use of another, or embezzles any of the moneys, funds, securities, credits, property, or assets of any registered investment company shall be deemed guilty of a crime .... *A judgment of conviction or acquittal on the merits under the laws of any State shall be a bar to any prosecution under this section for the same act or acts.* (Italics added.)

See also 18 United States Code § 659 (2000); 18 United States Code § 660 (2000); 18 United States Code § 2101 (2000).

17. An individual can, of course, be prosecuted by a state following his court-martial for the same offense, and *vice-versa*, because a military prosecution constitutes a federal proceeding for purposes of double jeopardy analysis (Childers v. Goldman, 2000).

18. *E.g.*, Amar & Marcus, *supra* note 4, at 4–27; Grant, *supra* note 12, at 1329–31; Sandra Guerra, *The Myth of Dual Sovereignty: Multijurisdictional Drug Law Enforcement and Double Jeopardy*, 73 The North Carolina Law Review 1159, 1209–10 (1995); Robert Matz, Note, *Dual Sovereignty and the Double Jeopardy Clause: If at First You Don't Convict, Try, Try Again*, 24 Fordham Urban Law Journal 353, 367–76 (1997); Pontikes, *supra* note 12, at 712–23.

19. *See also* Grant, *supra* note 12, at 1329–30; Matz, *supra* note 18, at 371–72.

20. *See also* Guerra, supra note 18, at 1207–08; Matz, *supra* note 18, at 374–75.

21. 1 *Annals of Congres* 434, 753 (Joseph Gales ed., 1789).

22. 1 Bishop, *supra* note 9, § 1009. *See also* Blackstone, *supra* note 8, at *335 ("[W]hen a man is *fairly* found not guilty upon any indictment, or other prosecution ... he may plead such acquittal in bar of any subsequent accusation for the same crime.") (italics added). *But see* Bacon, *supra* note 9, at 628 ("[I]f the acquittal in an indictment have [sic] been procured by a trick or fraud of the defendant, he may be punished for the trick or fraud; but ... the court cannot grant a new trial.").

23. *Corpus Juris Secundum, Criminal Law, supra* note 9, at 217. *See also The American & English Encyclopedia of Law, supra* note 9, at 593 ("A verdict of acquittal procured by a defendant by fraud is a nullity and does not put him in jeopardy, consequently it is no bar to a second trial for the same offense.").

24. The saga of Harry Aleman is recounted by two Chicago newspaper reporters in Maurice Possley & Rick Kogan, *Everybody Pays: Two Men, One Murder and the Price of Truth* (G.P. Putnam's Sons 2001).

25. 28 United States Code § 2254 (d) & (e)(1) (2000).

26. David S. Rudstein, *Double Jeopardy and the Fraudulently-Obtained Acquittal*, 60 Missouri Law Review 607 (1995).

27. If the prosecutor learns of the fraudulent conduct within the time allotted for an appeal, he theoretically could appeal the acquittal, claiming that the Double Jeopardy Clause would not bar the appellate court from reversing the judgment of acquittal and remanding for a new trial because the defendant obtained the acquittal through fraud; however, in making its decisions, an appellate court relies solely upon the record of the proceedings in the lower court and does not receive any "new" evidence or hold evidentiary hearings. In most cases involving allegations of fraud by the defendant, the trial court record will not contain any information concerning the alleged fraudulent conduct.

28. As explained earlier in this Analysis, the Double Jeopardy Clause does not apply in civil proceedings. For that reason, the collateral estoppel component of the Double Jeopardy Clause cannot bar a civil forfeiture proceeding even if that forfeiture proceeding involves an issue of ultimate fact actually and necessarily decided in a previous criminal action. As the Supreme Court explained in *One Lot Emerald Cut Stones v. United States* (1972), such a situation "involves neither two criminal trials nor two criminal punishments."

29. Justices Hugo L. Black and William J. Brennan, Jr., did not reach the merits of Jorn's claim. They believed that the Supreme Court lacked jurisdiction to hear the government's appeal from the trial judge's dismissal of the charges against Jorn on double jeopardy grounds. In their view, the trial judge's action in ending Jorn's first trial amounted to an acquittal and therefore deprived the judge of discretion to put Jorn in jeopardy again.

30. 31 United States Code § 3729 (1982 & Supp. II 1984).

31. Vikramaditya S. Khanna, *Double Jeopardy's Asymmetric Appeal Rights: What Purpose Do They Serve?*, 82 Boston University Law Review 341, 351 (2002).

Bibliographical Essay

In a lecture delivered in 1970 at the University of California School of Law (Boalt Hall), Justice Walter V. Schaefer of the Supreme Court of Illinois remarked that "[t]here has been enough written about double jeopardy to satisfy the most avid scholar."[1] Justice Schaefer, a former law professor and a scholar himself,[2] spoke these words less than a year after the United States Supreme Court held the Double Jeopardy Clause of the Fifth Amendment applicable to the States through the Due Process Clause of the Fourteenth Amendment (*see* Benton v. Maryland, 1969). Since then, the Supreme Court's flurry of activity in the double jeopardy arena during the 1970s and early '80s has spawned even more scholarly work on the subject, making Justice Schaefer's words as true today as when he spoke them.

Given the amount that has been written about the guarantee against double jeopardy, it is somewhat surprising that only a handful of books focus exclusively upon that protection. In researching the instant text, the author discovered only three: Jay A. Sigler, *Double Jeopardy: The Development of a Legal and Social Policy* (Cornell University Press 1969); Martin L. Friedland, *Double Jeopardy* (Clarendon Press, 1969); and George C. Thomas III, *Double Jeopardy: The History, The Law* (New York University Press 1998).

Friedland's work focuses upon double jeopardy law in England, so it is somewhat less valuable than the other two in dealing with the substantive protection afforded by the Double Jeopardy Clause of the Fifth Amendment. Nevertheless, his work contains a particularly illuminating chapter tracing the history of the protection against double jeopardy in English law. In addition, his criticism of various English rules governing double jeopardy helps in evaluating the United States Supreme Court's interpretation of the Fifth Amendment. For example, Friedland concludes that English law, contrary to American law, provides far too little protection to an accused against the premature termination of his trial by the improper declaration of a mistrial. At the opposite extreme, he believes that English law provides too much protection to an accused against a retrial following a successful appeal.

Like Friedland, Sigler begins his work with a chapter reviewing the history of the protection against double jeopardy. He not only examines its roots and its incorporation into English common law, but unlike Friedland, reviews the historical development of the protection against double jeopardy in America, both before and after the adoption of the Fifth Amendment. In the core of his text, Sigler examines the protection against double jeopardy afforded by the Fifth Amendment in federal criminal prosecutions and the protection afforded in state criminal prosecutions by comparable provisions in state constitutions and by the statutory and case law of the various states. His discussion of the policies and social purposes underlying the protection is quite helpful. Sigler wrote his book, however, before the United States Supreme Court held the Double Jeopardy Clause applicable to the States. The book therefore antedates the Supreme Court's increased activity in the area during the 1970s and beyond, and as a result does not discuss any of the significant double jeopardy cases decided by that Court in the past thirty-five years.

Thomas' book is much more recent than either Friedland's or Sigler's, and much more theoretical. Thomas focuses upon the meaning of the concepts of "same offense" and "second jeopardy." He rejects the notion that the Double Jeopardy Clause places substantive limits upon the number of punishments that the legislature can authorize for particular wrongdoing. He also rejects the alternative view that while the provision places no limits upon the legislature's authority to decree the number of punishments that can be imposed for the same offense in a single trial, it prohibits the legislature from allowing a prosecutor to attempt to obtain the authorized punishments in more than one trial. Instead, Thomas presents and defends the following thesis: Because "the legislature creates statutory criminal blameworthiness and the procedure for determining that blameworthiness, the legislature is the ultimate source of guidance on when offenses are the same and when the first jeopardy has ended" so that an additional proceeding for the same offense would constitute "double" jeopardy.

In addition to the books published about the Double Jeopardy Clause, there are hundreds of articles examining that provision. This Bibliographical Essay will discuss the most significant ones, merely mention others, and because of space limitations, entirely omit reference to still others. Because many of the significant articles address more than one distinct topic in double jeopardy law, they are discussed in several different sections of this Bibliographical Essay.

CHAPTER 1: A HISTORY OF THE GUARANTEE AGAINST DOUBLE JEOPARDY

An Introduction

One source pertinent to all five sections of the text is Jay A. Sigler, *Double Jeopardy: The Development of a Legal and Social Policy*. The first chapter of this book traces the development of the protection against double jeopardy from Greek and Roman times until shortly after the adoption of the Fifth Amendment.

In addition to Sigler's work, George C. Thomas III, at various points in his book, discusses the history of double jeopardy from ancient times until the present day. The book is: George C. Thomas III, *Double Jeopardy: The History, The Law*.

Origins of the Guarantee

No significant resources focus exclusively upon the protection against double jeopardy contained in ancient Jewish law or in early Greek or Roman law. A number of texts, however, focus on criminal law and procedure in those legal systems. Both Samuel Mendelsohn, *The Criminal Jurisprudence of the Ancient Hebrews: Compiled from the Talmud and other Rabbinical Writings, and Compared with Roman and English Penal Jurisprudence* (Hermon Press 2nd ed. 1968), and Hyman E. Goldin, *Hebrew Criminal Law and Procedure* (Twayne Publishers, Inc. 1952), examine the Talmud's system of criminal jurisprudence, including the various crimes recognized by ancient Jewish law and the procedure used to determine the guilt or innocence of an accused.

At least two texts contain useful information about early Greek criminal law and procedure. These are: Robert J. Bonner, *Lawyers and Litigants in Ancient Athens: The Genesis of the Legal Profession* (University of Chicago Press 1927), and J. Walter Jones, *Law and Legal Theory of the Greeks: An Introduction* (Clarendon Press 1956). Bonner's text traces the rise and development of the legal profession in ancient Athens. In the process, he discusses the organization of the courts and the legal practice and procedure of the time. Jones' text provides an overview of the Greek legal system.

A number of sources contain valuable information about criminal law and procedure in the Roman Republic and the Roman Empire. Among them are: H.F. Jolowicz, *Historical Introduction to the Study of Roman Law* (Cambridge University Press, 2nd ed.1952); Max Radin, *Handbook of Roman Law* (West Publishing Co. 1927); Pandias M. Schisas, *Offences Against the State in Roman Law* (University of London Press, Ltd. 1926); and James Leigh Strachan-Davidson, *Problems of the Roman Criminal Law* (Clarendon Press 1912).

Both Jolowicz and Radin focus primarily upon private law. Of particular interest are their discussions of the civil law of delicts, which in early Roman law encompassed a great deal of the field covered by modern criminal law. A delictual action was a private action brought by an individual against an alleged wrongdoer, seeking a penalty—not compensation—from the alleged wrongdoer. Roman citizens frequently used it in lieu of a criminal action by the state against the alleged wrongdoer. Both Jolowicz and Radin also include a brief chapter on criminal law and procedure in ancient Rome. Strachan-Davidson's two-volume work as well as Schisas' work focuses exclusively on criminal law and procedure.

R.H. Helmholz, *The Spirit of Classical Canon Law* (University of Georgia Press 1996) contains an entire chapter devoted to the law of double jeopardy. In that chapter, the author discusses the scope and meaning of the prohibition against double jeopardy as it existed in classical canon law, as well as the basis for the canon law's principle of double jeopardy.

English Common Law

The following sources contain useful information about the English common law system of criminal law and procedure, including the method of criminal prosecution by "appeal": William S. Holdsworth, *A History of English Law* (Metheun & Co., 7th ed. 1956); Theodore F.T. Plucknett, *A Concise History of the Common Law*, (Little, Brown and Company, 5th ed.1956); Frederick Pollack & Frederic William Maitland, *The History of English Law* (Cambridge University Press, 2nd ed.1923); and James Fitzjames Stephen, *A History of the Criminal Law of England* (MacMillan & Co. 1883). Three other valuable sources on English criminal law and procedure, which include discussions of the pleas of *autrefoits acquit* (a former acquittal), *autrefoits convict* (a former conviction), and pardon are the works of Coke and Hale in the seventeenth century, as well as Blackstone's monumental treatise written in the eighteenth century. These books are: William Blackstone, *Commentaries*; Edward Coke, *The Third Part of the Institutes of the Laws of England* (W. Lee & D. Parkman, 1644); and Matthew Hale, *The History of the Pleas of the Crown* (*Historia Placitorium Coronae*).

Martin L. Friedland, *Double Jeopardy*, contains an introductory chapter tracing the history of the protection against double jeopardy in English law from the time of the controversy between Henry II and the Archbishop of Canterbury, Thomas à Becket, in the twelfth century. Two important articles that follow the development of double jeopardy principles in English law are: Marion S. Kirk, *"Jeopardy" During the Period of the Year Books*, 82 University of Pennsylvania Law Review 602 (1934), and Jill Hunter, *The Development of the Rule Against Double Jeopardy*, 5 Journal of Legal History 3 (1984). A well-researched report to the Attorney General of the United States by the Justice Department's Office of Legal Policy discusses the history of the English common law rule against double jeopardy, focusing primarily upon appeals of acquittals by the crown. The report is: Office of Legal Policy, United States Department of Justice, *Report to the Attorney General on Double Jeopardy and Government Appeals of Acquittals, "Truth in Justice," Report No. 6* (1987), *reprinted in* 22 University of Michigan Journal of Law Reform 831 (1989).

A wealth of material exists concerning the twelfth-century controversy between Henry II and Thomas à Becket, the Archbishop of Canterbury. Among the most helpful texts are: Z.N. Brooke, *The English Church and the Papacy* (Cambridge University Press 1989); Martin Friedland, *Double Jeopardy*; Frederick Pollack & Frederic William Maitland, *The History of English Law*, 2d ed.; Austin Lane Poole, *From Domesday Book to Magna Carta 1087–1216* (Clarendon Press, 2nd ed.1955); and Goldwin Smith, *A Constitutional and Legal History of England* (Charles Scribner's Sons 1955). W.L. Warren's biography of Henry II is particularly illuminating. That text is: W.L. Warren, *Henry II* (University of California Press 1973).

In addition to these texts, an article by Charles Duggan provides thoughtful insight into the controversy. Duggan challenges the conventional view that canon law actually supported Henry's position in the dispute rather than Becket's. The article is: Charles Duggan, *The Becket Dispute and the Criminous Clerks*, 35 Bulletin of the Institute of Historical Research 1 (1962), *reprinted in* Charles Duggan, *Canon Law in Medieval England: The Becket Dispute and Decretal Collections* (Variorum Reprints 1982).

Double Jeopardy Protection in America Before the Adoption of the Fifth Amendment

A particularly useful source is Francis Newton Thorpe, *The Federal and State Constitutions, Colonial Charters, and Other Organic Laws of the States, Territories, and Colonies 1492–1908* (Government Printing Office 1909). This multivolume work, which was authorized by an Act of Congress, collects state constitutions, colonial charters, and other organic laws of each state.

Richard L. Perry & John C. Cooper, *Sources of Our Liberties: Documentary Origins of Individual Liberties in the United States Constitution and Bill of Rights* (Associated College Presses 1959), is a single-volume work compiled under the auspices of the American Bar Association. It contains reprints of historic documents constituting the major legal sources of the individual liberties of Americans, including Magna Carta, the English Bill of Rights of 1689, the Declaration of Independence, the first constitutions of various states following independence, the Constitution of the United States, and the Bill of Rights. Each document is preceded by an introductory editorial note on its origins and political background; its effectiveness in its own time; and its later significance in establishing individual liberties in America.

A number of sources discuss case law dealing with individual rights during the colonial period in America. These include: Julius Goebel, Jr., & T. Raymond Naughton, *Law Enforcement in Colonial New York* (Commonwealth Fund 1944); Arthur P. Scott, *Criminal Law in Colonial Virginia* (University of Chicago Press 1930); and Christopher Collier, *The Common Law and Individual Rights in Connecticut Before the Federal Bill of Rights*, 76 Connecticut Bar Journal 1 (2002).

The Adoption of the Fifth Amendment Guarantee Against Double Jeopardy

Several resources provide detailed information concerning the adoption of the Bill of Rights, in general, and the Double Jeopardy Clause, in particular. Volume I of the *Debates and Proceedings in the Congress of the United States* (Gales and Seaton 1834), popularly known as the *Annals of Congress*, contains the debates and proceedings in the House of Representatives during the First Congress. The *Annals* were not published contemporaneously, but compiled later, primarily from newspaper accounts. In the *Annals*, speeches are paraphrased, rather than presented verbatim. Volume I contains, among other things, James Madison's speech introducing the series of proposals that ultimately became the Bill of Rights and the debates on those proposals, including the limited discussion of the provision dealing with double jeopardy.

Neil H. Cogan, *The Complete Bill of Rights: The Drafts, Debates, Sources, and Origins* (Oxford University Press 1997), includes in one volume an array of reprinted primary materials. The author assigns each of the clauses of the Bill of Rights a separate chapter, except for the criminal clauses of the Sixth Amendment, which are grouped together. The first part of each chapter contains the texts of the drafts of the particular clause in the First Congress; proposals concerning the right in question made by the state conventions that ratified the Constitution; and the sources of the clause in question, such as state constitutions and laws and colonial charters and laws. The second part of each chapter features the discussions of the drafts and proposals in the First Congress, as well as in the Constitutional Convention, state conventions that ratified the Constitution, and newspapers and pamphlets. The final section of each chapter compiles excerpts from treatises and judicial decisions discussing the right in question.

The Bill of Rights: A Documentary History (Chelsea House Publishers in association with McGraw Hill Book Co. 1971), edited by Bernard Schwartz, is a two-volume work containing an array of reprinted primary materials, relating not only to the Bill of Rights, but also to the Constitution of the United States. This work contains: the English antecedents of the Bill of Rights, including Magna Carta and the Bill of Rights of 1689; colonial charters and laws; contemporaneous state constitutions and declarations; federalist and anti-federalist writings in favor of, and opposed to, the adoption of the proposed Federal Constitution; documents from state ratifying conventions; the "legislative history" of the Bill of Rights; and materials relating to the ratification of the Bill of Rights by the States. The publisher reissued the text several years later in a five-volume set: Bernard Schwartz, *The Roots of the Bill of Rights* (Chelsea House Publishers 1980).

In addition to texts containing reprints of primary materials, numerous secondary sources examine the origins of the Bill of Rights. Among them are Irving Brant, *The Bill of Rights: Its Origin and Meaning* (Bobbs-Merrill Co., Inc. 1965); Edward Dumbauld, *The Bill of Rights: And What It Means Today* (Greenwood Press 1979; originally published: University of Oklahoma Press 1957); and Robert Allen Rutland, *The Birth of the Bill of Rights, 1776–1791* (Northeastern University Press 1983; originally published: University of North Carolina Press 1955). Brant, as does Dumbauld, devotes a large portion of his book to the meaning of the various rights included in the Bill of Rights as of the time he wrote the book; however, both works are dated. Nevertheless, Dumbauld's work is particularly useful because of its appendices, which include a table providing the sources of the various provisions of the Bill of Rights; the proposals of the eight states that formulated amendments; the amendments offered in the First Congress by James Madison; the amendments reported to the House of Representatives by the Select Committee to which Madison's proposals were referred; the amendments passed by the House of Representatives and by the Senate; and finally, the amendments proposed by Congress to the States. Leonard W. Levy also provides a general history of the Bill of Rights, but unlike Brant and Rutland, he examines the antecedents of each of the major provisions of the Bill of Rights in a separate chapter. Levy devotes a brief chapter to the Double Jeopardy Clause. Francis Newton Thorpe, *The Constitutional History of the United States* (Callahan & Co. 1901), contains a chapter discussing the adoption of the Bill of Rights, which includes in the footnotes an outline listing the precedents for each of James Madison's proposals.

The Protection Against Double Jeopardy After Ratification of the Fifth Amendment

The Double Jeopardy Clause and State Criminal Prosecutions

Two articles in the same issue of the *Stanford Law Review* examine the relationship between the Bill of Rights and the Fourteenth Amendment. In his book-length article, Charles Fairman examines the events surrounding the drafting, passage, and ratification of the Fourteenth Amendment in an attempt to discover the original understanding of the Amendment. He focuses upon the views of those members of the Congress that proposed the Amendment, particularly those who sponsored and supported its passage, and the actions of the state legislatures when they considered ratification. Fairman concludes that the historical evidence is "overwhelmingly against" the conclusion that the Fourteenth Amendment was intended and understood to impose the first eight amendments upon the States. The article is: Charles Fairman, *Does the Fourteenth Amendment Incorporate the Bill of Rights? The Original Understanding*, 2 Stanford Law Review 5 (1949).

Stanley Morrison examines the cases decided between 1873 and 1947 in which the United States Supreme Court rejected the view that the Fourteenth Amendment incorporated the Bill of Rights and made them applicable to the States. Like Fairman, Morrison concludes that the historical evidence does not support the notion that the Fourteenth Amendment incorporated the first eight amendments. The article is: Stanley Morrison, *Does the Fourteenth Amendment Incorporate the Bill of Rights? The Judicial Interpretation*, 2 Stanford Law Review 140 (1949).

On the other hand, in a recent provocative article, Bryan H. Wildenthal concludes that in an 1873 case, the Supreme Court held that the Privileges and Immunities Clause of the Fourteenth Amendment—as opposed to the Due Process Clause of that Amendment—incorporates the Bill of Rights and applies it to the States. Wildenthal's reading of the case conflicts with the traditional understanding of the Supreme Court's holding in that case. The article is: Bryan H. Wildenthal, *The Lost Compromise: Reassessing the Early Understanding in Court and Congress on Incorporation of the Bill of Rights in the Fourteenth Amendment*, 61 Ohio State Law Journal 1051 (2000).

In a recent book, Akhil Reed Amar concludes that each of the three main approaches to incorporation—"total incorporation," as urged by Justice Hugo L. Black in his dissenting opinion in *Adamson v. California* (1947); "selective incorporation," as ultimately adopted by the United States Supreme Court (*see* Duncan v. Louisiana, 1968); and the "fundamental fairness" doctrine, as initially adopted by the Supreme Court (*see* Adamson v. California, 1947 (Frankfurter, J., concurring))—"contains both a deep insight and a fatal flaw." Amar proposes an approach, which he calls "refined incorporation," that synthesizes the three divergent approaches to incorporation. The book is: Akhil Reed Amar, *The Bill of Rights: Creation and Reconstruction* (Yale University Press 1998).

Developing the Contours of the Guarantee Against Double Jeopardy

This section of the text discusses the major United States Supreme Court cases interpreting the meaning of the Double Jeopardy Clause. The many works discussing the substantive provisions of the guarantee against double jeopardy will be discussed in the section of this Bibliographical Essay relating to the Analysis chapter of the text.

CHAPTER 2: ANALYSIS

Underlying Policies

The policies underlying the protection against double jeopardy are discussed in some depth by both Thomas and Sigler in their books. Other authors have discussed those policies while examining specific questions concerning the meaning and scope of the Double Jeopardy Clause. For example, the student author of a highly influential article in the *Yale Law Journal* discusses the underlying policies while attempting to formulate a test defining the "same offense" for purposes of double jeopardy analysis. The author maintains that four policies underlie the prohibition against double jeopardy: (1) "guilt should be established by proving the elements of a crime to the satisfaction of a single jury, not by capitalizing on the increased probability of conviction resulting from repeated prosecutions before many juries"; (2) "the prosecutor should not be able to search for an agreeable sentence by bringing successive prosecutions for the same offense before different judges"; (3) "criminal trials should not become an instrument for unnecessarily badgering individuals"; and (4) "judges should not impose multiple punishment for a single legislatively defined offense." The article is: Comment, *Twice in Jeopardy*, 75 Yale Law Journal 262 (1965).

One of the more detailed discussions of the values underlying the Double Jeopardy Clause appears in an article by Peter Westen and Richard Drubel in *The Supreme Court Review.* Westen and Drubel criticize the United States Supreme Court for its "conceptual confusion" and its failure to develop a fundamental theory of double jeopardy law. In formulating a general theory of double jeopardy, the authors identify three distinct interests served by the prohibition against double jeopardy, which they articulate in ascending degrees of importance: (1) an interest in finality; (2) an interest in avoiding double punishment; and (3) an interest in nullification, that is, in permitting the system to acquit an individual despite sufficient evidence of his guilt. They explain that each of these interests is loosely connected to the notion of ending litigation, a connection that provides justification for classifying them under the "rubric" of double jeopardy. Westen and Drubel first analyze each of these three interests in contexts in which they arise singly—reprosecution following mistrial, reprosecution following conviction, and reprosecution following acquittal, respectively—and then consider them in combination. The article is: Peter Westen & Richard Drubel, *Toward a General Theory of Double Jeopardy* (1978), The Supreme Court Review 81.

Westen again discusses these interests in a later article in the *Michigan Law Review.* There he rephrases the values underlying the Double Jeopardy Clause as: "(1) the integrity of jury verdicts of not guilty, (2) the lawful administration of prescribed sentences, and (3) the interest in repose." The article is: Peter Westen, *The Three Faces of Double Jeopardy: Reflections on Government Appeals of Criminal Sentences*, 78 Michigan Law Review 1001 (1980).

In a recent article examining the asymmetric appeal rights attached to the Double Jeopardy Clause, Vikramaditya S. Khanna articulates four functions served by the guarantee against double jeopardy: (1) decreasing the possibility of an erroneous conviction; (2) reducing or limiting the litigation costs of the accused; (3) protecting the right of jury nullification; and (4) constraining prosecuting attorneys from acting in their own self-interest or for politically-motivated reasons. Addressing this last function, Khanna contends that the double jeopardy provision and the restrictions it imposes upon the government's right to appeal an acquittal limit the ability of a prosecuting attorney to "wear down" an accused through successive prosecutions and that by doing so reduces the incentives of prosecutors to advance their own interests through the criminal process and of politically organized groups to lobby prosecutors to enforce the law in selective ways to benefit their particular group. The article is: Vikramaditya S. Khanna, *Double Jeopardy's Asymmetric Appeal Rights: What Purpose Do They Serve?*, 82 Boston University Law Review 341 (2002).

"Jeopardy"

The Nature of Jeopardy

According to the United States Supreme Court, the word "jeopardy," as used in the Double Jeopardy Clause, connotes "the risk that is traditionally associated with a criminal prosecution" (Breed v. Jones, 1975). The Supreme Court, however, has never discussed the origin of the word "jeopardy" or examined the intent of the drafters of the double jeopardy provision in using that word. Akhil Reed Amar and Jonathan L. Marcus, in an article in the *Columbia Law Review*, briefly discuss the origin of the word "jeopardy." They explain that the word derives from the French *jue-perdre*, a game that a person might lose, and from the Middle English *iuparti*, an uncertain game. The article is: Akhil Reed Amar & Jonathan L. Marcus, *Double Jeopardy Law After Rodney King*, 95 Columbia Law Review 1 (1995).

The United States Justice Department's Office of Legal Policy, in a report to the Attorney General, asserts that there is no clear indication that the word "jeopardy" (or, for that matter, the phrase "double jeopardy") was a legal term of art in the eighteenth century. In an attempt to ascertain the intent of the drafters of the Double Jeopardy Clause, the authors of the report resort to examining the definition of the word "jeopardy" in eighteenth and early-nineteenth century dictionaries. They find that neither Samuel Johnson's 1755 dictionary nor Giles Jacob's 1772 dictionary define the word "jeopardy." On the other hand, they discover that Noah Webster's dictionary, published in 1828, defines "jeopardy" as "[e]xposure to death, loss or injury; hazard; danger; peril." Relying upon this definition, the authors of the report suggest that the drafters of the double jeopardy provision intended the word "jeopardy" to mean "risk," "danger," or "peril," an interpretation consistent with that adopted by the United States Supreme Court. The report is: Office of Legal Policy, United States Department of Justice, *Report to the Attorney General on Double Jeopardy and Government Appeals of Acquittals, "Truth in Justice," Report No. 6* (1987), *reprinted in* 22 University of Michigan Journal of Law Reform 831 (1989).

Proceedings in Which the Protections Applies

Criminal Prosecutions

The United States Supreme Court held in *Ex Parte Lange* (1874) that despite the presence of the term "life or limb," the Double Jeopardy Clause extends its protection to all criminal offenses, both felonies and misdemeanors alike. Akhil Reed Amar, in an essay in the *Yale Law Journal*, agrees with the result reached by the Supreme Court in *Lange*. He contends that the phrase "life or limb" should be taken as a "vivid and poetic metaphor for all criminal punishment." He further contends that the words must be taken as a single unitary phrase "whose whole is greater than its parts." Appealing to logic, Amar rhetorically asks why the protection against double jeopardy should apply when the State wants to chop off a person's toes, a punishment meted out in seventeenth-century England, but not when it seeks to slit a person's nose, brand his skin, gouge his ears, or flay his back, other punishments imposed in England during that same period. With respect to imprisonment, he argues that while they may not *literally* deprive an individual of his limbs, chains and bars do deprive one of the free use of his limbs. For that reason Amar concludes that here, too, the spirit and purpose of the Double Jeopardy Clause apply. Amar believes that the "life or limb" imagery also should encompass petty criminal punishments, including criminal fines, because of the stigma that attaches to an individual following his conviction of a criminal offense. Contrasting the "life or limb" language in the Double Jeopardy Clause of the Fifth Amendment with the words "life, liberty, or property" contained in the Due Process Clause of that same amendment, Amar opines that the line should be drawn at criminal prosecutions and should not apply to civil suits involving only money. The essay is: Akhil Reed Amar, *Double Jeopardy Law Made Simple*, 106 Yale Law Journal 1807 (1997).

The Office of Legal Policy of the United States Justice Department, in its 1987 report to the Attorney General, states that it could not find a definition of the term "life or limb" in the eighteenth and early-nineteenth century dictionaries it inspected. After examining the definitions of the individual words "life" and "limb," it, like Amar, shies away from a literal reading of the term. It rejects the view that the phrase encompassed only proceedings that placed a person in peril of losing his life or having his limbs torn off. The authors of the report instead believe that the phrase "life or limb" was a term of art at the time of the adoption of the Double Jeopardy Clause and that it is highly probable that the drafters of that Clause intended it to refer to crimes punishable as felonies. Reaching a result contrary to that reached by the Supreme Court in *Lange*, the report concludes that the Double Jeopardy Clause, as written, does not apply to cases involving misdemeanors. The report is: Office of Legal Policy, United States Department of Justice, *Report to the Attorney General on Double Jeopardy and Government Appeals of Acquittals, "Truth in Justice," Report No. 6* (1987), *reprinted in* 22 University of Michigan Journal of Law Reform 831 (1989).

Judge Stephen N. Limbaugh, Jr., of the Supreme Court of Missouri disagrees with the interpretation of the Double Jeopardy Clause given by both Amar and the Office of Legal Policy, although he ultimately reaches the same result as that reached by the latter. In a recent article in *The American Criminal Law Review*, Judge Limbaugh critically examines the Supreme Court's decision in *Lange*. He acknowledges that few would disagree with the *policy* of affording double jeopardy protection for all offenses, a policy he calls "humane and just." Nevertheless, he believes that the Supreme Court reached the wrong result in *Lange*. Judge Limbaugh accuses the Supreme Court of acting as a super-legislature in that case, basing its decision purely on policy grounds. He argues that the Court ignored the language of the Fifth Amendment and in doing so disregarded the intent of the Founding Fathers. To them, he argues, "to be in 'jeopardy of life or limb' meant to be in jeopardy of capital punishment." Judge Limbaugh concedes that it is too late in the day to adopt the literal meaning intended by the Framers. He suggests instead that the Supreme Court acknowledge the error of *Lange* and redraw the double jeopardy line between felonies and misdemeanors. Such a line, he contends, is the one "most faithful to the Constitution (or more properly, the least unfaithful)." The article is: Stephen N. Limbaugh, Jr., *The Case of Ex Parte Lange (or How the Double Jeopardy Clause Lost its 'Life or Limb')*, 36 The American Criminal Law Review 53 (1999).

The United States Supreme Court has yet to determine whether the Double Jeopardy Clause applies to summary contempt of court proceedings. In a piece in the *Notre Dame Law Review*, the author of the instant text, David S. Rudstein, thoroughly discusses this issue. Rudstein reviews the decision of the Supreme Court in *United States v. Dixon* (1993), in which the Court, for the first time, held that the Double Jeopardy Clause applies in *nonsummary* contempt of court proceedings. He then examines the justifications given by lower courts for holding that the double jeopardy provision does not apply in *summary* contempt of court proceedings. Rudstein concludes, contrary to the result reached by the vast majority of lower courts, that the Double Jeopardy Clause applies to summary criminal contempt prosecutions. He also concludes, however, that under the Supreme Court's current definition of "same offense," the double jeopardy provision rarely will bar the government from prosecuting an individual for a substantive criminal offense based upon the same act for which he previously was convicted of contempt. The article is: David S. Rudstein, *Double Jeopardy and Summary Contempt Prosecutions*, 69 Notre Dame Law Review 691 (1994).

A number of student articles examine the United States Supreme Court's decision in *Monge v. California* (1998) holding the double jeopardy provision inapplicable to sentencing proceedings. One author asserts that the Supreme Court in *Monge* presented "no justifiable reason" for distinguishing between capital sentencing proceedings, to which the Double Jeopardy Court applies (Bullington v. Missouri, 1981), and non-capital sentencing proceedings. She concludes that had the Court properly applied its previous decision in *Bullington*, it would have held the double jeopardy provision applicable to the type of non-capital sentencing proceedings involved in *Monge*. She reasons that the enhancement proceedings in *Monge*, as in *Bullington*, "bore the hallmarks of a trial," and "because of the trial-like aspects, the sentencing phase required finality." "No person," she contends, "deserves to live in constant fear of the State lengthening a sentence whenever it finally gathers enough evidence." The article is: Eva Maria Floyd, Note, *Allowing the Prosecution a 'Second Bite at the Apple' in Non-Capital Sentencing: Monge v. California*, 53 Oklahoma Law Review 299 (2000).

Similarly, the author of an article in *The North Carolina Law Review*, after reviewing the decision in *Monge*, concludes that "[c]onstitutional protections for criminal defendants and public policy ... urge an extension of double jeopardy protections to include non-capital sentencing statutes ...." The article is: L. Alison Heller, Note, *Three Strikes, Two Bites at the Apple, and One Offense?: An Examination of Monge v. California and the Double Jeopardy Clause's Inapplicability to Three Strikes Law*, 77 The North Carolina Law Review 2007 (1999).

The *Monge* decision also is criticized by a student author in an article in the *Pepperdine Law Review*. The article is: Michael Kline, Note, *Wading in the Sargasso Sea: The Double Jeopardy Clause, Non-Capital Sentencing Proceedings, and California's 'Three Strikes' Law Collide in Monge v. California*, 27 Pepperdine Law Review 861 (2000).

Juvenile Court Proceedings

The 1977 reprint of a turn-of-the-century book by Timothy D. Hurley provides background material on the events leading to the establishment in 1899 of the first Juvenile Court in the country. The book is: Timothy D. Hurley, *Origin of the Illinois Juvenile Court Law: Juvenile Courts and What They Have Accomplished* (AMS Press, Inc., 3rd ed.1977; originally published: The Visitation and Aid Society 1907).

Several articles commemorate the recent centennial of the establishment of the first Juvenile Court. For example, Robert E. Shepherd, Jr., in an article in the *Family Law Quarterly*, traces the evolution of the juvenile justice system during its first 100 years. The article is: Robert E. Shepherd, Jr., *The 'Child' Grows Up: The Juvenile Justice System Enters Its Second Century*, 33 Family Law Quarterly 589 (1999). A student author in the *University of Hawaii Law Review* also traces the evolution of the Juvenile Court system and, in addition, examines its current operation. She suggests ways to improve the system and reflects upon the direction in which it is heading. The article is: Lisette Blumhardt, Comment, *In the Best Interests of the Child: Juvenile Justice or Adult Retribution*?, 23 University of Hawaii Law Review 341 (2000).

In an article in the *New York Law School Journal of Human Rights*, another student author outlines the nature and history of the juvenile justice system and examines aspects of the system that he thinks raise constitutional questions. The author concludes by making three alternative proposals to remedy the problems he believes plague the system: (1) abolish the juvenile justice system and return to the previous system under which the age of the offender would merely constitute a mitigating factor at sentencing; (2) legislatively amend the system to eliminate its shortcomings; and (3) establish a three-tiered juvenile justice system, with one tier for children, another for adolescents, and the third for adults. The article is: Claude Noriega, Note, *Stick a Fork in It: Is Juvenile Justice Done*?, 16 New York Law School Journal of Human Rights 669 (2000).

The United States Supreme Court's decision in *Breed v. Jones* (1975) holding the Double Jeopardy Clause applicable in juvenile delinquency proceedings is the subject of a number of student works. Among them are: Taunja Willis Miller, Case Comment, 78 West Virginia Law Review 428 (1976); Barry S. Mittenthal, Recent Case, 9 Akron Law Review 389 (1975); Marsha Ternus Rundall, Case Note, 25 Drake Law Review 503 (1975); and Charles B. Wayne, Case Note, 54 The North Carolina Law Review 89 (1975).

Prior to the Supreme Court's decision in *Breed*, several articles considered whether the double jeopardy provision applies to juvenile delinquency proceedings. For example, the author of the instant text, David S. Rudstein, argued that the guarantee against double jeopardy should apply in delinquency proceedings and should protect a juvenile in at least three situations: first, to bar successive delinquency proceedings based upon the same act; second, to prohibit a criminal prosecution of a juvenile for an act for which he already was adjudicated a delinquent; and, finally, to preclude the Juvenile Court from transferring jurisdiction to an adult criminal court once a hearing on the merits of a delinquency petition commences. The article is: David S. Rudstein, *Double Jeopardy in Juvenile Proceedings*, 14 William and Mary Law Review 266 (1972).

James G. Carr, in an article in *The University of Toledo Law Review*, also concluded that the Double Jeopardy Clause should apply in juvenile delinquency proceedings. He contended that when a delinquency petition is dismissed because the Juvenile Court finds the youth not to be delinquent, or when a delinquency proceeding is terminated in the absence of a "manifest necessity," the double jeopardy provision should bar the government from subsequently seeking an adjudication of delinquency against the youth based upon any act that was part of the "same transaction" that served as the basis for the first delinquency proceeding. In addition, Carr contended that double jeopardy principles should preclude the government from seeking review of a referee's decision that the facts in the case do not support a finding of delinquency when the referee reached that decision after a full delinquency hearing at which the government was able to present all its available evidence, a result contrary to that subsequently reached by the United States Supreme Court in *Swisher v. Brady* (1978). And, while Carr also concluded that the Double Jeopardy Clause should bar a Juvenile Court from transferring a child to an adult criminal court for prosecution *after* the Juvenile Court enters a final dispositional order retaining jurisdiction, he believed that transfer of a child to a criminal court for prosecution as an adult should be allowed after the commencement of an adjudicatory hearing, but *before* entry of a final dispositional order, a result contrary to that reached by Rudstein and later by the Supreme Court in *Breed*. The article is: James G. Carr, *The Effect of the Double Jeopardy Clause on Juvenile Proceedings*, 6 The University of Toledo Law Review 1 (1974).

Civil Actions Between Private Parties

Perhaps because the Double Jeopardy Clause clearly does not apply to civil actions brought by one private individual against another, little has been written on the subject. Several articles discuss the rule adopted by a few states, as a matter of state law, that a private individual who brings a tort (civil wrong) action cannot recover punitive damages from a defendant who has been, or is going to be, prosecuted criminally for the same act upon which the tort action is based. The student author of one of these articles suggests that punitive damages should be recoverable in a tort action, but that the defendant should be allowed to mitigate those damages if he previously was convicted of a criminal offense for the same act. The article is: Roger Gustafson, Note, 21 Notre Dame Lawyer 206 (1946). Another student author takes the same position and, in addition, proposes that if the civil trial precedes any criminal prosecution, the jury should assess the damages without regard to the possibility of a subsequent criminal trial, but that if punitive damages are assessed in the civil action and the government subsequently prosecutes and convicts the defendant, the trial judge in the criminal proceeding should consider the punitive damage award in meting out the criminal sentence. The author recognizes, however, that the Double Jeopardy Clause does not directly apply to the situation. The article is: N. Kent Smith, Note, *Double Jeopardy and the Rule Against Punitive Damages of Taber v. Hutson*, 13 Indiana Law Review 999 (1980). A third student writer argues that barring recovery of punitive damages because of the *possibility* of a future criminal prosecution may result in some defendants avoiding *all* punishment, such as when the prosecuting attorney decides not to bring a criminal action or when he brings such an action but fails to prove the defendant's guilt beyond a reasonable doubt. The writer also points out, rightly, that the rule prohibiting the recovery of punitive damages does not achieve one of the fundamental purposes of the protection against double jeopardy because it does not protect the defendant from having to undergo multiple trials—a civil tort action and a criminal prosecution—for the same act. The writer suggests that the courts abolish the rule barring recovery of punitive damages, at least as it applies to situations in which there exists the mere *possibility* of a subsequent criminal prosecution. The article is: Doyal E. McLemore, Jr., Comment, *Punitive Damages and Double Jeopardy: A Critical Perspective of the Taber Rule*, 56 Indiana Law Journal 71 (1980).

Civil Actions Brought by the Government

In a provocative essay in the *Buffalo Criminal Law Review*, Susan R. Klein relates some of the consequences of the United States Supreme Court's decision to classify all actions as either "criminal" or "civil" in nature and suggests that the Supreme Court consider alternative conceptualizations of forms of actions and the procedures applicable in those actions. Klein begins by setting forth the traditional understanding of what makes a particular proceeding criminal, as opposed to civil, and a sanction punitive, rather than remedial. She then outlines the social and legal changes over the past forty years that have, in her view, made the traditional distinctions "unstable and untenable." In particular, she focuses upon the increased use of civil actions to impose sanctions upon individuals for conduct also proscribed by the criminal law. Klein next traces the Supreme Court's responses to attempts by legislatures to achieve criminal justice goals in a civil action, beginning with its original "all-or-nothing" approach under which the Court either deemed a civil action "essentially criminal" and subject to all criminal procedural guarantees or accepted the legislature's designation of the action as "civil" and therefore subject to none of the criminal procedural guarantees, through its brief experiment during the late 1980s and early 1990s of permitting legislatures to impose punitive sanctions in civil actions but requiring some, but not all, of the constitutional protections accorded in criminal trials, and finally, its return in the late 1990s to its original "all-or-nothing" position. Klein criticizes a number of the Court's recent decisions, including *United States v. Ursery* (1996), *Hudson v. United States* (1997), and *Kansas v. Hendricks* (1997), which dealt with civil forfeitures of property, occupational debarments, and civil commitment of sexually dangerous individuals, respectively. She predicts that in the future, legislatures will transform an increasing number of formerly punitive sanctions imposed in criminal prosecutions into remedial ones that can be imposed in civil actions. Asserting that it is impossible today to separate all proceedings into one category or the other, she concludes that the Supreme Court's current approach of labeling an action either entirely civil or entirely criminal for purposes of determining a defendant's procedural rights is "misguided." She acknowledges, however, that "[t]he imposition of certain punishments in 'civil' trials may be necessary to ensure immediate compliance with the myriad of statutes and regulations in our increasingly complex world" and that "many sanctions, such as debarment and commitment, cannot be labeled punitive or remedial ...." With this in mind, Klein advocates that the Supreme Court recognize that some actions are hybrid and that certain criminal procedural protections are required in some of these hybrid actions. As to the Double Jeopardy Clause, she states that it "[c]ertainly" should apply "whenever the same governmental sovereign pursues both civil and criminal actions against the same individual or entity for the same underlying misconduct ...." Otherwise, she contends, the government would "reap the numerous and unfair advantages of simultaneous or successive criminal and civil proceedings for the same misconduct." The essay is: Susan R. Klein, *Redrawing the Criminal-Civil Boundary*, 2 Buffalo Criminal Law Review 679 (1999).

Neil P. Cohen provides useful background information concerning probation and parole in his two-volume book *The Law of Probation and Parole*. Cohen first sets forth a brief history of probation and parole and discusses their theoretical bases. He then examines in detail the law relating to the two. He includes a brief discussion of the current law concerning the Double Jeopardy Clause's applicability in probation and parole revocation hearings. The book is: Neil P. Cohen, *The Law of Probation and Parole* (West Group, 2nd ed. 1999).

Several student articles focus upon the applicability of the Double Jeopardy Clause to probation revocation and parole revocation hearings. The author of one of these articles explores whether the double jeopardy provision precludes the government from both attempting to revoke an individual's probation or parole and prosecuting him criminally on the basis of the same act. The author concludes that "it seems clear that the double jeopardy clause does not require the states to abandon altogether the use of dual proceedings in the conditional liberty context." Nevertheless, the author also concludes that "some of the double jeopardy interests infringed by holding dual proceedings might still be protected by the due process clause [of the Fourteenth Amendment]." Specifically, the author argues that when a court, or parole board, concludes that an individual's probation, or parole, should not be revoked on the basis of a particular act, due process should prevent relitigation of the individual's "guilt" in a subsequent criminal prosecution. The article is: Note, *Revocation of Conditional Liberty for the Commission of a Crime: Double Jeopardy and Self-Incrimination Limitations*, 74 Michigan Law Review 525 (1976).

Another article criticizes a decision of the Texas Court of Criminal Appeals allowing a second probation revocation hearing based upon the same act previously used as the basis for an unsuccessful probation revocation hearing. The author of the article contends that a probationer at a probation revocation hearing—like both a defendant in a criminal prosecution and a juvenile in a delinquency proceeding—faces the same risk of loss of liberty and the same burdens—financial costs, emotional strain, embarrassment, and lingering fear of prosecution—that the Double Jeopardy Clause is intended to protect against. The author concedes, however, that society has a legitimate interest in immediately protecting itself from a convicted offender who is not being rehabilitated. To accommodate these competing interests, the author urges that the Double Jeopardy Clause be interpreted to bar successive probation revocation hearings based upon the same act, but to permit a criminal prosecution following the revocation of probation based upon the same offense. The article is: Jim Ragan, *Texas Development*, 7 American Journal of Criminal Law 277 (1979).

An article in the *Brigham Young University Law Review* analyzes a case decided by the Washington Supreme Court holding that a parolee acquitted in a criminal prosecution in which his sole defense was an alibi could have his parole revoked on the basis of the same act that was the subject of the criminal prosecution. The court in that case based its decision upon the difference in the standards of proof in the two proceedings. The author of the article disagrees with the court's result. The author argues that even if proof beyond a reasonable doubt is not required in a parole revocation hearing, the collateral estoppel component of the Double Jeopardy Clause should prohibit revocation of parole based upon the same act for which the parolee was acquitted in a criminal prosecution whenever the revocation hearing would require relitigation of a fact decided against the government in the criminal prosecution. While acknowledging that a parole revocation hearing is not a criminal proceeding, the author reasons that it should be considered criminal in nature for purposes of double jeopardy analysis because it may ultimately result in imprisonment of the parolee and because the sanction is punitive in nature. The article is: Case Note, Brigham Young University Law Review 223 (1975).

A student commentator in the *Indiana Law Journal* examines whether the Double Jeopardy Clause applies to a criminal prosecution that follows a prison disciplinary proceeding based upon the same act, and *vice versa*. The commentator sets forth the traditional reasoning used by courts to reject a double jeopardy plea in such situations, namely, that a prison disciplinary proceeding is not "essentially criminal" and therefore does not place the prisoner in jeopardy. The commentator considers the traditional view to be unfair because it subjects a prisoner to successive prosecutions and multiple punishments. He accuses the courts of not giving the double jeopardy claim "thoughtful judicial scrutiny" and attacks them for being reluctant to reevaluate precedent in light of the more recent willingness of the judiciary to intervene in prison affairs. To implement the Double Jeopardy Clause's purposes of finality and fairness, the commentator suggests application of a broadened theory of the collateral estoppel component of double jeopardy to prelude relitigation in a prison disciplinary hearing—a concededly noncriminal proceeding—of issues actually determined in the prisoner's favor in a previous criminal prosecution. Prison disciplinary sanctions are punitive, not remedial, he argues, and therefore should be equated with a criminal prosecution for purposes of collateral estoppel analysis under the double jeopardy provision. The commentator also suggests application of the nonconstitutionally-based doctrine of collateral estoppel to preclude relitigation in a criminal prosecution of any issue actually determined in the prisoner's favor in a prison disciplinary proceeding. The article is: Joseph A. Colussi, Note, *An Application of Double Jeopardy and Collateral Estoppel Principles to Successive Prison Disciplinary and Criminal Prosecutions*, 55 Indiana Law Journal 667 (1980).

The Attachment of Jeopardy

Anne Bowen Poulin, in an article in the *Arizona State Law Journal*, discusses the point in a criminal prosecution when jeopardy "attaches." She does not take issue with the United States Supreme Court's conclusion in *Crist v. Bretz* (1978) that jeopardy attaches in a jury trial when the jury is impaneled and sworn. She reasons that the defendant's strong interest in a particular jury outweighs the interests of the public in a full and fair trial and in holding judges accountable for their actions. Poulin does not, however, believe that the same reasoning supports the early attachment of jeopardy in non-jury trials. Concerned about judges who might, because of corruption or error, manipulate the proceedings in a bench trial to cloak the defendant with double jeopardy protection, Poulin disagrees with the Supreme Court's rule that jeopardy attaches in a bench trial when the first witness is sworn. She argues that a defendant does not have as strong an interest in a particular judge as the selected fact finder as he does in a particular jury, because a jury—unlike a judge—clearly has authority to acquit against the evidence. On the other hand, she asserts, in a bench trial, the public has a strong interest in exposing as much of the judge's conduct as possible to the scrutiny of appellate courts and, in addition, its interest in the full and fair prosecution of criminal cases can be threatened by the early attachment of jeopardy. She proposes the following rule for the attachment of jeopardy in bench trials: jeopardy attaches if the prosecution in any way offers evidence to try to convict the defendant; but if the trial judge structures a procedure that *appears* to place the defendant in jeopardy, but *in fact* does not offer the government a realistic opportunity to present its case, then jeopardy should not be deemed to have attached. The article is: Anne Bowen Poulin, *Double Jeopardy and Judicial Accountability: When Is an Acquittal Not an Acquittal?*, 27 Arizona State Law Journal 953 (1995).

Akhil Reed Amar explores a broader question. He asserts that the appropriate inquiry in deciding whether a person has been placed twice in jeopardy is not when jeopardy "attaches," the approach taken by the United States Supreme Court, but rather the bifurcated inquiry of, first, "when does a jeopardy begin?" and, second, "when does that same jeopardy end?" Taking issue with the Supreme Court's holding in *Crist*, Amar notes that an individual is in peril even before the jury is empaneled and sworn, because a formal charge can trigger pretrial loss of liberty. "Surely," he states, "we should not say to someone acquitted of robbery that he may be reindicted for the same robbery and held pretrial because, unless and until his second jury is seated, he will not be twice 'in jeopardy.'" Amar also questions the right of judges to balance away the right contained in the Double Jeopardy Clause by allowing retrial following some mistrials, but not others. He suggests the following solution: "jeopardy" commences when an individual is indicted—the point at which a person's "life or limb" is at risk—but "jeopardy" may continue until "an error-free result is obtained." Under this approach, which supports the theory of continuing jeopardy articulated by Justice Oliver Wendell Holmes in his dissenting opinion in *Kepner v. United States* (1904), the government could seek appellate review of legal errors even after an acquittal and, if successful on appeal, could retry the defendant until an error-free result is reached. It would also allow retrials following an innocently-induced mistrial or one induced by non-egregious prosecutorial misconduct. When, however, the prosecutor induced the mistrial through "grave" misconduct, Amar would allow the trial judge, acting pursuant to principles of due process of law, to enter an acquittal for the defendant and terminate his jeopardy, thereby bringing the Double Jeopardy Clause into play and precluding a retrial. The essay is: Akhil Reed Amar, *Double Jeopardy Law Made Simple*, 106 Yale Law Journal 1807 (1997).

While examining the Double Jeopardy Clause in the context of mistrials, Stephen Schulhofer suggests that the current rule of when jeopardy "attaches" no longer has any basis in policy or logic. He contends that the rule does not provide sufficient protection to individuals in jury trials because it does not protect fully against governmental action that deprives the defendant of a potentially favorable jury when that action occurs when the panel is only partially constituted or before the selected jury is sworn. To provide such protection, Schulhofer proposes that jeopardy be deemed to attach at the opening of the jury *voir dire*, that is, when the process of selecting the jury begins. The article is: Stephen J. Schulhofer, *Jeopardy and Mistrials*, 125 University of Pennsylvania Law Review 449 (1977).

The Termination of Jeopardy

Not much has been written pertaining to the "termination" of jeopardy. As indicated in the preceding section of this Bibliographical Essay, Akhil Reed Amar proposes a type of "continuing jeopardy" under which jeopardy is deemed to terminate only after "an error-free result is obtained," an approach which the United

States Supreme Court consistently has rejected. The essay is: Akhil Reed Amar, *Double Jeopardy Law Made Simple*, 106 Yale Law Journal 1807 (1997).

One student commentator touches on the "termination" of jeopardy in an article in the *Virginia Law Review* attacking the United States Supreme Court's holding in *Richardson v. United States* (1984) that a defendant whose trial ends in a mistrial because of a hung jury cannot challenge the sufficiency of the evidence introduced against him at that trial. The commentator criticizes the Supreme Court for not providing "a principled mechanism for determining when jeopardy terminates," which, she asserts, has resulted in a lack of guidance for lower courts. The article is: Susan O. Wang, Note, *Insufficient Attention to Insufficient Evidence: Some Double Jeopardy Implications*, 79 Virginia Law Review 1381 (1993).

Another student commentator, in an article in the *Creighton Law Review*, criticizes the Supreme Court's decision in *Richardson*. He contends that the Court "erred in requiring facial termination of jeopardy," rather than asking "whether [jeopardy] *should have been* terminated by a directed verdict of acquittal" (italics added). The article is: Roger K. Johnson, Casenote, 18 Creighton Law Review 877 (1985).

The "Same Offense"

Factual Identity: The Same Act or Transaction

The student author of an article in the *San Diego Law Review* examines, among other things, whether the Double Jeopardy Clause places any restrictions upon a legislature's defining an ongoing offense in temporal terms, such as, to use one of the author's examples, making it an offense to park a motor vehicle in front of a fire hydrant and providing that each hour the vehicle remains parked in front of the hydrant constitutes a separate offense. Under such a statute, an individual's single act of parking in front of a fire hydrant could result in a series of separate offenses for which he could be convicted and punished. After discussing the United States Supreme Court's decisions in *Blockburger v. United States* (1932) and *Brown v. Ohio* (1977), the author concludes that the Double Jeopardy Clause prohibits more than one prosecution for the continuous violation of a statute *only* when the legislature does not clearly provide for temporal units of prosecution. "So long as a legislature is sufficiently clear," he asserts, "it may provide that a continuous act is divisible temporally for prosecution purposes" without running afoul of the double jeopardy provision. The article is: Jack Balderson, Jr., Comment, *Temporal Units of Prosecution and Continuous Acts: Judicial and Constitutional Limitations*, 36 San Diego Law Review 195 (1999).

Legal Identity: The Same Statutory Offense

The Blockburger (Same-Elements) Test

Akhil Reed Amar and Jonathan L. Marcus take issue with the United States Supreme Court's test for determining whether two offenses are the "same" for purposes of successive prosecutions. They take the position that the text of the Double Jeopardy Clause should be read literally, that is, two offenses are the "same" only when their elements are identical. Under their approach, a greater offense and a lesser-included offense do not constitute the "same offense" because the greater offense requires an element in addition to those required for the lesser-included offense. The authors concede that the Supreme Court ordinarily reaches the right result in cases involving successive prosecutions for greater and lesser-included offenses, but they contend that in doing so the Court gives the wrong reasons. Amar and Marcus suggest relying upon due process of law in conjunction with the double jeopardy provision. They propose "three simple rules" to reach the right results for the right reasons in these types of cases: (1) the double jeopardy provision means what it says—"'same' means 'same'"; (2) due process of law generally gives a defendant who prevails on any issue in a criminal trial the right to collaterally estop (*i.e.*, bar) the government from relitigating that issue in a subsequent criminal prosecution; and (3) even when two different offenses are involved, due process of law requires the government to have "good, nonvexatious reasons" for prosecuting them in two separate trials rather than one. The article is: Akhil Reed Amar & Jonathan L. Marcus, *Double Jeopardy Law After Rodney King*, 95 Columbia Law Review 1 (1995).

An article in the *Yale Law Journal* examines various tests for determining whether two offenses are the "same" for purposes of the Double Jeopardy Clause. After examining the policies underlying the guarantee against double jeopardy, the student author proposes that for purposes of successive prosecutions offenses should be deemed the "same" "whenever they could be prosecuted at a single trial." This rule would require the government to try together in a single proceeding all offenses that substantially overlap, unless the offenses are so complicated that the jury might confuse them, or the government would suffer prejudice by prosecuting them in a single trial. After the government tried an individual once, the Double Jeopardy Clause would bar it from trying that individual for any offense it could have brought in the first trial. As discussed in the text, the United States Supreme Court has adopted this view only with respect to greater and lesser-included offenses. With respect to multiple punishments in a single trial, the author points out that the primary purpose of the Double Jeopardy Clause is to limit the discretion of courts and prosecutors, not to limit the power of the legislature to define and punish offenses. Towards this end, he contends that the Double Jeopardy Clause permits cumulative punishment in a single trial for closely related offenses *only* when the legislature intended cumulative punishments for those offenses, the position subsequently taken by the United States Supreme Court. The article is: Comment, *Twice in Jeopardy*, 75 Yale Law Journal 262 (1965).

Peter Westen and Richard Drubel take a similar position in attempting to define "same offense" for purposes of multiple punishment. They conclude that in this context the Double Jeopardy Clause sets forth a "constitutional presumption against imposing multiple punishment [for two different statutory offenses] where the legislature may have intended a defendant to be punished for only one," a presumption that can be rebutted "by a clear and persuasive showing of legislative intent to the contrary." Thus, the authors assert, although primarily a protection against prosecutorial and judicial abuse, the double jeopardy provision acts as an indirect restraint upon legislatures, demanding a certain standard of clarity from the legislature before multiple punishment can be imposed for two offenses. The article is: Peter Westen & Richard Drubel, *Toward a General Theory of Double Jeopardy*, 1978 The Supreme Court Review 81.

The "Same-Conduct" Test

In an article in the *Rutgers Law Review*, Anne Bowen Poulin examines *Grady v. Corbin* (1990), the United States Supreme Court's decision adopting the "same-conduct" test as an additional test for determining whether two offenses are the "same" for purposes of successive prosecutions. Although Poulin criticizes the Supreme Court's reasoning in *Grady*, she believes the Court reached the "correct result" in that case. Poulin thinks the Court in *Grady* incorrectly focused upon the policies underlying the double jeopardy guarantee's prohibition against a prosecution following an *acquittal* for the same offense, which was not the factual setting involved in *Grady*. She nevertheless concludes that the "broader protection" afforded by the Court in *Grady* is justified by the defendant's interest in "closure," that is, in seeing an end to the proceedings against him. The Supreme Court's holding in *Grady* protects this admittedly limited interest by restricting (but not eliminating) the government's ability to fragment prosecutions. The article is: Anne Bowen Poulin, *Double Jeopardy: Grady and Dowling Stir the Muddy Waters*, 43 Rutgers Law Review 889 (1991).

The Supreme Court's decision in *Grady* is the subject of numerous student articles. Among them are: James K. Gatz, Note, *Grady v. Corbin: A New Approach for Insuring Defendants' Fifth Amendment Rights in Successive Prosecutions for Separate Offenses Arising from One Incident, or The Supreme Court Builds Another Twist in the Double Jeopardy Clause Maze*, 36 St. Louis University Law Journal 769 (1992); James M. Herrick, Note, *Double Jeopardy Analysis Comes Home: The 'Same Conduct' Standard in Grady v. Corbin*, 79 Kentucky Law Journal 847 (1991); Judith Stilz Ogden, Casenote, 20 American Journal of Criminal Law 281 (1993); Diane M. Resch, Note, "*High Comedy but Inferior Justice*": *The Aftermath of Grady v. Corbin*," 75 Marquette Law Review 265 (1991); and The Supreme Court, 1989 Term, 104 Harvard Law Review 1493 (1990).

United States v. Dixon (1993), the United States Supreme Court's decision overruling *Grady*, is commented upon in the following student articles: Aquannette Y. Chinnery, Comment, *United States v. Dixon: The Death of the Grady v. Corbin "Same Conduct" Test for Double Jeopardy*, 47 Rutgers Law Review 247 (1994); Kirstin Pace, Note, *The Adoption of the "Same Elements" Test: The Supreme Court's Failure to Adequately Protect Defendants from Double Jeopardy*, 84 The Journal of Criminal Law and Criminology 769 (1994); Kathryn A. Pamenter, Case Comment, *United States v. Dixon: The Supreme Court Returns to the Traditional Standard for Double Jeopardy Clause Analysis*, 69 Notre Dame Law Review 575 (1994); Scott Storper, Casenote, *Double Jeopardy's Door Revolves Again in United States v. Dixon: The Untimely Death of the "Same Conduct" Standard*, 49 University of Miami Law Review 881 (1995).

The "Same Transaction" Test

In addressing the United States Supreme Court's incorporation of the doctrine of collateral estoppel into the Double Jeopardy Clause in *Ashe v. Swenson* (1970), Justice Walter V. Schaefer of the Supreme Court of Illinois notes the shortcomings of that doctrine in criminal cases and implies that, as an alternative, the Supreme Court could protect individuals from abusive multiple prosecutions by adopting the "same transaction" test and thereby requiring the government to join in a single trial all offenses committed during the same course of criminal conduct. The article is: Walter V. Schaefer, *Unresolved Issues in the Law of Double Jeopardy: Waller and Ashe*, 58 California Law Review 391 (1970).

The "same transaction" test is the subject of a brief article by a student author in the *Wayne Law Review*. The author examines a case in which the Supreme Court of Michigan adopted the "same transaction" test as the measure of double jeopardy protection against successive prosecutions afforded by its state constitution. Under that test, successive prosecutions normally are barred if the defendant's conduct either constituted a single act or transaction or was motivated by a single intent. The author criticizes the test on several grounds. First, he contends that it will cause confusion in many cases because its operative terms, "act" and "transaction," "seem to defy separate definition," and because finding the "single intent" of an accused is "speculative at best." Next, he notes that a defendant tried for kidnapping, for example, cannot logically be said to have been in jeopardy in that trial for a rape that occurred during the same course of conduct. Finally, he argues that the exception created by the court when the prosecutor honestly did not know of the second crime until after the start of the defendant's trial on the first charge cannot be squared with the protection against double jeopardy. The author concludes that the main issue in cases involving several crimes committed during a single course of conduct is preventing prosecutors from abusing their discretion. He suggests that formulating a non-constitutional procedural rule of compulsory joinder requiring related offenses to be tried in a single proceeding would have been a more desirable way to achieve this goal than adopting the "same transaction" test as a matter of state constitutional law. The article is: John Lobur, *Recent Development*, 20 Wayne Law Review 1377 (1974).

The Dual Sovereignty Doctrine

Perhaps no issue in double jeopardy law has led to more scholarly commentary than the so-called dual sovereignty doctrine. Nearly all the articles written on the topic have been critical of the doctrine. In one of the earliest pieces, written about a decade after the United States Supreme Court formally adopted the doctrine in *United States v. Lanza* (1922), J.A.C. Grant asserts that the then-prevailing view on the Continent and the English common law rule against successive prosecutions both recognize a plea in bar based upon a previous prosecution in the courts of a foreign nation for the same wrongful act. Grant concludes that the international situation furnishes an exact parallel to the prosecution by the federal government following a trial for the same offense under a state law and that the Double Jeopardy Clause (which at the time placed restrictions only upon the federal government) should be interpreted to bar such a prosecution. Responding to the argument that such a rule would make the government powerless to punish an individual who violated one of its laws, he explains that the very "purpose of a bill of rights is to restrict sovereignty through placing limitations upon an otherwise legally omnipotent government." He also maintains that such a rule would not seriously hamper law enforcement. The article is: J.A.C. Grant, *The Lanza Rule of Successive Prosecutions*, 32 Columbia Law Review 1309 (1932). Nearly a quarter of a century later, in an article examining the law of England and the British Empire, including the federal systems of Canada and Australia, Grant repeats his criticism of the dual sovereignty doctrine. The article is: J.A.C. Grant, *Successive Prosecutions by State and Nation: Common Law and British Empire Comparisons*, 4 U.C.L.A. Law Review 1 (1956).

George C. Ponitkes, in an article written shortly after the Supreme Court reaffirmed the dual sovereignty doctrine in *Bartkus v. Illinois* (1959) and *Abbate v. United States* (1959), criticizes those decisions in light of English common law and the policies underlying the Double Jeopardy Clause. He concludes that when an individual commits an act that violates the laws of two sovereigns, and those laws embody substantially the same policy, there is but a single offense for double jeopardy purposes and that the prosecution of the individual by one of the sovereigns should, under the Double Jeopardy Clause, bar a subsequent prosecution by the other for an offense based upon the same act. The article is: George C. Ponitkes, *Dual Sovereignty and Double Jeopardy*, 14 Western Reserve Law Review 700 (1963).

In a more recent article generated by the federal civil rights prosecution of several white police officers after their acquittal in a California court for beating Rodney King, an African-American, Akhil Reed Amar and Jonathan L. Marcus argue that the dual sovereignty doctrine does not comport with the policies underlying the Double Jeopardy Clause. They propose that the dual sovereignty doctrine be abandoned in all but one situation. To prevent the impairment of federal power, they would allow the federal government to prosecute offenses committed by state officials after a state prosecution for the same conduct. In such situations, they argue, there is a need for the federal government to provide a check on state abuse of power. The authors find support for their exception in the Fourteenth Amendment. Amar and Marcus recognize that if the Supreme Court abandons the dual sovereignty doctrine, individuals still would not be protected from successive prosecutions by different sovereigns unless the Court also adjusts it definition of the "same offense" to take into account the fact that different legislatures typically do not use uniform language to describe an offense. They propose that in the dual sovereignty arena the statutory definition of each offense be subjected to a probing examination to discern whether the statutes in fact substantively describe the same offense with the same real elements. The article is: Akhil Reed Amar & Jonathan L. Marcus, *Double Jeopardy Law After Rodney King*, 95 Columbia Law Review 1 (1995).

Susan N. Herman is one of many scholars who have responded to Amar and Marcus' proposal to abolish the dual sovereignty doctrine except for federal prosecution of state officials. She agrees with them that the dual sovereignty doctrine should be abolished and for the same reasons, but she concludes that "[n]either the federal interests protected by the Fourteenth Amendment nor the Fourteenth Amendment's recalibration of the workings of federalism require even the limited dual sovereignty exception proposed." The article is: Susan N. Herman, *Reconstructing the Bill of Rights: A Reply to Amar and Marcus' Triple Play on Double Jeopardy*, 95 Columbia Law Review 1090 (1995).

Paul G. Cassell, in an article in the *UCLA Law Review*, also uses the Rodney King case as a vehicle for questioning the dual sovereignty doctrine. Examining the doctrine first from a policy standpoint, Cassell contends that it allows each sovereign to vindicate its own interests—interests that may well differ from one another—and that in some cases it helps to prevent miscarriages of justice. In addition, he asserts, the doctrine avoids undesirable "race[s] to the courthouse" by prosecutors from different sovereigns. Cassell opposes Amar and Marcus' proposal to abolish the doctrine except in cases involving civil rights prosecutions. Analyzing that proposal, he concludes that there is no principled basis for such an exception. Nevertheless, after examining English common law precedent, Cassell concludes that a "good case" can be made that "the Framers of the Double Jeopardy Clause did not intend to permit each of two sovereigns to prosecute a defendant for the same offense." The article is Paul G. Cassell, *The Rodney King Trials and the Double Jeopardy Clause: Some Observations on Original Meaning and the ACLU's Schizophrenic Views of the Dual Sovereign Doctrine*, 41 UCLA Law Review 693 (1994).

Among the other articles criticizing the dual sovereignty doctrine, or its application in certain contexts, are: Daniel A. Braun, *Praying to False Sovereigns: The Rule Permitting Successive Prosecutions in the Age of Cooperative Federalism*,

20 American Journal of Criminal Law 1 (1992); Walter T. Fisher, *Double Jeopardy, Two Sovereignties and the Intruding Constitution*, 28 The University of Chicago Law Review 591 (1961); Sandra Guerra, *The Myth of Dual Sovereignty: Multi-jurisdictional Drug Law Enforcement and Double Jeopardy*, 73 The North Carolina Law Review 1159 (1995); Note, *Double Prosecution by State and Federal Governments: Another Exercise in Federalism*, 80 Harvard Law Review 1538 (1967); Kevin J. Hellmann, Note, *The Fallacy of Dueling Sovereignties: Why the Supreme Court Refuses to Eliminate the Dual Sovereignty Doctrine*, 2 Journal of Law and Policy 149 (1994); Robert Matz, Note, *Dual Sovereignty and the Double Jeopardy Clause: If at First You Don't Convict, Try, Try Again*, 24 Fordham Urban Law Journal 353 (1997); and Taryn A. Merkl, Note, *The Federalization of Criminal Law and Double Jeopardy*, 31 Columbia Human Rights Law Review 175 (1999).

Leonard G. Miller is one of the few writers who defends the dual sovereignty doctrine. In a book written shortly after the United States Supreme Court's decisions in *Bartkus* and *Abbate* and focusing exclusively on successive prosecutions by state and federal authorities, Miller argues that the Constitution established a federal system that divides authority between the national government and the States—an institutional arrangement intended to maximize the enjoyment of individual liberty by having two governments serve and protect the people. Viewed from the perspective of individual freedom, however, federalism has its costs. One of these costs, Miller contends, is that an individual may be subject to overlapping or duplicate state and federal criminal statutes under which he may be subjected to successive state and federal criminal prosecutions and punishments for the same act. He asserts that the doctrine is not intrinsically unjust and "does not inevitably produce, or even unduly encourage, unjust results in specific cases." He concludes:

> When the issue presented to the [Supreme] Court is phrased in the stark terms of the constitutionality of successive prosecutions *per se*, a judgment sustaining such practices may be not only legitimate but perhaps even mandatory. The alternatives may be unacceptable; a rule invalidating successive prosecutions may be construed as either eroding the traditional law enforcing responsibilities of the states or as jeopardizing and imperilling federal supremacy. Furthermore, successive prosecutions might under certain circumstances be not only consistent with the dictates of justice but may be even necessary to serve the interests of justice. In the last analysis, justice requires at least as compellingly that the guilty not escape punishment on technicalities unrelated to the merits of the case as that the innocent not be convicted. It is fair to say that justice should not be reduced to an oversolicitous regard for the "rights" of the accused.

Miller suggests that the solution to the problem of successive prosecutions lies not with the Supreme Court, but rather with the states, Congress, and prosecutors. Legislatures could enact statutes precluding successive prosecutions, and prosecutors could exercise self-restraint in prosecuting an individual previously prosecuted in another jurisdiction for the same act. The book is: Leonard G. Miller, *Double Jeopardy and the Federal System* (University of Chicago Press 1968).

Two student articles criticize the United States Supreme Court's holding in *United States v. Wheeler* (1978) that Indian tribes are separate sovereigns from the United States for purposes of the Double Jeopardy Clause. In one article, the author briefly reviews the statutory history of the Indian Civil Rights Act as well as of the Major Crimes Act, which authorizes the United States to prosecute in federal court certain crimes committed by Native Americans within Indian country. After examining several Supreme Court decisions dealing with tribal sovereignty, including *Wheeler*, the author concludes that "under the current interpretation of the status of Native American's [sic] by the Supreme Court, it is impossible to argue that they are a sovereign and independent nation. History supports a conclusion that the federal government never contemplated the intention of allowing the Native Americans complete autonomy," so that "any attempt to prosecute criminal defendants in federal court subsequent to a tribal court ... would be a violation of double jeopardy." He proposes that Congress enact legislation allowing Indians to impose sentences commensurate with those imposed in federal courts for the same or similar offenses. Such a step, he argues, would alleviate the pressing need to prosecute Native Americans in federal courts. The article is: Fred Kantrow, Note, *Wheeler for Two, Do You Have A Reservation? The Supreme Court's Inconsistent Treatment of Tribal Sovereignty*, 17 Touro Law Review 801 (2001).

While lauding the decision in *Wheeler* for affirming tribal self-determination, the author of an article in the *American Indian Law Review* criticizes the decision for not protecting the double jeopardy rights of individual tribal members. He contends that the federal government, through its plenary power, can protect those rights while at the same time protecting its own important interests in the prosecution of major crimes on Indian reservations. The author suggests that Congress enact legislation restricting to special circumstances the federal prosecution of an Indian previously tried in a tribal court for the same conduct. He defines such "special circumstances" as those in which the tribal court proceedings could not, or did not, vindicate a strong federal interest in law enforcement on the reservation. The article is: Larry Alan Burns, Note, *Criminal Jurisdiction: Double Jeopardy in Indian Country*, 6 American Indian Law Review 395 (1978).

Writing shortly before the Supreme Court's decision in *Wheeler*, the student author of an article in the *Gonzaga Law Review* concluded that the rationale of the dual sovereignty doctrine applies to a tribal government the same as it applies to a state. He asserted that refusal to apply the doctrine to Indian tribes would be inconsistent with current views concerning tribal sovereignty, would create difficult problems concerning the legal status of tribal courts, and might interfere with federal interests in law enforcement on Indian reservations. He also expressed the concern that Congress might place further limits on tribal courts if the dual sovereignty doctrine did not apply to them. The author concedes that the doctrine may cause hardship to individual Indian defendants, but suggests that the Attorney General of the United States could takes steps to alleviate those hardships, for example, by requiring a federal prosecutor to obtain approval from an appropriate Assistant Attorney

General before prosecuting an Indian who already was prosecuted in a tribal court for the same conduct. The author suggests that such approval could be limited to cases in which the tribal court did not vindicate the federal interest in law enforcement or in which there was a deliberate effort to obstruct federal law. The article is: Ron Zobel, Comment, *Tribal Courts, Double Jeopardy and the Dual Sovereignty Doctrine*, 13 Gonzaga Law Review 467 (1978).

At least two articles discuss whether Puerto Rico should be considered a separate sovereign from the United States for purposes of the dual sovereignty doctrine. The first examines the acquisition of Puerto Rico by the United States and the initial relationship between the two. It then looks at the actions taken by Congress in the years 1950–52 granting Puerto Rico status as a Commonwealth. The student author of the article concludes that Congress, by this action, did not intend to relinquish any of its plenary powers over Puerto Rico, and he agrees with the Circuit Court of Appeals for the Eleventh Circuit that constitutionally, Puerto Rico remains a territory and therefore not a separate sovereign from the United States for purposes of the Double Jeopardy Clause. The article is: Raúl S. Mariani, *Sovereignty at Issue: Supreme Court's Ambiguity and the Circuits' Conflict on the Application of the Dual Sovereignty Doctrine to Puerto Rico*, 63 Revista Jurídica Universidad de Puerto Rico 807 (1994).

The student author of the second article reaches the same result, concluding that Puerto Rico remains an "unincorporated territory," governed by Congress through the Territorial Clause of the Constitution, and, with respect to the United States, is not a separate sovereign for purposes of the dual sovereignty doctrine. The article is: Carlos R. Soltero, Note, *Is Puerto Rico a "Sovereign" for Purposes of the Dual Sovereignty Exception to the Double Jeopardy Clause?*, 28 Revista Jurídica de la Universidad Interamericana de Puerto Rico 183 (1994).

Successive Prosecutions

Reprosecution Following a Conviction

The student author of a highly influential article in the *Yale Law Journal* states that the Double Jeopardy Clause prohibits reprosecution after a conviction so that the prosecutor cannot "search for an agreeable sentence by bringing successive prosecutions for the same offense before different judges." The article is: Comment, *Twice in Jeopardy*, 75 Yale Law Journal 262 (1965).

Peter Westen and Richard Drubel, on the other hand, submit in their article in *The Supreme Court Review* that the principle interest justifying the rule prohibiting the government from prosecuting an individual for an offense for which he already was convicted is not the individual's interest in "finality," which they contend is not a strong interest, but rather the individual's interest in avoiding double punishment for the same offense. The article is: Peter Westen & Richard Drubel, *Toward a General Theory of Double Jeopardy*, 1978 The Supreme Court Review 81.

Conviction of a Greater-Inclusive Offense or a Lesser-Included Offense

As discussed in the previous section of this Bibliographical Essay, Westen and Drubel assert that the double jeopardy provision prohibits a subsequent prosecution of an individual following his conviction for the same offense so it can protect the individual from being subjected to double punishment for the same offense. That concern does not, however, come into play, say the authors, when the individual is tried for a greater offense after first being tried and convicted for a lesser-included offense, as in *Brown v. Ohio* (1977). For in such circumstances the sentence for the greater offense can be adjusted to take into account the sentence initially imposed for the lesser-included offense. Nevertheless, explain the authors, no strong and justifiable societal interest in reprosecuting the individual exists in such situations, so that the individual's interest in finality, although not strong, should prevail. They thus argue that the Supreme Court reached the right result in *Brown*, but for the wrong reasons. The article is: Peter Westen & Richard Drubel, *Toward a General Theory of Double Jeopardy*, 1978 The Supreme Court Review 81.

In an article in the *Rutgers Law Review* analyzing the United States Supreme Court's decision in *Grady v. Corbin* (1990), Anne Bowen Poulin briefly discusses several exceptions to the general rule that the conviction of an individual for an offense bars his subsequent prosecution for a greater offense deemed to be the "same offense" for purposes of double jeopardy analysis. She points out that the "uncompleted offense" exception, which encompasses offenses not completed or despite due diligence not discovered at the time of the initial prosecution for the lesser offense, "has never been seriously challenged." She maintains that "[i]f events occurring after the initial prosecution make a more serious prosecution appropriate, society maintains a strong interest in permitting the prosecutor to pursue that prosecution." She concludes that the only interest the accused can advance in such a situation—seeing the matter concluded—is insufficient to outweigh the societal interest.

Poulin also briefly discusses the exceptions to the general rule that exist when the accused causes his prosecution to be separated into more than one proceeding, such as when—over the government's objection—he enters a plea of guilty to a lesser-included offense in a proceeding in which he is charged with both the greater and lesser offenses (see Ohio v. Johnson, 1984), or when he successfully moves for a severance of the greater and lesser-included offenses or successfully opposes the government's attempt to join the two offenses for trial together in a single proceeding (see Jeffers v. United States, 1977). Agreeing with the exception, Poulin states that a defendant who takes procedural steps leading to separate prosecutions cannot be heard to complain. The article is: Anne Bowen Poulin, *Double Jeopardy: Grady and Dowling Stir the Muddy Waters*, 43 Rutgers Law Review 889 (1991).

After a Conviction is Set Aside at the Behest of the Accused

The development of the United States Supreme Court's rationale for interpreting the Double Jeopardy Clause to allow a retrial after a conviction has been set aside at the behest of the defendant is briefly discussed by a student author in the *Virginia Law Review*. The article is: Note, *Twice in Jeopardy: Prosecutorial Appeals of Sentences*, 63 Virginia Law Review 326 (1977).

A number of short works by student authors comment favorably upon the United States Supreme Court's decision in *Burks v. United States* (1978) holding that the Double Jeopardy Clause bars retrial of an individual for the same offense when, at the behest of the individual, a reviewing court reverses his conviction on the ground that the evidence introduced by the government at his trial failed to prove him guilty beyond a reasonable doubt. Among the articles are: John R. Browning, Casenote, 1978 Texas Tech Law Review 184; James P. Naughton, Note, 53 Tulane Law Review 598 (1979); and Lambro Niforos, Note, *Burks v. United States: Redrawing the Lines in Double Jeopardy*, 1979 Detroit College of Law Review 193.

As discussed in the text, the United States Supreme Court held in *Lockhart v. Nelson* (1988) that the double jeopardy provision does not prohibit retrial of an individual whose conviction is set aside by a reviewing court because the trial court erroneously admitted certain evidence against him, even though the reviewing court also concludes that without the inadmissible evidence the government's case was insufficient to support a conviction. *Lockhart* is the subject of several short student works. These include: Thomas Collins, Note, *Double Jeopardy: Evidentiary Insufficiency v. Trial Error After Lockhart v. Nelson*, 1989 Detroit College of Law Review 283; John H. Draper IV, Case Comment, 23 Suffolk University Law Review 882 (1989); and Scott E. Schul, Comment, *Lockhart v. Nelson: Trial Error, Evidentiary Insufficiency, and Double Jeopardy*, 92 West Virginia Law Review 523 (1990).

Conviction in the First Tier of a Two-Tier System of Trial Courts

Very little has been written about the double jeopardy ramifications of an individual's trial *de novo* in a superior court following his conviction of the same offense in the first tier of a two-tier system of trial courts. The United States Supreme Court's decision in *Ludwig v. Massachusetts* (1976), which held that a trial *de novo* conducted at the request of a convicted defendant does not violate the Double Jeopardy Clause, is examined in Paul W. Manning, Case Comment, 12 New England Law Review 361 (1976). The author concludes that the Supreme Court "correctly" found that the Massachusetts *de novo* system does not violate the guarantee against double jeopardy.

Similarly, the author of a comment on *Justices of Boston Municipal Court v. Lydon* (1984) concludes that the United States Supreme Court's decision in that case allowing a trial *de novo* of a defendant convicted in the first tier of a two-tier system, despite the defendant's claim that the evidence introduced in the inferior court failed to prove him guilty beyond a reasonable doubt, was "wise and pragmatic." However, the author criticizes the Court's reliance on the theory of "continuing jeopardy" to reach that result. The article is: Adam N. Volkert, Case Note, 75 The Journal of Criminal Law and Criminology 653 (1984).

Conviction in a Court Lacking Jurisdiction

In her article in the *Rutgers Law Review*, Anne Bowen Poulin briefly discusses this exception to the general rule that the conviction of an individual bars his subsequent prosecution for the "same offense." She agrees that a conviction in a court that lacks jurisdiction should not bar the government from prosecuting the defendant in a court that has jurisdiction, even when the defendant was not responsible for initial court's erroneous belief that it possessed jurisdiction. She recognizes that the defendant, having suffered one trial, has "an interest in closure," that is, in seeing an end to the proceedings against him, but concludes that the government's interest in having one full and fair opportunity to convict outweighs the defendant's interest. The article is: Anne Bowen Poulin, *Double Jeopardy: Grady and Dowling Stir the Muddy Waters*, 43 Rutgers Law Review 889 (1991).

Conviction Procured Through Fraud or Collusion

Poulin also briefly discusses this exception to the general rule. She believes that the guarantee against double jeopardy should not permit a criminal defendant to frustrate society's "significant interest in law enforcement," either by colluding with a public official and exploiting the official's dishonesty, or by manipulating the legal system by misrepresenting the facts or taking advantage of the prosecuting attorney's ignorance of the facts. Poulin maintains that an accused who obtains a conviction against himself through collusion or manipulation cannot advance a strong interest in seeing an end to the proceedings against him. The article is: Anne Bowen Poulin, *Double Jeopardy:* Grady and *Dowling Stir the Muddy Waters*, 43 Rutgers Law Review 889 (1991).

Reprosecution Following an Acquittal

The General Rule: The Absolute Finality of an Acquittal

Peter Westen and Richard Drubel, in their article in *The Supreme Court Review*, seek the underlying rationale for the rule according absolute finality to a jury's verdict of acquittal. They conclude that the government cannot retry an individual following his erroneous acquittal "because the acquittal may be a product of the jury's legitimate authority to acquit against the evidence." The authors go on to explain:

> To say that an acquittal is erroneous may mean one of several things. It may mean that the verdict contradicts the overwhelming weight of the evidence. That, however, provides no basis for reversing such a verdict in a system like ours in which the jury may acquit against the evidence. An acquittal may also be erroneous if it is the product of defective fact-finding

either because items of prosecution evidence were wrongly excluded or because the jury was wrongly instructed. But, again, so long as the jury's role is not limited to simple fact-finding—so long as it has the authority to acquit a defendant in spite of the facts—these errors may be immaterial. There is no way of knowing whether a jury, which has acquitted a defendant following "defective" fact-finding, would not have come to precisely the same conclusion regardless of the facts and instructions.

They conclude that the Double Jeopardy Clause "allows the jury to exercise its constitutional function as the conscience of the community in applying the law: to soften, and in the extreme case, to nullify the application of the law in order to avoid unjust judgments." This is the only valid explanation, they insist, why an individual can be retried following an erroneous conviction, but not following an erroneous acquittal by a jury. With respect to bench trials, Westen and Drubel conclude that the double jeopardy provision protects an individual against retrial following an acquittal by a judge in a bench trial whenever a jurisdiction has chosen to vest its trial judges with the same authority to nullify the law that juries possess. The article is: Peter Westen & Richard Drubel, *Toward a General Theory of Double Jeopardy*, 1978 The Supreme Court Review 81.

In a subsequent article, Westen explains that because one cannot determine whether an "erroneous" acquittal by a jury resulted from legal error or from the jury's desire to nullify the law under which the government tried the defendant, one must choose between two alternatives: reject all "erroneous" jury verdicts, even though some of them will be based on the jury's desire to nullify, or accept all "erroneous" verdicts, even though some of them will be the product of legal errors. The law has chosen the second alternative, "reflecting the judgment," says Westen, "that it is ultimately better to err in favor of nullification than against it." The article is: Peter Westen, *The Three Faces of Double Jeopardy: Reflections on Government Appeals of Criminal Sentences*, 78 Michigan Law Review 1001 (1980).

In an essay in the *Yale Law Journal*, Akhil Reed Amar rejects the notion that an acquittal should be absolutely final. He suggests an approach to double jeopardy similar to the "continuing jeopardy" theory propounded by Justice Oliver Wendell Holmes in his dissenting opinion in *Kepner v. United States* (1904). Under Amar's approach, the government could seek appellate review of legal errors after an acquittal and, if successful on appeal, could retry the defendant until an error-free result is reached. The essay is: Akhil Reed Amar, *Double Jeopardy Law Made Simple*, 106 Yale Law Journal 1807 (1997).

Implied Acquittal

A student comment in the *Texas Law Review* briefly discusses the United States Supreme Court's holding in *Green v. United States* (1957) barring reprosecution following an implied acquittal. The author concludes that "by relieving ... defendants of the risk of reprosecution for a greater charge as a condition upon the right to appeal an erroneous conviction, the majority [in *Green*] adhered more faithfully to notions of fundamental fairness that pervade the Bill of Rights" than the dissenters, who weighed more heavily society's interest in the sound administration of justice. The article is: Scott J. Atlas, Comment, *Double Jeopardy and Government Appeals of Criminal Dismissals*, 52 Texas Law Review 303 (1974).

Green is the subject of a number of other short student works. Among them are: Ralph E. Boches, Recent Decision, 56 Michigan Law Review 1192 (1958); Philip A. Gragan, Case Note, 26 The George Washington Law Review 749 (1958); Stuart A. Simke, Case Note, 6 U.C.L.A. Law Review 321 (1959); James J, Thornton, Jr., Note, 32 Tulane Law Review 488 (1958); and Recent Case, 11 Vanderbilt Law Review 929 (1958).

Exceptions to the General Rule that an Acquittal Is Absolutely Final

Akhil Reed Amar and Jonathan L. Marcus consider whether an acquittal by a jury should always bar a subsequent prosecution for the same offense. Starting with the proposition that an acquittal procured by fraud or collusion is a nullity because the accused was not actually in jeopardy at the trial that resulted in the acquittal, they suggest that retrial perhaps should be allowed when error induced by the defendant undermines the status of the jury as a properly constituted body. They point to the Rodney King case, in which Caucasian police officers accused of assaulting an African-American succeeded in obtaining a change of venue to a predominantly Caucasian county where they were tried and acquitted by a jury on which no African-Americans served. The authors argue that "a [racially] stacked jury is, constitutionally speaking, no jury; its acquittal, no acquittal; and so defendant, as a result of his own race-stacking, was never constitutionally in jeopardy." The article is: Akhil Reed Amar & Jonathan L. Marcus, *Double Jeopardy Law After Rodney King*, 95 Columbia Law Review 1 (1995).

Several articles tackle head-on the question whether the Double Jeopardy Clause bars the government from retrying an individual for the same offense if the individual obtained that acquittal through bribery, blackmail, intimidation, or the like. In a piece in the *Missouri Law Review*, the author of the instant text, David S. Rudstein, concludes that the Double Jeopardy Clause applies to such acquittals. He contends that creating an exception to the rule that an acquittal, however erroneous, absolutely bars a subsequent prosecution for the same offense will require individuals—some of whom may well be innocent—to undergo additional personal strain and expense and will grant the government a means to harass *any* acquitted defendant. Perhaps, more importantly, he argues, such an exception would mean that *no* acquittal could ever be deemed final. For even years after a fact finder acquitted an accused, the government could again charge the individual with the same offense and allege that he obtained the acquittal through fraud. The article is: David S. Rudstein, *Double Jeopardy and the Fraudulently-Obtained Acquittal*, 60 Missouri Law Review 607 (1995).

Anne Bowen Poulin reaches the opposite conclusion with respect to bench trials. She suggests that courts recognize an exception to normal double jeopardy principles after an acquittal in a bench trial when the prosecution can prove beyond a reasonable doubt that the acquittal in the accused's first trial resulted from corruption of the judge. She contends that a defendant who tampers with the judicial process should be deemed to have consented to a subsequent trial necessitated by his improper conduct, or alternatively, courts should conclude that the defendant was never in jeopardy in the first proceeding because he was assured of an acquittal. By recognizing this limited exception, she reasons, courts would prevent the double jeopardy protection from frustrating the public's interest in the full and fair prosecution of criminal cases as well as its interest in holding trial judges accountable for their erroneous rulings or their misconduct, while at the same time protecting an individual's genuine interest in protection against double jeopardy. Like Rudstein, however, Poulin would not deviate from ordinary double jeopardy principles when the defendant corrupts members of a jury. She distinguishes bench trials from jury trials on two grounds. First, she asserts that in bench trials, the public has an interest in holding judges accountable for their actions. Second, she notes that because the judge in a bench trial acts as the sole fact finder, corrupting the judge gives the defendant greater certainty that the case will end in a result favorable to him than if the defendant attempts to corrupt a jury. The article is: Anne Bowen Poulin, *Double Jeopardy and Judicial Accountability: When Is an Acquittal Not an Acquittal?*, 27 Arizona State Law Journal 953 (1995).

Thomas M. DiBiagio, in a piece in *The Catholic University Law Review*, goes farther than Poulin, arguing that the government should be allowed to retry an individual for the same offense following an acquittal if it can show on appeal that the acquittal resulted from either a clear and obvious error of law by the trial court; tampering with or intimidating a member of the jury or a witness; or misconduct by the defense attorney. A judgment of acquittal obtained in such a manner, argues DiBiagio, calls into question the legitimacy and integrity of the criminal process and denies the public a fair opportunity to enforce its criminal laws. DiBiagio maintains that limited judicial review and retrial of, what he calls, a "faulty" judgment of acquittal would not violate the guarantee against double jeopardy because an appeal and retrial in such circumstances would not infringe upon the policies underlying the guarantee. Rather, it would merely be affording the government—and the public—an opportunity to convict the accused in an error-free trial. The article is: Thomas M. DiBiagio, *Judicial Equity: An Argument for Post-Acquittal Retrial When the Judicial Process is Fundamentally Defective*, 46 The Catholic University Law Review 77 (1996).

Collateral Estoppel

In a lecture presented in 1970 and reprinted in the *California Law Review*, Justice Walter V. Schaefer of the Supreme Court of Illinois discusses the then-recent decision of the United States Supreme Court in *Ashe v. Swenson* (1970) holding that the Double Jeopardy Clause encompasses the doctrine of collateral estoppel.

Justice Schaefer points out the shortcomings of that doctrine, namely, that it will not often be available to a criminal defendant because, in most cases, the defendant enters a general plea of not guilty and the jury returns a general verdict (*i.e.*, "guilty" or "not guilty"). If the jury acquits, it is not often possible to determine the basis for its decision. Justice Schaefer implies that the problem of protecting an individual from being harassed by multiple prosecutions could be resolved by the adoption of a rule of compulsory joinder of offenses committed during the "same transaction." Under such a rule, any related offenses that are omitted from the first prosecution of an individual could not thereafter be the subject of a second prosecution of that same individual. The article is: Walter V. Schaefer, *Unresolved Issues in the Law of Double Jeopardy: Waller* and *Ashe*, 58 California Law Review 391 (1970).

A student author writing in the *Drake Law Review* examines the doctrine of collateral estoppel in criminal cases. The author briefly traces the history of the doctrine and explores what he sees as the "rigid application" of that doctrine by courts. He contends that the United States Supreme Court reached the wrong result in *Ashe* when it held that the Double Jeopardy Clause encompasses the independent doctrine of criminal collateral estoppel. The author argues that by anchoring the doctrine of criminal collateral estoppel within the narrow confines of the Double Jeopardy Clause, the Supreme Court limited its usefulness to criminal defendants. He proposes three alternative ways for the Supreme Court to remedy the problem and allow the doctrine to be "a living, breathing doctrine capable of varying interpretations for varying situations." First, he suggests that the Supreme Court could overrule its decision in *Ashe* and hold that the doctrine is not a constitutional guarantee under the double jeopardy provision, but merely a principle of the common law. Second, the Court could hold that the Constitution embodies the doctrine not only in the Double Jeopardy Clause, but also in the more expansive requirement of "fundamental fairness" imposed by the Due Process Clause of the Fourteenth Amendment. Finally, the Court could adopt the "same transaction" test for determining whether two or more offenses are the "same" for purposes of double jeopardy analysis and, therefore, ordinarily must be tried together in the same proceeding. Such an interpretation, argues the author, would virtually eliminate the need for the doctrine of criminal collateral estoppel. The article is: Charles William Hendricks, Note, *100 Years of Double Jeopardy Erosion: Criminal Estoppel Made Extinct*, 48 Drake Law Review 379 (2000).

The Supreme Court's decision in *Ashe* has been examined in a number of student articles, including: Comment, *Ashe v. Swenson: Collateral Estoppel, Double Jeopardy, and Inconsistent Verdicts*, 71 Columbia Law Review 321 (1971); Bruce J. Downey III, Note, 49 The North Carolina Law Review 351 (1971); Howard P. Lucker, Comment, *Collateral Estoppel—An Attempted Transfusion Into the Guarantee Against Double Jeopardy*, 44 Temple Law Quarterly 377 (1971); Douglas S. Rich, Case Comment, *Collateral Estoppel: A Constitutional Guarantee*,

50 Boston University Law Review 604 (1970); and Recent Development, 69 Michigan Law Review 762 (1971).

Reprosecution Following a Mistrial

In an article in *The Supreme Court Review*, in which they attempt to formulate a general theory of the protection against double jeopardy, Peter Westen and Richard Drubel examine the double jeopardy rules governing retrial following a mistrial. Relying upon United States Supreme Court cases, they identify four values underlying the prohibition against double jeopardy: (1) protecting the defendant from embarrassment, expense, and ordeal; (2) protecting the defendant from having to live in a continuing state of anxiety and insecurity; (3) protecting the defendant from conduct by the government that would enhance the possibility that, though innocent, he may be found guilty; and (4) protecting the defendant's "valued right to have his trial completed by a particular tribunal." With respect to the last of these values, the authors reject the view that it means that "a defendant has a constitutional interest in having his case resolved by a tribunal that he perceives to be 'favorably disposed to his fate.'" Rather, they believe it means that the defendant has an interest in being able to end his confrontation with society once it has begun. This makes it essentially equivalent to the second value, which focuses upon the defendant's interest in finality. The authors do not believe that any of the values, taken by themselves, is sufficient to explain the rules governing mistrials, but that the second and third values, taken together, "provide a coherent rationale for mistrial cases." The authors concede, however, that a defendant's interest in finality may not always be sufficient to override the interest of the public in full and accurate criminal prosecutions. They conclude:

> [A] defendant has a constitutional interest in finality, a cognizable interest in seeing that criminal proceedings against him are resolved once and for all. But this interest is not absolute and must be balanced against society's interest in conducting further proceedings.... In the context of mistrials ..., where finality is balanced against "the public's interest in fair trials designed to end in just judgments," the defendant's interest can be relatively easily outweighed. Thus the defendant is not entitled to demand a mistrial with prejudice unless he can make a showing of deliberate harassment or overreaching. In all other cases, he is entitled to no more than to proceed with the first trial (subject always to being retried if he is convicted and his conviction is reversed on appeal), and even there his right to proceed with the first trial is limited to cases in which the defect in the first proceeding is capable of manipulation [in order to allow the government an opportunity to strengthen its case].

The article is: Peter Westen & Richard Drubel, *Toward a General Theory of Double Jeopardy*, 1978 The Supreme Court Review 81.

Mistrial Declared at the Request of the Defendant or With the Defendant's Consent

The United States Supreme Court's decision in *United States v. Dinitz* (1976), holding that the government can ordinarily retry a defendant whose trial ends in a mistrial declared upon his own motion, is briefly discussed by a student author in an article in *The American Criminal Law Review*. The article is: Kenneth M. Rosenzweig, Note, *Mistrials and Double Jeopardy*, 15 The American Criminal Law Review 169 (1977).

Several writers discuss the Supreme Court's holding in *Kennedy v. Oregon* (1982) that the Double Jeopardy Clause bars retrial of a defendant following a mistrial granted at his request only when he can show that the government engaged in action intended to "goad" the defendant into requesting the mistrial. For example, a student writing in the *Wayne Law Review* examines the standards adopted by two states, as a matter of state law, that grant defendants greater protection than *Kennedy*; however, she concludes that "the *Kennedy* standard adequately balances the interests of both the defendant and society." The article is: Cynthia C. Person, Note, *Prosecutorial Misconduct and Double Jeopardy: Should States Broaden Double Jeopardy Protection in Light of Oregon v. Kennedy*?, 37 Wayne Law Review 1699 (1991).

James F. Ponsoldt, on the other hand, in an article in the *Cornell Law Review*, concludes that *Kennedy* does not provide defendants with either adequate protection against government harassment, or a meaningful choice to complete their trial before the chosen jury. He proposes the adoption of a "plain error" standard under which a second trial would be barred whenever "'plain' government error, engaged in with the purpose of improperly seeking a conviction, ... results in a mistrial. ..." Moreover, Ponsoldt proposes the adoption of the same standard to govern the permissibility of a retrial following the reversal of a conviction on appeal. The article is: James F. Ponsoldt, *When Guilt Should be Irrelevant: Government Overreaching as a Bar to Reprosecution Under the Double Jeopardy Clause After Oregon v. Kennedy*," 69 Cornell Law Review 76 (1983).

Mistrial Declared Without the Defendant's Consent: The "Manifest Necessity" Standard

Stephen J. Schulhofer, in an article in the *University of Pennsylvania Law Review*, examines the "manifest necessity" rule governing the permissibility of a retrial following a mistrial declared without the consent of the defendant. After examining what he perceives to be the sources of difficulty underlying that rule, he proposes an approach to replace the "manifest necessity" rule, one that he asserts will eliminate some of the difficulties created by adherence to that rule and allow the propriety of retrial to be more meaningfully assessed. He acknowledges that his proposal "will not provide an automatic answer to every mistrial question that may arise," but claims that "it should permit resolution of these questions with considerably greater predictability, with due recognition for society's interest in an adequate opportunity to convict the guilty, and, above all, with assurance that the [recent] erosion of protection for the accused ... will not proceed into areas in which stringent double jeopardy safeguards remain necessary." Schulhofer proposes that once jeopardy attaches (which he would advance to the beginning of the jury-selection process), a relatively flexible standard should be used to determine the propriety of mistrial when difficulties occur at a point in the proceedings when the threat to double jeopardy interests is not particularly acute. This relatively flexible standard would merely require the judge to consider the possible alternatives to a mistrial and the disadvantages of those alternatives. Schulhofer would apply this relatively flexible standard in two circumstances:

> (1) before the opening of testimony, provided that jury selection has not been unusually difficult *and* there are no concrete indications that the panel might be unusually favorable to the defense; and
>
> (2) between the opening of testimony and the close of the government's case-in-chief, provided that the underlying difficulty is not attributable to the prosecution, the prosecution has suffered no specific tactical setback during the course of the trial, *and* jury selection has not been especially difficult or advantageous to the defense.

On the other hand, Schulhofer suggests that a more stringent standard should apply in situations involving an acute threat to double jeopardy interests. Specifically, he proposes that a "strict necessity" standard apply when a trial difficulty occurs:

> (1) before the opening of testimony, if jury selection has been unusually difficult or advantageous to the defense;
>
> (2) between the beginning of testimony and the close of the government's case, if the prosecution is responsible for the difficulty, if the proceedings have produced a specific tactical disadvantage for the prosecution, *or* if jury selection has been especially difficult or advantageous to the defense; and
>
> (3) after the close of the prosecution's case, regardless of the circumstances.

The article is: Stephen J. Schulhofer, *Jeopardy and Mistrials*, 125 University of Pennsylvania Law Review 449 (1977).

Reprosecution Following the Dismissal of a Charge

Distinguishing an Acquittal from a Dismissal

An "acquittal," whether by a jury or a judge, normally bars the government from prosecuting the defendant again for the same offense and from appealing the acquittal. A "dismissal," on the other hand, generally can be appealed by the government. Concerned about trial judges, either because of corruption or error, manipulating proceedings and insulating defendants from further prosecution, Anne Bowen Poulin urges that the definition of an acquittal be relaxed. Appellate courts should not, she argues, defer to the trial court's characterization of its ruling in a particular case as an acquittal, and they should refuse to treat as an acquittal any pro-defense ruling that ends a trial before the government has presented all its evidence, because such a ruling cannot rest upon a fair assessment of the sufficiency of the evidence. She reasons:

Whereas we have a strong tradition of and reasons for shielding factual acquittals from accountability, we have no comparable basis for shielding judicial rulings on matters of law. A legal ruling terminating the prosecution ought to be reviewable. To permit the trial judge to truncate the prosecution's presentation and then bar further proceedings by entering an order designated as an acquittal, places too little weight on the public interest in pursuing enforcement of the criminal laws through one full and fair opportunity to prosecute a criminal case. In addition, the approach undervalues the public interest in judicial accountability and grants too much deference to the trial court's decision to label its action as an acquittal, thereby insulating the ruling from appellate review.

The article is: Anne Bowen Poulin, *Double Jeopardy and Judicial Accountability: When Is an Acquittal Not an Acquittal?*, 27 Arizona State Law Journal 953 (1995).

Dismissal Before the Attachment of Jeopardy

Not much has been written pertaining to the prosecution of an individual following the trial court's dismissal of the charge against him at a point before jeopardy had attached. In an article written before the United States Supreme Court's decision in *Serfass v. United States* (1975), a student author writing in the *Loyola Law Review* concluded that double jeopardy principles do not bar the government from appealing a pretrial dismissal of a charge and prosecuting the accused anew if it succeeds in obtaining a reversal of the dismissal, the result subsequently reached by the Supreme Court in *Serfass*. The author reasoned that although an accused expends resources preparing for trial and experiences some social trauma and stigma during the pretrial stage of a criminal prosecution, "the extent of the authority granted to the trial judge in deciding a [pretrial] motion to dismiss is limited to the grant of a dismissal; and under no circumstances whatsoever is a defendant in fear of possible conviction at this point." Because the defendant is at no time in "'direct peril' of conviction," the Double Jeopardy Clause does not bar the government from prosecuting him anew if an appellate court reverses the trial court's order of dismissal. The article is: Susan L. Litzau, Comment, *Government Appeals of Pretrial Dismissals—The Implications of Double Jeopardy*, 21 Loyola Law Review 942 (1975).

Dismissal After the Attachment of Jeopardy

The United States Supreme Court's decision in *United States v. Scott* (1978), holding that the Double Jeopardy Clause does not bar the government from retrying a defendant after it succeeds in persuading an appellate court to reverse a trial court's judgment granting a defendant's midtrial motion to dismiss the charge against him on a ground unrelated to his factual guilt or innocence, is the subject of a student note in the *DePaul Law Review*. After criticizing the Supreme Court for overruling its three-year-old decision in *United States v. Jenkins* (1975), in which the Court reached the opposite result than in *Scott*, the author attacks the Court's reasoning in *Scott* as being logically flawed. He asserts that the Court erred in analogizing the motion to dismiss the indictment in *Scott* to a motion for a mistrial, first, because both the defendant and the trial judge in *Scott* believed the dismissal would be final, whereas a motion for a mistrial normally contemplates reprosecution of the accused; and second, because the declaration of a mistrial does not end the proceedings *favorably* to the defendant as did the dismissal of the indictment in *Scott*. The author also takes issue with what he calls the Court's "unduly restrictive definition of acquittal." He urges a return from the "nebulous balancing approach" adopted in *Scott* to the "clear test" articulated in *Jenkins*, a test that he believes "protected the constitutional rights of defendants, as well as those of society, with precision and clarity." The article is: Robert J. Ross, Case Note, 28 DePaul Law Review 485 (1979).

Other student authors have commented upon *Scott*; among them are: John K. Bennett, Note, 9 Seton Hall Law Review 579 (1978); Gary E. Jubber, Case Note, 1978 Brigham Young Law Review 742; and Larry L. Shupe, Note, 62 Marquette Law Review 289 (1978).

Sentencing Proceeding Following Conviction

A number of student works examine the United States Supreme Court's decision in *Schiro v. Farley* (1994) holding that the sentencing proceeding following a trial does not constitute a "second prosecution" for the purposes of double jeopardy analysis. The articles are: Patrick L. Edgerton, Casenote, *Schiro v. Farley: If at First You Don't Succeed, Trial and Trial Again; The Demise of the Double Jeopardy Clause Within the Context of Capital Punishment*, 16 Northern Illinois University Law Review 175 (1995); James R. Lane, Note, *The Covert Narrowing of Double Jeopardy Precedent: The Supreme Court's Real Reason for Hearing Schiro v. Farley*, 85 The Journal of Criminal Law and Criminology 909 (1995); Survey, 4 Seton Hall Constitutional Law Journal 817 (1994); and Nancy A. Wood, Casenote, *A Double-Take at Double Jeopardy: Schiro v. Farley*, 28 Creighton Law Review 445 (1995).

Multiple Punishments

In a Single Proceeding

Before the United States Supreme Court focused upon the role that the Double Jeopardy Clause plays in the context of multiple punishment in a single proceeding, a perceptive student commentator concluded in the *Yale Law Journal* that the Double Jeopardy Clause does not limit the power of the legislature to define and punish offenses, but rather limits the discretion of courts and prosecutors. Towards this end, he contended that the Double Jeopardy Clause permits cumulative punishment in a single trial for closely related offenses only when the legislature intended cumulative punishments for those offenses, the position subsequently taken by the United States Supreme Court. The article is: Comment, *Twice in Jeopardy*, 75 Yale Law Journal 262 (1965).

In Successive Proceedings

Following a Permissible Second Prosecution

Westen and Drubel, in their attempt to formulate a general theory of double jeopardy, discuss the concept of multiple, or double, punishment in some depth. They examine the relevant Supreme Court cases on the issue and assert that in the context of separate proceedings, an individual suffers multiple punishment in violation of the Double Jeopardy Clause only when he is subjected to punishment for the same offense in excess of that which the legislature intended. The article is: Peter Westen & Richard Drubel, *Toward a General Theory of Double Jeopardy*, 1978 The Supreme Court Review 81.

Sanctions Imposed in Both a Criminal Prosecution and a Civil Proceeding

In *United States v. Halper* (1989), the United States Supreme Court held that in any particular case a sanction imposed upon an individual in a civil action brought by the government could constitute "punishment" for purposes of double jeopardy analysis and that an individual who already had been punished in a criminal prosecution could not be subjected to any additional civil sanctions for the same conduct to the extent those sanctions constituted "punishment." Before the Supreme Court effectively overruled *Halper* in *Hudson v. United States* (1997), *Halper* generated a number of scholarly articles. For instance, in an article in the *Oklahoma Law Review*, the author of the instant text, David S. Rudstein, analyzed the Court's decision in *Halper* and explored a number of questions concerning the scope of the Court's holding. He concluded, first, that the principle enunciated in *Halper* applied regardless of the sequence of the civil and criminal proceedings, that is, even when the civil proceeding preceded the criminal prosecution. Second, he concluded that under *Halper*, the Double Jeopardy Clause precluded the government from both punishing an individual in a criminal action for unlawfully possessing illegal drugs and imposing a tax on the individual for possessing those same drugs, the result subsequently reached by the United States Supreme Court in *Department of Revenue of Montana v. Kurth Ranch* (1994). Third, Rudstein concluded that the principle articulated in *Halper* applied to the *in rem* forfeiture of real or personal property not in itself contraband, such as currency, automobiles, and a house (a result inconsistent with that subsequently reached by the United States Supreme Court in *United States v. Ursery* (1996)), and, perhaps, also to sanctions imposed upon inmates in prison disciplinary proceedings, but not generally to the suspension or revocation of an individual's driver's license or license to engage in a particular profession or business, or to the exclusion of an individual from participation in government programs. The article is: David S. Rudstein, *Civil Penalties and Multiple Punishment Under the Double Jeopardy Clause: Some Unanswered Questions*, 46 Oklahoma Law Review 587 (1993).

Halper was not without its critics, however. In an article in the *Washington University Law Quarterly*, Linda S. Eads concluded that *Halper* (1) did not give adequate guidance to either the executive or legislative branches of government in their tasks of formulating and enforcing appropriate civil sanctions; (2) would often force governments "to choose between civil and criminal remedies without having sufficient information to make a wise choice"; and (3) was unnecessary, because other provisions of the Constitution, such as the Due Process Clause of the Fourteenth Amendment and the Excessive Fines Clause of the Eighth Amendment, provided sufficient authority for dealing with the problem of a disproportionate civil penalty. The article is: Linda S. Eads, *Separating Crime from Punishment: The Constitutional Implications of United States v. Halper*, 68 Washington University Law Quarterly 929 (1990).

Among the other articles analyzing *Halper* are: Stanley E. Cox, *Halper*'s *Continuing Double Jeopardy Implications: A Thorn by any Other Name Would Prick as Deep*, 39 Saint Louis University Law Journal 1235 (1995); Lauren Orchard Clapp, Note, *United States v. Halper: Remedial Justice and Double Jeopardy*, 68 The North Carolina Law Review 979 (1990); Andrew Z. Glickman, Note, *Civil Sanctions and the Double Jeopardy Clause: Applying the Multiple Punishment Doctrine to Parallel Proceedings After United States v. Halper*, 76 Virginia Law Review1251 (1990); and Elizabeth S. Jahncke, Note, *United States v. Halper, Punitive Civil Fines, and the Double Jeopardy and Excessive Fines Clauses*, 66 New York University Law Review 112 (1991).

Susan R. Klein, in an article in the *Iowa Law Review*, criticizes the United States Supreme Court's decision in *United States v. Ursery* (1996) and explores the relationship between civil *in rem* forfeitures and the Double Jeopardy Clause. She contends that a civil forfeiture is punitive whenever the property owner is guilty of a criminal offense that would support the forfeiture, unless the property in question is illegal or dangerous for anyone to own, and that the Double Jeopardy Clause bars the government from bringing a criminal prosecution following a civil forfeiture proceeding, and *vice versa*, when the same illegal conduct constitutes the basis for both proceedings. She concludes:

> Because civil *in rem* forfeiture proceedings now apparently serve the punitive goals of criminal law, even if they are permissible civilly when that is the only action brought by the government against the property owner, they should not be permitted to follow or precede a more traditional criminal action against that property owner. The government should be forced to choose between punishing via a forfeiture action in a civil forum, with its advantageous procedural rules, and punishing via both incarceration and criminal forfeiture in a criminal forum, with its heavier procedural burdens.

She maintains that the Supreme Court, in holding otherwise in *Ursery*, "failed to consider the different values underlying each of the double jeopardy prongs and failed to recognize how recent developments in criminal law has [sic] endangered those values. The harm in parallel civil in rem forfeiture and criminal cases is that they enable the government to harass individuals through multiple proceedings." Klein suggests "a slightly modified version of the Double Jeopardy Clause's successive prosecution prong to bar whichever action is considered the second when both a civil forfeiture action against a piece of property and a substantive criminal charge against the property owner are brought concerning the same underlying illegal act." She rejects "the multiple punishment prong of double jeopardy—the theory applied by the Court in cases involving civil in personam monetary sanctions deemed punitive—as underprotective and ultimately illogical." She also touches upon "the possibility of expanding the 'same offense' test should legislators and prosecutors attempt to evade the mandates of [her] proposal by enacting duplicative statutes and artfully drafting indictments and civil forfeiture complaints." The article is: Susan R. Klein, *Civil In Rem Forfeiture and Double Jeopardy*, 82 Iowa Law Review 183 (1996).

A number of articles analyze the Supreme Court's decision in *Hudson v. United States* (1997), which in effect overruled *Halper*. For example, one student commentator concludes that "the *Hudson* Court adopted the appropriate analysis for distinguishing between criminal and noncriminal sanctions and proceedings," but that in refusing to evaluate whether the sanctions, as applied in the particular case, were punitive in character, the Supreme Court "failed to safeguard the individual liberties protected by the Double Jeopardy Clause." The article is: Troy D. Cahill, Note, *The Supreme Court's Decision in Hudson v. United States: One Step Up and Two Steps Back for Multiple Punishment Protection Under the Double Jeopardy Clause*, 33 Wake Forest Law Review 439 (1998).

Another student article criticizes the result reached by the Supreme Court in *Hudson* in light of its effect in the lower courts. The author concludes:

> [T]he decisions of appellate courts implementing *Hudson* reflect that under the current doctrine even very punitive civil sanctions will be considered "civil" and exempt from double jeopardy protection. Use of the ... test ... outlined in *Hudson* has continually resulted in a determination that: first, the sanction was intended to be civil by the legislature; and second, there was not the "clearest proof" required to show that the civil sanction should be regarded as "criminal" for double jeopardy purposes.

The article is: Lisa Melenyzer, Note, *Double Jeopardy Protection from Civil Sanctions After Hudson v. United States*, 89 The Journal of Criminal Law and Criminology 1007 (1999).

On the other hand, the student author of an article in the *American Journal of Criminal Law* concludes that the rule the Supreme Court adopted in *Hudson* "is a good one, clearing up much confusion and simplifying the task of finding when double jeopardy has occurred." The article is: John R. Weikart, Casenote, *A Second Look at Double Jeopardy: Hudson v. United States*, 25 American Journal of Criminal Law 631 (1998).

Enhancement of a Sentence Because of Previous Criminal Conduct

The United States Supreme Court's decision in *Witte v. United States* (1995) holding that the Double Jeopardy Clause does not bar the government from prosecuting an individual for an offense based upon conduct previously considered by a court to enhance the individual's sentence for a different offense is the subject of several student works, including: Brett J. Davis, Recent Development, *Witte v. United States: The Double Jeopardy Clause Does Not Bar Prosecution For Relevant Conduct Already Used to Enhance a Previous Sentence*, 22 Journal of Contemporary Law 145 (1996); Jason Ebe, Note, *Witte v. United States: Conduct May Be Considered for Multiple Punishments Without Violating Double Jeopardy*, 37 Arizona Law Review 1279 (1995); Christine H. Nooning, Recent Decision, 34 Duquesne Law Review 1147 (1996); and Elizabeth J. Wiet, Note, *Witte v. United States: Double Jeopardy and the United States Sentencing Guidelines*, 86 The Journal of Criminal Law and Criminology 1539 (1996).

Resentencing

Resentencing by the Trial Judge in the Same Proceeding

The United States Supreme Court's decisions in *Ex Parte Lange* (1874) and *In re Bradley* (1943) are briefly discussed by Gregory P. Dunsky in an article examining whether, consistent with the Constitution, an appellate court can increase a convicted defendant's sentence. The article is: Gregory P. Dunsky, *The Constitutionality of Increasing Sentences on Appellate Review*, 69 The Journal of Criminal Law and Criminology 19 (1978). A student author in an article on the same topic in the *Virginia Law Review* also discusses *Lange and Bozza v. United States* (1947). The article is: Note, *Twice in Jeopardy: Prosecutorial Appeals of Sentences*, 63 Virginia Law Review 325 (1977).

Resentencing Following Reconviction for the Same Offense

The Supreme Court's holding in *North Carolina v. Pearce* (1969) that the Double Jeopardy Clause does not prohibit imposition of a more severe sentence following an individual's reconviction for the same offense after the reversal of his initial conviction and sentence on appeal is briefly discussed by a student author in the Virginia Law Review. The article is: Note, *Twice in Jeopardy: Prosecutorial Appeals of Sentences*, 63 Virginia Law Review 325 (1977). *Bullington v. Missouri* (1981), which created an exception to *Pearce*'s general rule for certain capital sentencing proceedings, is the subject of two student articles. The articles are: John A. Chatzky, Comment, *Extending Double Jeopardy Protection to Sentencing*, 20 The American Criminal Law Review 127 (1982), and The Supreme Court, 1980 Term, 95 Harvard Law Review 112 (1981).

Resentencing Following an Appeal of the Initial Sentence

Gregory P. Dunsky, in an article in *The Journal of Criminal Law and Criminology*, discusses whether the Double Jeopardy Clause precludes an appellate court from increasing a convicted defendant's sentence on appeal. Dunsky examines the arguments on both sides of the issue in light of United States Supreme Court precedent and concludes that it does not, even when no new evidence supports the increase. The article is: Gregory P. Dunsky, *The Constitutionality of Increasing Sentences on Appellate Review*," 69 The Journal of Criminal Law and Criminology 19 (1978).

A student author in the *Mercer Law Review* criticizes the United States Supreme Court's holding in *United States v. DiFrancesco* (1980) that the Double Jeopardy Clause does not bar the government from appealing a sentence imposed upon a convicted defendant for the purpose of obtaining a more severe sentence. The author believes that the interests of society have diminished once it has obtained a conviction and therefore the defendant's interest in finality should prevail and the double jeopardy provision should prohibit the government from seeking an increased sentence. The article is: Thomas Michael Hackel, *United States v. DiFrancesco*: *Court Upholds State Initiated Sentence Appeals*, 32 Mercer Law Review 1261 (1981).

In addition to these works, some of the articles mentioned in the section of this Bibliographical Essay relating to appeals by the government of a convicted defendant's sentence also discuss resentencing following such an appeal.

Appeals

In a recent provocative article in the *Boston University Law Review*, Vikramaditya S. Khanna examines the purposes behind the asymmetric appeal rights attached to the Double Jeopardy Clause (*i.e.*, criminal defendants can appeal their convictions, but the right of the government to appeal is severely limited) and the likely effects of those asymmetric rights on the behavior of litigants and on the outcomes of trials. The justifications generally offered to support asymmetric rights to appeal are to reduce the number of erroneous convictions and to lessen the costs of litigation. Khanna finds, however, that by giving the government only one opportunity to obtain a conviction, asymmetric appeal rights may induce the government to spend even more in the defendant's initial trial than if appeal rights were symmetric and that such increased spending may, at least in some cases, increase the chances of an erroneous conviction and could increase the litigation costs of the defendant. He concludes that the overall effects of asymmetric appeal rights on erroneous convictions and litigation costs are ambiguous and may not be particularly dramatic. As a result, says Khanna, alternative justifications for asymmetric appeal rights, such as restraining self-interested prosecuting attorneys or politically motivated prosecutions, must be explored. The article is: Vikramaditya S. Khanna, *Double Jeopardy's Asymmetric Appeal Rights: What Purpose Do They Serve?*, 82 Boston University Law Review 341 (2002).

By the Accused

In researching this text, the author did not find any significant resources directly pertaining to the right of an accused to appeal immediately the denial of a pretrial motion to dismiss a charge on the ground that the proceeding placed him twice in jeopardy for the same offense.

By the Government

In an article in the *Columbia Journal of Law and Social Problems*, a student author briefly reviews the history of appeals by the United States in federal criminal cases. He points out that the United States Supreme Court held in 1892 that the United States government has no right to appeal any decision in a criminal case unless expressly authorized by statute to do so. This decision, he notes, led Congress to enact the first Criminal Appeals Act in 1907, which authorized the government to appeal certain decisions dismissing the charge against the accused. The statute proved confusing, however, because of Congress' use of language of common law pleading, such as "arrest of judgment" and "special plea in bar." As a result, many dismissals went unappealed. In an attempt to eliminate these problems and to broaden the right of the government to appeal in criminal cases to the constitutional limits imposed by the Double Jeopardy Clause, Congress enacted the Criminal Appeals Act of 1970. The author analyzes this statute in light of three decisions by the United States Supreme Court interpreting it: *United States v. Wilson* (1975); *United States v. Jenkins* (1975) (subsequently overruled by the Supreme Court); and *Serfass v. United States* (1975). He concludes that the Criminal Appeals Act of 1970 and the cases interpreting it "clarified the constitutional principles controlling double jeopardy and [g]overnment appeals." The article is: Kenneth A. Caruso, *Double Jeopardy and Government Appeals in Criminal Cases*, 12 Columbia Journal of Law and Social Problems 295 (1975).

James A. Strazzella, in a piece in the *Notre Dame Law Review*, discusses the relationship of double jeopardy principles to appeals by the government. He asserts that the guarantee against double jeopardy is designed to protect an individual against two trials, not to protect him against litigation in an appellate proceeding. According to Strazzella, the Double Jeopardy Clause does not itself bar appeals by the government, but does so only in combination with some additional legal principle. For example, if a state's own law precludes its appellate courts from issuing advisory opinions (as the United States Constitution does with the federal courts) and the remedy requested by the government in an appeal would be barred by the double jeopardy provision, then the case is one in which the appellate court's opinion on the merits of the government's position would be merely advisory and therefore prohibited by state law. Similarly, if the jurisdiction's own law expressly links an appeal by the government to double jeopardy—such as the current federal statute that makes government appeals contingent upon whether the Double Jeopardy Clause would bar further prosecution—the double jeopardy provision combined with the law governing appeals would bar an appeal whenever the appeal, if successful, would require further proceedings that would impermissibly place the accused in jeopardy a second time. Strazzella contends that in those few states that allow advisory opinions, prosecutors can seek to appeal a judgment in favor of the accused, even when double jeopardy principles preclude a new trial, by arguing that "an important and recurring trial level concern, which may well normally lead to acquittals, needs appellate resolution *limited to prospective cases*" (italics added). He also contends that the Supreme Court has not adequately focused upon this issue and, in fact, has made inaccurate statements about the scope of federal double jeopardy law creating the danger that "some states will be improperly precluded from effectuating a system actually allowed by the federal constitution: a system in which prosecutors can obtain an advisory opinion on the underlying issue, with the ruling applicable only to future cases." The article is: James A. Strazzella, *The Relationship of Double Jeopardy to Prosecution Appeals*, 73 Notre Dame Law Review 1 (1997).

Appeal Before the Attachment of Jeopardy

Little has been written pertaining to a government appeal of a pretrial order dismissing the charge against the defendant. One student author, writing before the United States Supreme Court's decision in *Serfass v. United States* (1975), concluded that the Double Jeopardy Clause does not prohibit the government from appealing such an order—the result subsequently reached by the Supreme Court in *Serfass*. The author acknowledged that an accused spends money preparing for trial and experiences a degree of social trauma and stigma during the pretrial stage of a criminal prosecution, but explains that a trial judge faced with a pretrial motion to dismiss a charge can only grant the motion to dismiss or deny it. She reasoned that because the defendant is not in danger of being convicted at that point in the proceedings, the double jeopardy provision would not bar the government from prosecuting him if the trial court's order of dismissal were reversed on appeal, and therefore an appeal by the government is constitutionally permissible. The article is: Susan L. Litzau, Comment, *Government Appeals of Pretrial Dismissals—The Implications of Double Jeopardy*, 21 Loyola Law Review 942 (1975).

Appeal After the Attachment of Jeopardy

In its 1987 Report to the Attorney General, the Office of Legal Policy of the United States Justice Department thoroughly examines the question of appeals by the government in criminal cases. After examining the history of the protection against double jeopardy, the Report concludes that the drafters of the Double Jeopardy Clause most likely intended it to bar the government from appealing an acquittal of a felony, for the purpose of obtaining a new trial, except in cases in which the initial trial court lacked jurisdiction; the initial indictment was defective; or the facts demonstrated that the accused committed a felony, but the court erroneously held that the conduct was not a felony. The Report also concludes that while the matter is not free from doubt, the drafters probably did not intend the Double Jeopardy Clause to bar the government from appealing an acquittal of a felony if a successful appeal would not result in a new trial. The Report then examines federal case law concerning government appeals. It concludes that under current case law, "acquittals" cannot be appealed by the government even when the acquittal results from errors of law made by the trial court, but that case law allows the government to appeal pretrial dismissals of charges; midtrial dismissals of charges on legal grounds unrelated to the factual guilt or innocence of the accused; and posttrial dismissals of charges following a conviction by the fact finder. After examining the treatment of government appeals of acquittals by the states and by various foreign countries, the Report considers the policy ramifications of the Double Jeopardy Clause's application to appeals of acquittals. It concludes that "a government right of appeal would tend to promote the fairness and expeditiousness of criminal trials, thus increasing the probability of correct verdicts and enhancing the efficiency of criminal adjudication," thereby promoting the search for truth in criminal justice. Nevertheless, it also concludes that "a general rule authorizing the government to appeal all acquittals—at least to the extent such appeals result in new trials—must be rejected on constitutional grounds." While recognizing that the Constitution could be amended to allow the government to appeal acquittals, it does not recommend such an amendment, because, "[g]iven the longstanding English and American legal tradition that looks upon appeals of acquittals with disfavor ..., an amendment authorizing appeals would predictably generate a furor." The Report recommends, instead, that the Department of Justice consider seeking an appropriate case to argue that the government can constitutionally appeal an acquittal rendered by a judge in a bench trial when correction of the error would allow a verdict of guilty to be entered without requiring a new trial. It states:

> We believe that the Department [of Justice] would stand an excellent chance of obtaining sanction for government appeals of errors of law in a bench trial, when findings of fact clearly support a guilty verdict. In a bench trial, an erroneous interpretation of law or a misapplication of law to the facts may yield a "legally defective" verdict of acquittal. If an appellate court determines that the trial judge actually resolved against the defendant all of the factual issues necessary to support a finding of guilt, and would have found him guilty under the correct legal standard, it would be appropriate for the higher court to order the entry of a verdict of guilty in place of the "mistaken" verdict of acquittal. By not requiring a new trial, such an action by the reviewing court would remain faithful to the apparent general purpose of the constitutional double jeopardy principle.

The report is: Office of Legal Policy, United States Department of Justice, *Report to the Attorney General on Double Jeopardy and Government Appeals of Acquit-*

tals, "Truth in Justice," Report No. 6 (1987), *reprinted in* 22 University of Michigan Journal of Law Reform 831 (1989).

As discussed earlier in this Bibliographical Essay, Akhil Reed Amar believes that "jeopardy" does not necessarily end with an acquittal. He contends that the government should be able to seek appellate review of legal errors even after an acquittal and, if successful on appeal, should be allowed to retry the defendant until an error-free result is reached. The essay is: Akhil Reed Amar, *Double Jeopardy Law Made Simple*, 106 Yale Law Journal 1807 (1997).

Taking issue with the definitions of "acquittal" used by the United States Supreme Court in various cases involving a decision by a trial judge terminating a jury trial in the defendant's favor, Westen and Drubel express their view why those definitions do not comport with the policies underlying the Double Jeopardy Clause. They suggest that the government be allowed to appeal any allegedly erroneous ruling in the defendant's favor by a trial judge if the consequence of the appeal would be to reinstate a valid finding of guilty by a jury. They also suggest that the government be allowed to appeal any such allegedly erroneous ruling so it can retry the defendant, unless retrial would be barred under the independent standards proposed by the authors to govern retrial following a mistrial. Westen and Drubel assert that these rules are consistent with the policies underlying the guarantee against double jeopardy as well as with the principal decisions of the United States Supreme Court. The article is: Peter Westen & Richard Drubel, *Toward a General Theory of Double Jeopardy*, 1978 The Supreme Court Review 81.

Vikramaditya S. Khanna, in a recent article in the *Boston University Law Review*, briefly addresses the situation in which a defendant obtains an acquittal through bribery of the fact finder. Khanna states that an exception to the otherwise absolute ban on government appeals of an acquittal "may arise when the defendant has bribed a juror or the judge." The article is: Vikramaditya S. Khanna, *Double Jeopardy's Asymmetric Appeal Rights: What Purpose Do They Serve?*," 82 Boston University Law Review 341 (2002). The articles by Rudstein, Poulin, and DiBiagio discussed in the section of this Bibliographical Essay dealing with the possible exception to the rule prohibiting reprosecution following an acquittal are also relevant to the right of the government to appeal an acquittal obtained through improper means.

Appeal of a Sentence

Several articles discuss the right of the government to appeal the sentence of a convicted defendant. In an article in the *Virginia Law Review* written before the United States Supreme Court's decision in *United States v. DiFrancesco* (1980) upholding a statutory provision allowing the government unilaterally to appeal a defendant's sentence for the purpose of increasing the sentence, the student author concluded that appellate review of sentencing at the behest of the government is "antagonistic to the interests and policies identified and protected by the Supreme Court in previous double jeopardy and due process decisions" and that "[o]nce the prosecution has secured a legally enforceable sentence, finality should attach to that decision in favor of the defendant." The article is: Note, *Twice in Jeopardy: Prosecutorial Appeals of Sentences*," 63 Virginia Law Review 325 (1977).

Peter Westen, also writing before the Supreme Court's decision in *DiFrancesco*, reached the opposite conclusion. He believed that such appeals do not violate the Double Jeopardy Clause. After identifying the three values he believes the double jeopardy provision protects, Westen argued that none of them are infringed by a government appeal of a sentence. First, he asserted that the rule that an individual cannot be prosecuted for the same offense following an acquittal does not encompass an appeal of a sentence. Next, he alleged that a government appeal of a sentence does not violate the rule prohibiting multiple punishments for the same offense, so long as the legislature clearly authorized the appeal and the increased sentence. Finally, he explained that a government appeal of a defendant's sentence would not impinge upon the defendant's interest in finality, even if the appellate court remands for a new sentencing hearing. The article is: Peter Westen, *The Three Faces of Double Jeopardy: Reflections on Government Appeals of Criminal Sentences*, 78 Michigan Law Review 1001 (1980).

As discussed earlier in this Bibliographical Essay, a student commentator in the *Mercer Law Review* examines the Supreme Court's decision in *DiFrancesco*. The author criticizes the Court's reasoning for focusing only upon the effect of a government appeal of a sentence upon one of the interested parties, the accused. He concludes that the Court should also have considered the interests of society after the trial judge imposes a sentence. The author believes that, like the interests of the accused, the interests of society have lessened after it has obtained a conviction because "the government has had its 'one bite at the apple.'" The article is: Thomas Michael Hackel, *United States v. DiFrancesco*: *Court Upholds State Initiated Sentence Appeals*, 32 Mercer Law Review 1261 (1981).

The Supreme Court's decisions in *DiFrancesco* and *Bullington v. Missouri* (1981) are discussed in an article in the *Harvard Law Review* reviewing the Court's decisions during its 1980-81 Term. The student author concludes that by holding in *Bullington* that a sentence of life imprisonment imposed in the sentencing stage of a bifurcated proceeding is final, so that the death penalty may not be imposed should the defendant be convicted again upon retrial, the Court "obscured [the] bright line" it drew in *DiFrancesco* when it held that the Double Jeopardy Clause allows the government to appeal a sentence when statutorily authorized to do so. Although the author agrees with the result reached by the Court in each of these cases, he attacks the Court's analysis as "perfunctory and misdirected" and criticizes it for being "unable to develop a coherent double jeopardy rationale capable of explaining why some sentences are constitutionally final while others are not." The article is: The Supreme Court, 1980 Term, 95 Harvard Law Review 112 (1981).

NOTES

1. Walter V. Schaefer, *Unresolved Issues in the Law of Double Jeopardy: Waller and Ashe*, 58 California Law Review 391 (1970).

2. See, e.g., Walter V. Schaefer, *The Suspect and Society: Criminal Procedure & Converging Constitutional Doctrines* (Northwestern University Press 1967); Walter V. Schaefer, *Federalism and State Criminal Prosecutions*, 70 Harvard Law Review 1 (1956); Albert E. Jenner, Jr., & Walter V. Schaefer, *The New Rules of the Illinois Supreme Court Under the Illinois Civil Practice Act*, 1 The University of Chicago Law Review 752 (1934).

Table of Cases

A

A.R. v. State, 678 S.W.2d 177 (Tex. Ct. App. 1984)
Abbate v. United States, 359 U.S. 187 (1959)
Abney v. United States, 431 U.S. 651 (1977)
Adamson v. California, 332 U.S. 46 (1947)
Adkinson, United States v., 135 F.3d 1363 (11th Cir. 1998)
Adoption of Iris, 427 Mass. 582, 695 N.E.2d 645 (1998)
Aguilar-Aranceta, United States v., 957 F.2d 18 (1st Cir. 1992)
Akins, State v., 867 S.W.2d 350 (Tenn. Crim. App. 1993)
Alabama v. Shelton, 535 U.S. 654 (2002)
Albanese, United States v., 195 F.3d 389 (8th Cir. 1999)
Albernaz v. United States, 450 U.S. 333 (1981)
Aldrich, Commonwealth v., 21 Mass. App. 221, 486 N.E.2d 732 (1985)
Aleman, People v., 281 Ill. App. 3d 991, 667 N.E.2d 615, 217 Ill. Dec. 526 (1996)
Aleman, United States *ex rel.* v. Circuit Court of Cook County, 967 F. Supp. 1022 (N.D. Ill. 1997)
Aleman v. Honorable Judges of the Circuit Court of Cook County, 138 F.3d 302 (7th Cir. 1998)
All Assets of G.P.S. Automotive Corp., United States v., 66 F.3d 483 (2d Cir. 1995)
Alston, State v., 82 N.C. App. 372, 346 S.E.2d 184 (1986)
Alston, United States v., 609 F.2d 531 (D.C. Cir. 1979)
Anderson v. United States, 481 A.2d 1299 (D.C. 1984)
Angel, State v., 132 N.M. 501, 51 P.3d 1155 (2002)
Angel v. Bullington, 330 U.S. 183 (1947)
Arena, United States v., 180 F.3d 380 (2d Cir. 1999)
Argersinger v. Hamlin, 407 U.S. 25 (1971)
Arizona v. Manypenny, 451 U.S. 232 (1981)
Arizona v. Rumsey, 467 U.S. 203 (1984)
Arizona v. Washington, 434 U.S. 497 (1978)
Arthurs v. Board of Registration in Medicine, 383 Mass. 299, 418 N.E.2d 1236 (1981)
Ashba v. State, 580 N.E.2d 244 (Ind. 1991)
Ashe v. Swenson, 397 U.S. 436 (1970)
Asher, *In re*, 772 A.2d 1161 (D.C. 2001)
Ashford v. Thornton, 1 B. & Ald. 405, 106 Eng. Rep. 149 (1818)
Ashley Transfer & Storage Co., United States v., 858 F.2d 221 (4th Cir. 1988)

B

B.D.T. v. State, 738 N.E.2d 1066 (Ind. Ct. App. 2000)
B.G., *In re*, 225 Ga. App. 492, 484 S.E.2d 293 (1997)
Baggett, United States v., 251 F.3d 1087 (6th Cir. 2001)
Ball, United States v., 163 U.S. 662 (1896)
Ball v. United States, 470 U.S. 856 (1985)
Ball v. United States, 140 U.S. 118 (1891)
Baranco, State v., 77 Haw. 351, 884 P.2d 729 (1994)
Barela v. People, 826 P.2d 1249 (Colo. 1992)
Barker, United States v., 681 F.2d 589 (9th Cir. 1982)
Barksdale, State v., 224 N.J. Super. 404, 540 A.2d 901 (App. Div. 1988)
Barron v. Mayor and City Council of Baltimore, 32 U.S. (7 Pet.) 243 (1833)
Bartkus v. Illinois, 359 U.S. 121 (1959)
Basile, United States v., 109 F.3d 1304 (8th Cir. 1997)
Bassing v. Cady, 208 U.S. 386 (1908)
Bates, United States v., 917 F.2d 388 (9th Cir. 1991)
Batey, People v., 183 Cal. App. 3d 1281, 228 Cal. Rptr. 787 (1986)
Bayer, United States v., 331 U.S. 532 (1947)
Beak v. Thyrwhit, 3 Mod. 194, 87 Eng. Rep. 124 (K.B. 1688)
Belcher, State v., 51 Conn. App. 117, 721 A.2d 899 (1998)
Belcher, United States v., 762 F. Supp. 666 (W.D. Va. 1991)
Bell, State v., 753 So. 2d 619 (Fla. Dist. Ct. App. 2000)
Bell, State v., 55 N.J. 239, 260 A.2d 849 (1970)
Belmarez, State v., 254 Neb. 467, 577 N.W.2d 264 (1998)
Benard v. State, 481 S.W.2d 427 (Tex. Crim. App. 1972)
Benton v. Maryland, 395 U.S. 784 (1969)
Beszborn, United States v., 21 F.3d 62 (5th Cir. 1994)
Betts v. Brady, 316 U.S. 455 (1942)
Beverly, *Ex parte*, 497 So. 2d 519 (Ala. 1986)
Beverly v. Jones, 854 F.2d 412 (11th Cir. 1988)
Black, State v., 153 N.J. 438, 710 A.2d 428 (1998).
Blockburger v. United States, 284 U.S. 299 (1932)
Bohmer, Commonwealth v., 374 Mass. 368, 372 N.E.2d 1381 (1978)
Booth v. State, 903 P.2d 1079 (Alaska Ct. App. 1995)
Booth v. State, 436 So. 2d 36 (Fla. 1983)
Bostwick, State v., 222 Neb. 631, 385 N.W.2d 906 (1986)
Bowden, State v., 93 Wis. 2d 574, 288 N.W.2d 139 (1980)
Bowling, State v., 712 So. 2d 798 (Fla. Dist. Ct. App. 1998)
Bowling, State v., 36 Ohio App. 3d 74, 520 N.E.2d 1387 (1987) (per curiam)
Bowling v. State, 298 Md. 396, 470 A.2d 797 (1984)
Bozza v. United States, 330 U.S. 160 (1947)
Bradley, *In re*, 318 U.S. 50 (1943)
Bradley v. State, 272 Ga. 740, 533 S.E.2d 727 (2000)
Bradshaw, State v., 593 S.W.2d 562 (Mo. Ct. App. 1979)
Branch, Commonwealth v., 417 Pa. Super. 571, 612 A.2d 1085 (1992), *overruled on other grounds by* Commonwealth v. Rosario, 545 Pa. 4, 679 A.2d 756 (1996)
Brancoccio, People v., 83 N.Y.2d 638, 634 N.E.2d 954, 612 N.Y.S.2d 353 (1994)

Brandon, People v., 40 Cal. App. 4th 1172, 47 Cal. Rptr. 2d 383 (1995)
Braxton v. United States, 395 A.2d 759 (D.C. 1978)
Breed v. Jones, 421 U.S. 519 (1975)
Breuhl, State v., 615 N.W.2d 375 (Minn. Ct. App. 2000)
Brickey, State v., 714 P.2d 644 (Utah 1986)
Brock, State v., 234 N.C. 392, 67 S.E.2d 282 (1951)
Brock v. North Carolina, 344 U.S. 424 (1953)
Brower, People v., 164 Mich. App. 242, 416 N.W.2d 397 (1987)
Brown, State v., 262 Or. 442, 497 P.2d 1191 (1972)
Brown v. Ohio, 432 U.S. 161 (1977)
Browning-Ferris Industries of Vermont, Inc. v. Kelco Disposal, Inc., 492 U.S. 257 (1989)
Brunet, State v., 806 A.2d 1007 (Vt. 2002)
Bugajewitz v. Adams, 228 U.S. 585 (1913)
Bullington v. Missouri, 451 U.S. 430 (1981)
Burks v. United States, 437 U.S. 1 (1978)
Burnett v. Commonwealth, 3 S.W.3d 359 (Ky. Ct. App. 1999)

C

Calhoun, State v., 18 Ohio St. 3d 373, 481 N.E.2d 624 (1985)
Camden v. Circuit Court of the Second Judicial Circuit, 892 F.2d 610 (7th Cir. 1989)
Campana, Commonwealth v., 452 Pa. 233, 304 A.2d 432, *vacated*, 414 U.S. 808 (1973), *on remand*, 455 Pa. 622, 314 A.2d 854 (1974)
Cardwell, *In re*, 50 P.3d 897 (Colo. 2002)
Carey, People *ex rel.* Mosley v., 74 Ill. 2d 527, 387 N.E.2d 325, 25 Ill. Dec. 669 (1979)
Carreon, United States v., 626 F.2d 528 (7th Cir. 1980)
Ceccolini, United States v., 435 U.S. 268 (1978)
Chaffin v. Stynchcombe, 412 U.S. 17 (1973)
Chastain, *In re*, 340 S.C. 356, 532 S.E.2d 264 (2000)
Childers v. Goldman, 110 F. Supp. 2d 576 (E.D. Mich. 2000)
Chukwurah v. United States, 813 F. Supp. 161 (E.D.N.Y. 1993)
Circuit Court of Cook County, United States *ex rel.* Aleman v., 967 F. Supp. 1022 (N.D. Ill.1997)
City of Cleveland v. Hogan, 92 Ohio Misc. 2d 34, 699 N.E.2d 1020 (Cleveland Mun. Ct. 1998)
Ciucci v. Illinois, 356 U.S. 571 (1958) (per curiam)
Clark, State v., 723 S.W.2d 17 (Mo. Ct. App. 1986)
Clark, United States v., 984 F.2d 319 (9th Cir.1993) (per curiam)
Coakley v. Daniels, 840 S.W.2d 367 (Tenn. Ct. App. 1992)
Cochran, State v., 51 Wash. App. 116, 751 P.2d 1194 (1988)
Codispoti v. Pennsylvania, 418 U.S. 506 (1974)
Coit v. Geer, 1 Kirby 269 (Conn. Super. Ct. 1787)
Colburn v. Tuscaloosa County Board of Education, 688 So. 2d 881 (Ala. Civ. App. 1997)
Collier v. State, 103 Nev. 563, 747 P.2d 225 (1987)
Collins v. Loisel, 262 U.S. 426 (1923)
Colten v. Kentucky, 407 U.S. 104 (1972)
Colton, State v., 234 Conn. 683, 663 A.2d 339 (1995)
Combs, United States v., 634 F.2d 1295 (10th Cir. 1980)

Commissioner of Social Services of New York *ex rel.* Denise R., *In re*, 219 App. Div. 2d 715, 631 N.Y.S.2d 431 (1995)
Comstock, State v., 168 Wis. 2d 915, 485 N.W.2d 354 (1992)
Consumer & Industry Services v. Greenberg, 231 Mich. App. 466, 586 N.W.2d 560 (1998) (per curiam)
Conway, State v., 661 P.2d 1355 (Okla. Crim. App. 1983)
Cooke v. United States, 267 U.S. 517 (1925)
Cooper, People v., 194 Ill. 2d 419, 743 N.E.2d 32, 252 Ill. Dec. 458 (2000)
Cordova-Perez, United States v., 65 F.3d 1552 (9th Cir. 1995)
Cornero v. United States, 48 F.2d 69 (9th Cir. 1931)
Correa, People v., 244 Ill. App. 3d 307, 614 N.E.2d 1246, 185 Ill. Dec. 561, *rev'd on other grounds*, 152 Ill. 2d 566, 623 N.E.2d 268, 191 Ill. Dec. 23 (1993)
Cox, State v., 109 Wash. App. 779, 37 P.2d 1240 (2002)
Crist v. Bretz, 437 U.S. 28 (1978)
Cross v. State *ex rel.* Linton, 419 N.E.2d 991 (Ind. Ct. App. 1981)
Crotwell, United States v., 896 F.2d 437 (10th Cir. 1990)
Cullen v. The King, [1949] S.C.R. 658
Cummings v. Commonwealth, 24 Va. App. 248, 481 S.E.2d 493 (1997)
Custody of a Minor, 375 Mass. 733, 379 N.E.2d 1053 (1978)
Cutshall v. Sundquist, 193 F.3d 466 (6th Cir. 1999)

D

Daff v. State, 317 Md. 678, 566 A.2d 120 (1989)
Dahlstrum, United States v., 655 F.2d 971 (9th Cir. 1981)
Daniels, State v., 780 So.2d 148 (Fla. Dist. Ct. App. 2000)
Dantzler v. Travis, 249 App. Div. 2d 841, 673 N.Y.S.2d 221 (1998)
Davenport v. State, 574 S.W.2d 73 (Tex. Crim. App. 1978)
Davis, *Ex parte*, 957 S.W.2d 9 (Tex. Crim. App. 1997)
Davis v. Brown, 87 N.Y.2d 626, 664 N.E.2d 884, 641 N.Y.S.2d 819 (1996)
Deems, People v., 81 Ill. 2d 384, 410 N.E.2d 8, 43 Ill. Dec. 8 (1980)
Delta School of Commerce, Inc. v. Harris, 310 Ark. 611, 839 S.W.2d 203 (1992)
Department of Revenue of Montana v. Kurth Ranch, 511 U.S. 767 (1994)
Despertt, State v., 73 Md. App. 620, 535 A.2d 963 (1988)
Detention of Garren, *In re*, 620 N.W.2d 275 (Iowa 2000)
Detention of Samuelson, *In re*, 189 Ill. 2d 548, 727 N.E.2d 228, 244 Ill. Dec. 929 (2000)
Dhinsa, United States v., 243 F.3d 635 (2d Cir. 2001)
Diaz v. United States, 223 U.S. 442 (1912)
Dickenson v. Israel, 644 F.2d 308 (7th Cir. 1981), *adopting* 482 F. Supp. 1223 (E.D. Wis. 1980)
Dickinson, United States v., 706 F.2d 88 (2d Cir. 1983)
DiFrancesco, United States v., 449 U.S. 117 (1980)
Dinitz, United States v., 424 U.S. 600 (1976)
Dinkane, United States v., 17 F.3d 1192 (9th Cir.1994)
Dinning v. State, 267 Ga. 879, 485 S.E.2d 464 (1997)
Discipline of Babilis, *In re*, 951 P.2d 207 (Utah 1997)
District of Columbia v. ______. *See opposing party.*

Dixon, United States v., 509 U.S. 688 (1993)
Donley v. Donley, 165 Vt. 619, 686 A.2d 943 (1996)
Douglas, United States v., 874 F.2d 1145 (7th Cir. 1989)
Dowling, Virgin Islands v., 633 F.2d 660 (3d Cir. 1980)
Downum v. United States, 372 U.S. 734 (1963)
Dowling v. United States, 493 U.S. 342 (1990)
Doyle, United States v., 121 F.3d 1078 (7th Cir. 1997)
Drakeford, *In re*, 32 N.C. App. 113, 230 S.E.2d 779 (1977)
Dreyer v. Illinois, 187 U.S. 71 (1902)
Duncan v. Louisiana, 391 U.S. 145 (1968)

E

Ebeling v. Morgan, 237 U.S. 625 (1915)
Echavarria, People v., 233 Mich. App. 356, 592 N.W.2d 737 (1999)
Edwards, *Ex parte*, 452 So. 2d 508 (Ala. 1984)
Edwards, People v., 97 Ill. App. 3d 407, 422 N.E.2d 1117, 52 Ill. Dec. 908 (1981)
Edwards v. Commonwealth, 233 Ky. 356, 25 S.W.2d 746 (1930)
Edwards v. State, 328 Ark. 394, 943 S.W.2d 600 (1997)
Elcock v. United States, 80 F. Supp. 2d 70 (E.D.N.Y. 2000)
Eliker v. Eliker, 206 Neb. 764, 259 N.W.2d 268 (1980)
Ellis v. State, 634 N.E.2d 771 (Ind. Ct. App. 1994)
Ewell, United States v., 383 U.S. 116 (1966)
Ex parte ______. See name of party.

F

Faber, United States v., 57 F.3d 873 (9th Cir. 1995)
Fariss v. State, 303 Ark. 541, 798 S.W.2d 103 (1990)
Farricielli, State v., 71 Conn. App. 1, 799 A.2d 1121 (2002)
Fassi v. State, 591 So. 2d 977 (Fla. Dist. Ct. App. 1991)
Fay, United States *ex rel.* Orlando v., 350 F.2d 967 (2d Cir. 1965)
Felix, United States v., 503 U.S. 378 (1992)
Ferguson, People v., 67 N.Y.2d 383, 494 N.E.2d 77, 502 N.Y.S.2d 972 (1986)
Ferreira, State v., 68 Haw. 238, 709 P.2d 607 (1985)
Finch v. United States, 433 U.S. 676 (1977) (per curiam)
Fitzpatrick, State v., 676 S.W.2d 831 (Mo. 1984)
Fitzsimmons v. State Bar of California, 34 Cal. 3d 327, 667 P.2d 700, 193 Cal. Rptr. 896 (1983)
Foley, State v., 610 N.W.2d 49 (N.D. 2000)
Fong Foo v. United States, 369 U.S. 141 (1962) (per curiam)
Forman v. United States, 361 U.S. 416 (1960)
Fox v. Ohio, 46 U.S. (5 How,) 410 (1847)
Francis, People v., 98 Cal. App. 4th 873, 120 Cal. Rptr. 2d 90 (2002)
Friend, Commonwealth v., 393 Mass. 310, 470 N.E.2d 788 (1984)

G

GAF Corporation, United States v., 884 F.2d 670 (2d Cir. 1989)
Gagnon v. Scarpelli, 411 U.S. 778 (1973)

Gallegos, People v., 914 P.2d 449 (Colo. Ct. App. 1995)
Gamble, United States v., 141 F.3d 621 (6th Cir. 1998)
Gannett Co. v. DePasquale, 443 U.S. 368 (1979)
Gantley, United States v., 172 F.3d 422 (6th Cir. 1999)
Garay-Burgos, United States v., 961 F. Supp. 1321 (D. Ariz. 1997)
Garrett v. United States, 471 U.S. 773 (1985)
Gary, United States v., 74 F.3d 304 (1st Cir. 1996)
Gault, *In re*, 387 U.S. 1 (1967)
Gaytan, United States v., 115 F.3d 737 (9th Cir. 1997)
Gedraitis, United States v., 690 F.2d 351 (3d Cir. 1982)
Gideon v. Wainwright, 372 U.S. 335 (1963)
Glover v. McMackin, 950 F.2d 1236 (6th Cir. 1991)
Gompers v. Buck's Stove & Range Co., 221 U.S. 418 (1911)
Goodnow, State v., 140 N.H. 38, 662 A.2d 950 (1995)
Goolsby v. Hutto, 691 F.2d 199 (4th Cir. 1982)
Gore v. United States, 357 U.S. 386 (1958)
Gori v. United States, 367 U.S. 364 (1961)
Govro, United States v., 833 F.2d 135 (9th Cir. 1987)
Grady v. Corbin, 495 U.S. 508 (1990), *overruled by* United States v. Dixon, 509 U.S. 688 (1993)
Grafton v. United States, 206 U.S. 333 (1907)
Grand Jury Proceedings (Horak), *In re*, 625 F.2d 767 (8th Cir. 1980)
Green, *Ex parte*, 548 S.W.2d 914 (Tex. Crim. App.1977)
Green, United States v., 139 F.3d 1002 (4th Cir. 1998)
Green v. United States, 355 U.S. 184 (1957)
Greene v. Massey, 437 U.S. 19 (1978)
Gregory, State v., 66 N.J. 510, 333 A.2d 257 (1975)
Greyson v. Kellam, 937 F.2d 1409 (9th Cir. 1991)
Griffin v. Wisconsin, 483 U.S. 868 (1987)
Grisanti, United States v., 4 F.3d 173 (2d Cir. 1993)
Grossfeld v. Commodity Futures Trading Commission, 137 F.3d 1300 (11th Cir. 1998)
Gryger v. Burke, 334 U.S. 728 (1948)
Guadagna, United States v., 183 F.3d 122 (2d Cir. 1999)
Guzman, United States v., 85 F.3d 823 (1st Cir. 1996)

H

H.J., *In re*, 854 P.2d 381 (Okla. Ct. App. 1993)
Halbert v. State, 18 Okla. Crim. 378, 195 P. 504 (1921)
Hale v. State, 336 Ark. 345, 985 S.W.2d 303 (1999)
Halper, United States v., 490 U.S. 435 (1989), *method of analysis disavowed by* Hudson v. United States, 522 U.S. 93 (1997)
Hamilton, State v., 107 N.M. 186, 754 P.2d 857 (Ct. App. 1998)
Hanahan, United States v., 798 F.2d 187 (7th Cir. 1986)
Hannaball v. Spalding, 1 Root 86 (Conn. Super. Ct. 1783)
Hansen v. Johns-Manville Products Corp., 734 F.2d 1036 (5th Cir. 1984)
Harding, People v., 443 Mich. 693, 506 N.W.2d 482 (1993)
Harisiades v. Shaughnessy, 342 U.S. 580 (1952)

Harris v. Oklahoma, 433 U.S. 682 (1977) (per curiam)
Harris v. United States, 382 U.S. 162 (1965)
Harris v. Washington, 404 U.S. 55 (1971)
Harrison, United States v., 918 F.2d 469 (5th Cir. 1990)
Harrison v. State, 767 S.W.2d 803 (Tex. Crim. App. 1989)
Harrocks, State v., 17 P.3d 1145 (Utah Ct. App. 2001)
Haynes, People v., 127 Misc. 2d 188, 485 N.Y.S.2d 929 (N.Y. City Crim. Ct. 1985)
Hazzard, State v., 743 S.W.2d 938 (Tenn. Crim. App. 1987)
Heath v. Alabama, 474 U.S. 82 (1985)
Heath v. Alabama State Tenure Commission, 401 So. 2d 68 (Ala. Civ. App. 1981)
Hecht, United States v., 638 F.2d 651 (3rd Cir. 1981)
Heffner, United States v., 85 F.3d 435 (9th Cir. 1996)
Hellems, State v., 13 S.W.3d 302 (Mo. Ct. App. 2000)
Helvering v. Mitchell, 303 U.S. 391 (1938)
Henderson v. State, 206 Ga. App. 642, 426 S.E.2d 264 (1992)
Herbert v. Billy, 160 F.3d 1131 (6th Cir.1998)
Hess, United States *ex rel.* Marcus v., 317 U.S. 537 (1943)
Hicks *ex rel.* Feiock v. Feiock, 485 U.S. 624 (1988)
Hoang v. State, 872 S.W.2d 694 (Tex. Crim. App. 1993)
Hodges, United States v., 211 F.3d 74 (3d Cir. 2000)
Hogg, State v., 118 N.H. 262, 385 A.2d 844 (1978)
Hollan, People v., 142 Ill. App. 3d 774, 491 N.E.2d 1372, 96 Ill. Dec. 912 (1986)
Holmgren, Commonwealth v., 421 Mass. 224, 656 N.E.2d 577 (1995)
Howell, State v., 220 S.C. 178, 66 S.E.2d 701 (1951)
Huang, United States v., 960 F.2d 1128 (2d Cir. 1992)
Hubbard, State v., 135 Ohio App. 3d 518, 734 N.E.2d 874 (1999)
Huddleston v. United States, 485 U.S. 681 (1988)
Hudson, State v., 121 N.H. 6, 425 A.2d 255 (1981)
Hudson v. Louisiana, 450 U.S. 40 (1981)
Hudson v. United States, 522 U.S. 93 (1997)
Hunt, United States v., 129 F.3d 739 (5th Cir. 1997)
Hunter, Commonwealth v., 449 Pa. Super. 493, 674 A.2d 306 (1996), *appeal dismissed,*
549 Pa. 571, 701 A.2d 1356 (1997)
Hunter v. State, 172 Ind. App. 397, 360 N.E.2d 588 (1977)
Hurtado v. California, 110 U.S. 516 (1884)
Hutchinson, Rex v., 3 Keble 785, 84 Eng. Rep. 1011 (1677)

I

Iannelli v. United States, 420 U.S. 770 (1975)
Illinois v. Allen, 397 U.S. 337 (1970)
Illinois v. Somerville, 410 U.S. 458 (1973)
Illinois v. Vitale, 447 U.S. 410 (1980)
In re ______. *See name of party.*
Innis, People v., 182 App. Div. 2d 641, 582 N.Y.S.2d 245 (1992)
INS v. Lopez-Mendoza, 468 U.S. 1032 (1984)
Isham, State v., 261 Neb. 690, 625 N.W.2d 511 (2001)

J

J.O., *In re*, 242 N.J. Super. 248, 576 A.2d 342 (App. Div. 1990)
Jackson, People v., 118 Ill.2d 179, 514 N.E.2d 983, 113 Ill. Dec. 71 (1987), *overruled on other grounds by* People v. Stefan, 146 Ill. 2d 324, 586 N.E.2d 1239, 166 Ill. Dec. 910 (1992)
James C.F., *In re*, 488 A.2d 118 (Del. Fam. Ct. 1984)
Jeffers v. United States, 432 U.S. 137 (1977)
Jefferson, People v., 248 App. Div. 2d 815, 670 N.Y.S.2d 239 (1998)
Jenkins, United States v., 420 U.S. 358 (1975)
Jines v. Seiber, 193 Ill. App. 3d 390, 549 N.E.2d 964, 140 Ill. Dec. 313 (1990)
John P., *In re*, 311 Md. 700, 537 A.2d 263 (1988)
Johnson, People v., 396 Mich. 424, 240 N.W.2d 729 (1976)
Johnson, State v., 248 S.C. 153, 149 S.E.2d 348 (1966)
Johnson, United States v., 537 F.2d 1170 (4th Cir. 1976)
Johnson v. Commonwealth, 201 Ky. 314, 256 S.W. 388 (1923)
Johnson v. United States, 529 U.S. 694 (2000)
Johnson v. United States, 763 A.2d 707 (D.C. 2000)
Johnson v. Zerbst, 304 U.S. 458 (1938)
Joiner v. State, 500 So. 2d 81 (Ala. Crim. App. 1986)
Jones, People v., 301 Ill. App. 3d 608, 703 N.E.2d 994, 234 Ill. Dec. 894 (1998)
Jones, State v., 7 Ga. 422 (1849)
Jones and Bever, Kely. 52, 84 Eng. Rep. 1078 (1665)
Jones v. Commonwealth, 379 Mass. 607, 400 N.E.2d 242 (1980)
Jones v. State, 843 S.W.2d 487 (Tex. Crim. App. 1992)
Jones v. Thomas, 491 U.S. 376 (1989)
Jones v. United States, 669 A.2d 724 (D.C. 1995)
Jorgenson, State v., 198 Ariz. 390, 10 P.3d 1177 (2000)
Jorn, United States v., 400 U.S. 470 (1971)
Justices of Boston Municipal Court v. Lydon, 466 U.S. 294 (1984)

K

Kahn, United States v., 822 F.2d 451 (4th Cir. 1987)
Kansas v. Hendricks, 521 U.S. 346 (1997)
Katz, *In re*, 638 A.2d 684 (D.C. 1994)
Keehner, State v., 425 N.W.2d 41 (Iowa 1988)
Keenan, Commonwealth v., 365 Pa. Super. 437, 530 A.2d 90 (1987)
Keerl v. Montana, 213 U.S. 135 (1909)
Keith, State v., 482 N.E.2d 751 (Ind. Ct. App.1985)
Kennedy v. Mendoza-Martinez, 372 U.S. 144 (1963)
Kenney, State v., 523 A.2d 853 (R.I. 1987)
Kent v. United States, 383 U.S. 541 (1966)
Kepner v. United States, 195 U.S. 100 (1904)
King, The, v. ______. *See opposing party.*
Klobuchir v. Pennsylvania, 639 F.2d 966 (3d Cir. 1981)
Knaff, State v., 128 Ohio App. 3d 90, 713 N.E.2d 1112 (1998)
Knights, United States v., 534 U.S. 112 (2001)
Koonce v. State, 654 S.W.2d 705 (Tex. Ct. App.1983)

Kwang Fu Peng, United States v., 766 F.2d 82 (2d Cir. 1985)

L

Lackes v. State, 274 Ga. 297, 553 S.E.2d 582 (2001)
Lange, *Ex parte*, 85 U.S. (18 Wall.) 163 (1874)
Lanni v. Engler, 994 F. Supp. 849 (E.D. Mich. 1998)
Lanza, United States v., 260 U.S. 377 (1922)
Lara, United States v., 124 S. Ct. 1628 (2004)
Large, State v., 607 N.W.2d 774 (Minn. 2000)
Lark, Commonwealth v., 548 Pa. 441, 698 A.2d 43 (1997)
LaRouche Campaign, United States v., 866 F.2d 512 (1st Cir. 1989)
Larsen, *In re*, 812 A.2d 640 (Pa. Spec. Trib. 2002)
Laverty v. State, 963 P.2d 1076 (Alaska Ct. App. 1998)
Lawson Mardon Flexible Packaging, Inc., Commonwealth v., 10 S.W.3d 488 (Ky. Ct. App. 1999)
LeCoure, State v., 158 Mont. 340, 491 P.2d 1228 (1971)
Lee, State v., 65 Conn. 265, 30 A. 1110 (1894)
Lee v. United States, 432 U.S. 23 (1977)
Leventhal on Behalf of Agosta, People *ex rel.* v. Warden, 102 App. Div. 317, 477 N.Y.S.2d 332 (1984)
Levy, United States *ex rel.* Rutz v., 268 U.S. 390 (1925)
Lippert, United States v., 148 F.3d 974 (8th Cir. 1998)
Livingston v. State, 266 Ga. 501, 467 S.E.2d 886 (1996)
Livingston v. State, 544 N.E.2d 1364 (Ind. 1989)
Local 28 of the Sheet Metal Workers' International Association v. Equal Employment Opportunity Commission, 478 U.S. 421 (1986)
Lockhart v. Nelson, 488 U.S. 33 (1988)
Logan v. State, 48 S.W.3d 296 (Tex. Ct. App. 2001)
Logan v. United States, 144 U.S. 263 (1892)
Lomax, *In re*, 367 A.2d 1272 (D.C. 1976), *vacated for other reasons*, 386 A.2d 1185 (D.C. 1978) (en banc)
Lopez Andino, United States v., 831 F.2d 1164 (1st Cir. 1987)
Louisiana *ex rel.* Francis v. Resweber, 329 U.S. 459 (1947)
Louisville Civil Service Board v. Blair, 711 S.W.2d 181 (Ky. 1986)
Love v. Morton, 112 F.3d 131 (3d Cir. 1997)
Lovinger v. Circuit Court of the 19th Judicial Circuit, 845 F.2d 739 (7th 1988)
Ludwig v. Massachusetts, 427 U.S. 618 (1976)
Lynn v. West, 134 F.3d 582 (4th Cir. 1998)

M

MacDonald, United States v., 435 U.S. 850 (1978)
Maggio v. Zeitz, 333 U.S. 56 (1948)
Malchow, People v., 193 Ill. 2d 413, 739 N.E.2d 433, 250 Ill. Dec. 670 (2000)
Malloy v. Hogan, 378 U.S. 1 (1964)
Malone v. State, 864 S.W.2d 156 (Tex. Ct. App. 1993)
Malufau, State v., 80 Haw. 126, 906 P.2d 612 (1995)
Malveaux, People v., 50 Cal. App. 4th 1425, 59 Cal. Rptr. 2d 371 (1996)

Manista, State v., 651 A.2d 781 (Del. Fam. Ct. 1994)
Manley v. State, 663 S.W.2d 881 (Tex. Crim. App. 1982)
Maples v. State, 565 S.W.2d 202 (Tenn. 1978)
Mapp v. Ohio, 367 U.S. 643 (1961)
Marcus, United States *ex rel.* v. Hess, 317 U.S. 537 (1943)
Marigold, United States v., 50 U.S. (9 How.) 560 (1850)
Marr, State v., 673 A.2d 452 (R.I. 1996) (per curiam)
Marrow, People v., 210 Mich. App. 455, 534 N.W.2d 153 (1995), *aff'd*, 453 Mich. 903, 554 N.W.2d 901 (1996) (table), *overruled on other grounds by* People v. Pasha, 466 Mich. 378, 645 N.W.2d 275 (2002)
Martin v. Reinstein, 195 Ariz. 293, 987 P.2d 779 (Ct. App. 1999)
Martin Linen Supply Co., United States v., 430 U.S. 564 (1977)
Martinez, United States v., 122 F.3d 1161 (9th Cir. 1997)
Mastrangelo, United States v., 662 F.2d 946 (2d Cir. 1981)
Mayes, United States v., 158 F.3d 1215 (11th Cir. 1998)
Maynard, State *ex rel.* Vance v., 177 W. Va. 251, 351 S.E.2d 437 (1986)
Maze, State v., 16 Kan. App. 2d 527, 825 P.2d 1169 (1992)
McAfee, *Ex parte*, 761 S.W.2d 771 (Tex. Crim. App. 1988)
McComb v. Jacksonville Paper Co., 336 U.S. 187 (1949)
McCrary v. Scully, 153 App. Div. 2d 629, 544 N.Y.S.2d 852 (1989) (memorandum)
McDermott, People v., 28 Cal. 4th 946, 51 P.3d 874, 123 Cal. Rptr. 2d 654 (2002)
McDowell, State v., 242 Conn. 648, 699 A.2d 987 (1997)
McFarland v. State, 68 Wis. 400, 32 N.W. 226 (1887)
McGee, Commonwealth v., 560 Pa. 324, 744 A.2d 754 (2000)
McKane v. Durston, 153 U.S. 684 (1894)
McKeeth, State v., 136 Idaho 619, 38 P.3d 1275 (2001)
McKeiver v. Pennsylvania, 403 U.S. 528 (1971)
McKinney, State v., 575 N.W.2d 841 (Minn. Ct. App. 1998)
Mesman, State v., 488 So. 2d 1296 (La. Ct. App. 1986)
Michael W., *In re*, 367 Md. 181, 786 A.2d 684 (2001)
Milenkovich, State v., 236 Neb. 42, 458 N.W.2d 747 (1990)
Miller, United States v., 797 F.2d 336 (6th Cir. 1986)
Mills, Commonwealth v., 447 Pa. 163, 286 A.2d 638 (1971)
Mirra, United States v., 220 F. Supp. 361 (S.D.N.Y. 1963)
Missouri v. Hunter, 459 U.S. 359 (1983)
Mitchell, State v., 712 A.2d 1033 (Me. 1998)
Mitchell G., *In re*, 226 Cal. App. 3d 66, 276 Cal. Rptr. 245 (1990)
Monge v. California, 524 U.S. 721 (1998)
Monk, State v., 132 N.C. App. 248, 511 S.E.2d 332 (1999)
Montana v. Hall, 481 U.S. 400 (1987)
Moore v. Illinois, 55 U.S. (14 How.) 13 (1852)
Moore v. Missouri, 159 U.S. 673 (1895)
Morris v. Mathews, 475 U.S. 237 (1986)
Morrissey v. Brewer, 408 U.S. 471 (1972)
Morton, State v., 971 S.W.2d 335 (Mo. Ct. App. 1998)
Morton, State v., 292 N.J. Super. 92, 678 A.2d 308 (App. Div. 1996)
Mosley, People *ex rel.* Carey v., 74 Ill. 2d 527, 387 N.E.2d 325, 25 Ill. Dec. 669 (1979)

Moyer, People v., 292 App. Div. 2d 793, 738 N.Y.S.2d 810 (2002) (memorandum)
Muldrow, State v., 348 S.C. 264, 559 S.E.2d 847 (2002)
Mundt, United States v., 846 F.2d 1157 (8th Cir. 1988)

N

Neff v. Commonwealth, 39 Va. App. 13, 569 S.E.2d 72 (2002)
Neil C., *In re*, 308 Md. 591, 521 A.2d 329 (1987)
Nelson, United States v., 277 F.3d 164 (2d Cir. 2002)
New Jersey State Parole Board v. Mannson, 220 N.J. Super. 566, 533 A.2d 58 (App. Div. 1987)
New York v. Hill, 528 U.S.110 (2000)
Nichols, United States v., 977 F.2d 972 (5th Cir. 1992)
Nicoletti v. State Board of Vehicle Manufacturers., Dealers and Salespersons, 706 A.2d 891 (Pa. Commw. Ct. 1998)
Nielsen, *In re*, 131 U.S. 176 (1889)
Nixon v. United States, 728 A.2d 582 (D.C. 1999)
North Carolina v. Pearce, 395 U.S. 711 (1969), *overruled on other grounds by* Alabama v. Smith, 490 U.S. 794 (1989)

O

O'Brien, State v., 857 S.W.2d 212 (Mo. 1993)
Offutt v. United States, 348 U.S. 11 (1954)
Ohio v. Johnson, 467 U.S. 493 (1984)
Ohm, State v., 107 Ohio Misc. 2d 19, 736 N.E.2d 121 (Akron Mun. Ct. 2000)
Oliver, *In re*, 333 U.S. 257 (1948)
Olson v. Walker, 162 Ariz. 174, 781 P.2d 1015 (Ct. App. 1989)
One Assortment of 89 Firearms, United States v., 465 U.S. 354 (1984)
One Lot Emerald Cut Stones v. United States, 409 U.S. 232 (1972) (per curiam)
Oregon v. Kennedy, 456 U.S. 667 (1982)
Orlando, United States *ex rel.* v. Fay, 350 F.2d 967 (2d Cir. 1965)
Osborn, State v., 345 Ark. 196, 45 S.W.2d 373 (2001)
Osteen, United States v., 254 F.3d 521 (4th Cir. 2001)
Owens, People v., 227 App. Div. 2d 256, 642 N.Y.S.2d 874 (1996)

P

P.H., People v., 145 Ill. 2d 209, 582 N.E.2d 700, 164 Ill. Dec. 137 (1991)
Paige, People v., 131 Mich. App. 34, 345 N.W.2d 639 (1983)
Palko, State v., 121 Conn. 669, 186 A. 657 (1936)
Palko v. Connecticut, 302 U.S. 319 (1937)
Parker v. Estelle, 498 F.2d 625 (5th Cir. 1974)
Patterson, United States v., 292 F.3d 615 (9th Cir. 2002)
Pavloyianis, United States v., 996 F.2d 1467 (2d Cir. 1993)
Peiffer v. State, 88 S.W.3d 439 (Mo. 2002) (per curiam)
People v. ______. *See opposing party.*
People *ex rel.* ______ v. ______. *See opposing party and relator.*
Peralta, *Ex parte*, 87 S.W.3d 642 (Tex. Ct. App. 2002)
Perez, United States v., 22 U.S. (9 Wheat.) 579 (1824)

Perkins, The King v., Holt. K.B. 403, 90 Eng. Rep. 1122 (1698)
Perry v. State, 213 Ga. App. 220, 444 S.E.2d 150 (1994)
Peterson, United States v., 268 F. 864 (W.D. Wash. 1920)
Petite v. United States, 361 U.S. 529 (1960)
Pettis v. State, 803 So. 2d 903 (Fla. Dist. Ct. App. 2002)
Pfortmiller, State v., 53 Or. App. 394, 632 P.2d 459 (1981)
Phillips, *In re*, 128 N.C. App. 732, 497 S.E.2d 292 (1998)
Pinkerton v. United States, 328 U.S. 640 (1946)
Poland v. Arizona, 476 U.S. 147 (1986)
Pontillo, People v., 267 Ill. App. 3d 27, 640 N.E.2d 990, 203 Ill. Dec. 840 (1994)
Pope v. Thone, 671 F.2d 298 (8th Cir. 1982)
Porter, People v., 156 Ill. 2d 218, 620 N.E.2d 381, 189 Ill. Dec. 413 (1993)
Preuss, People v., 920 P.2d 859 (Colo. Ct. App. 1995)
Price, State v., 333 S.C. 267, 510 S.E.2d 215 (1998)
Price v. Board of Fire and Police Commissioners of Beardstown, 139 Ill. App. 3d 333, 487 N.E.2d 673, 93 Ill. Dec. 848 (1985)
Price v. Georgia, 398 U.S. 323 (1970)
Price v. State, 104 Miss. 288, 61 So. 314 (1913)
Proctor v. State, 868 S.W.2d 669 (Tenn. Crim. App. 1992)
Puerto Rico v. ______. *See opposing party.*
Pursell, Commonwealth v., 555 Pa. 233, 724 A.2d 293 (1999)

Q

Quirk, *In re*, 705 So. 2d 172 (La. 1997)

R

R.A.C. v. State, 736 So. 2d 718 (Fla. Dist. Ct. App. 1999)
R.G., *In re*, 885 S.W.2d 757 (Mo. Ct. App. 1994)
R.L.K., *In re*, 67 Ill. App. 3d 451, 384 N.E.2d 531, 23 Ill. Dec. 737 (1978)
Racich v. Celotex Corp., 887 F.2d 393 (2d Cir. 1989)
Randy, United States v., 81 F.3d 65 (7th Cir. 1996)
Rankin v. State, 329 Ark. 379, 948 S.W.2d 397 (1997)
Rashed, United States v., 234 F.3d 1280 (D.C. Cir. 2000)
Rawles, Commonwealth v., 501 Pa. 514, 462 A.2d 619 (1983)
Read, The King v., 1 Lev. 9, 83 Eng. Rep. 271 (1660)
Reed v. Alcoholic Beverage Control Divisioon, 295 Ark. 9, 746 S.W.2d 368 (1988)
Renye v. State, 727 So. 2d 1003 (Fla. Dist. Ct. App. 1999) (per curiam)
Respublica v. ______. *See opposing party.*
Rex v. ______. *See opposing party.*
Rex Trailer Co. v. United States, 350 U.S. 148 (1956)
Reyes, United States v., 283 F.3d 446 (2d Cir. 2002)
Reynolds v. State, 4 S.W.3d 13 (Tex. Crim. App. 1999)
Rezaq, United States v., 134 F.3d 1121 (D.C. Cir. 1998)
Richards v. State, 108 Ark. 87, 157 S.W. 141 (1913)
Richardson v. State, 109 Tex. Crim. 403, 5 S.W.2d 141 (1928)
Richardson v. United States, 468 U.S. 317 (1984)
Ricketts v. Adamson, 483 U.S. 1 (1987)

Rinaldi v. United States, 434 U.S. 22 (1977)
Rincon, State v., 700 So. 2d 412 (Fla. Dist. Ct. App. 1997)
Rios v. State, 557 S.W.2d 87 (Tex. Crim. App. 1977)
Rivera v. Pugh, 194 F.3d 1064 (9th Cir.1999)
Rivera v. State, 716 S.W.2d 68 (Tex. Ct. App. 1986)
Roberts, *Ex parte*, 662 So. 2d 229 (Ala. 1995)
Robbins, People v., 223 Mich. App. 355, 566 N.W.2d 49 (1997)
Robinson, Virgin Islands *ex rel.* v. Schneider, 893 F. Supp. 490 (D.V.I. 1995)
Robinson v. Commonwealth, 18 Va. App. 814, 447 S.E.2d 542, *adopting* 17 Va. App. 551, 439 S.E.2d 622 (1994)
Robinson v. Neil, 409 U.S. 505 (1973)
Roche, The King v., 1 Leach 134, 168 Eng. Rep. 169 (Cr. Cas. 1775)
Roderick U., *In re*, 14 Cal. App. 4th 1543, 18 Cal. Rptr. 2d 555 (1993)
Rodriguez, State v., 198 Ariz. 139, 7 P.3d 148 (Ct. App. 2000)
Rollerson, United States v., 449 F.2d 1000 (D.C. Cir. 1971)
Rollerson, United States v., 308 F. Supp. 1014 (D.D.C. 1970)
Romero v. Justices of the Supreme Court, 237 App. Div. 2d 292, 654 N.Y.S.2d 803 (1997)
Rondberg v. Arizona Board of Chiropractic Examiners, 182 Ariz. 409, 897 P.2d 711 (Ct. App. 1995)
Rudi, People v., 103 Ill. 2d 216, 469 N.E.2d 580, 82 Ill. Dec. 936 (1984)
Rufo v. Simpson, 86 Cal. App. 4th 573, 103 Cal. Rptr. 2d 492 (2001)
Russo v. New Jersey Department of Corrections, 324 N.J. Super. 576, 737 A.2d 183 (App. Div. 1999)
Rutledge v. United States, 517 U.S. 292 (1996)
Rutz, United States *ex rel.* v. Levy, 268 U.S. 390 (1925)
Ryan, United States v., 810 F.2d 650 (7th Cir. 1987)

S

S.A. Healy Co. v. Occupational Safety & Review Commission, 138 F.3d 686 (7th Cir. 1998)
Sacher v. United States, 343 U.S. 1 (1952)
Salgado, People v., 88 Cal. App. 4th 5, 105 Cal. Rptr. 2d 373 (2001)
Sampson v. State, 478 N.W.2d 566 (N.D. 1991), *overruled on other grounds by* City of Fargo v. Hector, 534 N.W.2d 821 (N.D. 1995)
Sanabria v. United States, 437 U.S. 54 (1978)
Sanchez, People v., 276 App. Div. 2d 723, 714 N.Y.S.2d 521 (2000)
Sanchez, United States v., 992 F.2d 1143 (11th Cir.), *amended*, 3 F.3d 366 (11th Cir. 1993)
Sanders v. Shephard, 185 Ill. App. 3d 719, 541 N.E.2d 1150, 133 Ill. Dec. 712 (1989)
Sanford, United States v., 429 U.S. 14 (1976)
Sanges, United States v., 144 U.S. 310 (1892)
Sansone, People v., 18 Ill. App. 3d 315, 309 N.E.2d 733 (1974)
Santiago Soto, United States v., 825 F.2d 616 (1st Cir. 1987)
Santosky v. Kramer, 455 U.S. 745 (1982)
Sattazahn v. Pennsylvania, 537 U.S. 101 (2003)
Savage, State v., 933 S.W.2d 497 (Tex. Crim. App. 1996)

Schiro v. Farley, 510 U.S. 222 (1994)
Schneider, Virgin Islands *ex rel.* Robinson v., 893 F. Supp. 490 (D.V.I. 1995)
Scholz, United States v., 899 F. Supp. 484 (D. Nev. 1995)
Scott, People v., 15 Cal. 4th 1188, 939 P.2d 354, 65 Cal. Rptr. 2d 240 (1997)
Scott, United States v., 437 U.S. 82 (1978)
Scott v. Illinois, 440 U.S. 367 (1979)
Screws v. United States, 325 U.S. 91 (1945)
SEC v. Palmisano, 135 F.3d 860 (2d Cir. 1998)
Serfass v. United States, 420 U.S. 377 (1975)
Shaffer, Respublica v., 1 Dall. 236 (Pa. Ct. Oyer & Terminer 1788)
Sharp, *In re*, 674 A.2d 899 (D.C. 1996)
Sheaffer, *In re*, 655 N.E.2d 1214 (Ind. 1995)
Shell Co. (P.R.), Ltd., Puerto Rico v., 302 U.S. 253 (1937)
Shields v. State, 257 Md. 384, 263 A.2d 565 (1970)
Shields v. State, 722 So. 2d 584 (Miss. 1998)
Shillitani v. United States, 384 U.S. 364 (1966)
Shoels, *Ex parte*, 643 S.W.2d 761 (Tex. Ct. App. 1982)
Showery v. Samaniego, 814 F.2d 200 (5th Cir. 1987)
Shumate v. State, 718 N.E.2d 1133 (Ind. Ct. App. 1999)
Shute v. Texas, 117 F.3d 233 (5th Cir. 1997)
Silvers, United States v., 90 F.3d 95 (4th Cir. 1996)
Simeone, Commonwealth v., 222 Pa. Super. 376, 294 A.2d 921(1972)
Simmons v. United States, 142 U.S. 148 (1891)
Simpson, State v., 28 Minn. 66, 9 N.W. 78 (1881)
Simpson v. Florida, 403 U.S. 384 (1971) (per curiam)
Singleterry, United States v., 683 F.2d 122 (5th Cir. 1982)
Sir Henry Vane's Case, 6 How. St. Tr. 119; 1 Lev. 68, 83 Eng. Rep. 300 (1662)
Sisson, United States v., 399 U.S. 267 (1970)
Skipper, United States v., 74 F.3d 608 (5th Cir. 1996)
Smalis v. Pennsylvania, 476 U.S. 140 (1986)
Smith, Commonwealth v., 391 Pa. Super. 154, 570 A.2d 559 (1990)
Smith, Commonwealth v., 380 Pa. Super. 484, 552 A.2d 292 (1988)
Smith, Commonwealth v., 259 Va. 780, 529 S.E.2d 78 (2000)
Smith, State v., 81 S.W.3d 657 (Mo. Ct. App. 2002)
Smith, State v., 130 W. Va. 183, 43 S.E.2d 802 (1947)
Smith, United States v., 912 F.2d 322 (9th Cir. 1990)
Smith, United States v., 621 F.2d 350 (9th Cir. 1980)
Smith v. Doe, 538 U.S. 84 (2003)
Smith v. State, 307 Ark. 542, 821 S.W.2d 774 (1992)
Smith v. State, 219 Miss. 741, 69 So. 2d 837 (1954)
Snow, *In re*, 120 U.S. 274 (1887)
Solis, United States v., 299 F.3d 420 (5th Cir. 2002)
Soto-Olivas, United States v., 44 F.3d 788 (9th Cir. 1995)
Spaur v. Owens-Corning Fiberglas Corp., 510 N.W.2d 854 (Iowa 1994)
Spause, *In re*, 381 Pa. Super. 166, 553 A.2d 87 (1989)
Standefer v. United States, 447 U.S. 10 (1980)

State v. ______. *See opposing party.*
State *ex rel.* ______ v. ______. *See opposing party and relator.*
Stephens v. State, 806 S.W.2d 812 (Tex. Crim. App. 1990)
Stevens, State v., 126 Idaho 822, 892 P.2d 889 (1995)
Stevens, State v., 452 So. 2d 289 (La. Ct. App. 1984)
Stewart v. Roe, 776 F. Supp. 1304 (N.D. Ill.1991)
Stout v. State *ex rel.* Caldwell, 36 Okla. 744, 130 P. 553 (1913)
Stringer v. Williams, 161 F.3d 259 (5th Cir. 1998)
Stroud v. United States, 251 U.S. 15 (1919)
Sullivan v. State, 874 S.W.2d 699 (Tex. Ct. App.1994)
Superior Court (Williams), People v., 233 Cal. App. 3d 477, 284 Cal. Rptr. 601 (1991)
Swepson, State v., 79 N.C. 632 (1878)
Swisher v. Brady, 438 U.S. 204 (1978)

T

Tateo, United States v., 377 U.S. 463 (1971)
Taylor v. Hayes, 418 U.S. 488 (1974)
Terry, *Ex parte*, 128 U.S. 289 (1888)
Thangavelu v. Department of Licensing and Regulation, 149 Mich. App. 546, 386 N.W.2d 584 (1986)
Theodore W., *In re*, 4 Neb. App. 428, 545 N.W.2d 119 (1996)
Thompson, State v., 132 Ohio App.3d 755, 726 N.E.2d 530 (1999)
Thompson v. United States, 444 U.S. 248 (1980)
Thompson v. United States, 155 U.S. 271 (1894)
Tibbs v. Florida, 457 U.S. 31 (1982)
Tillis Trucking Co. v. Moses, 748 So. 2d 874 (Ala. 1999)
Tirrell, United States v., 120 F.3d 670 (7th Cir. 1997)
Todd, State v., 654 S.W.2d 379 (Tenn. 1983)
Tolliver, State v., 839 S.W.2d 296 (Mo. 1992)
Toney v. State, 15 Ala. App. 14, 72 So. 508 (1916)
Torres v. State, 614 S.W.2d 436 (Tex. Crim. App. 1981)
Totten, People v., 118 Ill. 2d 124, 514 N.E.2d 959, 113 Ill. Dec. 47 (1987)
Traficanti v. United States, 227 F.3d 170 (4th Cir. 2000)
Trammell, United States v., 133 F.3d 1343 (10th Cir. 1998)
Trono v. United States, 199 U.S. 521 (1905)
Tuckson, State v., 701 So. 2d 807 (La. Ct. App. 2001)
Turner, Kely. 30, 84 Eng. Rep. 1068 (1664)
Turner, People v., 186 Ill. App. 3d 849, 542 N.E.2d 935, 134 Ill. Dec. 589 (1989)
Turner v. Arkansas, 407 U.S. 366 (1972) (per curiam)
Turner v. Glickman, 207 F.3d 419 (7th Cir. 2000)
Turner v. United States Parole Commission, 934 F.2d 254 (10th Cir. 1991)
Tuttle v. Raymond, 494 A.2d 1353 (Me. 1985)
Twining v. New Jersey, 211 U.S. 78 (1908)

U

Ueno, *Ex parte*, 971 S.W.2d 560 (Tex. Ct. App. 1998)
United States, *In re*, 286 F.2d 556 (1st Cir. 1961)

Index

ABOUT THE AUTHOR

DAVID S. RUDSTEIN is Professor of Law, Illinois Institute of Technology, where he teaches courses in criminal law and criminal procedure.

www.ingramcontent.com/pod-product-compliance
Ingram Content Group UK Ltd.
Pitfield, Milton Keynes, MK11 3LW, UK
UKHW041640031026
15587UKWH00001B/395

9 780313 311802